GOD AT SINAI

Books in This Series

God at Sinai
God Is a Warrior
Grace in the End
Israel's Divine Healer
The Messiah in the Old Testament

STUDIES IN
OLD TESTAMENT BIBLICAL THEOLOGY

God at Sinai

COVENANT AND THEOPHANY IN THE BIBLE AND ANCIENT NEAR EAST

JEFFREY J. NIEHAUS

ZondervanPublishingHouse
Grand Rapids, Michigan

A Division of HarperCollinsPublishers

God at Sinai
Copyright © 1995 by Jeffrey J. Niehaus

Requests for information should be addressed to:
  Zondervan Publishing House
  Grand Rapids, Michigan 49530

Library of Congress Cataloging-in-Publication Data

Niehaus, Jeffrey Jay.
   God at Sinai : Covenant and theophany in the Bible and ancient Near East /
by Jeffrey J. Niehaus.
      p.   cm.—(Studies in Old Testament biblical theology)
   Includes bibliographical references and index.
   ISBN (invalid) 0-310-49471-0 (pbk.)
      1. Theophanies in the Bible. 2. Theophanies—Comparative studies.
   3. Revelation on Sinai. 4. Covenants—Religious aspects—Christianity—History
   of doctrines. 5. Covenants—Religious aspects—Judaism—History of doctrines.
   6. Middle East—Religion. 7. Bible. O.T.—Criticism, interpretation, etc. 8. Bible.
   N.T.—Relation to the Old Testament. I. Title. II. Series.
BS1199.T45N54   1995
231.7'4—dc20   94-40793
                                                                          CIP

All Scripture quotations, unless otherwise noted, are taken from the HOLY BIBLE:
NEW INTERNATIONAL VERSION® (North American Edition). Copyright ©
1973, 1978, 1984, by the International Bible Society. Used by permission of
Zondervan Publishing House. All rights reserved. In quoting the NIV, the author
substitutes *Yahweh* for LORD.

"NIV" and "New International Version" are registered in the Untied States Patent
and Trademark Office by the International Bible Society.

All rights reserved. No part of this publication may be reproduced, stored in a retrieval system, or transmitted in any form or by any means—electronic, mechanical, photocopy, recording, or any other—except for brief quotations in printed reviews, without the prior permission of the publisher.

Edited by Laura Weller

Printed in the United States of America

94 95 96 97 98 99 / ❖ DH / 10 9 8 7 6 5 4 3 2 1

*To my dear son, Paul,
who has seen
some of God's glory*

◆ Contents ◆

Acknowledgments	8
Abbreviations	9
Preface to Series	11
Author's Preface	13
1. Theology and Theophany	17
2. Sinai Tradition: Background of Scholarship	43
3. Ancient Near Eastern Parallels: *The Relationship of Egyptian, Hittite, Mesopotamian, and Canaanite Theophanies to the Biblical Tradition (Part 1)*	81
4. Ancient Near Eastern Parallels: *The Relationship of Egyptian, Hittite, Mesopotamian, and Canaanite Theophanies to the Biblical Tradition (Part 2)*	108
5. Pre-Sinai Theophanies	142
6. The Sinai Theophany	181
7. Post-Sinai Theophanies: *Theophanies Demonstrating Sinai Theophany Characteristics in Historical Books and Prophetical Accounts*	230
8. Memory, Imagination, and Eschatology: *Sinai-like Theophanies in the Psalms and Prophets*	280
9. Sinai Theophany: The New Testament and Beyond: *New Covenant Fulfillment of the Implications of the Sinai Theophanies*	333
Afterword	383
Bibliography	385
Scripture Index	399
Author Index	422

♦ Acknowledgments ♦

I would like to acknowledge the help of those people whose contributions to my life and work I have especially appreciated in the composition of this book. I give foremost thanks to our Lord, from whose Word I have learned and by whose Spirit I have sought to understand that Word. I thank him also for my wife, Margaret, who has faithfully stood in his service at home, taking the major share of the burden for homeschooling our sons, Paul and John, and providing a sane home setting in an increasingly unsound society. Her comments on various parts of this book as it progressed were a great help and encouragement. I cannot adequately acknowledge the blessing she has been and continues to be to me.

I am also thankful for Gordon-Conwell Theological Seminary and the context it provides for faithful biblical scholarship. I thank the school and its trustees for providing valuable sabbatical time toward the completion of this book. Among colleagues, I am especially grateful to Dr. Meredith Kline, whose teaching and writings have been an inspiration and in many ways a foundation for my own. His pioneering application of ancient Near Eastern materials to the Bible and his understanding of the Scriptures have been a great model and an encouragement. I express appreciation also to my colleague, Dr. Douglas Stuart, whose teaching has blessed me in the past and whose perusal of parts of the manuscript of this book produced helpful suggestions for its improvement. Thanks finally to Ms. Christine Kimball, my Byington research assistant, for her faithful work on the appendices. Like much work that is mechanical and tedious, it has produced something of clarity and value.

◆ Abbreviations ◆

ad loc.	In a commentary, under the verse discussed
AB	Anchor Bible
AfO	*Die Inschriften Tulkulti Ninurtas I. und seiner Nachfolger* (Weidner)
AHw	*Akkadisches Handwörterbuch* (von Soden)
AKA	*Annals of the Kings of Assyria* (King)
ANET	*Ancient Near Eastern Texts* (Pritchard)
ARI	*Assyrian Royal Inscriptions* (Grayson)
BA	*Biblical Archaeologist*
BASOR	*Bulletin of the American Schools of Oriental Research*
BDB	Brown, Driver, and Briggs, *Hebrew-English Lexicon of the Old Testament*
BO	*Bibliotheca Orientalis*
CAD	*Chicago Assyrian Dictionary*
CBQ	*Catholic Biblical Quarterly*
CH	Codex Hammurabi
CMHE	*Canaanite Myth and Hebrew Epic* (Cross)
CT	*Christianity Today*
CTA	*Corpus des tablettes en cunéiformes alphabétiques découvertes à Ras Shamra–Ugarit de 1929 à 1939* (Herdner)
EA	*Die El-Amarna Tafeln* (Knudtzon)
EBC	Expositor's Bible Commentary
HKAT	*Handkommentar zum alten Testament*
HPIA	*Historical Prism Inscriptions of Ashurbanipal* (Piepkorn)
HUCA	*Hebrew Union College Annual*
IB	*The Interpreter's Bible*
IDBSUP	*The Interpreter's Dictionary of the Bible Supplement*
Ibid.	Same book as the previous one cited
ICC	International Critical Commentary
IEJ	*Israel Exploration Journal*
JAOS	*Journal of American Oriental Society*
JBL	*Journal of Biblical Literature*
JEA	*Journal of Egyptian Archaeology*
JNES	*Journal of Near Eastern Studies*
JPOS	*Jounal of the Palestine Oriental Society*
JQR	*Jewish Quarterly Review*
JSOT	*Journal for the Study of the Old Testament*
JSOTSup	*Journal for the Study of the Old Testament Supplement*

KAT	Kommentar zum Alten Testament
KB	Koehler-Baumgartner, *Lexicon in Veteris Testament Libros*
KD	Keil and Delitzsch, *Commentary on the Old Testament in Ten Volumes*
KHAT	*Kurzer Handkommentar zum alten Testament*
MT	Masoretic Text
NICNT	New International Commentary on the New Testament
NICOT	New International Commentary on the Old Testament
NT	New Testament
OED	*Oxford English Dictionary*
OT	Old Testament
OTL	Old Testament Library
RA	*Revue d'assyriologie et d'archéologie orientale*
RAI	Rencontre Assyriologique Internationale. *Le palais et la royauté.* XIXe (Garelli, ed.)
RB	*Revue Biblique*
SAK	*Die Sumerischen und Akkadischen Königsinschriften* (Thureau-Dangin)
SBLDS	Society of Biblical Literature Dissertation Series
SJT	*Scottish Journal of Theology*
TB	*Tyndale Bulletin*
THw	Theologisches Handwörterbuch
TOTC	Tyndale Old Testament Commentary
TWOT	*Theological Wordbook of the Old Testament*
UT	*Ugaritic Textbook* (Gordon)
VAB	Vorderasiatische Bibliothek
VAS	Vorderasiatische Schriftdenkmäler der Königlichen Museen zu Berlin
VT	*Vetus Testamentum*
WBC	Word Biblical Commentary
ZA	*Zeitschrift für Assyriologie und Verwandte Gebiete*
ZAW	*Zeitschrift für die alttestamentliche Wissenschaft*

◆ Preface to Series ◆

The editors are pleased to announce the "Studies in Old Testament Biblical Theology" series, with the hope that it contributes to the field of Old Testament theology and stimulates further discussion. If Old Testament theology is the queen of Old Testament studies, she is a rather neglected queen. To write in the area of Old Testament theology is a daunting proposition, one that leads many to hesitate taking on the task. After all, Old Testament theology presupposes an understanding of all the books of the Old Testament and, at least as conceived in the present project, an insight into its connection with the New Testament.

Another reason why theology has been neglected in recent years is simply a lack of confidence that the Old Testament can be summarized in one or even a number of volumes. Is there a center, a central concept, under which the entire Old Testament may be subsumed? Many doubt it. Thus, while a number of articles, monographs, and commentaries address the theology of a source, a chapter, or even a book, few studies address the Old Testament as a whole.

The editors of this series also believe it is impossible to present the entirety of the Old Testament message under a single rubric. Even as important a concept as the covenant fails to incorporate all aspects of the Old Testament (note especially wisdom literature). Thus, this series will present separate volumes, each devoted to a different theme, issue, or perspective of biblical theology, and will show its importance for the Old Testament and for the entire Christian canon.

One last word needs to be said about theological approach. Gone are the days when scholars, especially those who work in a field as ideologically sensitive as theology, can claim neutrality by hiding behind some kind of scientific methodology. It is, therefore, important to announce the approach taken in this series. Those who know the editors, authors, and publisher will not be surprised to learn that an evangelical approach is taken throughout this series. At the same time, however, we believe that those who do not share this starting point may still benefit and learn from these studies.

The general editors of this series, Willem A. VanGemeren and Tremper Longman III, wish to thank the academic publishing department of Zondervan, particularly Stan Gundry and Verlyn Verbrugge, who will be working most closely with the series.

Willem A. VanGemeren
Professor of Old Testament and Semitic Languages
Trinity Evangelical Divinity School

Author's Preface

BACKGROUND

One may safely say that nothing is without a background except God himself. The Bible—the Old Testament—old as they are, yet have backgrounds. What God did at Sinai also has backgrounds. Consider the following poem:

> Adorned with a staff, trusted in the interior of Abzu,
> lord with no opposition in the temple tower and the house of Nanshe,
> the king, lord Hendursaga, brings with him
> these commands out of the house of Nanshe.
> Like heavy smoke they settle on the ground.
> This word spreads along the sky, a moving thundercloud.
> [With] the needle of matrimony he joins together,
> the king, lord Hendursaga, twists it apart.
> The just he places among the just.
> The evil he turns over to an evil place.
> He decides the right of the orphan.
> He enforces the right of the widow.
> He executes the right of mother and child.[1]

These lines from a Sumerian hymn celebrate the goddess Nanshe's theodicy. The song, which dates from ca. 2143–2119 B.C., shows a connection between the law or word of the deity and its theophanic promulgation.[2] That holy word is even hypostatized and "spreads along the sky" theophanically, "a moving thundercloud" (line 186). More: The goddess' law is mediated by a messenger who is "king" and "lord"—and to

---

[1] W. Heimpel, "The Nanshe Hymn," *Journal of Cuneiform Studies*, 33/2 (April 1981): 95.
[2] Heimpel, 67, dates the hymn either to the reign of Gudea of Lagash (2163–2144 B.C.) or to Urningirsu of Lagash (2123–2119 B.C.).

whom the judgment of all humans is entrusted. The Sumerian hymn is one of many ancient examples of theophanic lawgiving and judgment that antedate and anticipate what God did at Mount Sinai.[3]

The ancients could also expect a god to respond with thunderous power to human prayers. A good, relatively late example comes from Homer's *Odyssey*:

> [Odysseus] prayed: "O Father Zeus, if over land and water,
> after adversity, you willed to bring me home,
> let someone in the waking house give me good augury,
> and a sign be shown, too, in the outer world."
>
> He prayed thus, and the mind of Zeus in heaven
> heard him. He thundered out of bright Olympos
> down from above the cloudlands, in reply—
> a rousing peal for Odysseus. Then a token
> came to him from a woman grinding flour
> in the court nearby....
> She stopped, stayed her hand, and her lord heard
> the omen from her lips:
> > "Ah, Father Zeus
> almighty over gods and men!
> A great bang of thunder that was, surely,
> out of the starry sky, and not a cloud in sight.
> It is your nod to someone."[4]

In answer to Odysseus's prayer, Zeus (called νεφεληγερέτα, "the cloud-gatherer")[5] "thundered" (ἐβρόντησεν) from bright Olympus out of the clouds (ἐκ νεφέων)—much as the Canaanite god Baal (called *rkb ʿrpt*, "the cloud rider/gatherer") thundered (*qlh ... ytn*) from Zaphon.[6] Zeus's theophanic

---

[3] Not to mention later biblical themes!

[4] Homer, *Odyssey*, XX.97–114, trans. Robert Fitzgerald (New York: Doubleday, 1961), 378.

[5] Cf. Georg Autenrieth, *A Homeric Dictionary*, trans. Robert P. Keep, rev. Isaac Flagg (Norman: University of Oklahoma Press, 1958), 198.

[6] J. C. L. Gibson, *Canaanite Myths and Legends* (Edinburgh: T. & T. Clark, 1977), 65 (4.vii.29; cf. "the sounding of his [i.e., Baal's] thunder from the clouds" (*tn.qlh.bʿrpt*, 4.v.70).

thunder was the major answer to Odysseus's prayer, as the minor answer (the woman's interpretation of it) confirmed.

This Greek example from Isaiah's day shows a common assumption of the ancient world: that a god could thunder or respond in some other theophanic way to a mortal's request. That is why the prophets of Baal danced in vain on Carmel (1Ki 18:17–40). Moreover, the parallelism of terms—both with Canaanite Baal theophanies and Old Testament Yahweh theophanies—has noteworthy theological implications. It harks back to our first parents' encounter with God after the Fall. It also shows the persistence of memory of primordial theophany, in the realm of common grace.

Or does it? Another way to understand the ancient data is to take them as common grace revelation. Major biblical ideas surfaced in the ancient Near East (by God's common grace) before their appearance in the Bible. The "Nanshe Hymn" is one early example of a pagan text that adumbrates major Old Testament and New Testament themes. It conflates glory theophany, lawgiving, and judgment in a way later paralleled by the Sinai and wilderness accounts. It anticipates the confluence of the same themes in portrayals of the first and second comings of Christ.[7]

It may be that pagan theophanic accounts do both: that is, they echo primordial theophany and also display cases of common grace revelation. Both possibilities will appear as we study the biblical data.

THE PRESENT STUDY

What follows is a study of biblical glory theophany. It has an Old Testament focus (although the final chapter does explore New Testament implications). It engages the work of pre-

---

[7]The Homeric example follows the same ideological thread: the one who is "almighty over gods and men" communicates to his chosen one via storm phenomena.

vious scholars, some of whom display an unfavorable attitude toward the historicity of events recorded in the Old Testament accounts—an attitude not shared by the present study. It understands the Old Testament data against the background of similar ancient Near Eastern thought. Major theological parallels are explored, including a god/God as king; covenant relations between a god and a mortal king—including the covenantal relation of God with Adam and Eve and its implications for biblical theophany and eschatology. The study refers to biblical theophanies as "Sinaitic" or "Sinai-like," although God appeared in stormy glory before Israel's encounter at Sinai as well as afterward. God's descent upon that mountain added to what he had already make known by theophany, just as his later theophanies added more to what he had shown and done at Sinai. Why, then, do I call such theophanies "Sinaitic"? The Sinai theophany is taken as a touchstone for prior and subsequent glory theophanies in the Bible because the Sinai event was constitutive in Israel's history and crucial in salvation history. As God came to Sinai in the clouds to impart his law, so he will come again on the clouds of heaven to judge those who have broken that law.[8]

Until that day we are called to keep in step with God's Spirit, since we live by that Spirit. As we must also give an account for every unfounded word we have spoken (or written), I pray that this book may contain few such words. Since perfection is rare in human attainments, I would hope for more, but not expect it. But I am grateful to the Spirit of Christ for what good is in the following pages and grateful also to Jesus Christ, who has fulfilled the law for me and for all who believe in him.

J.J.N.

South Hamilton, Massachusetts

---

[8]So he came even to our first parents who broke his law (see below, chapter 5).

◆ 1 ◆

Theology and Theophany

> Fanatics have their dreams, wherewith they weave
> A paradise for a sect; the savage, too,
> From forth the loftiest fashion of his sleep
> Guesses at heaven. . . .
>
> John Keats, "Hyperion: A Vision," 1.1–4

The God of the Old Testament is a God who reveals himself. He is also a God who conceals himself. He reveals himself to those who are being saved. He conceals himself from those who are perishing.[1] In any case, he was not a God about whom Israel needed to guess. What Israel knew of God, it knew through his own self-disclosure.

A word commonly used for that self-disclosure is theophany, from the Greek compound θεοφάνεια, consisting of the noun θεός ("god") and the verb φαίνειν ("to appear"). The Greek original was used to describe a festival at Delphi at which the images of the gods were shown to the people.[2] The Hebrew lacks a precise translational equivalent, the closest

---

[1] Isaiah saw both truths: "Truly you are a God who hides himself, O God and Savior of Israel. All the makers of idols will be put to shame and disgraced" (Isa 45:15–16); "I am Yahweh. . . . I have not spoken in secret. . . . I have not said to Jacob's descendants, 'Seek me in vain'" (vv. 18–19).

[2] H. G. Liddell and R. Scott, *A Lexicon* (London: Oxford University Press, 1974), 315.

being the verb ראה ("to see"), in the Niphal, נראה ("to appear").³

As God of all creation, the God of the Old Testament could appear whenever and wherever he chose. According to the book of Exodus, he appeared on Mount Sinai to Moses in order to charge him as prophet and leader of the people. He also appeared to his people on that same mountain after he had brought them out of Egypt. In all of Israel's history, God's self-disclosure on Sinai was unique. Even if Yahweh also revealed himself on Zion (that other Old Testament mountain of which a singular theology may be predicated), it was at Sinai that he called Israel into covenant and founded this people as a theocratic state. So it is appropriate to speak of a "Sinai theology."

Yet again, just because God did reveal himself when and where he would, the theophany on Sinai does not stand exactly alone. God uniquely gave the law to Moses on Mount Sinai. But God did not uniquely appear there. He appeared in similar ways both before the events of Sinai and after. A small sample of passages makes this clear.

God appeared to Adam and Eve in the garden after they had sinned: "Then the man and his wife heard the thunder of Yahweh God going back and forth in the garden in the wind of the storm, and they hid from Yahweh God among the trees of the garden" (Ge 3:8, author's trans.). Such was the first Sinai-like theophany—the first storm theophany when God appeared as Judge of his guilty people.⁴

God also appeared at the dedication of Solomon's temple in a way that inevitably would remind people of his appearance on Sinai: "When the priests withdrew from the Holy Place, the cloud filled the temple of Yahweh. And the priests

---

³Cf. R. Rendtorff, "'Offenbarung' im Alten Testament," *Theologische Literaturzeitung* 85 (1960): col. 833.

⁴For discussion of this translation, see below, chap. 5.

could not perform their service because of the cloud, for the glory of Yahweh filled his temple. Then Solomon said, 'Yahweh has said that he would dwell in a dark cloud'" (1Ki 8:10–12).[5]

God appeared also to Ezekiel by the Kebar River—no less awesome (and perhaps more) than at Sinai: "I looked, and I saw a windstorm coming out of the north—an immense cloud with flashing lightning and surrounded by brilliant light. . . . This was the appearance of the likeness of the glory of Yahweh. When I saw it, I fell facedown, and I heard a voice like thunder" (Eze 1:4–28, author's trans.).[6]

Old Testament writers separate in time and space portrayed the appearance of Yahweh in remarkably similar ways. As God, he could appear as he wanted and when he wanted. Sometimes he appeared as a man.[7] Sometimes he appeared as or in the person of "the angel of Yahweh"[8] or "the angel of God."[9] But more than once he chose to appear in glory—as in the above passages.

Because God appeared in glory on several occasions and at more places than Sinai, it is appropriate to see the Sinai theophany (or, more properly, Sinai theophanies) in the broader context of those other appearances of God.[10] As we

---

[5]Cf. Lev 16:2, "Yahweh said to Moses, . . . 'I appear in the cloud.'" The passage is also evocative of Ex 40:34–35.

[6]"A voice like thunder" translates Heb. קוֹל ("thunder, voice"). Some such translation is best for theophanic contexts and is usually missed. Note the NT: "Then a voice [φωνή] came from heaven, 'I have glorified it, and will glorify it again.' The crowd that was there and heard it said it had thundered [βροντὴν γεγονέναι]; others said an angel had spoken to him" (Jn 12:28–29).

[7]E.g., Ge 18:1–2ff.; 32:24–30.
[8]E.g., Ge 16:7–14, Ex 3:2–6.
[9]E.g., Ge 31:11–13, Ex 14:19–24.
[10]There is no compelling reason to discredit the actuality of these appearances. J. Lindblom, "Theophanies in Holy Places in Hebrew Religion," *HUCA* 32 (1961): 91–106, after a discussion with brief allusions to extrabiblical examples, claims that these theophanies were "hallucinatory expe-

do so, a number of characteristics appear. Some of these characteristics are unique to Sinai-like theophanies. Some of them overlap with other theophanies.

CHARACTERISTICS OF OLD TESTAMENT THEOPHANIES

Divine Initiation

One characteristic common to all Yahweh theophanies is that they are divinely initiated. As J. Kenneth Kuntz remarks, "The theophany in the Old Testament is initiated by, and only by, the deity himself."[11] This point is made in contradistinction to other religious practices in the ancient Near East that often involved strenuous efforts to evoke the desired deity. The futile efforts of 450 prophets to force a manifestation of Baal on Mount Carmel (1Ki 18:16–29) is a good example.[12] Yahweh often "appeared" (ראה, Niph.) in the Old Testament, but never once did human effort "cause [him] to appear" (ראה, Hiph.)[13]

Temporariness

A Yahweh theophany is a temporary event. Yahweh may appear when and where he will, but he is not always apparent at one sole place. H. Wheeler Robinson has noted, "The

---

riences with many analogies at all stages of human life" (p. 106). J. K. Kuntz, *The Self-Revelation of God* (Philadelphia: Westminster, 1967), 32, n.19, appropriately observes that "one may justifiably have reservations as to the propriety of [Lindblom's] expression, 'hallucinatory experiences.'"

[11]Kuntz, *Self-Revelation of God,* 32. This observation is also Kuntz's point of departure in a discourse on theophanic characteristics to which the following discussion is indebted, but from which it also departs in significant ways. Cf. also L. Köhler, *Old Testament Theology,* trans. A. S. Todd (Philadelphia: Westminster, 1957), 103; H. H. Rowley, *The Faith of Israel* (Philadelphia: Westminster, 1956), 23.

[12]The fact that satanists perform various rituals and incantations to conjure up demons in the present day is a related phenomenon.

[13]Cf. Kuntz, *Self-Revelation of God,* 33.

theophany is a transient manifestation of deity, and, as such, to be distinguished from the continuous revelation of Him in all Nature."[14] This fact does not contradict God's omnipresence, which is clearly asserted elsewhere: "Where can I go from your Spirit? Where can I flee from your presence?" (Ps 139:7; cf. vv. 8–10). Nor does it absolutely differentiate between Yahweh and false gods, for pagan gods were also portrayed theophanically. They also were held to be revealed in natural phenomena—Baal in the storm, Yam in the sea, and Shamash in the sun, for example. Yahweh theophanies, then, like pagan theophanies, are temporary. God appears for a purpose, accomplishes that purpose, then disappears.

The Old Testament does image forth a time beyond time when Yahweh's theophany will be continuous:

> The sun will no more be your light by day,
>   nor will the brightness of the moon shine on you,
> for Yahweh will be your everlasting light,
>   and your God will be your glory.
>
> (Isa 60:19)

Such a presence of God is visionary and eschatological. Nowhere in the Old Testament does God actually appear in such a way. Indeed (for reasons to be discussed below) he cannot.

To Save and to Judge

When Yahweh does appear, he comes to save. God's self-disclosure in the Old Testament implies *Heilsgeschichte,* and *Heilsgeschichte* entails theophany. Moses lays down the principle in the first of his three final discourses in Deuteronomy:[15]

> Has any other people heard the voice of God speaking out of fire, as you have, and lived? Has any god ever tried to

---

[14]H. W. Robinson, *Inspiration and Revelation in the Old Testament* (Oxford: Clarendon, 1946), 39.

[15]The three Mosaic discourses that largely structure Deuteronomy from a rhetorical standpoint are, respectively, Dt 1:6–4:43, 4:44–28:68, 29:1–30:20.

take for himself one nation out of another nation, by testings, by miraculous signs and wonders, by war, by a mighty hand and an outstretched arm, or by great and awesome deeds, like all the things Yahweh your God did for you in Egypt before your very eyes?

You were shown these things so that you might know that Yahweh is God; besides him there is no other. (Dt 4:33-35)[16]

Yahweh revealed himself in mighty acts to save his people. He also spoke to them out of fire in theophany. These facts make it clear that Moses connects theophany and *Heilsgeschichte*.

But the same glorious appearance that brings salvation can also bring judgment, as is distinctly shown in Job 40:6-14 (emphasis mine):

Then the Lord spoke to Job out of the *storm*:
. . . .

"Do you have an *arm* like God's,
    and can your *voice thunder* like his?
Then adorn yourself with *glory* and *splendor*,
    and *clothe* yourself in *honor* and *majesty*.
Unleash the fury of your wrath,
    look at every proud man and bring him low,
look at every proud man and humble him,
    crush the wicked where they stand.
Bury them all in the dust together;
    shroud their faces in the grave.
Then I myself will admit to you
    that your own *right hand* can save you."

According to Job, Yahweh's appearance can mean both salvation and judgment.[17] Not only do verses 11-12 remind one of

---

[16]The same principle appears in the NT: "Jesus did many other miraculous signs in the presence of his disciples, which are not recorded in this book. But these are written that you may believe that Jesus is the Christ, the Son of God, and that by believing you may have life in his name" (Jn 20:30-31). In both cases, the manifestation of God or of God's power occurs so that salvation may come to his people.

[17]It is axiomatic, biblically speaking, that salvation implies judgment.

THEOLOGY AND THEOPHANY

Yahweh's judgment appearance in Isaiah 2:9–22 to humble all who are lofty and proud, but the whole passage is rich in theophanic terms used elsewhere in the Old Testament for God's appearance as Savior or Judge. Yahweh spoke to Job out of the "storm" (סְעָרָה),[18] his "voice thundered" (קוֹל ... תַּרְעֵם),[19] he adorned himself with "glory" (גָּאוֹן)[20] and "splendor" (גֹּבַהּ),[21] and he was "clothed" (לבשׁ)[22] with "honor" (הוֹד) and "majesty" (הָדָר).[23] God challenged Job's ability to save himself and used the terms "arm" (זְרוֹעַ)[24] and "right hand" (יָמִין),[25] the same terms used elsewhere of Yahweh's ability to save (most notably

---

[18] Job 40:6 repeats Job 38:1. For סְעָרָה ("storm"), cf. 2Ki 2:1–11 (assumption of Elijah); Isa 29:6 (Yahweh in theophany fighting against the enemies of Jerusalem), 40:24 (in metaphor of Yahweh's judgment against princes and rulers, cf. 41:16); Jer 23:19 and 30:23 (the "storm of Yahweh," which descends like a whirlwind on the wicked); Eze 1:4 (Yahweh in theophany as he commissions Ezekiel to warn Israel of impending judgment).

[19] The word קוֹל ("voice") is a common theophanic term, e.g.: Ge 3:8 (Eden theophany); Ex 19:16 (Sinai theophany); Pss 29:3, 4, 5, 7, 8, 9; 46:7(6); 77:19(18); Joel 2:11; 3:16 (4:16); et al. The verb רעם ("thunder") and the cognate noun (רַעַם) are sometimes used in conjunction with קוֹל, e.g.: Pss 29:3 (the verb); 77:19(18); 104:7.

[20] גָּאוֹן ("glory") describes Yahweh's judgment appearance against opposing Egyptians (Ex 15:7); his theophanic judgment appearance on the day of Yahweh (Isa 2:10, 19, 21); his salvific appearance after eschatological world judgment (Isa 24:14); and possibly in a judgment oracle against Israel at Am 8:7– cf. J. Niehaus, *Amos*, in T. E. McComiskey, ed., *The Minor Prophets: An Exegetical and Expository Commentary* (Grand Rapids: Baker, 1992), 1:472.

[21] גֹּבַהּ ("splendor/height") appears at Job 22:12 in the context of God's ability to judge the wicked (vv. 13ff.).

[22] לבשׁ ("clothe") is used with Yahweh as subject in theophanic glory at Pss 93:1; 104:1 הָדָר and (הוֹד), creation psalms that imply his ability to save (cf. Pss 135, 136).

[23] הוֹד ("honor") and הָדָר ("majesty") appear as a stock pair in the context of Yahweh's saving work in Israel's history (1Ch 16:27; Pss 11:3; 145:5).

[24] Cf. Ex 6:6: "I will ... redeem you with an outstretched arm and with mighty acts of judgment." Frequently זְרוֹעַ occurs in the phrase "בְּיָד חֲזָקָה וּבִזְרוֹעַ נְטוּיָה" ("with a mighty hand and an outstretched arm"), e.g., Dt 4:34; 5:15; 7:19; et al.; 2Ki 17:36. For Yahweh's arm working salvation, cf. Isa 53:5; 59:16.

[25] E.g., Ex 15:6, 12. The Psalms extol Yahweh's ability to save with his right hand, e.g., Pss 17:7; 20:7(6); 21:9(8); 60:6(5); 108:7(6); 138:7.

in the Exodus accounts of the deliverance of Israel from Pharaoh so that they could worship Yahweh at Mount Sinai).

The logic of the passage may be stated as follows: If Job could appear in the splendor of God, he could both deliver himself and destroy the wicked–just as Yahweh does. Since Job lacks the theophanic glory, he also ipso facto lacks the ability to save and to judge.

This reasoning points to another fact about theophany in the Old Testament that I suggested above and will now state as follows: *The mere revelation of God both saves and judges.* Theophany in the Old Testament is not merely an apparition. It is not neutral; it is defining.[26] So it was when God revealed himself to Moses: "Do not come any closer. . . . Take off your sandals, for the place where you are standing is holy ground" (Ex 3:5). The self-revelation of a holy God defines Moses immediately.

God's appearance began to define not only Moses, but the future of Israel as well. God undertook that future by further revealing himself: he disclosed his name. From that disclosure we learn that only God is essentially self-determining. Only he can say of himself, "I will be what I will be" (אֶהְיֶה אֲשֶׁר אֶהְיֶה, Ex 3:14, author's trans.). The divine name is the first person (Qal imperfect) form, of which the name Yahweh is the third person form ("He is/will be"). Cassuto has pointed out that it is God's name in covenantal relation with Israel.[27] But it is also the name God explained to Moses out of the burning bush theophany. The context of that theophany envisioned Yahweh's deliverance of Israel out of Egypt and his judgment of Pharaoh (Ex 3:7–22). In other words, the significance of Yahweh's name–the One who "is what he is/will be what he will be"–was given in a context that spoke of salvation (for Israel)

---

[26]Cf. Jn 3:16–21.
[27]U. Cassuto, *The Documentary Hypothesis* (Jerusalem: Magnes, 1961), 15ff.

and judgment (for Egypt). In Yahweh's first appearance to Moses a collocation was made between Yahweh's self-revelation and his role as Savior and Judge.[28]

Impartation of Holiness

Another fact appears in this first Sinai theophany: *God is holy, and he imparts holiness where and for as long as he appears.* Yahweh warns Moses that he is standing on "holy ground." As long as Yahweh is there, the ground is holy because his presence sanctifies it. Later the Lord's holiness is an attribute communicated to his messenger–the commander of Yahweh's army–who similarly warns Joshua, "Take off your sandals, for the place where you are standing is holy" (Jos 5:15). Yahweh's holiness consecrates the Tent of Meeting, as he says to Moses, "There I will meet you and speak to you; there also I will meet with the Israelites, and the place will be consecrated [נִקְדַּשׁ, 'made holy'] by my glory" (Ex 29:42–43).

The same holy presence descends upon and fills the temple (1Ki 8:10–11) when Solomon dedicates it; and Yahweh's

---

[28]The NT makes the same collocation. The NT equivalent of the name Yahweh (or, to put it another way, of the divine self-naming of Ex 3:14) is the affirmation that "as the Father has life in himself, so he has granted the Son to have life in himself" (Jn 5:26). In the next verse we read, "And he [the Father] has given him authority to judge" (v. 27). Here, as in Ex 3, God's *aseity* is connected with his authority to judge (the authority is illustrated descriptively in Ex 3 and stated propositionally in Jn 5). True, the verse concludes with the clause "because he is the Son of Man." This is not simply a statement of his identification with humanity, however. It is a messianic title with divine implications (cf. Da 7:13). To the extent that Jesus' humanity is mentioned here as a reason for his appointment as Judge, it agrees with Ac 17:31 (and cf. Heb 4:15). However, if Jesus' sinless humanity is a necessary condition of his appointment as Judge of all, it is not a sufficient condition. Ultimately the sufficient condition is that he is God, for it is God alone who is "Judge of all the earth" (Ge 18:25). The most important point for our purposes is that Jesus' identity as Judge *follows upon* his identity as divine–as possessing the divine *aseity*.

presence (his "Name") is what makes the temple holy:²⁹ "I have heard the prayer and plea you have made before me; I have consecrated [הִקְדַּשְׁתִּי] this temple, which you have built, by putting my Name there forever" (1Ki 9:3). God's holiness is not a quality that lingers when God departs (Eze 10), nor does it somehow bind God to the place (Jer 7:9–15). God's presence is what makes the place holy–but only as he remains there.³⁰

Revealer-Concealer

The fact that a Yahweh theophany is not spiritually neutral but defining relates to another quality of those theophanies. *When Yahweh does reveal himself, he does not only reveal himself, he also conceals himself.* The revelation comes in flashes of glory that resemble lightning. The concealment takes the form of a thick, dark cloud. God's holiness is the reason for this twofold phenomenon. Because of his holiness, a full revelation of God's glory would be unendurable. Once Adam and Eve had sinned in Eden, God appeared as a storm–partly revealed, partly concealed. So he appeared on Sinai–with flashes of lightning yet veiled in a thick cloud.

Human Fear

Another aspect of Yahweh theophanies closely related to his holiness is human reaction. *The human reaction to theophany in the Old Testament is one of fear.* Old Testament examples make this doctrine clear: "Moses hid his face, because he was afraid

---

²⁹For the significance of the divine "name," cf. J. Niehaus, "The Central Sanctuary: Where and When?" *TB* 43, no. 1 (May 1992): 3–30, esp. 22–27 and sources there cited. See earlier G. J. Wenham, "Deuteronomy and the Central Sanctuary," *TB* 22 (1971): 103–18.

³⁰G. von Rad, *Old Testament Theology*, trans. D. M. G. Stalker (New York: Harper & Row, 1961), 1:272, notes that this holiness comes from God himself, whether it involves the consecration of a place or of the people (cf. Ex 19:6, 10, 14; Nu 11:1; Jos 3:5; 7:13).

to look at God" (Ex 3:6); Israel was "afraid of the fire and did not go up the mountain" (Dt 5:5); Elijah "pulled his cloak over his face" in the presence of God (1Ki 19:13). *Mysterium tremendum* this may be.[31] Yet it is neither mystery nor power alone that frightens mortals in the presence of Yahweh's glory—it is God's holiness.[32] Mortals can only respond in fear and awe (not because they are human, but because they are fallen) even in the presence of the God who saves them.

Natural Upheaval

Not only does humankind react when God appears, but *nature also is disturbed*.[33] Perhaps the best example is Elijah's encounter with God on Mount Horeb (Sinai):

> Yahweh said, "Go out and stand on the mountain in the presence of Yahweh, for Yahweh is about to pass by." Then a great and powerful wind tore the mountains apart and shattered the rocks before Yahweh, but Yahweh was not in the wind. After the wind there was an earthquake, but Yahweh was not in the earthquake. After the earthquake came a fire, but Yahweh was not in the fire. And after the fire came a thunderous voice. When Elijah heard it, he pulled his cloak over his face and went out. (1Ki 19:11–13)[34]

Yahweh is not in the wind, earthquake, or fire. Rather his advance causes these natural convulsions. Other descriptions of natural disruption at his appearing may be more purely literary

---

[31]Cf. W. Eichrodt, *Theology of the Old Testament*, trans. J. A. Baker (Philadelphia: Westminster, 1967), 2:269.

[32]Cf. ibid., 268ff.; Th. C. Vriezen, *An Outline of Old Testament Theology* (Oxford: Basil Blackwell, 1958), 135.

[33]Cf. J. Jeremias, *Theophanie: Die Geschichte einer alttestamentlichen Gattung*, Wissenschaftliche Monographien zum Alten und Neuen Testament (Neukirchen-Vluyn: Neukirchener Verlag, 1965 [hereafter *Theophanie: WMANT*]), who calls this phenomenon "der Aufruhr der Natur" (pp. 7ff.).

[34]For the translation of קוֹל דְּמָמָה as "thunderous voice," see J. Lust, "A Gentle Breeze or a Roaring Thunderous Sound?" *VT* 25 (1975): 110–15.

(e.g., Jdg 5:4; Ps 18:7ff.). But passages such as 1Ki 19:11–13 (cf. Ge 3:8; Ex 19:16–19; et al.) portray stormy atmospheric disruptions attendant upon actual theophany.

To some extent the storm-cloud nature of these appearances is accounted for by God's self-concealment. He chooses to garb himself in a thick cloud because a full revelation of his holy presence would destroy the onlooker. As he told Moses, "You cannot see my face, for no one may see me and live" (Ex 33:20). But self-concealment alone does not account for the storm-cloud language in every case. Sometimes the stormy language seems calculated to enhance the supernatural power of the great Judge, whose appearance thus has implications even for the natural order. Perhaps that is why David reported that when God heard his cry for help:

> The earth trembled and quaked,
>   and the foundations of the mountains shook;
>   they trembled because he was angry.
>
> . . . .
>
> He parted the heavens and came down.
>
> (Ps 18:7–9)

So Micah said that as Yahweh comes to judge Israel,

> The mountains melt beneath him
>   and the valleys split apart,
> like wax before the fire,
>   like water rushing down a slope.
>
> (Mic 1:4)

Although such is the language of poetry, it is not just poetic language. On the one hand, it describes Yahweh's advance—either to save or to judge—in terms evocative of the Sinai theophany. On the other hand, it portrays the advent of the great Judge in terms found also in Old Testament eschatology (cf. Isa 24:17–23).

Adumbrated Eschatology

Another characteristic of any Sinaitic theophany, therefore, is that *it anticipates the eschatological revelation of Yahweh.* The manner of God's theophany at Sinai foreshadows the manner of his appearance when he will come to "punish the powers in the heavens above / and the kings on the earth below" (Isa 24:21).

Theophanic Words

God is not silent when he appears as Savior or as Judge. As one scholar has remarked, "God appears *in order* to speak."[35] God's words are an essential part of his self-disclosure in every case. Gerhard von Rad has put the matter forcefully: "With an Old Testament theophany everything depends upon the pronouncement: the phenomena which accompany it are always merely accessories."[36] This is perhaps an overstatement. In the very act of revealing himself, God conceals himself with a good purpose, even a saving purpose, as we have seen, and he uses accompanying phenomena (thick cloud) to do so. His appearance can also cause severe natural dislocations: a mode of theophany by which God shows his power over nature and foreshadows the manner of his eschatological return. These phenomena are not just accessories. They are significant consequences of God's advent. They have their own story to tell of God's superhuman holiness and supernatural power. Yet God's pronouncement is all-important. Everything does depend upon it, for without the pronouncement, the phenomena of theophany would go unexplained. So when Yahweh revealed himself in a fiery theophany to Abram,

---

[35] M. Burrows, *An Outline of Biblical Theology* (Philadelphia: Westminster, 1946), 28. Emphasis added.
[36] Von Rad, *Old Testament Theology*, 2:19.

he explained that he was there to make a covenant with him (Ge 15:17–21).[37] When Yahweh appeared to Moses, it was to raise him up as prophet and leader of the people (Ex 3:10ff.)– and later to establish his covenant with all Israel (Ex 19–24). When Yahweh appeared to Isaiah (Isa 6) and Ezekiel (Eze 1), it was to ordain them as prophets to carry God's covenant lawsuit against his rebellious people. The visual component in all of these theophanies was important, even awesome. But the heart of the matter in each case was what Yahweh had to say.

FORM CRITICISM

In the Old Testament many of God's utterances appear in a certain form. This fact has been well-documented in form-critical studies of second millennium international treaties (covenants) and their bearing on the structure and date of Deuteronomy.[38] The same has been demonstrated with regard to Old Testament covenant lawsuit literature.[39] The covenant lawsuit form found in the Old Testament also appears in extrabiblical literature. It is now clear that strong formal parallels exist between the ancient Near Eastern and Old Testament materials in these genres.[40]

---

[37] It was a covenant that implicated both the covenant of Moses and the covenant of Christ. See below, chap. 5.

[38] Cf. M. Kline, *Treaty of The Great King* (Grand Rapids: Eerdmans, 1963); K. A. Kitchen, *The Bible in Its World* (Exeter: Paternoster, 1977), 79–85.

[39] Cf. H. B. Huffmon, "The Covenant Lawsuit in the Prophets," *JBL* 78 (1959): 285–95; E. W. Nicholson, *Preaching to the Exiles* (Oxford: Basil Blackwell, 1970). See especially the seminal chapter by G. E. Wright, "The Lawsuit of God: A Form-Critical Study of Deuteronomy 32," in *Israel's Prophetic Heritage*, ed. B. W. Anderson and W. Harrelson (New York: Harper & Bros., 1962), 26–46.

[40] Cf. Niehaus, *Amos*, 318–19, for comparative discussion of Old Testament and ancient Near East covenant lawsuit materials especially.

Can the same be said for Old Testament theophanies and for Sinaitic theophanies in particular? Do they have an identifiable literary form, and does one find the same in extrabiblical materials?

Both questions may be answered in the affirmative even though the history of the recognition of the forms is fairly recent. Hermann Gunkel, generally credited as the father of Old Testament form criticism, took patriarchal theophanies into account in his Genesis commentary (1901).[41] He did not, however, explore their form in any detail. Julian Morgenstern furthered the study of pentateuchal theophanies in a lengthy study (1911, 1913), but without adding significantly to the form criticism of the genre.[42] Eduard Norden, in his signal work, *Agnostos Theos* (1913),[43] contributed to the study of certain recurring formulae in theophanies.

The most significant recent work has been done by Jörg Jeremias[44] and by J. Kenneth Kuntz.[45] Kuntz in particular appears to have identified the fundamental components of this literary *Gattung*, which may be stated as follows:

1 Introductory description in the third person
2 Deity's utterance of the name of the (mortal) addressee
3 Response of the addressee
4 Deity's self-asseveration
5 His quelling of human fear

---

[41] H. Gunkel, *Genesis*, 6th ed. (Göttingen: Vandenhoeck & Ruprecht, 1964).
[42] J. Morgenstern, "Biblical Theophanies," *ZA* 25 (1911): 139–93; 28 (1913): 15–60.
[43] E. Norden, *Agnostos Theos: Untersuchungen zur Formengeschichtliche religiöser Rede* (Leipzig/Berlin: B. G. Tuebner, 1913).
[44] Jeremias, *Theophanie: WMANT.* For more detailed discussion of Jeremias's work, see chap. 2.
[45] Kuntz, *Self-Revelation of God*; cf. below, chap. 2, for further bibliography.

6   Assertion of his gracious presence
7   The *hieros logos* addressed to the particular situation[46]
8   Inquiry or protest by the addressee
9   Continuation of the *hieros logos* with perhaps some repetition of elements 4, 5, 6, 7, and/or 8
10 Concluding description in the third person[47]

Any proposed *Gattung* is a distillation of actual examplars, and the above is no exception. Not every element will appear in every theophany. Kuntz observes, "The Hebrews were not rigid in their utilization of a literary form."[48] For that matter, neither were other nations of the ancient Near East. However, the regularity with which the above elements recur in Old Testament theophanies argues strongly for the adoption of this form.[49]

Like the international treaty form and the covenant lawsuit form mentioned above, the theophanic *Gattung* occurs in both the Old Testament and the ancient Near East. Subsequent study of Old Testament and extrabiblical examples will be

---

[46]"*Hieros logos*," Gk. for "holy word"—a word from God (or, in pagan theophanies, from the god/goddess) to the human recipient.

[47]Adapted from Kuntz, *Self-Revelation of God,* 60.

[48]Ibid., 47.

[49]Kuntz's book, and especially chap. 2, "The Form of Theophanic Disclosure in the Old Testament," is worthwhile reading in this regard. Kuntz illustrates the structure of Genesis 26:23–25, e.g., as follows (p. 59):

1	Introductory description	[23]From there he went up to Beer-Sheba. [24]And Yahweh appeared to him the same night and said,
2	Divine self-asseveration	"I am the God of Abraham your father;
3	Quelling of human fear	Fear not,
4	Assertion of gracious divine presence	For I am with you,
5	*Hieros logos*	And I will bless you, and multiply your descendants for my servant Abraham's sake."
6	Concluding description	[25]And he built an altar there and called upon the name of Yahweh....

more extensive, but a brief survey at this point will show the applicability of the form.

The Yahweh theophany at Genesis 3:8–24 illustrates the essential elements of the proposed *Gattung*:

Formal Element	**Genesis 3:8–24**
1 Introductory description in the third person	3:8
2 Deity's utterance of the name of the (mortal) addressee	3:9
3 Response of the addressee	3:10
4 Deity's self-asseveration[50]	
5 His quelling of human fear[51]	
6 Assertion of his gracious presence[52]	
7 The *hieros logos* addressed to the particular situation	3:11
8 Inquiry or protest by the addressee	3:12
9 Continuation of the *hieros logos* with perhaps some repetition of elements 4, 5, 6, 7, and/or 8:	
hieros logos	3:13a
protest	3:13b
hieroi logoi	3:14–19
to the serpent	3:14–15
to the woman	3:16
to Adam	3:17–19
10 Concluding description in the third person	3:20–24

---

[50]This element is present in later Yahweh theophanies but lacking here. The reason appears to be that the man and woman already knew God from previous occasions (unmarred by sin, e.g., Ge 1:28–30; 2:16–17) and had no doubt as to who was now addressing them.

[51]This element, common in later Yahweh theophanies, is also lacking here. The reason appears to be that Yahweh's later appearances to people are also *hieroi logoi* of deliverance. His appearance to Adam and Eve, by contrast, initiates covenant lawsuit procedures and eventuates in judgment.

[52]This element, the gracious assertion, "[for] I am with you" or the like, is also common in later Yahweh theophanies. It is missing here (perhaps) for reasons similar to the omission of element 5.

Form is not everything even if it does implicate content.[53] Much more needs to be said about matters of covenant background and theology. But the analysis of Genesis 3:8–24 shows that the proposed *Gattung* articulates well the essential structure of the passage.

The same may be said of extrabiblical theophanies. A good example comes from the annals of Ashurbanipal (668–627 B.C.), the last great king of Assyria. Apparently while Ashurbanipal was staying in Arbela to attend a feast of the goddess Ishtar and to "worship her great divinity," word came to him of a rebellious vassal. Teumann the Elamite was marching to do battle with Assyria. The Assyrian king took the report of Teumann's revolt before Ishtar in her temple, bowed down before her, and prayed for her intervention against the Elamite. The response to his prayer was a theophany of the goddess:

v. 46 Ishtar heard the sighs I emitted, and
v. 47 she said, "Fear not!" and comforted me in my heart:
v. 48 "Because of the raising of your hands which you have raised,
[because of] your eyes, filled with tears,
v. 49 I have had mercy upon you."
During that very same night in which I approached her
v. 50 a certain seer lay down and saw a dream vision.[54]

The seer's "dream vision" follows this account of an actual theophany of Ishtar. In context, the third-person conclusion of vv. 49b–50 also provides a transition and part of the

---

[53]Cf. S. Mowinckel, *The Psalms in Israel's Worship*, trans. D. R. Ap-Thomas (New York: Abingdon, 1962), 1:25: "There exists no form without a content, and no content without a form."

[54]Translation adapted from A. C. Piepkorn, *Historical Prism Inscriptions of Ashurbanipal* [hereafter *HPIA*] (Chicago: University of Chicago Press, 1933), 1:64–67.

longer introduction to the vision itself (see below). Be that as it may, Ashurbanipal's Ishtar theophany has the following form:

Formal Element	vv. 46–50
1 Introductory description in the third person	vv. 46–47
5 Ishtar's quelling of human fear	v. 47
7 The *hieros logos* addressed to the particular situation	vv. 48–49a
10 Concluding description in the third person	vv. 49b–50

As is often the case in the Old Testament, the Assyrian pericope does not contain every possible element of the theophanic *Gattung*. It does, however, contain enough to be a good basic illustration of the form. Ishtar is introduced in the third person (she comes to Ashurbanipal in response to his sighs and prayers).[55] She encourages him to "Fear not!" The encouragement comes because (as in Old Testament theophanies) deity has come to save the favorite, not to destroy him. She gives a *hieros logos* directly appropriate to the situation: "Because of the raising of thy hands ... I have had mercy upon thee." Ashurbanipal has prayed to his goddess, and she is about to answer his prayer. (A more detailed version of the goddess's answer comes in the dream-vision theophany that follows.) The theophany to Ashurbanipal concludes with a third-person account of a seer's dream-vision of Ishtar that took place on the same night as the Ishtar theophany.

The Assyrian theophanic account is cast in the same literary form as the biblical examples. More will be said later about the theological ramifications of this fact. Before we look at theology, however, we must take another look at form criticism and, in particular, the form-criticism of visions.

---

[55]This does not contradict the point made above, that deity, and not human, initiates theophany. Ashurbanipal prayed to Ishtar, but he did not try to make her appear. Her appearance was unasked for, unexpected, and entirely on her own initiative.

The form criticism of visions is relevant to a discussion of Sinaitic theophanies. For example, Genesis 15 (a visionary chapter of unusual theological importance for both the Old and New Testaments) contains a theophany of the Sinai type.

One appropriate analysis of Genesis 15 shows the same literary form as the examples above.[56] In fact, the form repeats itself no less than four times within the passage.[57] We will further discuss this complex chapter later. At the present, an analysis of one small section (Ge 15:7–11) will serve to illustrate the point:

	Formal Element	Genesis 15:7–11
1	Introductory description, third person	15:7a
4	Deity's self-asseveration	15:7b
7	*Hieros logos*	15:7c[58]
3	Inquiry or protest of addressee	15:8
9	Continuation of *hieros logos*	15:9
10	Concluding description, third person	15:10–11

This small pericope is part of the larger vision (introduced at Ge 15:1) in which Yahweh speaks to Abram. Like other parts of the vision, it contains a number of essential elements of the theophanic *Gattung*. This is an important fact to establish simply because it shows the legitimacy of applying the same kind

---

[56] I say, "one appropriate analysis," because Ge 15, like some other OT passages, may be analyzed in different ways for structure, each one appropriate and each one able to teach us something of the meaning of the passage. See below, chap. 5.

[57] Namely, Ge 15:1–6; 15:7–11; 15:12–16; and 15:17–18.

[58] One might argue that the phrase "to give you this land to take possession of it" is properly a part of the self-asseveration of Yahweh, since it depends on the foregoing, "I am Yahweh, who brought you out of Ur of the Chaldeans." However, the phrase not only makes a promise of land, but also raises a questioning response or protest from Abram. It should therefore be considered a prophetic *hieros logos*.

of formal analysis to both kinds of theophany, spatial and visionary. If the same kind of analysis applies, the same kind of conclusions may result (see below).

The same form applies not only to Old Testament visionary theophanies, but also to extrabiblical ones. A good example is the dream vision of Ashurbanipal's seer mentioned above. The account runs as follows:

v. 49 During that very night in which I [Ashurbanipal] approached her [Ishtar],
v. 50 a certain seer lay down and saw a dream-vision.
v. 51 When he awoke he recounted the vision which Ishtar had revealed to him
v. 52 to me, declaring, "Ishtar dwelling in Arbela
v. 53 entered, and right and left she bore quivers;
v. 54 she held a bow in her hand;
v. 55 she unsheathed a sharp sword for battle.
v. 56 You stood before her. Like the mother of a
v. 57 child she talked with you.
v. 58 Ishtar, the exalted of the gods, addressed you, giving you this counsel:
v. 59 'You behold a direction to go to war.
v. 60 Where my face is set, there do I go forth.'
v. 61 You said to her, 'Where you go
v. 62 I will go with you, O Lady of Ladies!'
v. 63 She repeated to you: 'Here you
v. 64 shall stay, where you are dwelling.
v. 65 Eat food, drink wine,
v. 66 provide music, revere my divinity,
v. 67 until I go and do this deed [and]
v. 68 make you attain the desire of your heart.
v. 69 Your face shall not turn green, your feet shall not tire,
v. 70 your strength shall not fail you in the heat of the battle.'

v. 71 In her kindly embrace she enfolded you and
v. 72 protected your entire stature.
v. 73 From her face fire flared forth,
v. 74 angrily she went off shining brightly and strode forth to conquer her foe.
v. 75 Against Teumann, king of Elam,
v. 76 with whom she was angry, she set her face."[59]

The passage may be outlined as follows:

	Formal Element	v. 49–76
1	Introductory description, third person	vv. 49b–58
7	The *hieros logos*	vv. 59–60
3	Inquiry or protest of addressee	vv. 61–62
9	Continuation of the *hieros logos*	vv. 63–70
10	Concluding description, third person	vv. 71–76

The Ashurbanipal dream vision is slightly more complex than Genesis 15:7–11 because part of the "introductory description" consists of the reporting speech of "a certain seer" (vv. 52b–58). When this is taken properly into account, it appears that the Assyrian and patriarchal dream visions have the same overall structure. The only real exception may be the "divine self-asseveration," which appears to be lacking in the Ashurbanipal account. However, this element is probably supplied functionally by the seer's own assertion that "Ishtar, exalted of the gods, addressed you" (v. 58).

Not every item must be exactly parallel. In fact, there is not always exact parallelism between any two Old Testament theophanic accounts. But the close formal parallel shows that both Old Testament and ancient Near Eastern visionary theophanies may be understood in terms of the same *Gattung*. Such theophanic accounts involve not only a literary form, however, but also an experiential content. Both form and content, in turn, have theological implications.

---

[59]Translation adapted from Piepkorn, *HPIA,* 66–67.

FORM CRITICISM AND THEOLOGY

Form and content are two words that represent two distinct ideas. They may be considered apart, but they must ultimately be understood together. Mowinckel aptly said, "There exists no form without a content, and no content without a form."[60] In a poem, a play, or a theophany, form and content cooperate to impact the audience of the work.

When the "work" is or purports to be a theophany—or rather an account of a theophany—what then is the relevance of the *Gattung* by which the account is structured? What does that structure tell about the faith of the author? What does it say about the theophany itself?

It may be, as Kuntz says, that "to lay bare literary form ... is to travel a good measure of the distance that is required for an understanding of the faith itself that is articulated."[61] But what can scholars who aim to "get at" the faith of Israel say when a Yahweh theophany and an Ishtar theophany are cast in the same *Gattung*? How is the faith of Ashurbanipal different from that of Abraham? Or of Moses—or better yet of Joshua, to whom Yahweh spoke words of warlike encouragement (Jos 1:2–9), much as Ishtar did to Ashurbanipal?

Perhaps the best way to answer these questions is to ask yet another question—namely, What lay behind these theophanies? Or, to put it another way—What actually happened? Such a question is unavoidable, if only because theophanic accounts—both biblical and extrabiblical—purport to tell about something that really happened, that is, they appear to be historical.

To illustrate that fact one can subject a historical account that entails no theophany to the same form-critical analysis used above. The interview between King David and Mephi-

---

[60]Cf. above, n. 50.
[61]Kuntz, *Self-Revelation of God,* 49.

bosheth, son of Jonathan (2Sa 9:6–11), lends itself well to such an analysis:

Formal Element	2 Samuel 9:6–11
1 Introductory description, third person	9:6a David said
2 Utterance of name of addressee	9:6b "Mephibosheth!"
3 Response of the addressee	9:6c "Your servant," he replied
5 Quelling of human fear	9:7a "Don't be afraid," David said to him,
6, 7 Assertion of gracious presence + *"hieros logos"*	9:7b "for I will surely show you kindness for the sake of your father Jonathan. I will restore to you all the land that belonged to your grandfather Saul, and you will always eat at my table."
8 Inquiry or protest by addressee	9:8 Mephibosheth bowed down and said, "What is your servant, that you should notice a dead dog like me?"
9 Continuation of the *"hieros logos"* + elements 4, 5, 6, 7, and/or 8	9:9–11a David conveys to Ziba the *hieroi logoi* announced to Mephibosheth
10 Concluding description, third person	9:11b So Mephibosheth ate at David's table like one of the king's sons. (Continued in 9:12–13.)

There are, of course, differences. David is not God, and his very appearance cannot inspire fear as God's does. Yet he is a king and one who (because of Saul's sins against him) might have had good reason to seek the life of Saul's grandson. Therefore, when Mephibosheth finds himself in the presence of the king, a gracious word from David appropriately quells his fear. Because David is not God, his words are not really "*hieroi logoi*" in that sense. But his words do play the same role in the structure of the account that God's *hieroi logoi* play: they convey in a detailed way the gracious plans and provisions of the great king for his servant.

What is outstanding about the above analysis is that it parallels in every way the structure of theophanic interviews. This parallel indicates the historical verisimilitude of the theophanies. They are described in just the way one would describe a historical encounter between a person of great, even dreadful, power, who plans to bless, and a more humble recipient of unexpected favor.

Theophanic accounts, therefore, both biblical and extrabiblical, not only partake of the same *Gattung,* they also share that *Gattung* with historical accounts of interviews between humans. And if, for instance, such an interview did take place between David and Mephibosheth in the manner described, we may say that a historical event gave rise to the *Gattung* in that case. The author of the account wrote what happened, and the sequence of events and words in large part suggested the form of the account. And if the theophanic *Gattung* is the same, it follows that there, too, in each case, the sequence of events and words suggested the form of the account. This holds only for actual theophanies and for theophanic visions, and not for poetically embellished accounts such as Psalm 18:7ff. that draw upon past theophanies and even upon the treasury of Canaanite Baal poetry for emphatic language.

Theophanies from the Old Testament and from the ancient Near East are, therefore, actually cast in a mode of historical reportage. And if we ask what actually happened, the answer must be twofold. One half of the answer is that the authors would have us believe that what they reported is what happened. We may call this a matter of faith, or of propaganda. To Israel, Assyrian claims probably sounded like propaganda (cf. 2Ki 18:19–25). The other half of the answer is that we have no other real information in any one case. Although the theophanies and visions have much in common, each one finally stands on its own and tells its own story.

2

Sinai Tradition: Background of Scholarship

> Look on my works, ye Mighty, and despair!
> Percy Bysshe Shelley, "Ozymandias"

Old Testament theophanies are hardly a new topic of study. Several books on the subject have appeared in the last few decades. Jörg Jeremias's *Theophanie*,[1] J. Kenneth Kuntz's *The Self-Revelation of God*,[2] Frank Moore Cross's *Canaanite Myth and Hebrew Epic*,[3] and Thomas W. Mann's *Divine Presence and Guidance in Israelite Traditions*,[4] have explored a number of Old Testament theophanies in detail, with some valuable results. All four scholars approach the biblical data with assumptions that ultimately limit the theological value of their work (see below). Meredith G. Kline has also taken a general approach to Old and New Testament theophanies in two works, *Images of the Spirit*[5] and *Kingdom Prologue*.[6] His work does not focus on the

---

[1] Neukirchen: Neukirchener Verlag, 1965.
[2] Philadelphia: Westminster, 1967.
[3] Cambridge: Harvard University Press, 1973 [hereafter *CMHE*].
[4] Baltimore: Johns Hopkins Press, 1977.
[5] Grand Rapids: Baker, 1980.
[6] South Hamilton: Gordon-Conwell Seminary Press, 1986.

events of Mount Sinai, but he understands the Sinai theophany in relation to other Old Testament theophanies in a covenantal context. Kline is above all a biblical theologian, and his volumes are major contributions to that field, both in terms of biblical anthropology and covenant theology. Kline stands in a tradition of biblical theology, exemplified by Geerhardus Vos, that assumes that the events portrayed in both Testaments took place as described.[7] Such an assumption governs the present study.

HISTORICAL SCIENCE AND BIBLICAL THEOLOGY

The governing assumption that the events portrayed in both the Old and New Testaments took place as described is not naive. Nor is it unscientific, for we define science to include the proposition that God exists and has revealed himself in both the natural realm and in the Bible.

Many scholars—and a long tradition of scholarship—would argue the error of this approach. It has been said that history in the modern "scientific" sense cannot be found where supernatural events are reported. Narratives of the supernatural are actually the domain of primitive mythmaking, legend, or saga. Literary critics from W. M. L. de Wette to the present day have held essentially this view. Hermann Gunkel, the father of form criticism, believed that "any other conclusion" was "impossible."[8] Many Old Testament scholars, whose work forms an im-

---

[7]G. Vos, *Biblical Theology* (Grand Rapids: Eerdmans, 1948).

[8]H. Gunkel, *The Legends of Genesis* (New York: Schocken, 1964), 8: "Any other conclusion is impossible from the point of view of our modern historical science, which is not a figment of imagination but is based upon the observation of facts. And however cautious the modern historian may be in declaring anything impossible, he may declare with all confidence that animals—serpents and she-asses, for instance—do not speak and never have spoken, that there is no tree whose fruit confers immortality or knowledge, that angels and men do not have carnal connexion, and that a world-conquering army cannot be defeated—as Genesis xiv. declares—with three hundred and eighteen men."

portant background to the present area of study, have shared this perspective.

Although our task is not to produce a philosophy of science, a prefatory comment on the issue may be helpful for the sake of orientation. Alfred North Whitehead, a signal modern philosopher of science, has cogently argued that the rise of Western science, far from excluding the supernatural, has depended radically on *faith*: "The faith in the order of nature *which has made possible the growth of science* is a particular example of a deeper faith. This faith cannot be justified by any inductive generalisation."[9] Whitehead sees the roots of this faith in "the medieval insistence on the rationality of God, conceived as with the personal energy of Jehovah and with the rationality of a Greek philosopher."[10] He argues that whatever contributions pagan cultures may have made to European and even world culture, it was the idea of God that made possible the rise of modern science and the civilization that arose with it. Whitehead's argument has implications for biblical studies. After all, if the biblical idea of God has made modern science possible, then (one might argue) the historical study of the Bible, to be scientific, ought to include God as the Bible portrays him.

Historicity and Theology

If theology is meant to tell us facts about God—as opposed to human guesses about him—then scholars who discount the supernatural take an approach to theophany, and to revelation in general, that renders theology proper (the study of the nature of God) almost impossible. Such a result is inevitable because they rule out the biblical portrayals of God as unhistorical.[11]

---

[9] A. N. Whitehead, *Science and the Modern World* (New York: Free Press, 1967), 18. Emphasis added.
[10] Ibid., 13.
[11] While some may call such an approach a "theology" of sorts, it is in fact no such thing, because, although it implies what theologians call "practical atheism" (which is a theological stance in itself), it tells us nothing about God.

Liberal scholarship of the Pentateuch, and consequently of the Sinai events as well, finds itself in this situation.

Duane Garrett, in his book *Rethinking Genesis*,[12] has shown in a concise and intelligent way many of the pitfalls of such Pentateuchal scholarship. He has done so by drawing upon literary evidence from the ancient Near East; he has also used ancient Near Eastern evidence to argue an alternative view of the documentary origins of the book of Genesis consonant with Mosaic authorship.[13] Perhaps a similar book is needed to demonstrate the attitude of some liberal scholars toward the supernatural events recorded in the Old Testament.

Garrett is the latest of a long line of scholars whose books have shown the inadequacy of the documentary, oral-traditionist, and traditio-historical approaches to Old Testament, and especially Pentateuchal, materials. The Old Testament commentaries of C. F. Keil and F. Delitzsch;[14] the apologetic works of A. H. Sayce,[15] James Orr,[16] and O. T. Allis;[17] Old Testament introductions by E. J. Young[18] and R. K. Harrison;[19] *The Pentateuch in Its Cultural Environment* by G. Herbert Livingston;[20] and various more recent commentaries[21] have all

---

[12] Grand Rapids: Baker, 1991.

[13] His work to some extent builds upon that of I. M. Kikawada and A. Quinn, *Before Abraham Was* (Nashville: Abingdon, 1985). Kikawada and Quinn compare the primeval history (Ge 1–11) with the Akkadian "Atrahasis Epic" as well as Sumerian, Homeric, and Zoroastrian examples to show a generic structure to primeval histories. They thus argue the unity of Ge 1–11, as opposed to the Documentary Hypothesis. Cf. Garrett, *Rethinking Genesis*, 108–25.

[14] *Commentary on the Old Testament in Ten Volumes* (Grand Rapids: Eerdmans, 1978).

[15] *Monument Facts and Higher Critical Fancies* (London: Religious Tract Society, 1904).

[16] *The Problem of the Old Testament* (New York: Scribners, 1907).

[17] *The Five Books of Moses* (Nutley: Presbyterian and Reformed, 1943); *The Old Testament: Its Claims and Its Critics* (Grand Rapids: Baker, 1972).

[18] *An Introduction to the Old Testament* (Grand Rapids: Eerdmans, 1949).

[19] *Introduction to the Old Testament* (Grand Rapids, Eerdmans, 1969).

[20] 2d ed. (Grand Rapids: Baker, 1987).

[21] Cf. G. Wenham, *Genesis 1–15* (Waco: Word, 1987); P. C. Craigie, *The*

shown, in one way or another, both the internal inconsistencies of more liberal approaches and their failure to use what we now know of ancient Near Eastern literary methods as controls. Nonevangelical scholars who have pioneered in ancient Near Eastern studies have demonstrated the same—most notably Umberto Cassuto[22] and Cyrus Gordon,[23] both of whom recognized from their studies of Ugaritic and other ancient Near Eastern literature that the criterion of different divine names as hallmarks of different Pentateuchal documents—the foundational premise of the documentary approach—cannot stand. Their conclusion has damaging implications for subsequent approaches, such as redaction criticism and tradition-history, which build upon the fundamental distinguishing criteria of the older Documentary Hypothesis.

The goal of this book is not to produce an exhaustive critique of liberal Old Testament or Pentateuchal scholarship.[24] Yet the attitude of documentary, form-critical, redaction-critical, and traditio-historical scholars toward historicity, as well as toward the supernatural, can hardly be ignored when they have contributed so much to the scholarship of the passages we must study. The Documentary Hypothesis developed in the

---

Book of Deuteronomy (Grand Rapids: Eerdmans, 1976); M. H. Woudstra, *The Book of Joshua* (Grand Rapids: Eerdmans, 1981).

[22]U. Cassuto, *The Documentary Hypothesis* (Jerusalem: Magnes, 1961).

[23]C. Gordon, "Higher Critics and Forbidden Fruit," *CT* 4 (1949).

[24]For a useful recent critique of documentary, form-critical, and traditio-historical methods, cf. R. N. Whybray, *The Making of the Pentateuch,* JSOT Supplement Series 53 (Sheffield: JSOT Press, 1987). Whybray himself, however, is quite prepared to see the Pentateuch as the work of an author who prepared it "as a supplement (i.e., a prologue) to the work of the Deuteronomistic Historian.... He had at his disposal a mass of material, most of which may have been of quite recent origin and had not necessarily formed part of any ancient Israelite tradition. Following the canons of the historiography of his time, he radically reworked this material, probably with substantial additions of his own invention, making no attempt to produce a smooth narrative free from inconsistencies, contradictions and unevenness. Judged by the standards of ancient historiography, his work stands out as a literary masterpiece" (p. 242).

last two centuries forms the foundation upon which later scholarship has built, or to which it has at least felt the need to pay lip service. Since documentary work on the Pentateuch received a major reformulation at the hands of W. M. L. de Wette, we turn first to his efforts in a review of the scholarship of Sinai.

De Wette

The work of Wilhelm Martin Leberecht de Wette (1780–1849) was to some extent revolutionary. Because his classic work is unavailable in English, we quote him generously in translation. De Wette, who inherited the nascent Documentary Hypothesis from Astruc, Eichhorn, and others, not only furthered their approach, but also argued in new ways against the Mosaic authorship of Deuteronomy.[25] For him, documentary analysis of the Pentateuch went hand in hand with a dismissal of supernatural occurrences as myths. De Wette believed that the first Sinai theophany—God's appearance to Moses in a burning bush—was poetry, not history.[26] Whatever the source of the burning bush idea may have been, he said, we have no way of asserting that such an event actually took place.[27]

---

[25]W. M. L. de Wette, *Dissertatio critica qua Deuteronomium a prioribus Pentateuchi libris diversum alius cuiusdam recentioris opus esse monstratur* (Jena, 1805).

[26]W. M. L. de Wette, *Kritik der Israelitischen Geschichte, Erster Theil: Kritik der Mosäischen Geschichte* (Halle: Schimmelpfenning: 1807), 184: "This conversation [of Yahweh] with Moses is not to be taken in a literal sense. One must take it as ideas which arose and mutated into Moses. Later days then clothed it with the form of this conversation. So, if one takes this portrayal as poetry, one can then throw out the tale as it now stands before us."

The German text reads: "...das Gespräch Gottes mit Mose nicht in eigentlichem Sinn zu nehmen sei; man nimmt es für die in Mose aufsteigenden und wechselnden Gedanken; die spätere Tage habe sie dann in dieses Gespräch eingekleidet. Also nimmt man diese Darstellung für Poesie, man verwirft die Relation, wie sie vor uns liegt."

[27]Ibid., 186: "If one asks how the poet got the idea of letting God appear in a burning bush, I answer: We do not know, and we cannot know. That

When de Wette related the Sinai theophany to the theophany in Genesis 15, as biblical theology also must do, he reached similar conclusions:

> Apparently the poet, who on other occasions introduces theophanies in very simple terms, now allowed Jehovah to appear in this most important epoch in the greatest majesty, with thunder and lightning. Or else a later poet did so, just as an imitator of Genesis 15 also adorned the simple myth of God's covenant with Abraham in Genesis 17.... We may not regard this [i.e., the Sinai theophany] any differently than we have regarded the earlier myths. If we found that the covenant sacrifice of Abraham and the concommitant theophany was a piece of pure poetry, we must also regard this theophany on Sinai as such. Can we expect anything else? Have we any more ground, in the case of Sinai, to accept some aspect of it as factual?[28]

According to such an approach, a literary analysis of the Pentateuchal data results in a dismissal of its supernatural content. As I said earlier, such an avenue can have little value for orthodox theology, for it assumes that God does not inject him-

---

(of course) lies totally hidden behind the veil of history. We only know what the poet relates—not where he got it or how he developed it."

The German text reads: "Fragt man, wie der Dichter dazu gekommen, Gott in einem brennenden Dornstrauch erscheinen zu lassen? so antworte ich: das wissen wir nicht und können es nicht wissen; dies liegt ja ganz hinter dem Schleier der Geschichte. Wir wissen nur was der Dichter erzählt, nicht woher er es nahm, und wie er es ausbildete?"

[28]Ibid., 237. The German text reads: "Wahrscheinlich liess unser Dichter, der sonst die Theophanieen ganz einfach einführt, hier in dieser wichtigsten Epoche den Jehovah in der größten Majestät erscheinen, in Donner und Blitz. Oder ein späterer Dichter thats, so wie auch ein Nachahmer Gen. 15. die simpele Mythe vom Bunde Gottes mit Abraham Cap. 17. ausschmückte ... so können wir sie doch nicht anders betrachten, als wir die frühern Mythen betrachtet haben. Fanden wir, daß das Bundesopfer Abrahams und die damit verbundene Theophanie eine reine Dichtung sei, so müssen wir auch diese Theophanie auf Sinai als eine solche betrachten. Können wir etwas anders erwarten? Haben wir hier mehr Grund etwas Faktisches anzunehmen?"

self theophanically into history. That is why all reports of his doing so are categorized as "myths" one can then ignore, omit, redefine, or—in de Wette's words—"throw out."

Julius Wellhausen

Almost a century later Julius Wellhausen (1844–1918), who built upon the work of de Wette and others, gave the Documentary Hypothesis what many consider its classic formulation. Wellhausen stands at the latter end of a century of scholarship in which literary criticism of the Pentateuch and implicit or explicit dismissal of its supernatural content go hand in hand.[29] The linkage of literary method with rejection of historicity appears with an overtone of sarcasm in Wellhausen's evaluation of the events at Mount Sinai:

> But the miracle of the covenant making on Sinai is in the most profound sense unrealistic. Who can seriously believe that Yahweh wrote the ten commandments on stone with his own hand—yes, and even thundered them down at the assembled people with his own voice from the mountaintop out of the thundercloud, and afterward, way up there, had an intimate conversation with Moses for forty days! . . . [Rather], it suited poetical necessity to elevate the constitution of the people of Yahweh to a dramatic act upon a sublime stage.[30]

As in the case of de Wette, Wellhausen's handling of the text reflects an underlying attitude that affects other aspects of historical reconstruction. For instance, the Old Testament always

---

[29]Cf. J. G. Eichhorn, *Einleitung in das Alte Testament* (Göttingen: K. E. Rosenbusch, 1823); J. W. Colenso, *The Pentateuch and Book of Joshua Critically Considered* (London: Longmans, Green & Co., 1875); A. Kuenen, *The Origin and Composition of the Hexateuch*, P. H. Wicksteed, trans. (London: Macmillan, 1886). For a good overview and philosophical commentary on this scholarly tradition and reactions to it, cf. R. K. Harrison, *Introduction to the Old Testament* (Grand Rapids: Eerdmans, 1969), 11–61.

[30]J. Wellhausen, *Israelitische und jüdische Geschichte*, zweite Ausgabe (Berlin: Georg Reimer, 1895), 12–13. The German text reads: "Im innersten Wesen

represents the theophany and lawgiving at Mount Sinai as unique events in the history of the world. In an unprecedented way, Yahweh came to Moses and Israel atop Mount Sinai, and God's holiness rendered the place itself holy (Ex 3:5). But Wellhausen rejected the historicity of the Exodus narratives. He believed that the holiness of Mount Sinai originally had nothing to do with the creation of Israel as God's people: "In reality the holiness of Sinai is totally independent of Yahweh's covenant-making with Israel, and does not point to the peculiarity of Israelite religion.... Sinai was the seat of Deity—the holy mountain—not merely for the Israelites, but for all the tribes in the area."[31] This last statement may seem to be a strange assertion. It is an extrapolation based apparently on the fact of Jethro's priesthood (Ex 2:16; 3:1).[32] However, there are no biblical or extrabiblical data to suggest that Mount Sinai was locally thought to be a seat of deity (a sort of Arabian Zaphon or Olympus).

It appears that Wellhausen had a radically skeptical attitude toward God's miraculous involvement in history. The same attitude toward the biblical data is not hard to find today. Virtually any commentary that takes a liberal approach to the Pentateuch also discounts the miraculous narratives to some

---

unwirklich aber ist das Wunder von der Bundschliessung am Sinai. Wer mag im Ernste glauben, dass Jahve mit eigener Hand die zehn Gebote auf Stein geschrieben, ja sie sogar mit eigener Stimme von der Bergspitze herab zugedonnert und darnach noch hoch droben vierzig Tage lang mit Moses vertraute Zwiesprache gehalten habe! ... Es waltete das poetische Bedürfnis, die Constituirung des Volkes Jahve zu einem dramatischen Akte auf erhabener Bühne zuzuspitzen."

[31]Ibid., 12. The German text reads: "In Wirklichkeit ist die Heiligkeit des Sinai ganz unäbhangig von der Bundschliessung Jahves mit Israel, sie weist nicht auf die Besonderheit der israelitischen Religion hin.... Der Sinai war der Sitz der Gottheit, der heilige Berg, nicht bloss für die Israeliten, sondern für alle Stämme der Umgegend."

[32]Cf. ibid., 12: "Von dem dortigen Priestertum wurde das Priestertum Moses abgeleitet, dort war ihm Jahve im brennenden Dornbusch erschienen," etc.

extent and seeks naturalistic explanations for them all.³³ For instance, the burning bush is regarded as a bush whose leaves reflected the sunset, causing Moses to think it was aflame, or else as St. Elmo's fire.³⁴ Yahweh's appearance atop Mount Sinai is assumed to have been a misunderstood volcano.³⁵

---

³³The situation that faces evangelical scholarship today continues to be the same as M. F. Unger, *Introductory Guide to the Old Testament* (Grand Rapids: Zondervan, 1951), described it more than forty years ago, that the "long succession of able scholars by whom the documentary theory was elaborated, have been unbelievers in supernatural revelation and divine miracle" (p. 270). Unger went on to say, "It is accordingly evident that the critical theory has been deliberately fabricated and foisted on Old Testament scholarship to explain away the supernatural, whether in revelation, miracle or fulfilled prophecy. This is its fundamental error" (p. 271).
³⁴Cf. M. Noth, *Exodus* (Philadelphia: Westminster, 1962), 39.
³⁵An interpretation aptly refuted by N. M. Sarna, *Exploring Exodus* (New York: Schocken, 1986), 132. H. Gunkel, *Schöpfung und Chaos in Urzeit und Endzeit* (Göttingen: Vandenhoeck und Ruprecht, 1895), 104-7, advanced the thesis that those passages that portrayed conflict between Yahweh and the sea were derived from the Babylonian creation myth, while those that made use of volcanic imagery stemmed from the (volcanic) experience narrated in Ex 19. Further on the volcano hypothesis, cf. W. J. Pythian-Adams, "The Volcanic Phenomena of the Exodus," *JPOS* 12 (1932): 89ff. Noth, *Exodus*, 109, says that "smoke rising like a cloud and fire are features of the theophany on Sinai (19:18 J), and the phenomenon of the pillars of cloud and fire presumably goes back to observation of an active volcano, to which allusion is without doubt made in the account of the events on Sinai," but also avers that "we cannot obtain any completely reliable reference to the situation of Sinai even from the existence of the volcano-tradition" (p. 160). J. C. Rylaarsdam, "Introduction and Exegesis to the Book of Exodus," *IB* 1:976, gives a fair representation of current scholarly opinion on the matter when he says, "It seems impossible to decide definitely whether this description is based on an actual recollection of meteorological conditions at Sinai or represents a literary portrayal in metaphors that were considered appropriate to a theophany. Inasmuch as these are widely used stock metaphors, and inasmuch as this account, at least in its written form, must be several centuries removed from the event, the latter seems much more probable." S. R. Driver, *The Book of Exodus* (Cambridge: University Press, 1911), followed the "poetical" interpretation of de Wette and Wellhausen: "The literal truth was that God spoke to the heart of Moses: the poetic truth was that He spoke in thunder and lightning from the crest of Sinai" (p. 177).

DOCUMENTARY INFLUENCE ON MORE RECENT SCHOLARSHIP

A documentary view of the Pentateuch inevitably discounts the historicity of its narratives, because the putative documents date from centuries after the supposed events. Form criticism, to the extent that it shares Gunkel's assumptions about oral tradition, produces the same result, because the narratives are seen as the end result of centuries of oral transmission and mutation (see below, pp. 55–80).

Both of these approaches heavily influence study of the Sinai materials today. Major liberal contributors to the discussion still assume the basic documentary division developed in the nineteenth century. That division sees Genesis and Exodus as composed primarily of two traditions, the Elohistic and the Jehovistic/Yahwistic along with Deuteronomistic and Priestly elements or redactions.

The background of these developments can be seen in the nineteenth century and followed as the century turned. De Wette and Eberhard Schrader, for example, saw Exodus as divided into two Elohistic documents (an earlier and a later), and a Yahwistic document, which they respectively designated the "Annalistic Narrator" ("Annalistische Erzähler"), the "Theocratic Narrator" ("Theokratische Erzähler"), and the "Prophetic Narrator" ("Prophetische Erzähler").[36] According to them, Exodus 19:1–2ab (itinerary notice of Israel's arrival at Sinai) was from the "Annalistic" narrator (E_1); whereas Exodus 3:1–6, 9–14 (the burning bush theophany and warning to Moses to remove his sandals; Moses' commission) and Exodus 19:20–25 (warning to Moses to set limits so that the people may not rashly approach the mountain) belonged to the "Theocratic" narrator (E_2); and Exodus 3:7–8, 15–22 (Yahweh's notice of

---

[36]W. M. L. de Wette and E. Schrader, *Lehrbuch der historisch-kritischen Einleitung in die kanonischen und apokryphischen Bücher des Alten Testaments* (Berlin: Georg Reimer, 1869), 274.

Israel's distress in Egypt and promise to deliver them) and Exodus 19:3c–19 (Yahweh's review of his past deliverance of and promises to Israel; and the promise that he will descend upon Sinai) came from the "Prophetic" narrator, or Yahwist.[37] The use of divine names, Elohim and Yahweh, as well as other vocabulary, affected the assignment of the verses to the individual documents.[38]

Early in this century the state of the art remained essentially the same, as evidenced in the work of J. Estlin Carpenter and George Harford, *The Composition of the Hexateuch* (1902), which analyzed Genesis–Joshua into composite documents. For them, the Elohist was responsible for Exodus 3:1, 4b, 6, 9b–13, 15, 19–21 and Exodus 19:2b–3a, 7–11a, 14–17, 19, 23; the Jehovist for Exodus 3:2–4a, 7–9a, 14, 16–18, and Exodus 19:3b–6, 11b–13, 18, 20–22, 24; and the Priestly writer for Exodus 19:2a.1.[39] Well-known Oxford scholar S. R. Driver, in *An Introduction to the Literature of the Old Testament* (1913), analyzed these chapters in an only slightly different way. For him, the Elohist was responsible for Exodus 3:1, 4b, 6, 9–15, 19–22 and Exodus 19:3a, 10–11a, 14–17, 19; the Jehovist for Exodus 3:2–4a, 5, 7–8, 16–18 and Exodus 19:3b–9, 11b–13, 18, 20–25; the Priestly writer accounted for Exodus 19:1–2a.[40] Otto Eissfeldt, in his *Einleitung in das Alte Testament* (1934)—a work which is still a standard in Old Testament scholarship—gave an analysis consistent with the results of earlier documentary research. In addition to the traditional J, E, and P sources, however, Eissfeldt identified an "L" ("Lay") source, consisting of a residuum

---

[37]Ibid., 280–81.

[38]Ibid., 281–86.

[39]J. E. Carpenter and G. Harford, *The Composition of the Hexateuch* (London: Longmans, Green & Co., 1902), 515–17.

[40]S. R. Driver, *An Introduction to the Literature of the Old Testament*, 9th ed. (Edinburgh: T. & T. Clark, 1913), 22–33. Driver remarks, "The structure of JE's narrative of the transactions at Sinai ... is complicated, and there are parts in which the analysis (so far as concerns J and E) must be regarded as provisional only. Nevertheless, the composite character of the narrative seems to be unmistakable" (p. 32).

which he felt remained after J, E, and P had been assigned all materials that reasonably could be attributed to them.[41]

DOCUMENTARY SOURCES AND CULTIC ORIGINS

With the work of Sigmund Mowinckel, Gerhard von Rad, and Martin Noth, a new development took place in the handling of the Sinai materials. The concern shifted from the study of putative original documents (Documentary Hypothesis) to the study of tradition history. The J and E "documents" were now seen as later written sources that presupposed oral traditions—in particular, "cult legends" or "creeds" that grew out of cultic celebrations of the Exodus, the Conquest, and God's appearance at Sinai. This approach has been adopted in some degree by many scholars.[42] Among them are J. Kenneth Kuntz and Jörg Jeremias, each of whom has devoted a book to the subject of theophany in the Old Testament. Although the newer approach complicates the analysis of sources, it does not draw us much closer to what actually happened on Mount Sinai (or in the Pentateuch, for that matter) according to these scholars.

S. Mowinckel, G. von Rad

Gerhard von Rad, in 1938, produced a work on "The Form-Critical Problem of the Hexateuch," which still employed

---

[41]O. Eissfeldt, *Einleitung in das Alte Testament* (Tübingen: J. C. B. Mohr, 1934), 217ff.; cf. the English translation by P. R. Ackroyd: O. Eissfeldt, *The Old Testament—An Introduction* (New York: Harper & Row, 1965), 194ff.

[42]Cf. R. Rendtorff, *Das überlieferungsgeschichtliche Problem des Pentateuch*, Beihefte zur *ZAW* 147 (Berlin: de Gruyter, 1977). A good recent example is T. B. Dozeman, *God on the Mountain,* SBL Monograph Series 37 (Atlanta: Scholars Press, 1989). Dozeman discovers an original "Mountain of God" tradition that "represents a cultic theology of divine presence" (pp. 29–30) and more specifically "reflects Zion-Sabaoth theology" (p. 30). He then goes on to discuss the Deuteronomistic (pp. 37–86) and Priestly (pp. 87–143) redactions of this traditional material. See further S. J. De Vries, "A Review of Recent Research in the Tradition History of the Pentateuch," SBL Abstracts and Seminar Papers 26 (1987): 459–502.

the results of documentary scholarship as tools for understanding the provenance of the "Sinai tradition."[43] But von Rad also followed an attempt by Sigmund Mowinckel to derive the JE account of Sinai from the festival-cult at Jerusalem.[44] According to Mowinckel, the events at Sinai were none other than an account of the Jerusalem New Year's Festival, translated into the language of literary mythology: "What J and E recount as a narrative of the events of Sinai is nothing other than the description of a cult festival celebrated at a more recent epoch, more precisely in the temple in Jerusalem."[45] After Mowinckel's work, von Rad agreed that "there can be no doubt of the fact" that the Sinai narratives "were originally deeply rooted in the cultus."[46] He concluded that the Exodus–Conquest tradition and the Sinai tradition originally had nothing to do with each other. Both grew out of creeds, which, while they had some "historical rootage," did not necessarily reflect historical events: "Doubtless they have been overlaid with much historically 'credible' material, yet once the basic facts of hexateuchal history are enumerated, it is exclusively of the *faith* of Israel that they speak."[47] Each tradition had its own *Sitz im Leben*. The Exodus–Conquest tradition was associated with

---

[43]Cf. G. von Rad, *The Problem of the Hexateuch and other Essays* (Edinburgh: Oliver & Boyd, 1966), 1–78. The work in question, "The Form-critical Problem of the Hexateuch," appeared originally in *Beiträge zur Wissenschaft vom Alten und Neuen Testament*, fourth series, vol. 26, Stuttgart, 1938.

[44]S. Mowinckel, *Le décalogue, Etudes d'histoire et de philosophie religieuses* (Paris: F. Alcan, 1927). Mowinckel's approach was anticipated by that of P. Volz, who in 1912 posited an autumnal New Year festival (Tabernacles) parallel to the Babylonian Akitu festival and including an epiphany of God in the cult, a ritual combat with his foes, reinstatement of his kingship, and covenant renewal; cf. E. Lipinski, *La Royauté de Yahwé dans la poésie et le culte de l'ancien Israël* (Brussels: Paleis der Academiën, 1965), 47.

[45]Ibid., 120. The French text reads: "Ce que J et E rapportent come récit des événements du Sinai n'est autre chose que la description d'une fête cultuelle célébrée à une époque plus récente, plus précisément dans le temple de Jérusalem."

[46]Von Rad, *Problem*, 21.

[47]Ibid., 2.

the shrine at Gilgal; it grew out of the brief historical creed found there (Dt 6:20–24; 26:5ff.), the festival-legend of the Feast of Weeks.[48] The Sinai tradition was associated with the covenant renewal ceremony at Shechem (cf. Jos 24); it, too, grew out of a festival-legend ("the Feast of Booths of the ancient Yahwistic amphictyony") and reflected the pattern of the cult at Shechem.[49] According to von Rad, the Sinai tradition was a later addition to the Exodus–Conquest materials: "The earliest example of the interpolation of the Sinai story into the canonical story of redemption is found in the great prayer of *Neh.* IX.6ff."[50] At a later stage, after the two traditions had been separated from their cultic origins, the Yahwist combined them.[51]

Although the comments above are brief, they do present an overview of the key points of von Rad's analysis. Whatever else one may say of the avenue taken by Mowinckel and von Rad (see below), it's implications for historicity are clear. Their approach allows one to maintain a critical distance from the historicity of the supernatural events of Mount Sinai, as did the purely documentary approach of earlier scholars.

M. Noth

Like von Rad, Martin Noth believed that the Sinai tradition had historical rootage: "There is no doubt that the Sinai tradition, the basic substance of which is unique and unrelated

---

[48]Ibid., 3–13, 41–48. Von Rad followed A. Alt, *Die Landnahme der Israeliten in Palästina* (Reformationsprogramm der Universität Leipzig, 1925) in his view of the Conquest, which argued a gradual settlement of Palestine by Israelites, rather than the sweeping military campaign portrayed in the book of Joshua.

[49]Ibid., 33–40. Von Rad termed the Sinai tradition "the cult-legend of the ancient Yahwistic ceremony of the renewal of covenants at the Feast of Booths" (p. 53; cf. p. 41).

[50]Ibid., 12.

[51]Ibid., 48ff.

to any other phenomena in the history of religion, derived from an actual event."[52] But he also agreed that "after von Rad's studies it is scarcely necessary to repeat . . . that the Sinai tradition was based on the legend used in a festival of *covenant-making* or *covenant-renewal.*"[53] One consequence of Noth's analysis was the "negative conclusion" that the Decalogue never existed in the original narratives of the Sinai theophany, but was subsequently inserted.[54] He carried analysis of the hexateuchal data further than von Rad and believed that major themes such as the Exodus ("Guidance out of Egypt"),[55] the Conquest ("Guidance into the Arable Land"),[56] the "Promise to the Patriarchs,"[57] the "Guidance in the Wilderness,"[58] and the "Revelation at Sinai"[59] were originally independent traditions, which ultimately go back to expressions of faith—that is, "creeds"—that were rooted in the cult. Noth also suggested that the Exodus-Conquest and Sinai themes may have been brought together in a common basis or *Grundlage* (G) upon which the Elohist and Yahwist built. He felt that one must postulate such a *Grundlage* in order to account for the numerous parallels between J and E.[60] Noth's work, therefore, building on the efforts of Wellhausen, von Rad, and others, reached

---

[52] M. Noth, *The History of Israel,* 2d ed. (New York: Harper & Row, 1960), 128.

[53] M. Noth, *Überlieferungsgeschichte des Pentateuch* (Stuttgart, 1948); we reference the English translation by B. W. Anderson: M. Noth, *A History of Pentateuchal Traditions* (Englewood Cliffs: Prentice-Hall, 1972), 60.

[54] Noth, *Exodus,* 154ff.

[55] Noth, *Pentateuchal Traditions,* 47–51.

[56] Ibid., 51–54.

[57] Ibid., 54–58.

[58] Ibid., 58–59.

[59] Ibid., 59–62.

[60] Ibid., 38–41. Noth remarks that "in those elements of the tradition where J and E run parallel, they concur to such an extent that their common *Grundlage* must already have existed in a fixed form, either one fixed in writing or one which had already been quite distinctly formed according to structure and content in oral transmission" (p. 39).

negative conclusions similar to theirs about the historicity of the Sinai (and other Old Testament) narratives.

W. Beyerlin

More recently, Walter Beyerlin, in *Herkunft und Geschichte der ältesten Sinaitraditionen* (1961), has also employed assumptions of documentary analysis coupled with an attribution of cultic origins in a study of tradition history, but he has reached a somewhat different conclusion.[61] He believes that the Yahwistic and Elohistic Sinai traditions underwent three stages of development: one during the desert-period, one during the period between the invasion of Palestine and the formation of a state, and one during the period of the monarchy.[62] Beyerlin's comments on the first period are of special interest.

During the desert (Mosaic) period, the Decalogue originated in written form at Kadesh as a second millennium covenantal document between Yahweh and Israel. It originated in written form because "this was in accord with the view which was fairly widespread throughout the Ancient Orient that the written record of a treaty contributed to its realisation and served to attest its conclusion."[63] The public recital of this treaty was repeated as "freshly incoming groups of Hebrews were admitted into the Sinaitic covenant," and these repetitions "led to well-established forms and the beginnings of a cultic *tradition*."[64] During this period also, sacrifices to Yahweh developed, so that "the tradition of the covenant-meal on the mount of God in Exod xxiv.11b was rooted in a practice

---

[61](Tübingen: J. C. B. Mohr); we reference the English translation by S. Rudman: Walter Beyerlin, *Origins and History of the Oldest Sinaitic Traditions* (Oxford: Basil Blackwell, 1965).
[62]Beyerlin, *Origins*, 145ff.
[63]Ibid., 147.
[64]Ibid., 148–49.

of the desert period."⁶⁵ In fact, "The tradition of the making of the covenant in Exod xxiv.5, in describing the sacrifice of . . . burnt offerings and peace offerings . . . is probably referring to the cultic situation of the Kadesh-community."⁶⁶ Thus, Beyerlin argues, "it is probable that several elements in the Yahwistic-Elohistic tradition of Sinai had their origin in the initial stages of the cult of Yahweh, which everything points to having first developed at Kadesh."⁶⁷

During the period between the invasion of Canaan and the establishment of the monarchy, various additions were made to the tradition. The invasion itself was a "complicated and somewhat prolonged process" in which Israelites entering Palestine found other Israelites already settled there and joined with them in a sacral tribal union in which all bore the name Israel.⁶⁸ This view, noted above, was shared by von Rad and Noth⁶⁹ and has since been advocated by G. E. Mendenhall⁷⁰ and others.⁷¹ G. E. Wright⁷² and Y. Yadin,⁷³ among others,⁷⁴ have supported a contrary scenario more in accord with the biblical portrayal.

---

⁶⁵Ibid., 150.
⁶⁶Ibid., 150.
⁶⁷Ibid., 150–51.
⁶⁸Ibid., 151. Cf. A. Alt, *Die Landnahme der Israeliten.*
⁶⁹Cf. M. Noth, *History of Israel,* 68–97; *Das System der zwölf Stämme Israels, Beiträge zur Wissenschaft vom Alten und Neuen Testament,* 4:1 (Stuttgart: W. Kohlhammer, 1930).
⁷⁰G. E. Mendenhall, "The Hebrew Conquest of Palestine," *BA* 25, no. 3 (Sept. 1962): 66–87; reprint, *The Biblical Archaeologist Reader 3* (New York: Anchor Books, 1970), 100–120.
⁷¹Cf. M. Weippert, *Die Landnahme der israelitischen Stämme in der neueren wissenschaftlichen Diskussion* (1967).
⁷²G. E. Wright, "The Literary and Historical Problem of Joshua 10 and Judges 1," *JNES* 5 (April 1946), 105–14.
⁷³Y. Yadin, "Military and Archaeological Aspects of the Conquest of Canaan in the Book of Joshua," *'EL HA'AYIN* (Jerusalem, 1960), 1–13.
⁷⁴Cf. J. Niehaus, "*Pa'am 'eḥāt* and the Israelite Conquest," *VT* 30, no. 2 (April 1980): 236–39.

The cultic development of the Sinai tradition continued into the monarchical period and eventually came to appear in J and E. This does not mean that, as von Rad argued, a long period of oral transmission predated their emergence in any written form. Beyerlin takes issue with von Rad on this point and also concerning the separation of the Exodus-Conquest and Sinai traditions. He believes the two traditions belong together, because he finds them combined in Old Testament passages structured after the second-millennium international treaty form:

> As far as its relation to the Exodus-tradition goes, it remains to confirm that the two traditions were linked together from the very beginnings of the covenant with Yahweh: the covenant-form attested in Hittite state treaties of the 14th and 13th centuries B.C., which also underlies the Decalogue, the basic law of the Sinaitic covenant . . . contains a historical prologue which describes the beneficent acts of the author of the covenant. If this treaty-form was already in use in Mosaic times, as may be assumed, it must have referred in its preface to Yahweh's saving act in delivering the Israelites from Egypt.[75]

This is a good use of form critical data—as far as it goes. An actual literary, legal form, whose existence in the ancient Near East has been documented beyond doubt,[76] is applied to Old Testament passages to demonstrate their character and even their date. The method has already been fruitfully applied to the whole book of Deuteronomy, as well as to significant portions of Exodus and Leviticus.[77] The proper use of such a tool

---

[75]Beyerlin, *Origins,* 169. Beyerlin also points to the union of the Exodus and Sinai traditions in Ex 19:3b–8, which follows the second millennium covenant form.

[76]Cf. G. E. Mendenhall, "Covenant Forms in Israelite Tradition," *BA* 17 (1954): 49–76.

[77]Cf. M. Kline, *Treaty of the Great King* (Grand Rapids: Eerdmans, 1963), and the two valuable books by K. A. Kitchen, *Ancient Orient and Old Testament* (Chicago: InterVarsity Press, 1973), and *The Bible in Its World* (Downers Grove: InterVarsity Press, 1978).

obviates a good deal of speculation about the credal sources of Old Testament historical accounts. Form critical evidence alone, in this case, suggests that the methodology of cultic source attribution is deeply flawed.[78] It bears no demonstrable relation to the way people actually kept historical records in the ancient Near East. But just because it has shaped so much recent scholarship, it merits further critical attention.

J. Kenneth Kuntz

J. Kenneth Kuntz's book *The Self-Revelation of God* has made a valuable contribution to the study of Old Testament theophanies in the area of form criticism. He has discerned an Old Testament theophanic *Gattung* that will apply in the following pages.[79]

Kuntz's work also shares the approaches outlined above. On the one hand, like von Rad and Noth, Kuntz avers that "biblical interpreters have rightly discerned a historical nucleus in the Sinaitic theophany and covenant ceremony."[80] On the other hand, "the very ordering of the various incidents at Sinai by both the J and E strata attests the effective influence of the cult."[81] The formative role of the cult in the tradition is so great that "the materials of Ex., chs. 19 to 24, are primarily cultic in character."[82] Consequently, "not even the earliest of these traditions, namely those which have been incorporated into the

---

[78] For further discussion of the problems with the cult-legend approach, cf. R. W. L. Moberly, *At the Mountain of God*, JSOT Supplement Series 22 (Sheffield: JSOT Press, 1983), 116–40.

[79] See above, chap. 1.

[80] Kuntz, *The Self-Revelation of God*, 74.

[81] Ibid., 74. Kuntz cites "the prefatory ceremonies of purification, the anticipated advance toward God at the sound of the horn (šôpār), the deity's significant disclosure of his nature and will, and the sealing of the covenant by sacrificial rite" as evidences of cultic shaping of the tradition (p. 74).

[82] Ibid., 73–74.

J and E narratives, can be understood as exactly representing a historical happening as sheer event."[83]

Documentary analysis attributed the Sinai data to J, E, and P, and Kuntz follows this tradition. To E he attributes Exodus 19:2b–8 (the invitation of the people and their response), 19:10–11a, 14–15 (the sanctification of the people), 19:16–17, 19 (the appearance of deity), 20:18–21 (the fear of the people and their request that Moses mediate), 20:1–17 (the self-asseveration of the deity and proclamation of his will), and 24:3–8 (the establishment and sealing of the covenant).[84] The cultic background of the E stratum is apparent in such features as the exact timing of God's theophany[85] and the sound of the horn.[86] To the J stratum Kuntz attributes 19:9a (Yahweh's promise to Moses that he will come in a dense cloud), 11b–13 (the warning to set limits for the people), and 24:1–2, 9–11 (Yahweh's invitation to Moses alone, from among Aaron, Nadab, Abihu, and the elders, to come near; the covenant meal Moses, Aaron, Nadab, Abihu, and the elders share in God's presence). The Yahwist's account has three chief characteristics: first, the "cult-oriented concern for the appropriate

---

[83]Ibid., 73.

[84]Ibid., 75–76.

[85]Ibid., 81. Kuntz remarks, "The efficacy of a given event in the Israelite cult depended much upon its execution at the proper moment. The event was not to be evoked prematurely. Rather, it was to be anticipated through correctly instituted cultic preparation. Thus the received tradition of the theophany to which the Elohist had access is plainly a cultic tradition" (p. 81). Cf. Beyerlin, *Origins,* 140; H. Ringren, *Israelite Religion,* trans. D. E. Green (Philadelphia: Fortress, 1966), 35, 71.

[86]Ibid., 84: "In the E stratum, however, theophanic visitation is further proclaimed through a conspicuous cultic element, the sound of the horn ($\check{s}\hat{o}$-$p\bar{a}r$), that has been infused into the Sinai tradition." In this Kuntz follows Beyerlin, *Origins,* who argued that the horn was used to impart God's presence dramatically in the cult: "The epiphany of the God whom no man could look upon . . . and who remained hidden in the cloud of incense . . . could only be perceived by the cultic community in terms of such dramatic representation" (pp. 135ff., cf. pp. 156–57).

preparation for, and conduct during, theophanic meeting";[87] second, the fact that Yahweh's approach to Mount Sinai is seen as a "descent by means of the cloud vehicle from his heavenly residence" (as contrasted to the Elohist's view that God's abode was on Mount Sinai);[88] and third, "a preference for the visual effects of the theophany" (as contrasted to the Elohist's emphasis on the "horn," etc.).[89] The Yahwist's handling of the Sinai theophany is shorter and more fragmentary than the Elohist's, "owing primarily to his losing out in the competition of subsequent redaction," but for all that "it is . . . not lacking in significance."[90] However short the Yahwist's contribution may be, the Priestly writer's is even shorter. Kuntz follows earlier documentary scholars in allotting him only the annalistic introduction, Exodus 19:1–2, and a few verses in Exodus 24 (24:15b–18a, which call our attention to: the period of waiting before the theophany, the audible summons to Moses to come hear God's words, and the visual manifestation of the theophany to the people).[91]

For Kuntz, as for scholars before him, the methods of documentary analysis and traditio-historical cultic source attribution go hand in hand with doubt as to God's actual appearance on Mount Sinai. For him it is an open question "whether the theophanic event here depicted be thought of as original happening in later dress or as cultic reenactment."[92] The same is true of the volcanic or meteorological modes of accounting for the theophanic glory: "Whether or not the reality depicted here is meteorological in fact or metaphorical in description is

---

[87] Ibid., 95. An example would be the notice that the theophanic encounter would occur "on the third day" (Ex 19:11b).

[88] Ibid., 98. The Yahwist sees Yahweh descending upon Sinai from heaven, as opposed to the Elohist who imagines that Mount Sinai itself is God's perpetual home (pp. 84, 93, 98).

[89] Ibid., 99.
[90] Ibid., 95.
[91] Ibid., 101–2.
[92] Ibid., 81.

not the major issue."⁹³ Similarly, the historicity of Moses' encounter with God in the E stratum is not a matter of concern. What matters is that such an encounter is needed to complete the story (i.e., the narrative structure): "It is not a question of whether or not some direct encounter between Moses and the deity might have taken place. Rather, the narrative requires that it must take place, and take place now through divine speech."⁹⁴

Jörg Jeremias

Jeremias's book, *Theophanie*, is a detailed study of Old Testament theophanies that deserves to be translated into English. Although Jeremias is concerned with form criticism and tradition-history, he controverts the efforts of Mowinckel, Beyerlin, and others to find the source of theophanic narratives in the cult. His general argument is worth note:

> Indeed, their hypothesis is already rendered unlikely on the basis of obvious, even fundamental considerations: proper to the cultic realm are the static, the constant, the regular, but proper to the coming of Yahweh in a theophany are the sudden, the unanticipated, the agitated. Lightnings convulse, thunder rolls, the clouds drive on, the earth quakes, rain pours down, the deep roars upward. All this does not point to the cult as its place of origin. An unbiased reader of the individual theophanic portrayals could hardly hit upon the thought that these portrayals grew out of the life of the cult.⁹⁵

---

⁹³Ibid., 83. He adds, "The natural phenomena as a whole have served to make unmistakably real for the witnessing community the dreadful yet unseen presence of the deity. The thunder in particular *has impressed itself upon the people* as the divine voice that addresses them, although the specific content of divine speech has not been theirs to know" (p. 88). Emphasis added.
⁹⁴Ibid., 89.
⁹⁵Jeremias, *Theophanie: WMANT,* 122. The German text reads: "Ja, ihre Hypothese ist schon aus naheliegenden grundsätzlichen Erwägungen unwahrscheinlich: Dem Kultischen eignet das Statische, Stetige, Regelmässige,

Jeremias's point is well taken. Whatever other evidence one may adduce against a cultic origin of theophanic portrayals, such a source seems improbable on the most elementary considerations.[96] But if the cult is not the place of origin of Sinai-like theophanies, what is? Jeremias believes that the form of all other Old Testament theophanic portrayals originated in the "Victory Celebrations" (*Siegesfeiern*) of Israel, of which the "Song of Deborah" is the earliest example.[97] A basic form or theophanic *Gattung*—made up of two elements—may be discerned in Deborah's song: first, a coming of Yahweh (*das Kommen Jahwes*), and second, an upheaval of the natural realm (*der Aufruhr der Natur*).[98] The two elements function as cause and effect: "The cause is the coming of Yahweh, the effect is . . . the upheaval of earth, the heavens and mountains."[99] According to Jeremias, the two elements are traceable to different sources.

The source of the second element, the upheavel of nature, is easy to locate: "Israel took it over from *the peoples of her environment*. The peoples adjacent to Israel praised the power and might of their gods by telling how heaven, earth, and moun-

---

dem Kommen Jahwes in einer Theophanie das Plötzliche, Unberechenbare, Bewegte. Blitze zucken, Donner rollt, die Wolken ziehen dahin, die Erde erbebt, Regen prasselt nieder, Tehom brüllt auf: das alles weist nicht auf den Kultus als Entstehungsort. Ein unbefangener Leser der einzelnen Theophanieschilderungen wird kaum auf den Gedanken verfallen können, daß diese Schilderungen aus dem kultischen Leben erwachsen sind."

[96]It is unlikely, for example, that the awesome storm theophanies reported in the Old Testament would have had as their source the incense of the temple (cf. Beyerlin, *Origins*, 135ff.).

[97]Jeremias, *Theophanie: WMANT,* 7, says: "We believe that behind the portrayal of the theophany of the Song of Deborah a form may be recognized out of which the forms of all other theophanic portrayals of the Old Testament have developed." The German text reads: "wir meinen, daß hinter der Theophanieschilderung des Deboraliedes eine Form zu erkennen gibt, aus der sich die Formen aller anderen Theophanieschilderungen des AT entwickelt haben." Cf. pp. 142ff.

[98]Ibid., 137.

[99]Ibid., 7. The German text reads, "Die Ursache ist das Kommen Jahwes, die Wirkung ist . . . der Aufruhr der Erde, der Himmel und Berge."

tains quaked before the gods. They wanted to show, thereby, that nothing could withstand their gods."[100] Jeremias founds his conclusion on a detailed comparison of extrabiblical theophanic accounts with those in the Old Testament. From a form-critical standpoint, the comparisons are worthy of note. It is one of the longest such efforts in print.[101] Yet, although there are many points of contact—and even phrase-borrowing from the pagan world on the part of Old Testament authors—there is a better explanation of those parallels than that which Jeremias has tendered.[102]

Jeremias does not locate the source of the second motif, the "coming of Yahweh" in the mythology of the ancient Near East. This is because Yahweh's "coming" also involves some portrayal of his "going forth" to execute judgment or to fight for his people.[103] Verbs of going forth typically appear in such portrayals. For instance, in the "Song of Deborah" (Jdg 5:4), "The verb יצא refers to Yahweh's departure from his abode."[104] Jeremias finds scant evidence of such terminology in the ancient Near East and none at all in the Akkadian realm.[105] But a very appropriate example from the Akkadian realm does lie at hand and has already been noted: a dream vision related to the Assyrian king Ashurbanipal.[106] In Ashurbanipal's annals

---

[100] Ibid., 151. The German text reads: "Israel übernahm es von den *Völkern seiner Umwelt.* Die Israel benachbarten Völker priesen die Kraft und Stärke ihrer Götter dadurch, daß sie davon sprachen, wie Himmel, Erde und Berge vor den Göttern bebten. Sie wollten damit zu erkennen geben, daß nichts ihren Göttern zu widerstehen vermöge."

[101] Ibid., 73ff., esp. 73–97.

[102] See below, chap. 3.

[103] Ibid., 152ff. Yahweh's warfare for his people is, of course, itself an act of judgment on Israel's foes, as Jeremias notes.

[104] Ibid., 7. The German text reads, "Das Verb יצא weist auf das Aufbrechen Jahwes von seiner Wohnung hin."

[105] Ibid., 153. He remarks, "I could find no analogy to it at all in the Akkadian texts." The German reads, "In den akkadischen Texten konnte ich keinerlei Analogien zu ihr finden."

[106] See above, chap. 1, 37–38.

he tells how a certain seer had a vision in which the goddess Ishtar appeared and embraced the king and spoke comforting words to him. She appeared with bow, arrows, and a sharp sword, and she promised to do battle on Ashurbanipal's behalf against a rebellious vassal. Then we read: "From her face fire flared forth, angrily she went off shining brightly and *strode forth* to conquer the foe."[107] The Akkadian verb, "strode forth" (*tattaṣi*, root *waṣû*), is cognate with Hebrew יצא. This parallel, and any others like it that may be found, does not prove that Israel took from the pagan world the idea of Yahweh's "coming." It does suggest that the idea was not unique to Israel.[108]

Unable to accept a pagan background as the source for the idea of Yahweh's coming,[109] Jeremias turns at last to the Sinai tradition: "After all has been said, it is in the highest measure probable that the kernel of the first member of the theophanic portrayal, that spoke of the coming of Yahweh from his abode—more precisely, from Sinai—is indebted to the influence of the Sinai tradition for its origin."[110] This is so because "in the transmission of the Sinai tradition Israel testifies that it has experienced a first-time and one-time appearance of Yahweh that was . . . decisive."[111] As further evidence he cites Judges 5:5; Psalm 68:9, 18b; and Deuteronomy 33:2, which offer the oldest traditio-historical examples of Sinai as Yahweh's abode—the mountain from which he departs to do battle.[112]

---

[107]Piepkorn, *HPIA* (Chicago: University of Chicago Press, 1933), 1:66–67. See discussion above, chap. 1, 37–38.

[108]Contra Jeremias, *Theophanie: WMANT*, 152–54.

[109]Jeremias also rejects an ad hoc creation of such an idea, p. 154.

[110]Ibid., 155. The German text reads: "Nach alledem ist es in hohem Maße wahrscheinlich, dass der Kern des ersten Gliedes der Theophanieschilderungen, der von einem Kommen Jahwes von seiner Wohnung—präziser: vom Sinai-sprach, den Einflüssen der Sinaitradition seine Entstehung verdankt."

[111]Ibid., 154. The German text reads: "In der Überlieferung der Sinaitradition bezeugt Israel, dass es ein erstmaliges und einmaliges Erscheinen Jahwes erlebt hat, das . . . entscheidend war."

[112]Ibid., 155; cf. 115ff.

According to Jeremias, the theophanic *Gattung* first appeared in Israel's "Victory Celebrations" and drew upon the pagan world and the Sinai tradition for its constitutive elements. Such was its *Sitz im Leben.* Jeremias follows A. Alt in his definition of the latter term as "'the regular events and needs of life' . . . from which the *Gattung* of the theophany texts developed and to which they owe their 'particular content' and 'particular forms of expression.'"[113] This definition, which may be adequate in itself, poses a problem for Jeremias's reconstruction, because there is actually little evidence that such songs were regular in Israel's life or that they regularly had theophanic components. Jeremias at once admits and avoids the problem: "Although we have no explicit examples, all probability favors the idea that 'Victory Celebrations' such as those at which the 'prophetess' Deborah sang her song, were regularly celebrated after victorious Yahweh-wars."[114]

On the basis of such a putative origin, Jeremias is able to sketch a history of the *Gattung's* development. He argues that Israel's victory celebrations must have changed during the monarchy, "since the celebrations of an army made up largely of hirelings must necessarily have assumed a profane character."[115] After that, the *Gattung* was cut loose, as it were, from its original *Sitz im Leben.* It appears subsequently in the prophetic

---

[113]Ibid., 136; cf. p. 3. The German text reads: "'die regelmäßigen Ereignisse und Bedürfnisse des Lebens' . . . aus denen die Gattung der Theophanietexte erwuchs und denen sie ihre 'bestimmten Inhalte' und 'bestimmten Ausdrucksformen' verdankt." Jeremias references A. Alt, *Die Ursprünge des israelitischen Rechts,* Berichte über die Verhandlungen der Sächsischen Akademie der Wissenschaften zu Leipzig, Phil.-hist. Klasse, Bd. 86, H.1 (Leipzig, 1934), 11.

[114]Ibid., 158. The German text reads, "Obwohl wir keine ausdrücklichen Belege haben, spricht alle Wahrscheinlichkeit dafür, daß Siegesfeiern wie diejenige, bei der die 'Prophetin' Debora ihr Lied sang, regelmäßig nach siegreichen Jahwekriegen gefeiert wurden."

[115]Ibid., 158. The German text reads, "da die Feiern des zum Großteil aus Söldnern bestehenden Heeres zwangsläufig profanen Charakter annehmen mußten."

literature—in oracles of judgment and salvation—and in apocalyptic.[116] It has no place in prose theophanic accounts (1Ki 19:11ff.; Eze 1:4ff., and those of the Sinai tradition), which are a completely independent development, although they may have borrowed now and then from the *Gattung*.[117]

Jeremias's book is a major recent effort to understand the form and the background of Old Testament theophanies. It contains valuable form-critical comparisons with theophanies reported in ancient Near Eastern literature. But it suffers from the same tendency toward ungrounded hypothetical reconstruction noted in earlier scholarship. Jeremias rejects the approach of cultic source attribution as a way of accounting for the tradition history of theophanic materials but then does essentially the same as those he criticizes when he postulates an undemonstrable regular "Victory Celebration" as the origin of the *Gattung* in premonarchical Israel. Whether one sees the origin of theophanic accounts in the incense, candles, and horns of a cultic celebration, or in the exuberant hyperbole of a victory song after a battle, the conclusion for the historicity of these supernatural appearances remains, to use Noth's word, "negative."[118]

---

[116]Ibid., 158; cf. pp. 130–35.
[117]Ibid., 135–36, 162–63.
[118]T. W. Mann, *Divine Presence and Guidance in Israelite Traditions* (Baltimore: Johns Hopkins Press, 1977), 8–9, accurately describes both the virtues and the faults of Jeremias's approach: "Jeremias's study is most impressive in its comprehensive treatment of the theophanic material throughout the Old Testament. At least a descriptive analysis is offered of all the major texts, and the principal traditions commonly associated with theophany are taken into account. Nevertheless, one cannot help being at first puzzled and finally frustrated by his line of argument. He has reconstructed a *Form* that by his own admission is not attested, then has used it as a rigorous standard by which to judge every other occurrence of the *Gattung* as having secondary accretions or deletions. . . . In short, Jeremias's study is a classic case of overextended form-critical method."

SINAI TRADITION: BACKGROUND OF SCHOLARSHIP

Frank Moore Cross

Frank Moore Cross's book *Canaanite Myth and Hebrew Epic* has been called "by far the most comprehensive and energetic attempt to utilize the fruits of Near Eastern research as the basis for a new approach to Israel's historical traditions."[119] Actually Cross draws primarily on the Ugaritic data and even declares, "Any discussion of the language of theophany in early Israel must begin with an examination of the Canaanite lore."[120] Accordingly his main critique of Jeremias's work is that he did not consider "the Canaanite *Gattung*" of theophany.[121] Cross analyzes the *Gattung*, which he calls an "archaic mythic pattern," as follows:

1. Battle of the divine warrior against a chaos figure
2. Convulsive reaction of nature to the warrior's wrath
3. Return of the warrior to his mountain to assume kingship of the gods
4. Utterance of the warrior's voice from his temple and revival of nature[122]

It is immediately obvious that such a schema has much in common with Babylonian myth. Cross also finds a mutated form of the *Gattung* in Israelite poetic and cultic traditions. In the poetry, elements 1 and 2 have been replaced by the Exodus and Conquest and the march from Egypt to Sinai, element 3 has been replaced by the Sinai theophany, and both 3 and 4 appear in various psalms.[123] This according to Cross is the historical sequence of events. By contrast, the cultic form consists of two major parts: a reenactment of the Exodus–Conquest events and a renewal of the covenant at Sinai. It is ultimately to the cult that we owe the Sinai traditions:

---

[119] Ibid., 13.
[120] Cross, *CMHE*, 147.
[121] Ibid., 147, n. 1.
[122] Ibid., 162–63.
[123] Ibid., 160–64.

> There can be little doubt, however, that the Sinai traditions ultimately stem from the preleague cult, as well as historical memory, and are "correctly" located in epic tradition. In other words, the cultus of the twelve-tribe league (covenant renewal ceremonies in variant forms at the great sanctuaries) presented the events of Exodus and Conquest as a single continuity to be reenacted in a single act, preceding formally the covenant ceremony in which the tribes bound themselves anew in community.[124]

Whatever there may be of "historical memory," what we now have by way of Sinai tradition reflects the various cultic covenant renewal ceremonies. These would have included hymns that are antecedent to extant prose accounts: "The theophanic language of the prose sources of the Sinai revelation is secondary, derived from the hymns of the Wars of Yahweh, where the (Exodus-) Conquest motif is naturally and primitively linked with theophany."[125] The Yahwist in particular, or "J" source, was active in the subsequent reworking of such materials.[126]

Although Cross draws on ancient Near Eastern and particularly Ugaritic data in a stimulating way, his approach is distorted by documentary presuppositions and relies heavily on cultic source attribution. In fact, when he attributes the source of sinaitic theophanic language to ancient "hymns of the Wars of Yahweh," he comes remarkably close to Jeremias's unfounded proposal that the source of the theophanic *Gattung* in the Old Testament was the "Victory Celebrations" regularly celebrated after victorious "Yahweh wars."[127] In any case, there is no real evidence that such covenant renewal ceremonies took place in variant forms at the great sanctuaries, or that they were the source of the Old Testament prose theophanic accounts.

---

[124]Ibid., 85.
[125]Ibid., 86.
[126]Ibid., 85–86.
[127]See above, p. 69–70.

Thomas W. Mann

Thomas W. Mann has produced a book that is at once a fine study of some ancient Near Eastern theophanies and an attempt to relate these to various Old Testament theophanies. His work *Divine Presence and Guidance in Israelite Traditions* builds upon a typology developed by William W. Hallo—the "typology of exaltation"—in the latter's book *The Exaltation of Inanna*.[128]

Hallo's book presents a transliteration and translation of a poem in Sumerian, "The Exaltation of Inanna," by Enheduanna, daughter of Sargon I and priestess of Inanna. Hallo develops a typology according to which the goddess Inanna pursues warfare victoriously—with attendant storm theophany language—and is then exalted. Hallo saw this typology as rooted in historical events—namely, Sargon's actual military successes and his own subsequent exaltation. He suggested that the same might be said of the Reed Sea events: "Events at the Reed Sea and God's exaltation are closely related, and this relationship, which deserves further study, can materially help to date the former while strengthening the historical character of the latter."[129] The discovery of "exaltation typology" in the Reed Sea events would "strengthen" their "historical character," because, according to Hallo, such typology in the ancient world appears to be rooted in historical events—as in the case of Sargon and Inanna. The following chapter will deal more extensively with Hallo's contribution to our grasp of the ancient Near Eastern data.

Mann extends Hallo's approach to a number of ancient Near Eastern theophanic passages from Sumer, Assyria, Babylon, and Ugarit, and demonstrates exaltation typology in them

---

[128]Wm. W. Hallo and J. J. A. van Dijk, *The Exaltation of Inanna*. Yale Near Eastern Researches 3 (New Haven: Yale University Press, 1968).
[129]Ibid., 68.

all.[130] His work shows in a most lucid way the viability of the paradigm developed by Hallo and is a strong contribution to our appreciation of this aspect of ancient Near Eastern literature. Mann concludes that two major features characterize the typology of exaltation. The first is historical rootage: most of the texts "reflect an historical situation that is intricately involved with the founding and/or renaissance of an empire."[131] The second is what he calls the "vanguard motif," according to which a god or goddess goes in the vanguard, waging war against the enemy who is foe simultaneously to the deity and to the human king who serves the deity.[132] The texts that "utilize the motif of the divine vanguard" are also "often accompanied by the language of storm phenomena."[133]

The problem comes when Mann applies Hallo's typology to Old Testament theophanies. A great contrast obtains between the clarity and fluency of his analyses of ancient Near Eastern texts on the one hand and the much more involved and even ponderous analyses of Old Testament passages on the other. The reason for the contrast is clear. The Old Testament discussions are encumbered by discussions of tradition history and cultic origins. For instance, of Exodus 19 he says, "It goes without saying that in its present form, this material provides a number of different levels of tradition and interpretation, not the least of which is the intrusive nature of the Decalogue."[134] This means, among other things, an acceptance of traditional source-critical methodology with all of its criteria for subdividing texts. For example:

> It is interesting that Exod 19:9 stresses auditory aspects—the people are to hear Yahweh speak to Moses (cf. vs. 19). It is

---

[130]Mann, *Divine Presence,* "Part I," 25–117. He draws far less on Hittite and Egyptian sources, but cf. p. 109 (Hittite), and pp. 169–70 (Egyptian).
[131]Ibid., 51.
[132]Ibid.
[133]Ibid.
[134]Ibid., 136.

tempting to assign this verse to E and to see here a different orientation concerning divine presence from that of J who, as in Exod 14.13, 30–31, emphasizes the visual.[135]

Mann routinely takes such criteria into account, and they burden his discussion unnecessarily. He also employs the methodology of cultic source attribution, with a remarkable misuse of ancient Near Eastern evidence. For example:

> Alongside the use of the vanguard motif, the story of the Jordan crossing also has a strong resemblance to the cultic texts we have examined in the Near Eastern material. As in the latter, we have a processional march that is led by a physical representation of the presence of the deity. The analogy supports the hypothesis that Joshua 3–5 is the description of an actual cultic procession that was celebrated repeatedly at Gilgal.[136]

Mann assumes that because divine emblems were foremost in cultic processions, a cultic origin must (or at least may) account for the forward position of the ark in the Jordan crossing account. He correctly calls this a "hypothesis," which by definition is a proposition that has not been proven. Nor can it be. But an equally reasonable alternative may be proposed that also draws on ancient Near Eastern practice. That is the practice of ancient kings, according to which their armies proceeded with divine emblems (standards, etc.) in the vanguard, as Mann himself points out.[137] The presence of the ark in the vanguard of Israel's Jordan crossing may be understood as a historical fact, analogous to the ancient Near Eastern use of divine emblems—just as Deuteronomy employs a suzerain-vassal treaty form for God's suzerainty covenant with Israel, analogous to ancient Near Eastern treaties between human

---

[135]Ibid., 137.
[136]Ibid., 197.
[137]Ibid., 74–75, 170–71.

suzerains and their vassals. In both cases God employs a culturally current form his people can appreciate.

One piece of Old Testament evidence for the pagan attitude toward such divine emblems is the reaction of the Philistines when the Israelite army in Eli's day received the ark into its midst:

> When the ark of Yahweh's covenant came into the camp, all Israel raised such a great shout that the ground shook. Hearing the uproar, the Philistines asked, "What's all this shouting in the Hebrew camp?"
>
> When they learned that the ark of Yahweh had come into the camp, the Philistines were afraid. "A god has come into the camp," they said. "We're in trouble!" (1Sa 4:5–7).[138]

The Philistines clearly understood that some divine emblem or standard had entered the Hebrew camp. For them, and erroneously for Israel, this was tantamount to the god himself coming into the camp.

Evidence from the Old Testament and from the ancient Near East is sufficient to show that there is no need to attribute a cultic source for the Jordan crossing. The same may be said of other attempts to attribute Old Testament historical accounts to cultic sources (see below, 77–80).

A simultaneous strength and weakness of Mann's work is its focus on "exaltation typology" as a paradigm for understanding Old Testament theophanies. Although it is relevant to a number of Old Testament passages, it fails to take into account many significant ones. This is because the typology is usually rooted in battles.[139] He does not therefore deal with theophanies that are similar in character—that is, Sinaitic "glory" theophanies—but different in purpose, for example

---

[138]The Philistines also remark, "Nothing like this has happened before," by which they mean simply that Yahweh's ark has never been brought against them before in battle (cf. 1Sa 4:8–9).

[139]Mann, *Divine Presence*, 50–51.

God's covenant-initiatory presence at Creation (Ge 1:2) and in Abram's vision (Ge 15), God's judgment parousia in the garden (Ge 3:8–10), God's departure from his temple (Eze 8–11), his appearance to certain prophets (e.g., Elijah, Isaiah, and Ezekiel), and so on.[140]

It is time to turn from a review of past scholarship to some final comments on the approach to the Sinai data taken by Mowinckel, von Rad, and a number of subsequent scholars. Some observations are necessary concerning the avenue of cultic source attribution in particular that these scholars have taken.

METHODOLOGY OF CULTIC ATTRIBUTION

The attribution of Old Testament traditions to cultic sources has arisen as a major tool in liberal scholars' handling of the biblical data. This traditio-historical approach may be regarded as a mutation of the older Documentary Hypothesis. The assumption now is that creeds originating in the cult eventually formed the basis of historical traditions that J and E, for example, much later put down in writing.

Whatever its attractions may be, this procedure is a peculiar way of dealing with the biblical materials. Martin Noth refers to the evolution from creed to historical account as a "historicizing" process.[141] What actually seems to be going on is the very opposite. That is, scholars of this persuasion are taking historical accounts and "credalizing" them. For instance, Leviticus 23:42–43 tells Israel that at the Festival of Booths all native-born Israelites must live in booths for seven days (v. 42) so that their descendants will know that Yahweh had the Israelites live in booths when he brought them out of Egypt (v. 43). According to Noth the reverse is true: because a

---

[140]Mann does notice such passages, of course, but only gives them very brief mention, mostly noting some theophanic terms that occur in them. Cf. his "Index of Biblical Citations," ibid., 288ff.

[141]Noth, *Pentateuchal Traditions*, 60.

Festival of Booths existed, somehow a "historical" account arose that claimed that Yahweh once had Israel live in booths when he brought them out of Egypt. This he refers to as the "'historicizing' of the 'feast of tabernacles.'"[142] The methodology he employs is the same as that seen in Mowinckel, Beyerlin, von Rad, and others.

This is a method that uproots biblical passages from their literary and historical context and attributes them to a later, cultic setting. Is such a procedure appropriate? What knowledge can it yield of the origin of biblical materials? To answer these questions it is important to keep in mind that the Old Testament is, among other things, a text (or collection of texts) from the ancient Near East. Yet such an approach to other ancient Near Eastern texts would have difficulty finding acceptance among scholars. Take for example the annals of the kings of Assyria. Assyrian kings frequently attributed their success in battle to the help of their gods. One might lift one of those brief paeans out of its context in the annals, attribute it to a cultic setting, and claim that the annalistic account in which it now appears was simply a historicizing of the original creed. For instance, Tiglath-pileser I (ca. 1115–1077 B.C.) claimed that the god Aššur helped him win victory over the rebellious land of Ishdish: "With the onslaught of my fierce weapons by means of which Ashur, the lord, gave me strength and authority I took thirty of my chariots escorting my aggressive personnel carriers, my warriors trained for successful combat. . . . I destroyed the land Ishdish [so that it looked] like ruin hills [created by] the deluge."[143]

Nothing would be easier than to posit a cultic setting as the origin of this account. In a sacred ceremony, an Assyrian king attributes his weapons to the god Aššur. He confesses that

---

[142] Ibid., 60.

[143] A. K. Grayson, *Assyrian Royal Inscriptions* [hereafter *ARI*] (Wiesbaden: Harrassowitz, 1976), 2:8.

these weapons will give him the "strength and authority" to win the battles to which Aššur calls him. This is the creed. Gradually arising out of this putative cultic creed, a "historical" account develops some time later, attributing a particular conquest in the past (the subjugation of Ishdish) to the weapons and help of Aššur. The presence of the first person in the narrative may be a literary device to enhance its historical flavor, or it may reflect the cultic root of the account in the individual's credal confession of help from the god Aššur. Such is the methodology of cultic attribution. The approach is excluded in the case of Tiglath-pileser's annals because they were inscribed in stone within five years of the events they record and were not the product of any gradual "historicizing" of cultic creeds.[144] Moreover, the attribution of success to one's gods was commonplace in the ancient Near East and formed a regular part of historical accounts (royal annals) written shortly after the events themselves.[145] The same is true of accounts of miraculous interventions on the part of the national gods.[146]

No good reason has been put forward why the Old Testament record should be accorded any less credence than other ancient Near Eastern historical accounts. In fact, if the Old Testament data are accorded that respect, what comes into question is not their historicity. Rather it is the putative creeds that lack firm evidence: for their seminal role in the evolution of the biblical histories and in some cases for their very existence. An example from Noth illustrates the problem. According to Noth, the Sinai tradition is supposed to be rooted in a covenant renewal ceremony at the Shechem cult. But Noth himself is compelled to ask, "Why do we learn so little

---

[144]L. W. King, *Annals of the Kings of Assyria*, ed. E. A. Wallis Budge [hereafter *AKA*] (London: Harrison and Sons, 1902), 1:lxv.

[145]Cf. passim R. Borger, *Einleitung in die assyrischen Königsinschriften*, erster Theil (Leiden: Brill, 1961); W. Schramm, *Einleitung in die assyrischen Königsinschriften*, zweiter Theil (Leiden: Brill, 1973).

[146]See below, chap. 3.

definite in the Old Testament about that festival of covenant-making or covenant-renewal, which one is supposed to regard as an event of fundamental and central significance . . . if indeed a reactualization of this event took place regularly in a cultic festival?"[147] The obvious answer is that on the biblical data there never was such a regular cultic "reactualization of this event." Noth has postulated a regular festival on an evidential basis that would never obtain in dealing with other ancient texts. As a result, however, he can maintain a critical avoidance of what actually happened on Mount Sinai.

The same is substantially true of all the liberal scholars and scholarly traditions examined above. Whatever their approach—whether putative J, E, and P are considered to have been original documents that survive only in fragmentary form as we now have them in the Hexateuch; or whether J, E, and P have actually put down in written form the latter fruits of centuries of oral/credal tradition—all of these scholars agree on the wide gap that separates the biblical data from anything that one could call history.

These scholarly traditions are subjective, and the methods they employ go hand in hand with a bias against the supernatural as the Old Testament portrays it. Although that bias could be further documented with ease, enough has been said to differentiate the approaches of liberal scholars from the present endeavor.

One area that has drawn attention from many scholars of the Old Testament—whatever their methodological or theological orientations—is the world of the ancient Near East. In that world we find many parallels to the thought and the theophanic portrayals of the Old Testament. We also find significant differences and an important reason for those differences.

---

[147]Noth, *Pentateuchal Traditions*, 60. Cf. the remarks of Jeremias on the similar lack of evidence for his putative regular "Victory Celebrations," above, n. 106.

3

Ancient Near Eastern Parallels:

The Relationship of Egyptian, Hittite, Mesopotamian, and Canaanite Theophanies to the Biblical Tradition (Part 1)

> Oh! Blessed rage for order, pale Ramon,
> The maker's rage to order words of the sea,
> Words of the fragrant portals, dimly-starred,
> And of ourselves and of our origins,
> In ghostlier demarcations, keener sounds.
>
> Wallace Stevens, "The Idea of Order at Key West"

Humanity does have a "rage for order," and it is blessed. The "rage" exists because God is a God of order—of cosmos— and he made human beings to be compatible with the cosmos he created. As a result, humanity longs for this God who made all things. So Augustine could say, "*Nos fecisti ad te, et inquietum est cor nostrum donec requiescat in te.*" That divinely placed unquiet was well known to the people of the ancient Near East. For that reason the vast bulk of ancient Near Eastern literature demonstrates a religious point of view. It assumes the existence of gods and goddesses who must be adored and served, or of spirits that must be invoked,[1] exorcised,[2] or protected against.[3]

Those pagan religions–characterized by polytheism (or henotheism at best)[4] and idolatry–represent a *Weltanschauung* that is degraded from the truth. The apostle Paul put pagan religion in perspective when he portrayed it as a result of the Fall. According to Paul, humanity knew God from the beginning but chose not to glorify him or give thanks to him, and as a result, "their foolish hearts were darkened" and "they became fools and exchanged the glory of the immortal God for images made to look like mortal man and birds and animals and reptiles" (Ro 1:21–23).[5]

Paul's genealogy of pagan religion accounts for many of the analogies one can find between the religious thought of the

---

[1] Cf. O. R. Gurney, *Some Aspects of Hittite Religion*. The Schweich Lectures 1976 (Oxford: Oxford University Press, 1977), 53.

[2] Cf. the collection of incantations for exorcizing demons, E. Reiner, *Šurpu, A Collection of Sumerian and Akkadian Incantations*, *AfO* Beiheft 11 (Graz, 1958).

[3] Cf. the collection of Aramaic incantations for protection against demons, Ch. D. Isbell, *Corpus of the Aramaic Incantation Bowls* (Missoula: Scholars Press, 1975).

[4] As in the reign of Akh-en-Aton (ca. 1380–1362 B.C.) in Egypt; cf. the useful if somewhat romantic characterization of his reign and his efforts to introduce what Breasted calls "solar monotheism," J. H. Breasted, *Development of Religion and Thought in Ancient Egypt* (Philadelphia: University of Pennsylvania Press, 1972), 312–43; cf. *ANET*, 3d ed., 365–72.

[5] Interestingly, the ancients thought of the idols as man-made forms that the spiritual gods entered, thus becoming available to the human worshiper. Such was clearly the case in Egypt and Mesopotamia. Cf. Breasted, *Development of Religion*, 46, where it is said of the Egyptian god Ptah-Tatenen, "He installed the gods in their holy places.... He made likenesses of their bodies to the satisfaction of their hearts. Then the gods entered into their bodies of every wood and every stone and every metal." For Mesopotamian evidence, cf. A. L. Oppenheim, *Ancient Mesopotamia, Portrait of a Dead Civilization* (Chicago: University of Chicago Press, 1964), 184.

ancient Near East and Old Testament portrayals of God and his behavior. Consequently, one may use the Old Testament as a touchstone by which to understand parallel materials from the ancient Near East. Such a procedure is empirical, not imperialistic.[6] It does not mean, for example, that the ancient Near Eastern data cannot illuminate the Bible. Recent scholarship has amply shown how customs, laws, and legal forms (as well as other literary forms) from the ancient world enhance one's appreciation of the narrative and legal materials of the Old Testament. But only the Old Testament (and, as it relates, the New Testament) can afford theological illumination to the ultimate nature and value of ancient Near Eastern religious matter—whether it be a hymn to Aton or a divine titulary in an Assyrian royal inscription.

MAJOR OLD TESTAMENT THEMES AS BACKGROUND TO THEOPHANY

The Old Testament contains a hierarchical set of themes that form a background to Old Testament theophanies. A parallel set of themes appears in the ancient Near East. In the Bible they appear in a revealed form, with great clarity and force. They can be arranged hierarchically because that is their natural theological order. I set them forth now as the organizing themes of this chapter. Although abundant biblical evidence attests the appropriateness of the scheme employed here, I will cite only enough biblical data to demonstrate its reality. A fully developed argument in its favor would be

---

[6]We need not, therefore, agree with Oppenheim's lament that "Western man seems to be both unable and, ultimately, unwilling to understand such religions except from the distorting angle of antiquarian interest and apologetic pretenses" (*Ancient Mesopotamia,* 183). A proper appreciation of polytheism in light of revealed truth is not an apologetic pretense, and an understanding of its spiritual dimensions vis á vis a revealed God (who is Spirit) is not just of antiquarian interest.

beyond the scope of this chapter.⁷ The hierarchy of ideas is as follows: God as King, God's Kingdom, God's Covenant(s), and God's Covenant Administration.⁸ The order of the ideas is both logical and biblical; and it will become clear that all Old Testament theophanies take place against the background—or within the matrix—of these governing ideas. I will now demonstrate them from the Old Testament, with parallels from the ancient Near East.

God as King

The Old Testament portrays God as a great king, as does the New (cf. Mt 5:35). Old Testament evidence for this idea is both indirect and direct. The book of Genesis contains at least two major indirect evidences of God's kingship: the Genesis 1 Creation account and Abraham's characterization of God before Sodom and Gomorrah. The Creation account, Genesis 1:1–2:3, follows the pattern of a second-millennium suzerain-vassal treaty.⁹ In this arrangement, God is the Suzerain or Great King, and man is the vassal. The literary form of the passage therefore implies God's suzerainty. Later in Genesis, Abraham characterizes Yahweh as the "judge of all the earth" (Ge 18:25), using a term ("judge," שֹׁפֵט) routinely used of rulers, including kings, in the Old Testament (cf. Judges, passim; 2Ki 15:5 [King Jotham of Judah]; Ex 16:5 [the messianic king]; Am 2:3 [Moab's king]).¹⁰ Consequently, form-critical and terminological evidence point to Yahweh's kingship early in Genesis.

---

⁷Such an argument will form part of a work in progress, in which I hope to use the hierarchical scheme presented here as an organizing and illuminating principle for many ancient Near Eastern parallels to the Old and New Testaments.

⁸Because of the magnitude of the scheme, a separate chapter (pt. 2, chap. 4) is dedicated to the last topic, God's Covenant Administration.

⁹As I will show in chap. 5; cf. already M. Kline, *Kingdom Prologue*, "The Covenant of Creation" (South Hamilton: Gordon-Conwell Seminary Press, 1986), 12–17.

¹⁰For a Mesopotamian parallel, cf. J. Niehaus, *Amos*, in T. E. McComiskey, ed., *The Minor Prophets: An Exegetical and Expository Commentary*

One early direct statement of Yahweh's royal nature is found in Deuteronomy 33 and is closely linked to Yahweh's appearance at Sinai:

> Yahweh came from Sinai
>   and dawned over them from Seir . . .
> . . . from you they receive instruction,
> the Torah that Moses gave us,
> He became king [מֶלֶךְ] in "righteous-nation" [Jeshurun][11]
>   when the leaders of the people assembled,
>   along with the tribes of Israel. (Dt 33:2–5, author's trans.)

Moses' poem employs a shift of person (he/you) characteristic of Hittite treaties[12] and other ancient Near Eastern literature[13] to emphasize Yahweh's personal involvement with Israel: he appeared at Sinai not only to give them laws, but even more, to become their King. In fact, one thing that a good king did in the ancient Near East was to give just laws to his people; Hammurapi of Babylon boasted such a claim in his famous law code.[14]

Later in Israel's history, explicit reference to Yahweh as King includes the application of the noun "king" (מֶלֶךְ) or the verb "to be king" (מָלַךְ). Samuel calls Yahweh Israel's king (מֶלֶךְ, 1Sa 12:12), and David celebrates Yahweh as his King (מֶלֶךְ, Pss 5:2[3]; 10:16; 24:8–10; 29:10; et al.). The related verb, "to be king," is used of Yahweh in celebration of the Reed Sea crossing (Ex 15:18) and of Yahweh in other theophanic portrayals (Isa 24:23; Pss 93:1; 96:10; 97:1; 99:1).

(Grand Rapids: Baker, 1992), 1:359. For the broad sense of the verb, with examples, cf. *TWOT* 2:947–48.

[11]Cf. C. F. Keil, *The Fifth Book of Moses*, in C. F. Keil and F. Delitzsch, *Commentary on the Old Testament in Ten Volumes* (Grand Rapids: Eerdmans, 1978), 1:499.

[12]Cf. K. Baltzer, *Das Bundesformular* (Neukirchen: Neukirchener Verlag, 1960); English version, *The Covenant Formulary*, trans. D. E. Green (Philadelphia: Fortress, 1971).

[13]Cf. J. Sperber, "Der Personenwechsel in der Bibel," *ZA* 21 (1918/19): 23–33.

[14]Cf. *ANET*, 3d ed., 163–80 (cf. esp. p. 165, vv.10ff.).

Both indirect and direct evidence clearly indicate that Yahweh was considered a king in the Old Testament. The fact that he was a king—even a great king or suzerain—has implications for everything else in the Bible, including theophanies.

Pagan Gods as Kings

Pagan inscriptions also ascribed kingship to various gods. Their royalty could involve suzerainty or authority over humans or over other gods. Examples from Egypt, Sumeria, Hatti, Assyria, Babylon, and Ugarit provide ready parallels to the Old Testament idea of divine kingship.

One of the earliest indications of this idea is found in Egypt, in a creation account from ca. 2000 B.C. or earlier, which says of the god Re (the sun god), "Re, when he began to rule that which he had made . . . Re began to appear as a king."[15] The meaning is that the god Re (who is also called "Lord of all") created all things and thus appeared as king over what he had made. The combination of the attributes of creator and king in one god parallels the Old Testament data, including the Genesis 1:1–2:3 Creation account. In an evidently older text (ca. 2700 B.C.), divine kingship of a particular land—Egypt—is apparent. Geb, the earth god, allots monarchies to the two gods Horus and Seth: "He made Seth the King of Upper Egypt . . . [and] made Horus the King of Lower Egypt."[16] In a later hymn (ca. 1775–1575 B.C.), Amon-Re is

---

[15]*ANET*, "Another Version of the Creation by Atum," 3d ed., trans. J. A. Wilson, 4. Re is another name for Atum; that is, both Atum and Re are "phases of the sun," p. 3, n. 2. Breasted, *Development of Religion,* 14ff., points out that the sun god came to be conceived of as a former king of Egypt and that as a result, "the qualities of earthly kingship were easily transferred to Re." Among his evidence Breasted cites a five-thousand-year-old hymn to Re (pp. 16–17).

[16]*ANET*, "The Theology of Memphis," 3d ed., trans. J. A. Wilson, 4. Wilson notes that "the extant form of this document dates only to 700 B.C., but linguistic, philological, and geopolitical evidence is conclusive in support of its derivation from an original text more than two thousand years older."

"King of Upper and Lower Egypt."[17] More examples are available,[18] but it is already clear that ancient Egypt thought of a god as both creator and king over all creation, and of gods as kings over particular lands.[19] These ideas parallel the concepts of God as Creator and King, and as King over Israel (and ultimately over the world), all of which are major themes of the Old Testament.

Examples of divine kingship are also found in Mesopotamia, from the Sumerian culture onward. Lugalsilasi of Lagaš (who flourished sometime between 2500 and 2350 B.C.)[20] has left us a lapis lazuli tablet dedicated to "An, king of all lands," and other deities.[21] Lugalzagesi of Umma (ca. 2300 B.C.) calls Enlil "king of all lands."[22] The "Sumerian King List," which dates from the reign of Utu-hegal of Uruk (2116–2109 B.C.), declares that kingship itself was lowered down from heaven, and that one of the primordial kings among men was Dumu-zi (Tammuz), who was also a shepherd and a god.[23] Other evidence shows that Sumerian and later Mesopotamian idols "lived the life of a king" which, to cite a few examples, could include a morning *lever du roi*, ceremonial meals at which the high god Anu and his divine court were served hot meals on golden plates, marriage festivals between deities, the transportation of the god Nabu's image into a game park to hunt,

---

[17] *ANET*, "A Hymn to Amon-Re," 3d ed., trans. J. A. Wilson, 365.

[18] Cf. Breasted, *Development of Religion*, 3–48; *ANET*, 3d ed., 3–36, 365–82.

[19] Compare the apparently evil angels who are termed the "prince of Persia," the "king of Persia," and the "prince of Greece" in Da 10:13, 20; cf. Dt 32:8.

[20] J. S. Cooper, *Sumerian and Akkadian Royal Inscriptions, I*, Presargonic Inscriptions (New Haven: The American Oriental Society, 1986), p. 3. In a later inscription, Eanatum of Lagaš (ca. 2400 B.C.) calls Enlil the "king of heaven and earth," 35 (La 3.1.xivff.).

[21] Ibid., 21–22 (Ki 8).

[22] Ibid., 94 (Um 7.1.i).

[23] Cf. T. Jacobsen, *The Sumerian King List* (Chicago: University of Chicago Press, 1939), 70–71; *ANET*, 3d ed., 265–66.

and so on.[24] Such were a part of what Oppenheim has called "the care and feeding of the gods."

The Hittites also ascribed royalty to the gods. Among them were the sun god, who was "king of the lands," and Erishkigal, or the "sun goddess of the earth (i.e., underworld)," the queen of the chthonic deities.[25] The sun goddess of Arina could also be called "queen of all the countries."[26] The myth "Kingship in Heaven" tells of a battle between the weather god Teshub and the "Primeval Gods," in which Teshub wins the supremacy over Alalus, the king of heaven, and banishes him and the other gods to the underworld, thus becoming king himself.[27] The picture is complicated in Hatti by the idea that a human king became a god upon his death. Hence Muršiliš II (ca. 1325 B.C.) could declare in traditional fashion that his father "became god" (that is, died).[28] In fact, a Hittite funerary ritual for a dead king ends with the prayer, "Be kind to your children! Your kingdom shall endure for your grandchildren and great-grandchildren." The prayer takes into account the potential menace posed by the soul of the dead, especially when the dead is a royal personage who has now become a god, and seeks to propitiate it by an elaborate rite of passage.[29]

Royal terminology from Assyria and Babylon is also abundantly applied to gods. The Akkadian cognate to Hebrew

---

[24]Cf. Oppenheim, *Ancient Mesopotamia,* 183–98.

[25]O. R. Gurney, *Some Aspects of Hittite Religion.* The Schweich Lectures 1977 (Oxford: Oxford University Press, 1977), 4–5. Gurney notes that Erishkigal is a Sumerian name sometimes applied to the Sun goddess.

[26]Ibid., 18.

[27]*ANET,* 3d ed., 120–21; H. A. Hoffner, Jr., *Hittite Myths.* SBL Writings From the Ancient World 2 (Atlanta: Scholars Press, 1990), 40–43 (Text 14, "The Song of Kumarbi"). Cf. Gurney, *Aspects of Hittite Religion,* 4–23, for a careful reconstruction of the evolution and permutations of the Hittite pantheon under Sumerian, Babylonian, Hurrian and other influences.

[28]A. Götze, *Die Annalen des Muršiliš* (Darmstadt: Wissenschaftliche Buchgesellschaft, 1967), 14–15.

[29]Gurney, *Aspects of Hittite Religion,* 62.

מֶלֶךְ, which is *malku*, means "prince, ruler," and occurs as a divine epithet (e.g., of Enlil, Shamash, and others).[30] The Akkadian word, *šarru(m)*, which actually denotes "king" in the Old Testament sense (cf. Heb. שַׂר, "prince"), occurs very often as a divine epithet in Akkadian (e.g., of Tammuz [already noted], Anu, Sin, Shamash, Adad, Marduk, and others).[31] Adad is "king of the gods."[32] Aššur is "king of the totality of the great gods."[33] Shamash, Anu, and Enlil are all called "king of all humanity."[34] Shamash is "king of the evil night-demons," and so on.[35] The title, "King of kings" (cf. Rev 19:16), is applied to the gods Enlil and Aššur.[36] Akkadian legend attributes the creation of the world to Marduk, who is also called "the king of the gods."[37] Assyrians considered the god Aššur to be king of the gods and the national god of Assyria; Babylonians claimed the same attributes for the god Marduk.[38] Mesopotamia thus amply attests an assumption from the Sumerian period onward that gods were kings. The idea of a god who was both national and universal is also well attested.

Ugaritic poetry shows a similar if less variegated picture. Two gods, El and Baal, stand out as "kings." El is the head of the pantheon, and Baal is the storm god who dies and is raised again from the domain of Mot (the god of death; cf. Heb. מוֹת, "to die"). Cognate with Hebrew, the noun "king" (*mlk*) and the verb, "to be king" (*mlk*) are used of the gods. El, the high god

---

[30] K. Tallqvist, *Akkadische Götterepitheta* (Helsinki: Druckerei–A.G. der finnischen Literaturgesellschaft, 1938), 129.
[31] Ibid., 232–33.
[32] Ibid., 233.
[33] Ibid., 233.
[34] Ibid., 232–33.
[35] Ibid., 235.
[36] Ibid., 237.
[37] *ANET,* 3d ed., 68. Cf. "The Creation Epic," 60–72.
[38] For a study of the relation between the national gods and their lands in the ancient Near East, cf. D. I. Block, *The Gods of the Nations.* ETS Monograph Series 2 (Jackson: Evangelical Theological Society, 1988), 7–23.

in Ugaritic, is called "the King, [the] Father of Years" (compare El as a name for God in the Old Testament, and the biblical epithet of God, "the Ancient of Days," Da 7:9).[39] El, as head of the pantheon, has authority to bestow kingship on other gods. The god Athtar is portrayed as possessing a kingship that El intends to bestow upon the god Yam (the personified sea, cf. Heb. ם׳, "sea"), who is also called "Judge River."[40] El also asks the goddess Athirat to let him make one of her sons king upon the death of Baal.[41] But the gods in assembly also declare, "Mightiest Baal is our King, over whom there is none,"[42] a sentiment that Baal also affirms: "I alone am he that is King over the gods."[43] And Baal is again king after his resurrection.[44]

The data from Egypt, Sumer, Hatti, Assyria, Babylon, and Ugarit are in substantial agreement. In each case, various gods were called "king" or were said "to be king." One reason for the plurality of kings is that each god had a certain domain or kingdom. In Ugarit, Yam ruled over the sea, Baal ruled over the sky, and El ruled over all. In Mesopotamia, Sin was the god of the moon (and of wisdom and of change), Shamash the god of the sun (and of covenants and legal arrangements), and so on. Another reason for the plurality is that the same domains were attributed to various gods in different places and over time. In Assyria and Babylonia Anu, Enlil, Aššur, and Marduk were supreme at different periods and in different ways. Where there was overlap it was, at least in part, because of the variety and inconsistency inherent in polytheism. W. F. Albright has noted that Canaanite deities have a remarkable fluidity of function, "a fluidity that makes it exceedingly hard

---

[39]J. C. L. Gibson, *Canaanite Myths and Legends* (Edinburgh: T. & T. Clark, 1978), 37 (2.iii.5).
[40]Ibid., 37–38; cf. Gibson's commentary on the text, pp. 3–4.
[41]Ibid., 75 (6.i.43–46).
[42]Ibid., 54 (3.E.40–41).
[43]Ibid., 66 (4.vii.49–50).
[44]Ibid., 79 (6.v.5–6).

to fix the domains of different gods or to determine their relation to one another."[45] To some extent the same may be said of polytheism in general.[46]

God's Kingdom

The Old Testament speaks of God's kingdom, as does the New (cf. Mt 6:33; et al.). The concept of God's kingdom is implicit in the Suzerain-vassal arrangement of Genesis 1:1–2:3, as was the concept of God as King. Wherever God is called a king, his kingdom is also implied. But there is also explicit reference to his kingdom in the Old Testament. The operative terms are "kingdom" in Hebrew (מַלְכוּת, מְלוּכָה) and Aramaic (מַלְכוּ). David declared that "Yahweh has established his throne in heaven, and his kingdom rules over all" (מַלְכוּת, Ps 103:19; cf. Ps 145:13). The "Sons of Korah" sang to God, "Your throne, O God, will last for ever and ever; a scepter of justice will be the scepter of your kingdom" (מַלְכוּת, Ps 45:7[6]). Obadiah prophesied that "the kingdom will be Yahweh's" (מְלוּכָה, Ob 21 = Ps 22:29[28]). Later in Israel's history, the prophet Daniel declared in a theophanic portrayal of God that the "Ancient of Days" had a kingdom that would be eternal (מַלְכוּ, Da 7:9–14).

---

[45]W. F. Albright, *Archaeology and the Religion of Israel* (Baltimore: Johns Hopkins Press, 1942), 71.

[46]As Oppenheim, *Ancient Mesopotamia,* 194ff., points out, other historical reasons for the overlap and polyvalence observed in polytheistic systems include development over a long period, which produces "layers of divine names," fusions that create a number of "hybrid figures," and the "fluctuations of the popularity of the individual deities." Although his remarks are centered on Mesopotamian religion, I believe they apply with similar force to other ancient Near Eastern polytheistic environments. More broadly and theologically considered, one may say that as human beings turned from God, they fractionalized his attributes into various false gods, who came to have fluid functions and overlapping qualities. Any of a host of these gods might at some time or other be exalted as a "king."

Pagan Gods and Their Kingdoms

The idea of a king naturally entails the idea of a kingdom. Both ideas are important as a background for covenantal thought in the Old Testament and the ancient world. The overall picture is that gods were kings, had kingdoms, and could bestow kingdoms both on other gods and on mortals whom they chose.

In Egyptian royal ideology, those who were kings also had kingdoms. In fact, kingdom might be said to be a corollary of royal authority—rooted in the sun god's authority as Creator of all things, and imparted both to other gods and to his pharaonic offspring.[47]

In Mesopotamia it was normal to recognize gods as kings over the earth, who in turn bestowed kingship on chosen mortals. Uru'inimgina of Lagaš said that "Ningirsu, warrior of Enlil, granted the kingship of Lagash to Uru'inimgina."[48] King Gudea of Lagaš (2143–2124 B.C.) in effect styles himself the vassal of the god Ningirsu when he declares, "O my king, Ningirsu."[49] The "Sumerian King List" is a record of human kings (and one who was a god) who ruled earthly kingdoms on authority from heaven. The Hittite deities mentioned above were also rulers over the earth and the underworld. Hittite gods allocated royal dominion to the Hittite emperors—and the emperors themselves became gods upon their death. In an Old Hittite text, for example, the king declares, "To me, the king, have the gods—Sun-god and Weather-god—entrusted the land and my house. I, the king, will rule over the land and my house."[50] Among the Hittites indeed, "the death of a king or

---

[47]Cf. Breasted, *Development of Religion,* 15ff., 39ff., 251ff. and examples there cited.
[48]Cooper, *Royal Inscriptions,* 71 (La 9.1.viiff.). The king's name was formerly read *Urukagina,* cf. ibid., 70.
[49]Cf. Mann, *Divine Presence and Guidance in Israelite Traditions,* 80.
[50]Gurney, *Aspects of Hittite Religion,* 9; *ANET,* 3d ed., 357ff.

queen seems to have been regarded as a violation of the divine order of things."[51] The Akkadian term for "kingdom, royal authority" (šarrūtum) was used for nearly two millennia for everything from the "kingdom of heaven" to the imperium of Assyrian and Babylonian kings chosen by the gods.[52]

The gods of Ugarit could also have kingdoms. One passage tells how El, the head of the pantheon, planned to overturn the throne of the god Athtar's "kingdom" (mlk).[53] El himself of course had "kingdom" (mlk) and "dominion" (drkt),[54] and as a god and king could bestow kingdoms upon others. King Pabil of Udm, for example, said that the city-state over which he ruled was "the gift of El, and a present from the Father of mankind/Adam (ʾab ʾadm)."[55]

According to the data from the ancient world, many gods were kings and had kingdoms. They also elevated humans to royalty, bestowing kingdoms upon them. This simple structure of ideas forms a backdrop for covenantal thought in the ancient Near East and the Old Testament. The royal idea in particular is foundational because covenants were normally made between kings, usually in the form of suzerain-vassal treaties. Such treaties were overseen by gods who were also kings and had bestowed kingship on the mortal kings. (Even where a private covenant was made, a god was invoked as overseer of its provisions—compare David's and Jonathan's covenant and invocation of Yahweh, 1Sa 20:12–17.) Because the Old Testament God was King, he was able to make covenants with mortals whom he had created. By so doing he showed himself to be their Suzerain. Similar ideas obtained in the ancient Near East.

---

[51]Ibid., 59.
[52]Wolfram von Soden, *Akkadisches Handwörterbuch* (Wiesbaden: Harrassowitz, 1974), 3:1190–91.
[53]Gibson, *Canaanite Myths and Legends,* 38 (2.iii.17–18). "Throne" (ksʾa) occurs with "kingdom" (mlk) in the Ugaritic verse, as does כִּסֵּא with מַלְכוּת in Ps 103:19.
[54]Ibid., 83 (14.i.41–43).
[55]Ibid., 86 (14.iii.135–36).

God's Covenants

So much has been written about God's covenants with his people that a lengthy discussion is not necessary here.[56] The major covenants in the Old Testament are the Creation covenant (Ge 1:1–2:3), the Noahic covenant (Ge 9:1–17), the Abrahamic covenant (cf. especially Ge 15:7–21), the Mosaic covenant (cf. especially the book of Deuteronomy), and the Davidic covenant (cf. 2Sa 7:1–17). The Old Testament covenants are cast in the form of a second-millennium treaty.[57] Accordingly they contain a title identifying the Suzerain, a historical prologue, stipulations, and blessings and curses.[58] Perhaps the two outstanding facts about God's covenants are his impartation of them and their legal content. The same is true of covenants between gods and humans in the ancient Near East. Gods could appear as suzerains in covenants that demanded a vassal's obedience to laws. One important subordinate feature of covenants between gods and humans was that the vassal king was chosen to shepherd a god's people. The Davidic covenant affirms that God chose David to be a shepherd of God's people (cf. Ps 78:70–71; 2Sa 7:8). This theme is of obvious theological importance and can be explored in its ancient Near Eastern context.

Pagan Gods and Covenants

Covenants With Their Elect Kings and People

Like Israel, other peoples of the ancient Near East considered their gods to be great suzerains. One right of a suzerain

---

[56]Cf. the works by Vos and Kline, cited above in chap. 2.

[57]No doubt because they were written down in that form during the time of Moses—with the exception of the Davidic covenant, which stands at the end of the second millennium and the beginning of the first.

[58]For a full discussion of the form as it applies to OT passages, cf. M. Kline, *Treaty of the Great King* (Grand Rapids: Eerdmans, 1963); K. A. Kitchen, *The Bible in Its World* (Downers Grove: InterVarsity Press, 1978), 79–85.

was the election of a subordinate king. Just as one god could choose another god to be a king among gods, so a god could chose a human to be a king among humans. As suzerains the gods could also ordain rules for human conduct, both royal and popular. As Dennis J. McCarthy has noted, "Semitic Mesopotamia at least was convinced that the world and human activity in it were governed by a law which was guarded by the gods and which consequently was above and beyond the will of man and formed the measure of human action, even the action of the king."[59] The involvement of gods in Egyptian and Hittite treaties shows that his observation applies outside ancient Mesopotamia as well. Cross has suggested that "in Akkadian and Amorite religion as also in Canaanite, 'Ēl frequently plays the role of 'god of the father,' the social deity who governs the tribe or league, often bound to league or king with kinship or covenant ties."[60]

The gods who guarded the world's legal order chose human kings and gave them laws. In both capacities the gods apparently entered into covenantal arrangements. The evidence for such covenants is not abundant—partly because the covenants themselves form a small proportion of the national literature, and partly (perhaps) because much ancient literature still lies beneath the earth. Yet the data apparently parallel what we find in the Old Testament.

Divine election of kings was a well-understood doctrine in the ancient Near East. The question hardly arose in Egypt, since the pharaoh was the son of the sun god and ruled in that authority.[61] Mesopotamian kings also claimed to be divine offspring.[62] The earliest known example, an inscription of Eana-

---

[59] D. J. McCarthy, *Treaty and Covenant.* Analecta Biblica 21A (Rome: Biblical Institute Press, 1978), 134.
[60] Cross, *CMHE,* 43.
[61] This was so from at least 2750 B.C. onward; cf. Breasted, *Development of Religion,* 15–16.
[62] Cf. S. N. Kramer, "Kingship in Sumer and Akkad: The Ideal King," *RAI* 19, pp. 163–66. As Mann, *Divine Presence,* 83, notes, Gudea of Lagaš

tum of Lagaš (ca. 2400 B.C.), dramatically illustrates both divine paternity and election:

> [Lor]d [Ni]ngirsu, [war]rior of [En]lil ... Ni]n[gir]su [imp]lanted the [semen] for E[a]natum in the [wom]b ... and ... rejoiced over [Eanatum]. Inana accompanied him, named him Eana-Inana-Ibgalakakatum, and set him on the special lap of Ninḫursag. Ninḫursag [offered him] her special breast. Ningirsu rejoiced over Eanatum, semen implanted in the womb by Ningirsu. Ningirsu laid his span upon him for [a length of] five forearms he set his forearm upon him: [he measured] five forearms [cubits], one span! Ningirsu, with great joy, [gave him] the kin[gship of Lagash].[63]

The account portrays the god Ningirsu as the father of King Eanatum (the goddess Ninḫursag is his mother). Ningirsu sired him, gave him his span, and made him king of Lagaš. It is an ancient adumbration of that historically later paternity and of that Father who later said, "This is my Son, whom I love; with him I am well pleased" (Mt 3:17).

The Sumerians thought that kingship itself was lowered down from heaven; the gods chose where and by whom it would be exercised.[64] Eanatum of Lagaš said as much of himself: "Eanatum, ruler of Lagaš, nominated by Enlil, granted strength by Ningirsu, chosen in her heart by Nanshe."[65]

---

recognized no father or mother but the goddess Gatumdu. Note also the description of the Assyrian king Tukulti-Ninurta I in W. G. Lambert, "Three Unpublished Fragments of the Tukulti-Ninurta Epic," *AfO* 18 (Graz, 1957–68): 50–51:

> By the fate assigned by Nudimmud his form is reckoned as divine nature,
> By the decree of the Lord of the Lands his forming proceeded smoothly *inside* the divine womb,
> He is the eternal image of Enlil.

[63]Cooper, *Royal Inscriptions,* 34 (La 3.1.iv–v).
[64]H. Frankfort, *Kingship and the Gods: A Study of Ancient Near Eastern Religion as the Integration of Society and Nature* (Chicago: University of Chicago Press, 1948), 237.
[65]Cooper, *Royal Inscriptions,* 41 (La 3.5.i–ii).

Uru'inimgina of Lagaš claimed that the god Ningirsu granted him the kingship of that city, "selecting him from among the myriad people."⁶⁶ As noted above, King Gudea of Lagaš effectually styled himself the vassal of the god Ningirsu when he declared, "O my king, Ningirsu."⁶⁷ Lugalzagesi of Umma called himself the "nominee of Utu."⁶⁸ Hittite kings, as we have seen, were also chosen by the gods. Assyrian kings thought that they were the gods' elect rulers. Tiglath-pileser I (ca. 1115–1077 B.C.) styled himself the "beloved prince, your [i.e., 'the gods'] select one, attentive shepherd, whom in the steadfastness of your hearts you chose."⁶⁹ Assyrian kings from Shamshi-Adad I (1814–1782 B.C.) to Ashurbanipal (668–627 B.C.) made similar claims.⁷⁰

The idea of the royal shepherd, alluded to by Tiglath-pileser I, was also a common idea among Israel's neighbors and predecessors. Pharaonic iconography typically portrays the king with a shepherd's crook in one hand, symbolic of this royal function. The concept of a royal shepherd, chosen by the gods, is well attested in Mesopotamia from very ancient times. Lugalzagesi of Umma boasted his divine election and prayed, "May I always be the leading shepherd!"⁷¹ Hammurapi (1792–1750 B.C.) said that he was called to shepherd the people

---

⁶⁶Ibid., 71 (La 9.1.viiff.).
⁶⁷See above, n. 21.
⁶⁸Ibid., 94 (Um 7.1.i).
⁶⁹King, *AKA*, 30.18ff.; Grayson, *ARI*, 2:5.
⁷⁰Cf. A. K. Grayson, *Assyrian Rulers of the Third and Second Millennia B.C. The Royal Inscriptions of Mesopotamia, Assyrian Periods*, vol. 1 (Toronto: University of Toronto Press, 1987), 48 (1.1–17, Shamshi-Adad I); p. 183 (1.22–26, Shalmaneser I); Ernst Weidner, *Die Inschriften Tukulti Ninurtas 1. und seiner Nachfolger* [hereafter *AfO* 12] (Graz, 1959), 1.I.21–31 (Tukulti-Ninurta I); *AKA*, 260.17ff. (Ashurnaṣirpal II); R. Borger, *Die Inschriften Asarhaddons Königs von Assyrien* [hereafter *AfO* Beiheft 9] (Graz, 1956), § 65.vv. 1–12 (Esarhaddon); A. C. Piepkorn, *HPIA* 28.1–13 (Ashurbanipal).
⁷¹Cooper, *Royal Inscriptions*, 94 (Um 7.1.iii [30]ff.).

of Babylon by the gods Anu and Enlil,[72] and the phrase, "the people of the god, Enlil," is attested from Sharkalisharri of Akkad (2212–2188 B.C.) to Ashurbanipal (668–627 B.C.), who claims, "I shepherded the people of the god, Enlil."[73]

Evidence suggests that ancient royalty were shepherds not only by election, but also by covenant. Such covenantal arrangements with the god(s) involved stipulations or laws that governed popular life. Uru'inimgina of Lagaš (twenty-fifth/twenty-fourth century B.C.) made a covenant with the god Ningirsu that emphasized the human observance of laws: "When Ningirsu, warrior of Enlil, granted the kingship of Lagash to Uru'inimgina, selecting him from among the myriad people, he replaced the customs of former times, carrying out the command that Ningirsu, his master, had given him."[74] As already noted, the passage claims divine election to kingship. It also implies covenant in that Uru'inimgina carries out the "commands" of his "master" just as vassal kings must do—just as Moses and the people did in Yahweh's covenant. Among the legal advances of Uru'inimgina's rule we read: "Uru'inimgina promised Ningirsu that he would never subjugate the waif and the widow to the powerful."[75] The Sumerian king's statement illustrates the sort of "advanced humanism" sometimes erroneously cited as evidence for a late date for Deuteronomy with its similar concern for the "orphan and widow."[76]

Somewhat later in Mesopotamian tradition Ur-Nammu (2112–2095 B.C.), the son of the goddess Ninsun, gave laws to

---

[72]H. Winckler, *Die Gezetze Hammurabis* [hereafter *CH*] (Leipzig: J. C. Hinrichs, 1903), I.1–25; cf. 24.R.10–15.

[73]Cf. Tallqvist, *Akkadische Götterepitheta*, 182–83.

[74]Cooper, *Royal Inscriptions,* 71 (La 9.1.viiff.); cf. earlier, F. Thureau-Dangin, *Die Sumerischen und Akkadischen Königsinschriften* [hereafter *SAK*] (Leipzig: Hinrichs, 1907), 52ff.

[75]Cooper, *Royal Inscriptions,* 73 (La 9.1.xii).

[76]E.g., M. Weinfeld, *Deuteronomy and the Deuteronomic School* (Oxford: Clarendon, 1972), 290.

his people "in accordance with the true word of Utu [i.e., the sun god]."⁷⁷ Apparently similar in intent is the iconography of Hammurapi's law code in which Shamash gives Hammurapi the law, that he might "bring justice to prevail in the land, to destroy the wicked and evil, that the strong may not injure the weak ... to enlighten the land and to further the welfare of men ... that orphans and widows may be protected in Babylon."⁷⁸ A great Hittite sun hymn celebrates Shamash, the sun god, as "just lord of judgment" who rules all lands and "establishes custom and contract of the land."⁷⁹ From Hatti also comes the remarkable record of a covenant between an apparently private individual and the god Sanda (a pestilential god, written with the logogram MARDUK) and "the Violent Gods." The covenant ritual involves the slaughtering of a goat and the smearing of its blood on a drinking vessel, as well as the offering of the sacrificial animal to the gods and the consumption of it in a communal meal.⁸⁰ From Babylon, in the so-called "Prophetic Speech of Marduk" (probably from the reign of Nebuchadnezzar I, 1127–1105 B.C.), the god Marduk foretells that he will make a covenant with a human king whom he will raise up: "That prince will rule all lands. And/But I, O gods all, have a *covenant* with him. He will destroy Elam. Its cities he will cast down."⁸¹ The text is important because it shows a divine-human covenant that involves a king's conquest and rule of all lands. Such royal rule would also involve laws, and it is clear from the ancient Near East that laws came from the gods. The suggestion is strong, therefore, that laws

---

⁷⁷*ANET,* 3d ed., 523.
⁷⁸*CH* I.30–45; 24.R.60.
⁷⁹H. G. Güterbock, "The Vocative in Hittite," *JAOS* 65 (1945): 251.
⁸⁰Gurney, *Aspects of Hittite Religion,* 29–30. Gurney parallels the ritual to "the covenant of Moses (Exod. 24:5–8)."
⁸¹Cf. D. I. Block, *Gods of the Nations,* 175. Cf. the discussion by Tremper Longman III, *Fictional Akkadian Autobiography* (Winona Lake: Eisenbrauns, 1991), 132–42.

were given by gods to humans in the context of some sort of covenantal understanding. Another suggestive bit of evidence comes from Ashurnaṣirpal II (883–859 B.C.), who relates, "I founded the temples of the great gods within the city, and established the *covenant* of the great gods, my lords, within them."[82] The content of that covenant is not known, but it is significant that the king mentions its deposition in the temples as part of routine Assyrian royal temple construction/renovation. This is the closest analogy extant from the ancient Near East to the deposition of Yahweh's covenant with Israel in the tabernacle.

A related phenomenon to divine lawgiving is a divine impartation of wisdom and instruction (*torah*) to the chosen king. For example Eanatum of Lagaš claims that he was "given a fine name by Inana, granted wisdom by Enki."[83] Lugalzagesi also claimed that he was "granted wisdom by Enki.[84] Like Ur-Nammu and Hammurapi, Tukulti-Ninurta I (1244–1208 B.C.) of Assyria claims divine instruction for being a good ruler when he says, "[Aššur] taught me righteous judgment."[85] Six centuries later, Esarhaddon says that the gods Sin (the god of the moon and of wisdom) and Shamash (the sun god and overseer

---

[82]D. J. Wiseman, "A New Stela of Aššur-naṣir-pal II," *Iraq* 14 (1952): 34 (col. ii, left Rev., 59–60). We translate *mamītu* "covenant," i.e., "sworn agreement." Wiseman, with some doubt, translates, "the spell (?) of the great gods." But *mamītu* + *kunnu* is used of covenant establishment. Cf. two examples from the *Tukulti-Ninurta Epic*: R. C. Thompson and R. W. Hutchinson, "The Excavations of the Temple of Nabu at Nineveh," *Archaeologia*, 79 [2d series, vol. 29] (1929): 130, 133–"v." 16, *u-kin-nu ma-mi-ta*, where the covenant oath is in view; R. C. Thompson and M. E. L. Mallowen, "The British Museum Excavations at Nineveh," *University of Liverpool Annals of Archaeology and Anthropology* 20 (1933): 120, 124–"iv." 9, "I will read aloud the tablet of the covenant/sworn agreement (*mamītu*) between us and the Lord of heaven" (cf. *CAD,* vol. 10, pt. 1, p. 190).

[83]Cooper, *Royal Inscriptions,* 41 (La 3.1.r.v; 3.5.ii).

[84]Ibid., 94 (Um 7.1.i).

[85]*AfO* 12.1.I.32–33.

of covenants) appointed him "to give just and righteous judgment to the land and the people."[86]

Royalty in the ancient Near East claimed to be chosen by their gods to rule the people of their gods. They were also given divine laws—divine *torah*, so to speak—by which to rule. Such instruction was clearly given, in some cases at least, in some sort of covenant relationship, although more evidence in this area is needed to complete the picture. Because the calling and authority of royalty were understood in this way, the ancient Near East provides an ideological background for the cutting of covenant and impartation of laws atop Mount Sinai.[87] If Mesopotamian covenants between gods and vassals did not include portrayals of a dramatic theophany such as Moses and Israel saw, the reason appears to be that no theophany actually occurred (cf. 1Ki 18:16–29, esp. 27–29).

Covenants With Conquered Peoples

There is some evidence that pagan gods had covenants with their own elect kings and people. They were also involved in covenants with nations conquered by their chosen kings. As D. J. McCarthy has remarked:

> The gods governed such relations, directing them by their word or that of their viceregent, the overlord. One assured the effectiveness of this governance by specifying the obligations involved in the relationship and imposing them under oath. A properly ordered relationship was a brotherhood. These are the ideas and usages basic to all ancient Near Eastern treaties.[88]

---

[86] *AfO* Beiheft 9 § 2.I.31–34.

[87] With the significant difference that in the OT the Sinai covenant was cut with all Israel, whereas in the ancient Near East the god apparently made a covenant with the king alone—although such a covenant also obligated the people to the obedience of covenantal laws, perhaps under a principle of federal headship.

[88] McCarthy, *Treaty and Covenant*, 32.

Much has been written about such treaties. My concern is to explore the role of the gods, and especially of theophanies, in relation to them.

As noted, the treaties were created to establish legally a suzerain-vassal relationship. But such a relationship was only possible because one kingdom had conquered another. And when one king set out to conquer another, it was understood that his god(s) also waged war against the god(s) of the opposing king (cf. 2Ki 18:33–35). Another possibility was that the gods of the defeated king had abandoned him as an act of judgment (see pt. 2). Ultimately the victory was achieved by the gods, who waged war for their elect king just as Yahweh waged war for Israel. The purpose of such warfare was to establish the dominion of the god. In Assyria, for example, as McCarthy notes, "the vassal treaty system was deliberately used to achieve the universal dominion of Ashur."[89]

Ancient people believed that theophanic intervention and miraculous aid occurred in royal campaigns against foreign lands; and the conquest of other nations led to the initiation of covenants overseen by the gods. The gods were seen as very involved in the initial conquest of vassals. This complex of ideas is extremely ancient, as early Sumerian evidence shows.

A Sumerian account of Eanatum of Lagaš tells how the god Ningirsu commanded Eanatum to subdue Umma. He promised that "the sun-(god) will shine at your right," and that as a result Eanatum would produce a mountain of slaughtered foes: "Their myriad corpses will reach the base of heaven."[90] Eanatum succeeds, and the leader of Umma must swear an oath, "By the life of Enlil, king of heaven and earth!" The

---

[89]Ibid., 134. McCarthy goes on to remark that "this is an idea without parallel in Hatti." There are hints of it in Hittite annals, however. At least Hittite vassals always lived subject to the judgments and the vengeance of the Hittite covenant gods. Cf. Götze, *Annalen,* passim.

[90]Cooper, *Royal Inscriptions,* 34 (La 3.1.vii).

leader of Umma agrees to abide by certain terms. Eanatum then pronounces a treaty curse: "After what he has declare[d] and has reiterated [to my master Enlil], if any leader in Umma reneges against the agreement, when he opposes or contests the agreement, whenever he violates this agreement, may the great battle net of Enlil, by which he has sworn, descend upon Umma!"[91] The leader of Umma then swears a series of self-imprecatory oaths.[92] The end of the account declares, "Eanatum, who subjugates foreign lands for Ningirsu."[93] The account is the earliest Sumerian narrative of a divinely mandated and assisted subjugation, persecuted with divine aid and followed by an "agreement" overseen by gods of the victorious elect suzerain.

Somewhat later in Sumerian tradition, Lugalzagesi portrays a similar state of affairs:

> When Enlil, king of all lands, gave to Lugalzagesi the kingship of the nation, directed all eyes of the land [obediently] toward him, put all the lands at his feet, and from east to west made them subject to him; then, from the Lower Sea [along] the Tigris and Euphrates to the Upper Sea, he [Enlil] put their routes in good order for him. From east to west, Enlil permitted him no [riv]al; under him the lands rested contentedly, the people made merry, and the suzerains of Sumer and rulers of other lands conceded sovereignty to him at Uruk.[94]

Lugalzagesi paints a more far-flung suzerainty, but all of it is granted by Enlil–from the vassal obedience of his own people to the vassaldom of the "suzerains of Sumer" and "rulers of other lands."

Assyrian kings also claimed to be chosen by the gods, not only to rule their people, but also to extend the borders of their

---

[91] Ibid., 35 (La 3.1.xviiff.).
[92] Ibid., 35–37 (La 3.1.xvii–r.ivff.).
[93] Ibid., 37. For the same epithet in other inscriptions, cf. 38–47.
[94] Ibid., 94 (Um 7.1.i.30–ii.30).

land.⁹⁵ The gods were often portrayed as commanding the king to march against the foe. Sennacherib declared, "At the command of Aššur I blew over the enemy like the onrush of a raging storm."⁹⁶ His theophanic pretensions are also characteristic of ancient Near Eastern kings. Tiglath-pileser I is a good example. In one battle account the Assyrian king declared, "Terror and fear of the *splendor* of Aššur, my Lord, overwhelmed [the enemy]."⁹⁷ According to the annalist, Aššur came in theophany and terrified the foe: he appeared in his "splendor" (*melammu*), a term often used of theophanic glory in Assyrian annals.⁹⁸ But the Assyrian king also possessed theophanic glory on the field. Tiglath-pileser I said of his foe that "The *splendor* [*melammu*] of my valor overwhelmed them."⁹⁹ The god Aššur is also pictured as actively engaged in combat: "They fled before the terrible weapons of Aššur, my lord."¹⁰⁰ But likewise the king's enemies "were afraid before my terrible weapons."¹⁰¹ The same phraseology is used to portray both Aššur and his chosen king. As Morton Cogan has shown, such parallelism was meant to show an affinity between the two.¹⁰² The Old Testament attests similar phraseological parallels between Yahweh and those he favors, be it Joshua, all Israel, or even the sons of Esau.¹⁰³

---

⁹⁵E.g., *ARI* 2:6 (Tiglath-pileser I); *AfO* Beiheft 9 § 27 Ep. 3.30–31 (Esarhaddon).

⁹⁶*CAD* 13 (Q): 246 (*qibītu*). The claim is traditional.

⁹⁷Cf. Jeffrey Niehaus, "Joshua and Ancient Near Eastern Warfare," *JETS* 31, no.1 (March 1988): 42–43, n. 21.

⁹⁸See *CAD*, 10 (M Pt. 2): 9–12.

⁹⁹Niehaus, "Joshua," 42, n. 20.

¹⁰⁰Ibid., 43, n. 23.

¹⁰¹Ibid., 43, n. 22.

¹⁰²M. Cogan, *Imperialism and Religion*. SBL Monograph Series 19 (Missoula: Scholars Press, 1974), 45: "The interchangeability of terms points to functional equivalence. Swearing to serve the king was at the same time acknowledging the rule of the Assyrian god."

¹⁰³E.g., Dt 2:12 ("And the children of Esau destroyed them from before them") and Dt 2:21 ("Yahweh destroyed them from before them"); both

The data make it clear that the gods who commanded war also fought on behalf of their chosen kings and even came to their aid in a theophanic splendor that terrified the foe.

Once victorious, the king made his newly won vassal swear the "oath of the great gods" (or "by the great gods" or the like)—i.e., enter into a suzerain-vassal treaty under the gods' guardianship. A good example comes from the reign of Tukulti-Ninurta I (1244–1208 B.C.), who says:

> When Aššur, my lord, faithfully chose me to worship him, gave me my sceptre for my office of shepherd . . . granted me excellence so that I might slay my enemies [and] subdue those who did not fear me . . . I marched to the land of the Uq[umenu]. . . . Trusting in Aššur and the great gods, my lords, I struck [and] brought about their defeat. . . . The hordes of princes of Abulê, king of the land of the Uqmenu, I captured and brought them bound to my city, Aššur. I made them swear by the great gods of heaven [and] underworld, I imposed upon them the [exacting] yoke of my lordship, [and then] I released them [to return] to their lands. . . . Annually I receive with ceremony their valuable tribute in my city, Aššur.[104]

The Assyrian king goes on to say how he shook the shrines of his enemy "like an earthquake," reminiscent of theophanic Adad/Haddu.[105] Finally he claims that the great gods allotted to him for conquest all the lands about which his inscription has given an account.[106]

Such claims are part of the stock-in-trade of the Assyrian tradition and form the ideological background of covenant relations in the ancient Near East. They may shed light on a

---

Joshua (Dt 1:38; 3:28) and Yahweh (Dt 12:10; 19:3) as subjects of נחל (Hiph.); both Israel (Dt 1:41, 42) and Yahweh (Dt 1:30; 3:22) as subjects of לחם (Niph.).

[104]Grayson, *Assyrian Rulers*, 234–35 (1 i 21–ii 40).
[105]Ibid., 235 (1 iii 21–27).
[106]Ibid., 236–37 (1 iv 24–36).

fascinating Ugaritic passage that portrays a triumphant campaign by the storm god Baal before entering his new palace:

> He marched from [city] to city,
> he turned from town to town;
> he captured sixty-six cities,
> > seventy-seven towns;
> Baal sacked eighty,
> > Baal sacked ninety;
> then Baal returned to his house . . .
> [he] opened a rift in the clouds.
> Baal sounded his holy voice,
> > Baal repeated it from his lips;
> he uttered his holy voice and the earth quaked . . .
> the earth's high places shook.
> Baal's enemies fled to the woods,
> > Hadad's haters took to the mountains.[107]

The Ugaritic myth is not given any clear historical anchorage. But Baal's triumphant campaign, which makes him master of many cities, is a perfect portrayal of divine conquest in the ancient Near East. Human kings conquered lands and cities. But those conquests were portrayed as the conquests of the gods who favored the human kings. It may be that the Ugaritic pas-

---

[107]Cf. Gibson, *Canaanite Myths and Legends,* 64–65 (4 vii 7–12, 27–37). For a popular translation, cf. M. D. Coogan, *Stories from Ancient Canaan* (Philadelphia: Westminster, 1978), 104–5. P. D. Miller, *The Divine Warrior in Early Israel.,* Harvard Semitic Monographs, 5 (Cambridge: Harvard University Press, 1973), 33–34, thinks the passage describes a "triumphal procession of the victorious god to his palace" to assume kingship. He believes (pp. 34–35) it is "quite probable that Baʿal was accompanied by his various military hosts" (i.e., a vanguard of warrior gods, like Marduk's in *Enuma eliš)* of which, however, there is no evidence. Cross, *CMHE,* 93, n. 9, gives the following summary of the passage: "Baʿal's going on the warpath (7–14), a return to his temple, theophany (29–35), and proclamation of kingship." Mann, *Divine Presence,* 99, says rather guardedly, "This text describing Baal's 'march' possibly could be interpreted as referring to historical events, or at least to terrestrial 'cities' and 'towns,' but the context is so fragmentary that such an interpretation would be shaky." It is, however, the most likely, since ancient Near Eastern gods and goddesses were routinely involved in the conquest of human cities and towns.

sage portrays such a conquest from a strictly theological point of view, just as Judges 5:4–5 portrays Yahweh alone as the one who marches against the forces of Jabin of Hazor:

> O Yahweh, when you went out from Seir,
> when you marched from the land of Edom,
> the earth shook, the heavens poured,
> the clouds poured down water.
> The mountains quaked before Yahweh, the One of Sinai,
> before Yahweh, the God of Israel.

Similar theophanic portrayals, also recalling Sinai, occur at Deuteronomy 33:2 and Psalm 68:8–9, 18–19 (7–8, 17–18) and will be examined in detail later.

Upon his defeat, a foe was forced to enter into a suzerain-vassal treaty. According to such a treaty, he must pay tax and tribute to his conqueror. In Assyria, such impost was often termed "the tribute due to Aššur."[108] A defeated foe could even be called a vassal to his conqueror's god.[109] Tiglath-pileser I typically declared of a group of vanquished foes, "I imposed upon them tribute and impost [and] regarded them as vassals of the god Aššur, my lord."[110]

Such vassaldom was often galling, and rebellions were not uncommon. Hittite and Assyrian annals are largely devoted to accounts of royal campaigns to subdue rebellious vassals. Some of the most vivid portrayals of divine activity on the suzerain's behalf also appear in those accounts. Such royal and divine actions form part of a god's covenant administration—a topic to which we now turn.

---

[108] *CAD* 2 (B): 229–36 (*biltu*). Tiglath-pileser I says that a vassal "held back the tribute and gifts due to my lord Aššur" (p. 235); "he (Aššur) imposes tribute and the bringing of gifts on . . . all the regions of the world" (p. 236).

[109] Cogan, however, *Imperialism and Religion,* 42–61, argues that Assyrian vassals were free of any cultic obligations toward their master.

[110] Grayson, *ARI,* 2:11.

◆ 4 ◆

Ancient Near Eastern Parallels:
The Relationship of Egyptian, Hittite, Mesopotamian, and Canaanite Theophanies to the Biblical Tradition (Part 2)

> Those masterful images because complete
> Grew in pure mind, but out of what began?
> A mound of refuse or the sweepings of a street,
> Old kettles, old bottles, and a broken can,
> Old iron, old bones, old rags, that raving slut
> Who keeps the till. Now that my ladder's gone,
> I must lie down where all the ladders start,
> In the foul rag-and-bone shop of the heart.
>
> William Butler Yeats, "The Circus Animals' Desertion"

THEOPHANY AND GOD'S COVENANT ADMINISTRATION

The idea that God judged his people for their covenant trespasses in the Old Testament does not need elaboration. But the role of theophany in God's covenantal arrangements is another matter. Detailed discussion of that role occupies the subsequent chapters of this book. God appeared in theophanic glory as part of his covenant administrations primarily in four ways. He appeared to initiate a covenant (e.g., at the Creation,

Ge 1; with Abraham, Ge 15; with Moses and Israel, Ex 3–4, 19). He appeared to instruct, encourage, or correct his covenant vassal (e.g., during the wilderness wanderings; via "angelic" appearances, as to Joshua, Jos 5:13–15; in theomachy, as at 1Ki 18:16ff.).[1] He appeared to commission or encourage a prophet in covenant lawsuit (e.g. to Elijah, 1Ki 19:9b–18; to Isaiah, Isa 6; to Ezekiel, Eze 1). And he appeared to bring covenantal judgment on rebellious vassals (e.g., to the fallen man and woman, Ge 3:8–19; eschatologically, Joel 2:1–11; et al.). Data from the ancient world in general are more scattered and uneven than those of the Old Testament. But there are points of contact between the Old Testament and the ancient Near East.

PAGAN THEOPHANIES TO INITIATE A COVENANT

Data from the ancient Near East show or suggest the existence of covenants between gods and humans. But there appears to be little evidence of anything like a "storm theophany" or "glory theophany" as a god initiates such a covenant. The portrayal of Shamash giving the law to Hammurapi suggests a glorious theophany of some sort. And gods were seen in dreams, or in storms or wind as part of their action on behalf of a chosen earthly king. But covenant initiatory theophanies are not much attested, and few may ever be found. The most natural reason for this lack is apparently that such theophanies never occurred. Noth has remarked, "There is no doubt that the Sinai tradition, the basic substance of which is unique and unrelated to any other phenomena in the history of religion, derived from an actual event."[2] Without embracing Noth's

---

[1] Of course God's theophanic fire on Mount Carmel was not only a corrective lesson to Israel, but also a proof to Baal worshipers that he alone is God.

[2] M. Noth, *The History of Israel*, 2d ed., 128.

idea of a "Sinai tradition," we may affirm the unparalleled nature of what happened on Sinai.

The ancients did portray gods as creators, however, and it may be that the ancient creation myths contain the fundamental substance of a primordial covenant between god(s) and humans, even if they lack the literary form of such a covenant. The Egyptian "Pyramid Text" theology of Atum is an example. The fact that the god was the creator meant that he was also king. As king he ruled the world, and humanity was thereby in fealty to him and owed him tribute. Such an arrangement is implicitly covenantal.

Babylon offers a creation myth that may have covenantal overtones. The Old Babylonian poem "Enuma Elish" (which actually has Sumerian antecedents) portrays the sky god Marduk as victor over Tiamat, a vicious sea dragon goddess with a host of demon subordinates. After Marduk slays Tiamat, he cuts her body in two, and from it he fashions the heavens and the earth:[3]

> When he [Marduk] had subdued her [Tiamat], he destroyed her life;
> He cast down her carcass [and] stood upon it.
> . . . .
> He split her open like a mussel [?] into two [parts];
> Half of her he set in place and formed the sky [therewith] as a roof.
> . . . .
> And a great structure, its counterpart, he established, [namely,] Esharra.[4]

---

[3] H. Gunkel, in his *Schöpfung und Chaos in Urzeit und Endzeit* (Göttingen: Vandenhoeck und Ruprecht, 1895), identified the various monsters Rahab, Leviathan, and Tannin with the sea. He argued that Yahweh's original battle with the sea-monster was connected with Creation and also with the eschaton, as an allegory of the battle that would preceed the new creation (pp. 84–87).

[4] A. Heidel, *The Babylonian Genesis,* 2d ed. (Chicago: University of Chicago Press, 1951), 40–41 (IV:103–4), 42–43 (IV:137–38, 144). Heidel notes,

Marduk also created humans on the earth and ordained that humanity should serve the gods. The term for "servant" (*wardum*, equivalent to Heb. עֶבֶד) may be compared to the term used for vassals in international covenants.[5] Compare Goliath's taunt to Israel: "If he [an Israelite hero] is able to fight and kill me, we will become your *servants* [i.e., "vassals," עֲבָדִים]; but if I overcome him and kill him, you will become our *servants* [עֲבָדִים] and *serve* [עֲבַדְתֶּם] us" (1Sa 17:9). The gods in effect have humanity for their vassals. Marduk declares that Babylon shall be built along with a temple for the gods—Esagila.[6] Heidel has shown that a good many parallels exist between the Babylonian poem and the Creation account of Genesis. There are also significant differences that go far to suggest that both the Old Testament and Babylonian accounts are recalling an actual creation event independently (contra Delitzsch and others who have insisted on seeing the Genesis account as dependent on the Babylonian materials).[7] Among the parallels between the Old Testament and Babylonian accounts may be an implicit covenant obligation to worship the creator god. A possibly related fact is that the same Akkadian term used for "tribute" in suzerain-vassal relations is also used of offerings to the gods.[8]

Excursus: Storm God and Sea God

A pattern that has literary and theological importance in the Old Testament—and, indeed, the Bible—emerges here. According to this pattern, a storm or sky god (Marduk) battles and vanquishes a sea monster (Tiamat). He then fashions

---

"Esharra in this passage is a poetic designation of the earth, which is pictured as a great structure, in the shape of a canopy, placed over the *Apsû*" (p. 43, n. 96).

[5]Cf. *AHw*, 3:1464–66 (*[w]ardu[m], [w]ardūtu[m]*); *CAD*, vol. 1, pt. 2 (*ardu, ardūtu*), 243–53.

[6]Heidel, *Babylonian Genesis*, 48 (VI:57ff.).

[7]F. Delitzsch, *Babel and Bible* (New York: G. P. Putnam's Sons, 1903), 47ff.

[8]See chap. 3, n. 108.

heaven and earth and humanity, and causes a holy city and a temple to be constructed. This pattern also has parallels in Ugaritic myth.[9]

The Ugaritic story involves Baal, the storm god, and Yam, the sea god.[10] Gibson has noted, "Yam-Nahar was the chief Ugaritic counterpart of the Babylonian Tiamat, defeated by Marduk."[11] Baal does battle with Yam and soundly defeats him by using two magical clubs. Baal's mistress Anat later claims the victory over Yam and boasts:

> Did I not destroy Yam the darling of El?
> did I not make an end of Nahar the great god?
> was not the dragon captured [and] vanquished?
> I did destroy the wriggling serpent [*bṯn ʿqltn*],
> the tyrant with seven heads.[12]

The portrayal of the "dragon" as a "wriggling serpent" appears in an expanded form in another Ugaritic poem as part of a description of the sea monster Lītānu/Leviathan.[13] Mot the god of death is irate against the storm god Baal—partly at least because Baal vanquished Lītānu (apparently an ally of Yam, who harbors him):

> Because you smote Lītānu the *slippery serpent [bṯn brḥ]*
> [and] made an end of the *wriggling serpent [bṯn ʿqltn]*,
> the tyrant with seven heads . . .
> . . . .
> Indeed you must come down into the throat of divine Mot.[14]

---

[9] Cf. M. K. Wakeman, *God's Battle With the Monster* (Leiden: E. J. Brill, 1973), 45–47, for a discussion of a Hittite myth that is, however, only parallel in part.

[10] Cf. ibid., 37ff., for a reconstruction of the Ugaritic data in connection with other ancient theomachies.

[11] Gibson, *Canaanite Myths and Legends*, 7.

[12] Ibid., 50 (3.D.iii.35–39).

[13] For the vocalization Lītānu, instead of the usual Lotan, see J. A. Emerton, "Leviathan and *LTN*: the Vocalization of the Ugaritic Word for the Dragon," *VT* 32, fasc. 3 (1982): 327–31.

[14] Gibson, *Canaanite Myths and Legends*, 68 (5.i.1–3, 6–7).

Mot (god of death), Yam (god of the sea), and Lītānu are thus allied in Ugaritic myth. This passage has a remarkable Old Testament parallel–Isaiah's eschatological vision of Yahweh's victory over all powers of watery chaos:

> In that day,
> Yahweh will punish with his sword,
>   his fierce, great and powerful sword,
> Leviathan the *slippery serpent* [נָחָשׁ בָּרִחַ],
>   Leviathan the *coiling serpent* [נָחָשׁ עֲקַלָּתוֹן];
> he will slay the monster of the *sea* [יָם].
>
> (Isa 27:1, emphasis mine)

The verbal parallel alone between the Ugaritic and the Hebrew is astonishing: Lītānu/Leviathan (Ugar. *ltn*; Heb. לִוְיָתָן); "slippery/twisted serpent" (Ugar. *bṯn brḥ*; Heb. נָחָשׁ בָּרִחַ); and "wriggling/coiling serpent" (Ugar. *bṯn ʿqltn*; Heb. נָחָשׁ עֲקַלָּתוֹן).[15] It shows how stock phrasing can survive over many centuries–a common enough phenomenon in the ancient Near East, the more remarkable here because of an intercultural context.[16]

Isaiah's vision of eschatological victory is followed by a portrayal of the restoration of God's people to "worship Yahweh on the holy mountain in Jerusalem" (Isa 27:13). The Isaianic pattern echoes the Canaanite and also the Mesopotamian. Yahweh is victor over the sea monster. His victory is followed if not explicitly by temple construction at least by an event associated with temples: God's people will come and worship him on his "holy mountain." This same pattern appears in Exodus 15, where Yahweh's theophanic supremacy over the sea (Ex 15:8–10) is followed by anticipation that Yah-

---

[15] Cf. Wakeman, *God's Battle*, 58, n. 3, for a discussion of the translation options for *brḥ*.

[16] For similar examples, especially of persistent divine epithets; cf.: for Akkadian, Tallqvist, *Akkadische Götterepitheta;* for Hittite, Gurney, *Some Aspects of Hittite Religion*; and for royal epithets brought down into Akkadian from Sumerian, Thureau-Dangin, *Die Sumerischen und Akkadischen Königsinschriften.*

weh will lead his people to "the mountain of [Yahweh's] inheritance . . . the sanctuary, O Yahweh, your hands established" (Ex 15:17).[17]

Important differences exist between the Old Testament and ancient Near Eastern accounts. Yahweh is one God but not the chief of a pantheon and not the god of one natural power predominantly (that is, he is not, like Baal, a storm god). Yahweh does show his power over the sea, but only as he has shown his supremacy over other aspects of nature earlier, during the plagues of Egypt. God's enemy in the Reed Sea crossing is not a sea dragon goddess like Tiamat, nor is it a dragon like Lītānu/Leviathan; however, the Old Testament does later pick up the Canaanite terminology as a poetic description of Yahweh's foe.[18] His enemy is Pharaoh and all that Pharaoh represents. According to Egyptian theology, Pharaoh was the son of the sun god and thus a god himself. Yahweh's victory over both the sun god (cf. the three-day-long plague of darkness, Ex 12:21–23) and the son of the sun god—that is, Pharaoh—shows that Yahweh alone is truly God.[19]

In the Babylonian and Ugaritic tales, the storm or sky god's victory over the dragon or serpent results in a housebuilding. Marduk founds Babylon and the E-sagilla temple; and the craftsman god Kothar-wa-Ḥasis (cf. Hephaestos/Vulcan) builds a palace for Baal on Mount Zaphon.[20] After Marduk's triumph over the chaos dragon, the god creates heaven and earth from her carcass. This does not happen in Ugaritic myth, and with good reason. In Ugarit El and not Baal is the

---

[17]Cf. Gibson, *Canaanite Myths and Legends,* 49, where Baal uses the parallel phrase, "the rock of my inheritance" (*ǵr nḥlty*) as an epithet for his "holy place," "my rock El Zephon" (3 c 26–27). Similarly, Memphis is the "land" of Kothar-wa-Ḥasis' inheritance (*'arṣ nḥlth,* p. 55 [3 F vi 16]); "filth" is the "land" of Mot's "inheritance" (*'arṣ nḥlth,* p. 66 [4 viii 13–14]).

[18]Cf. Wakeman, *God's Battle,* 56ff.

[19]Cf. J. J. Davis, *Moses and the Gods of Egypt,* 2d ed. (Grand Rapids: Baker, 1986), 133–36.

[20]Gibson, *Canaanite Myths and Legends,* 46–67.

"creator of creatures" (*bny bnwt*).[21] Consequently the creation is not an immediate backdrop to Baal's temple-building.[22] But in other respects the Ugaritic story echoes the Babylonian.

Note also that the divine pattern of battle-victory-temple/palace building in the ancient Near East had a parallel in the activity of human kings. The earliest example of this comes from a boulder inscription of Enanatum I of Lagaš (ca. 2400–2350 B.C.):

> [When Lu]galurub granted the kingship of Lagash to Enanatum, put all foreign lands in his control, and [set] the rebellious lands at his feet, then Enanatum [bui]lt the I[bgal] for Inana. . . . For his master who loves him, Lugalrub, he built the "palace" of Urub, decorated it for him with gold and silver, and furnished it.[23]

The passage contains familiar ancient Near Eastern theology. The god Lugalurub has granted kingship to Enanatum, and put all foreign lands under his control. Once the mortal king has subdued his enemies round about, he builds temples for his gods and goddesses. On the human plain this pattern follows the mythological archetype, whereby the god defeats his supernatural foes and then builds a palace. The pattern repeats itself again and again, e.g., in the Assyrian annalistic tradition. It provides a broad background for the account of David's desire to build a temple for Yahweh: "After the king was settled in his palace and Yahweh had given him rest from his enemies around him, he said to Nathan the prophet, 'Here I am, living in a palace of cedar, while the ark of God remains in a tent'" (2Sa 7:1–2).

---

[21]Ibid., 56 (4 ii 11).

[22]Ibid., 7. Gibson remarks further, "Evidently to the people of Ugarit the sustaining of the seasons and the guaranteeing of the world's order were more important properties than the original creation of things, and it was therefore the god who embodied those active properties and not the venerable and remoter creator-father El who in their mythology slew the monster of old and overcame the forces of chaos."

[23]Cooper, *Sumerian and Akkadian Royal Inscriptions, I,* 51 (La 4.9.iii–iv).

The pattern finds its ultimate fulfillment in the New Testament, where Jesus, who is both God and man, King of Kings and Lord of Lords, defeats his foe and then builds his temple—the church. It is one of many ancient Near Eastern ideas that finds expression in the New Testament, and we will return to it again.

In the ancient Near East, a god's palace was considered his home. But an earthly temple of the god was the home of his idol. The earthly temple was meant to reflect the pattern of the heavenly palace, just as the idol was meant to reflect the god's presence. In that temple the god's people offered sacrifices to him in fealty; they also obeyed the laws that he had given through a chosen king. In return for all this, the king and the people expected the god's protection and help. That is where the covenantal dimension of ancient Near Eastern temple-building and divine lawgiving appears, to the extent that it can be discerned from the extant data.[24]

Since some of the early Yahweh theophanies occurred at the Tent of Meeting, and since Moses built that tent according to the pattern shown him on Mount Sinai, the divine tent motif deserves some comment at this point. The tabernacle idea is an ancient one. Ugaritic poetry tells us that El, supreme god of the Canaanite pantheon, lived in a tent:[25]

> They set face
> Toward El at the sources of the Two Rivers,
> In the midst of the pools of the Double-Deep.
> They entered the tent[s] of El and went into
> The tent-shrine of the King, Father of Years.[26]

---

[24]Cf. above, chap. 3.
[25]The most detailed discussion at present is that by R. J. Clifford, *The Cosmic Mountain in Canaan and the Old Testament* (Cambridge: Harvard University Press, 1972), 48–54.
[26]Ibid., 48.

The term for "tent" here is *qrš* (cf. Heb. קֶרֶשׁ), and will receive further comment below. But El was not alone in having a tent. The craftsman god, Kothar, also inhabited a tent:

> *tbʿ.ktr l'ahlh.*   "Kothar did depart to his tent,
> *hyn.tbʿ.lmsknth.*   Heyan did depart to his dwelling"[27]

The other gods of Canaan also lived in tents:

> *t'ity.'ilm.l'ahlhm*   "The gods returned to their tents,
> *dr 'il.lmsknthm*   the race of El to their habitations"[28]

The Ugaritic gods, El and his pantheon, dwelt in tents, just as El/Elohim, the God of Israel, dwells in a heavenly tabernacle (cf. Ex 25:9, 40; 26:30; 27:8; Heb 8:5). Clifford goes on to observe:

> Other evidence links the [Old Testament] Tent of Meeting to the tent of El. In the Tent of Meeting, *qᵉrašim*, "tent-frames," describes part of the structure. The Old Testament use is not completely clear, but apparently the word describes the wood frame on which the tent fabrics were hung. The word also describes El's tent in Ugaritic. The tent of Israel is to be made by the divinely gifted and commissioned craftsman Bezalel (Ex. 31:3). The temple of Baal is constructed by the craftsman god Koshar wa-Khasis. In Ex. 28:33–34, the skirts of the priests are to have golden bells and pomegranates suspended from the edge. The dress of the priest is considered part of the equipment of the tent. At Ras Shamra, a circular pedestal of bronze has been found, under the rim of which were decorations shaped like pomegranates. They were suspended like the pomegranates of Ex 28.[29]

The idea that a god should inhabit a tent was thus an old one, even in the days of Moses.

---

[27] Gibson, *Canaanite Myths and Legends*, 107 (17.v.31–33).
[28] Ibid., 92 (15.iii.18–19).
[29] R. J. Clifford, "The Tent of El and the Israelite Tent of Meeting," *CBQ* 33, no. 2 (April 1971): 226.

To Instruct, Encourage, or Correct:

Gods of Tabernacle/Temple Pattern

Yahweh instructs Moses to build a tabernacle after the pattern shown him on Mount Sinai. As we have noted, the temple of a god, both in Mesopotamia and Canaan, was considered a replica of the god's heavenly dwelling-place. It "reproduced and made present the heavenly prototype."[30] Richard J. Clifford adds that "in Canaanite religion, the earthly shrine could be considered the copy of a heavenly prototype. Baal's [earthly] temple at Ras Shamra had a window in the roof as did Baal's [heavenly] temple on Mount Zaphon."[31] The ancient world provides ample evidence of this theology.[32] But in light of it the question naturally arises, "How did people discover the true form of the putative heavenly dwelling in order to pattern the earthly tabernacle/temple after it?" The data available to answer this question are not as abundant as one might wish. But it is clear that a god could prescribe the pattern of his temple to his worshiper.

Divine revelation to chosen kings about temple construction is well-attested in Assyria. Because Assyria's cult was long established, the issue often was not so much building a temple as it was renovating a temple where the god had already established his presence. The procedure was described with stock phrasing in Assyrian tradition. The kings said that the gods, "who love my priesthood,"[33] "commanded me to rebuild

---

[30] Ibid., 225.

[31] Ibid., 225.

[32] Assyrian royal inscriptions, for example, routinely compare the interiors of newly built or renovated temples to the heavenly dwelling place of the gods. Cf. CH II.31 (Hammurapi); A. K. Grayson, *Assyrian Rulers of the Third and Second Millennia B.C.* The Royal Inscriptions of Mesopotamia, Assyrian Periods (Toronto: University of Toronto Press, 1987), 1:254–55, 11.15–57 (Tukulti-Ninurta I); *AKA* 97ff., col. VII.90ff. (Tiglath-pileser I); *AfO* Beiheft 9, p. 96, § 2 V.39 (Esarhaddon); *HPIA* 28.21 (Ashurbanipal).

[33] E.g., *AKA*, 288, col. I.99 (Ashurnasirpal II); Luckenbill, *Annals*, p. 107.48 (Sennacherib); *AfO* Beiheft 9, p. 96, § 65 Vs.1 (Esarhaddon).

their shrine."³⁴ A more explicit case of divine command for temple-building comes with the Assyrian king Tukulti-Ninurta I (1244–1208 B.C.), who relates that the god Aššur commanded him to build a great cult city, Kar-Tukulti-Ninurta, across the river from his city Ashur: "At that time Aššur, my Lord, requested of me a cult centre on the bank opposite my city . . . and he commanded me to build his sanctuary."³⁵ Divine revelation—in the form of a building command—precedes the king's construction of the temple. The nature of such commands is not clear. Perhaps they came by way of oracle, perhaps by dream vision. It is also not clear whether the gods gave Assyrian kings architectural patterns for the temples.

The most explicit evidence is also the most ancient. It comes from a Sumerian inscription of Gudea of Lagaš (2143–2124 B.C.). Gudea declares, "I am the shepherd, the kingship has been given me as a gift!"³⁶ He also informs us that the great destinies of the god Enlil's city and its *e-ninnu* temple have all been divinely determined. Then he tells how he had a dream, and, not understanding it, described it to the goddess Nina:

> In the dream a man, whose stature reached up to heaven [and] reached down to earth, who according to the *tiara* around his head was a god, at whose side was the divine bird Imgi[g], at whose feet was a storm, to whose right and left a lion was at rest, commanded me to build his house [i.e., temple]. . . . A second [man], like a warrior . . . held in his hand a tablet of lapus-lazuli, [and] outlined the pattern of a temple.³⁷

The goddess Nina explains Gudea's dream to him. It was a vision of her brother Ningirsu, who has commanded Gudea to

---

³⁴*AKA*, p. 96, col. VII.74–75 (Tiglath-pileser I). Cf. Luckenbill, *Annals*, p. 137.30 (Sennacherib); *AfO* Beiheft 9, p. 16, § 11 Ep. 14.41–45 (Esarhaddon).
³⁵Grayson, *Assyrian Rulers,* 277, 25 rev. 9ff.
³⁶*SAK,* 90–91(Cylinder A, 1, 26).
³⁷Ibid., 94–95 (Cylinder A, 4, 14–5, 4).

build his temple. The second god was Nindub, who has shown Gudea the pattern for the temple.[38]

This exemplar—in which a pagan god prescribes for his worshiper the pattern after which his temple is to be built—shows that the concept of a heavenly archetype for an earthly temple is very ancient. More significantly, it shows the antiquity of the concept of direct divine revelation of the temple pattern. When Yahweh revealed the pattern of the tabernacle to Moses on Mount Sinai, he was doing something that a pagan god had supposedly done for Gudea of Lagaš some eight or nine hundred years before. The evidence indicates that the concept of such divine revelation persisted in the ancient Near East into the second and first millennia.

The Light of God's Countenance

A temple in the ancient world was an earthly home for the god. He was present there in the form of his idol. A human worshiper could encounter the god in that place via the idol. To be thus in the god's presence was considered a great privilege. Among other things, a favorable encounter with a god was thought to impart vitality to the worshiper. These ideas appear in both the Old Testament and the ancient Near East. A significant factor in both domains is the association of light with the god's countenance.

The association of fire and theophany in the Old Testament is no accident. This phenomenon, encountered again and again, points to the fact that God is not only indestructible life, but also powerful light. God's luminous countenance has an effect on the man who encounters it. Moses is the best example because of his unusual encounters with God. Moses was unique as God's servant partly because he saw God's form and spoke with him "mouth to mouth" (NIV "face to face"; cf. Nu

---

[38]Ibid., 94–95 (Cylinder A, 5, 12–6, 5).

12:6–8). Indeed, "Yahweh would speak to Moses face to face, as a man speaks with his friend"(Ex 33:11). A similar testimony about Moses comes at the end of Deuteronomy: "Since then, no prophet has risen in Israel like Moses, whom Yahweh knew face to face" (Dt 34:10).[39]

One memorable result of Moses' encounters with God was that the prophet's face shone afterward (Ex 34:29–30, 34:34–35). The Hebrew idiom translates roughly, "The skin of his face sent out horn(s) [i.e., of light]" (קָרַן עוֹר פָּנָיו, Ex 34:29, 30; cf. 34:35).[41] The glow of Moses' face came from encounters with the living God, the source of all light and life. But there are further implications of this phenomenon.

Because he saw God, Moses' face shone as a reflection of God's luminous visage. To that extent, however briefly (cf. 2Co 3:7, 11, 13), Moses took on something of the nature of God. A related fact is the Aaronic blessing commanded by Yahweh:

> May Yahweh bless you and keep you.
> May Yahweh make his face to shine upon you,
>   and be gracious to you.
> May Yahweh lift up his countenance upon you,
>   and give you wholeness ["peace," i.e., שָׁלוֹם].
>
> (Nu 6:24–26, author's translation)

---

[39]These claims for the uniqueness of Moses' encounters with Yahweh are true, but they must be taken in a modified sense; cf. Ex 33:18–23 (author's translation):

> Moses said, "I pray, show me your glory." And he said, "I will make all my goodness pass before you, and I will proclaim before you my name, 'Yahweh.' . . . But . . . you cannot see my face; for man shall not see me and live." And Yahweh said, "There is a place by me where you shall stand upon the rock; and while my glory passes by I will put you in a cleft of the rock, and I will cover you with my hand until I have passed by; then I will take away my hand, and you shall see my back; but my face shall not be seen."

[40]Cf. *A Hebrew-English Lexicon of the Old Testament*. Trans. F. Brown, S. R. Driver, and C. A. Briggs (Oxford: Clarendon Press, 1952), 902. [Hereafter BDB.]

The formula calls upon Yahweh to make his face shine upon his people, and the consequence of this event will be "wholeness" (שָׁלוֹם). After this comes a notable commentary by God upon the blessing itself: "So they will put my name on the Israelites, and I will bless them" (Nu 6:27). In other words, when Aaron and his sons call upon Yahweh to make his face shine upon his people, they will also be invoking his Name upon them, and this will result in his blessing. Yahweh's blessing upon the people and the radiance of his face upon them are parallel, and thus to a considerable extent equivalent. But to call God's Name upon them is to invoke upon them something of the character of Yahweh himself, since the Name is tantamount to the character.[41] Just as Moses reflected something of God's nature as a result of his self-revelation to Moses, so the people can reflect something of God's nature when he "makes his face to shine upon" them.

A similar idea occurs in second millennium Mesopotamian literature. What God gave to Moses and meant for all his people was claimed by ancient Near Eastern royalty as a fact. An inscription of Samsuiluna (1749–1712 B.C.), son of Hammurapi, says that Samsuiluna was privileged to speak with gods face to face. Enlil, the supreme god, sent Zababa and Ishtar (two lesser deities) with a message to the king. Zababa and Ishtar "lifted their radiant, life-giving faces (*bu-ni-šu-nu ša ba-la-tim*) toward Samsuiluna . . . and they spoke to him with glee" (ll.62–69).[42] Via these emmisaries, the high god commissioned Samsuiluna to conquer various foes, to build the wall of Kish (the holy city) higher than it was before, and to enhance the city's temple complex. All of these tasks were meant

---

[41]See *Theological Wordbook of the Old Testament,* ed. R. L. Harris, G. L. Archer, Jr., and B. K. Waltke (Chicago: Moody Press, 1980), 2:2404–5 (sub שֵׁם, *name).* [Hereafter *TWOT.*]

[42]E. Sollberger, "Samsu-iluna's Bilingual Inscriptions C and D," *RA* 63, no. 1 (1969): 29–43.

to make the divine authority more manifest than before, in addition to being an honor and a blessing to the king and his people. A god's blessing is never without a purpose in the ancient Near East: namely, to make manifest the authority of the god, so that others may fear—that is, worship—him. So it was in Israel. But the remarkable parallel in this case is that the impartation of blessing is portrayed as a revelation of divine countenance, the "radiant, life-giving faces" of Zababa and Ishtar—just as it is in the Aaronic blessing.

Notable in the Samsuiluna passage is the brightness of the divine countenances involved in the face-to-face communication with the Mesopotamian king. As was the case with Yahweh, that brightness has to do with the presence of life in the gods themselves. Theirs are "radiant, life-giving faces [lit., 'radiant faces of life']."

Imagery of divine radiance appears again and again in Mesopotamian tradition. For instance, Ashurbanipal (668–627 B.C.) declares, "With their bright countenances and lifting their beautiful eyes through which they view the world, Ashur and Ninlil looked joyfully upon Ashurbanipal, the delight of their hearts."[43] This inscription from the last of the great Assyrian kings shows a traditional association of radiant faces with gods and goddesses in Mesopotamia. It also illustrates the persistent idea that the gods looked upon mortal kings whom they loved with those same radiant, life-giving faces. One result of such divine regard was that the kings enjoyed extraordinary vitality —something like that of the gods who looked upon them.

For this reason, perhaps, it was not only gods who took the initiative in facing kings whom they loved. Ashurbanipal could also take such initiative and pray, "Let me [Ashurbanipal] look at your [Aššur's] face, let me bow before you."[44] Because the king wanted some of that godly vitality, it was very im-

---

[43] *CAD* B, 320 (Thompson, *Esarhaddon*, pl. 18 vi.12).
[44] *CAD* B, 320 (Bauer, *Asb.*, 2 83 r.21).

portant for him to look at the god's face. So much so that some kings had statues of themselves made and placed in temples, so that by a sort of sympathetic magic the king could be always gazing upon his god and vice-versa. The Sumerian king Enmetena (ca. 2400 B.C.) records, "Enmetena fashioned his statue, named it 'Enmetena Whom Enlil Loves,' and set it up before Enlil in the temple."[45] Almost two thousand years later, Nebuchadnezzar (604–562 B.C.) prays, "[O Shamash] look with your radiant countenance, your happy face joyfully upon the precious work of my hands, my good works, [and] my royal statue and inscription."[46] Nebuchadnezzar's prayer reflects a very ancient tradition in Mesopotamia.

No doubt the joyfulness of the gods who look upon the kings indicates divine favor toward the king so regarded. So the term "joyfully" (*ḫadîš*) is also sometimes translated "with favor."[47] Does this mean that portrayals of the god's countenance as "radiant" simply indicate the joy—or favorable bearing—of the god toward the king? The Samsuiluna C inscription, coming early in Mesopotamian tradition, shows the contrary: the faces of Zababa and Ishtar are both "radiant" and "life giving." And late in Mesopotamian tradition the same connection between radiant faces and supernatural vitality, or *shalom,* is indicated. A suppliant of the Babylonian king Merodach-baladan (= Marduk-apal-iddina II, 721–710 B.C.; cf. 2Ki 20:12; Isa 39:1) says that "the king, his lord, looked on him with favor, his face *radiant like a god's.*"[48] The divine radiance of the king's face implies also the divine power of life within him.

---

[45]Cooper, *Royal Inscriptions,* 63 (La 5.17.iii–1v).
[46]S. Langdon, *Die Neubabylonischen Königsinschriften,* VAB 4 (Leipzig: J. C. Hinrichs, 1912): 258, ii.21.
[47]Cf. *CAD* B, 320–21.
[48]*CAD* B, 320 (VAS 1.37.iii.40).

To Bring Covenantal Judgment:

Gods of Thunder

God thundered through the Garden of Eden after his man and woman sinned, he thundered atop Mount Sinai, he thundered before Elijah and Ezekiel, and he thundered from Mount Zion in eschatological glory. But God is not the only god who thundered. It was thought throughout the ancient Near East that thunder was a holy utterance of some god or other. Sumerian, Hittite, Akkadian, Egyptian (Amarna), and Ugaritic evidence makes this clear. What also becomes apparent as we survey the evidence is that theophany or theophanic language in the ancient Near East often happened because a god was said to appear as a part of covenant administration—namely, to thunder against covenant breakers.

Sumerian Inanna

William W. Hallo and J. J. A. van Dijk have produced an edition of a hymn from the days of Sargon I (2329–2274 B.C.) entitled "The Exaltation of Inanna."[49] The hymn is not a purely theological piece but has a distinct historical rootage in Sargon's victorious career, as Hallo has demonstrated (see below). It was composed by Sargon's daughter Enheduanna, who was a princess, priestess, and poetess. It exalts Inanna—who was early equated with the stormlike Akkadian Ishtar[50]—as one who appears in the storm:

1	Lady of all the me's,[51]	resplendent light,
2	Righteous woman clothed in radiance . . .	beloved of Heaven and Earth,

---

[49]See above, chap. 2, 73.

[50]Wm. W. Hallo and J. J. A. van Dijk, *Exaltation*, Yale Near Eastern Researches 3 (New Haven: Yale University Press, 1968), 9, note that "Sargon equated the Sumerian Inanna with the Akkadian Ištar to lay the theological foundations for a united empire of Sumer and Akkad."

[51]Sumerian ME is tantamount to "divine attribute"; cf. ibid., 4, 49–50.

> 5 Whose hand has attained   [all] the "seven"
>   me's . . .
> 9 Like a dragon you have deposited venom on the land
> 10 When you roar at the earth like Thunder, no vegetation
>   can stand up to you.
> 11 A flood descending from its mountain,
> 12 Oh foremost one, you are the Inanna of heaven and
>   earth!
> 13 Raining the fanned fire   down upon the nation,
> 14 Endowed with me's by An,   lady mounted on a
>   beast,
> 15 Who makes decisions   at the holy command
>   of An.
> 16 [You] of all the great rites,   who can fathom what
>   is yours?

According to the poem's exordium Inanna possesses standard ancient Near Eastern theophanic qualities. She is "resplendent light" (1). She "roars at the earth like Thunder" (10). She can "rain down fire upon the nation" (13)—just as Yahweh does upon Sodom and Gomorrah. And she is even associated with or compared to a "flood" (11).[52]

Inanna's stormy advent has an ordained purpose. The high god An has endowed her with "me's" (divine attributes)—she even has the perfect number of them, "seven" (5)—and she is enabled to make decisions "at the holy command of An" (14–15).[53]

According to the poem, judgment has been decreed upon humans who have not obeyed or honored the gods. Inanna carries out the judgment:

---

[52]Compare her description a few lines later:
> 28 In the guise of a charging storm   you charge.
> 29 With a roaring storm   you roar.
> 30 With Thunder you   continually thunder.

Ibid., 18–19.

[53]Cf. the "sevenfold Spirit" or "seven spirits" of God in theophany (Rev 4:5).

17	Devastatrix of the lands,	you are lent wings by the storm.
18	Beloved of Enlil,	you fly about in the nation.
19	You are at the service	of the decrees of An.
20	Oh my lady, at the sound of you	the lands bow down.
21	When mankind	comes before you
22	In fear and trembling	at [your] tempestuous radiance,
23	They receive from you	their just deserts.

Inanna moves according to the "decrees of An" (19). As a divine bringer of judgment according to those decrees, she gives men "their just deserts" (23). Perhaps the phrase applies to men who have withheld homage from the goddess (cf. vi.43, "In the mountain where homage is withheld from you vegetation is accursed"). Elsewhere in the poem it is clear that the gods communicate to people through their priestess (in this case Enheduanna). But Enheduanna has been driven by an enemy from her role as priestess; she laments, "I may no longer reveal the pronouncements of Ningal to man" (119). The gods communicate their will to the people, and that should bring blessing. But those who interfere with such divine revelation must be punished. The punishment Inanna brings can also apply more broadly to any who are rebellious:

125 That you devastate the– rebellious land	be it known!
126 That you roar at the land–	be it known!

The historical background to the poem includes Sargon's defeat of Lugalzagesi, his principal opponent for the rule of Sumer and Akkad.[54] In terms of the historical context, then, the "re-

---

[55]Hallo and van Dijk, *Exaltation*, 7–10.

bellious" are those who have not yet submitted to Sargon and the divine powers who back him. Such submission in the ancient Near East would have involved a formalization of relations by a covenant overseen by the gods. Although the latter cannot be demonstrated from the poem, it is clear that divine retribution for human law-breaking—human transgression of divine standards—is in view.[55]

Storm God of Hatti

Hittite emperors often had to quell revolts by vassals who strove to throw off the imperial yoke. The emperor, who styled himself "the Sun [god]"—itself a theophanic appellation—marched forth with the aid of his gods to put down any insurrection. Such events took place under a covenantal aegis, and the gods were overseers of the covenants.

A good example comes from the *Annals* of Muršiliš II (ca. 1325 B.C.) Shortly after the emperor ascended the throne, a number of vassal states rebelled against him.[56] The emperor raised his hands in prayer to the "Sun goddess of Arina, my Lady," and bewailed this attempt to take away her territories.[57] The phrasing indicates that the sun goddess was overseer of covenants between Hatti and the vassals. The emperor called upon her to enact covenantal judgment, which she did, enabling him to subdue the rebel lands within ten years.[58]

Muršiliš also got help from "the proud Weather god, my Lord," in the course of his campaign against one of the rebel states, Arzawa. The help came in the form of a theophanic thunderbolt that shattered the foe:

---

[55]For another example involving Inanna in the vanguard of battle, cf. T. W. Mann, *Divine Presence and Guidance in Israelite Traditions* (Baltimore: Johns Hopkins Press, 1977), 33–35 (the "Nur-Adad Letter").
[56]A. Götze, *Die Annalen des Muršiliš* (Darmstadt: Wissenschaftliche Buchgesellschaft, 1967), 14–21.
[57]Ibid., 20–23.
[58]Ibid., 22–23.

> The proud Weather god, my Lord, showed his divine power, and he violently threw down a thunderbolt. And my army saw the thunderbolt, and Arzawa land saw it, too, and the thunderbolt went forth and smote Arzawa land, and also smote Apasa, the city of Uhha-LU-iš [the leader of the revolt].[59]

Muršiliš even reported that the rebel leader became ill as a result of the thunderbolt—so much so that the weather god's theophany led to his defeat and eventual death.[60]

Such drastic theophanic intervention was appropriate because vassals had broken a divinely ordained covenant. In another such campaign Muršiliš declared, "The covenant gods showed their divine power,"[61] and "The covenant gods must have their vengeance"[62]—an assertion that strongly resembles Yahweh's word against covenant breakers: "Vengeance is mine, and retribution" (Dt 32:35, author's translation).[63]

Perhaps the most resonant example from Hatti also comes from the reign of Muršiliš. It is an account of what happened when the emperor set out against rebellious Malazzija land.

> The proud Weather god, my Lord, stood by me. It rained the whole night, so that the enemy could not see the camp fires of my troops. But as it became light, the proud Weather god, my Lord [. . .] In the early part of the day, a stor[m *and darkness*] suddenly arose. . . . And as long as I [*marched*] against [. . . lacking, but presumably, *Malazzija*], the storm went before my troops and [*made them invisible*]. But as soon as I arrived in Malazzija land, the storm broke up.[64]

The emperor goes on to tell how the foe was caught unawares and rapidly defeated. For a reader of the Old Testament the

---

[59]Ibid., 46–47 (17.16–19).
[60]Ibid., 48–49, 60–61 (Vs II.13–14, Rs III B 40–41).
[61]Ibid., 112–13 (Vs I.46).
[62]Ibid., 112–13 (Vs II.10–11).
[63]Cf. Ps 94:1; Isa 34:8.
[64]Götze, *Annalen*, 194–97 (11–19).

passage is evocative. The storm and darkness go before the Hittite army during the day and cloak its approach to the foe until the army is close enough to have the advantage of surprise and accomplish covenantal vengeance upon those rebellious vassals. All is seen as the glorious work of the "proud Weather god," the Hittite emperor's "lord." The passage shows a theology of divine intervention not unlike that of Exodus, where a pillar of cloud and of fire goes before Israel during the day and night, and even helps destroy the Egyptian army by keeping it at bay until Israel can cross the Sea of Reeds.[65]

Akkadian Storm Theophanies

Ancient Near Eastern monarchs often went to battle against rebellious vassals. When they did, they commonly portrayed themselves as thundering in theophany against the foe. Their thunder alone was envisaged as an awesome weapon that might defeat the enemy or quash rebellion. A good example comes from the Amarna correspondence. In a letter from Abdimilki of Tyre to the pharaoh Akhenaton, the pharaoh is compared with Baal, "who thunders" (lit., "gives his voice," *id-din ri-ig-ma-šu)* in the heavens, like Adad, so that the whole land trembles at his thunder (lit., "from his voice," *iš-tu ri-ig-mi-šu).*[66] Note the replacement of Akkadian *šagāmu* ("to thunder") by an often used Akkadian theophanic idiom, *rigma nadānu* ("to give voice"), just as in Hebrew רעם ("to roar" [Qal]; "to thunder" [Hiph.]) is often replaced by נתן קול. In the *Atra-Ḥasis* epic, *šagāmu* and *rigmu* are used synonymously, just

---

[65]An important difference is that Yahweh's judgment on Egypt is not a judgment on a state in vassaldom to his chosen Israel. More broadly considered, however, it is a judgment of Egyptian idolatry and insubmissiveness to a God who stands in covenant relation (both Adamic and Noahic) to all people and nations.

[66]J. A. Knudtzon, ed., *Die El-Amarna Tafeln* (Leipzig: Otto Zeller, 1915), 608–9 (147.13–15).

like רעם and נתן קול in Hebrew.⁶⁷ Likewise in Akkadian *rigmu*, "voice," is used to mean "thunder," just like קול in Hebrew. We read for instance of the storm god Adad, "at whose thundering [*ša ina rigim pîšu*, lit., 'at the voice/thunder of whose mouth'] the fields are ruined, the plain shakes [*iḫillu*, cf. Heb. חים]."⁶⁸ Though not Canaanizings of Akkadian (as the example from *Atra-Ḫasis* shows), these idioms are compatible with Canaanite usage and equivalent to Ugaritic *ytn ql* and Hebrew נתן קול.

Mesopotamian royal ideology sometimes illumines Mesopotamian theology. Oppenheim has observed that the Mesopotamian gods lived like kings.⁶⁹ But Mesopotamian kings also thundered like gods. When a Mesopotamian king made war against the foe, his advance was often portrayed as an awesome theophany—especially a theophany of the storm god, Adad. The verb normally used to portray such a theophanic advance was the verb "to thunder" (*šagāmu*). Shalmaneser I (1274–1245 B.C.) styled himself "the one who thunders in battle against his foes."⁷⁰ In the Assyrian "Tukulti-Ninurta Epic," Tukulti-Ninurta I (1244–1208 B.C.) appears like the storm god: "As when Addu bellows, the mountains tremble."⁷¹ Tiglath-pileser I (1115–1077 B.C.) declared of one enemy, "I brought about the destruction of their extensive army like a storm of the god Adad."⁷² To give visual impact to his Adad-like victories, he fashioned bronze lightning-bolts and

---

⁶⁷W. G. Lambert and A. R. Millard, *Atra-Ḫasis* (Oxford: Clarendon, 1969), 92–93 (III.ii.49–50). For Hebrew examples, cf. Job 37:4; 40:9; Ps 29:3; and esp. Ps 18:14(13).

⁶⁸*CAD*, vol. 6 (H), p. 55 (*ḫalu* B); cf. vol. 13 (Q), p. 213 (*qerbetu* 2.e).

⁶⁹A. L. Oppenheim, *Ancient Mesopotamia, Portrait of a Dead Civilization* (Chicago: University of Chicago Press, 1964), 186ff.

⁷⁰Grayson, *Assyrian Rulers*, 182, 1.11–12. Grayson translates the verb *šagāmu* rather weakly in this case, "makes resound the noise of battle with his enemies (*mu-ul-ta-aš-gi-mu qa-bal ge-ri-šu*)."

⁷¹W. G. Lambert, "Three Unpublished Fragments of the Tukulti-Ninurta Epic," *AfO* 18 (Graz, 1957–58): 50–51.

⁷²*AKA*, 67.

inscribed some of his conquests on them as a memorial.[73] Ashurnaṣirpal II (883–859 B.C.) claimed, "Like Adad [the god] of the storm I thundered against them."[74] Sargon II (721–705 B.C.) said, "Against that city, the thunder of my great army like Adad I made thunder."[75] Likewise Sennacherib (704–681 B.C.) asserted that he "thundered" against the enemy "like Adad."[76] According to a long tradition in Mesopotamia, Assyrian kings as they went to war compared themselves with theophanic Adad.[77] That warfare was always either to conquer new lands or to punish rebellious vassals. It was as though the Storm god himself were involved in such covenantal punishment. Indeed an ancient curse of Assyrian king Adad-nārāri I (1307–1275 B.C.) against anyone who alters his monumental inscriptions declares: "May he [Adad] make his land [look] like ruin hills [created by] the deluge."[78] Such monumental inscriptions included records of victorious battles and covenant oaths sworn by the defeated.[79]

---

[73] Ibid., 79–80. For the translation "lightning bolts," cf. A. K. Grayson, *Assyrian Royal Inscriptions* (Wiesbaden: Harrassowitz, 1976): 2:15 (par. 38). The Akkadian word is *birqu* (cf. Heb. ברק).

[74] Ibid., 233.

[75] F. Thoreau-Dangin, *Une relation de la huitième campagne de Sargon* (Paris, 1912), 52–53 (l. 343).

[76] Luckenbill, *Annals of Sennacherib,* 44.

[77] In light of such evidence, it may be that Jer 4:13–16 portrays the advance of a Mesopotamian army in theophanic terms consistent not only with Mesopotamian tradition but also with OT judgment theophany:

> Look! He advances like the clouds,
>   his chariots come like a whirlwind. . . .
> A besieging army is coming from a distant land,
>   *and they thunder* against the cities of Judah.

We translate "and they thunder" (וְיִתְּנוּ . . . קוֹלָם), rather than the traditional "raising a war cry" (NIV).

[78] Grayson, *Assyrian Rulers,* 1:143, 9.32–33.

[79] Ibid., 136, 3.4ff. Cf. especially the typical claim, "I made him take an oath and then allowed him to return to his own land" (3.11). The oath was a standard covenant "oath of the great gods," by which the defeated swore vassaldom to both Aššur and the Assyrian king.

One example of Adad (and other gods) involved in storm theophanies against covenant-breakers comes from the "Tukulti-Ninurta Epic." Here Aššur, Enlil, Anu, Nannar Sin, Adad, Šamaš, Ninurta, and Ishtar form the vanguard in battle against Kashtiliash IV of Babylon, who has broken covenant with Tukulti-Ninurta I of Assyria. Tukulti-Ninurta follows the divine vanguard to victory:

23 The fighting line was spread out on the field of battle; fighting commenced.
24 A great commotion set in among them; the servants trembled.
25 Assur led in the vanguard; he kindled a biting flame against the foes.
26 Enlil danced (?) in the midst of the enemy; he fanned the burning flame.
27 Anu set a relentless weapon against the evil ones.
28 Nannar Sin forced against them the pressure of battle.
29 Adad the hero sent down a flood-wind against their fighting line.
30 Šamaš, Lord of judgment, dimmed the eyes of the forces of Sumer and Akkad.
31 Ninurta, the warrior, leader of the gods, shattered their weapons.
32 And Ishtar beat her skipping rope which drove their warriors mad.
33 Behind the gods, his helpers, the king in the vanguard of the army began the fight.[80]

A consortium of deities goes before the king and wages war against the foe. The warfare is portrayed in terms reminiscent of Yahweh judgments: Aššur sends "biting flame"; Enlil fans the "burning flame"; Adad sends a "flood-wind" against them. Adad's flood-wind sheds some theological light on another

---

[80]Mann, *Divine Presence*, 40–41.

common boast of Assyrian kings, that they left a rebellious city in ruins, "like a ruin heap after a flood/the Flood/Deluge."[81] Such use of flood imagery in passages of judgment will appear again in our discussion of the Noahic flood.

Later in Assyrian tradition Esarhaddon records an intriguing case of divine warfare against a disobedient vassal.[82] The king of Šubria has been insubordinate in every way to his suzerain Esarhaddon. Smitten with his sin he clothes himself with sackcloth and goes about in mourning. He writes to Esarhaddon and begs for mercy. He admits, "I committed a heavy sin against the god Aššur when I failed to obey the word of my lord the king."[83] But Esarhaddon shows him no mercy. He marches against his insubordinate vassal and builds a siege rampart against his royal city Upumme. He then reports:

> While I marched about victoriously through that district, they splashed the siege rampart which I had erected against his royal city Upumme . . . in the still of the night with naphtha and set fire to it. But at the command of Marduk, the King of the gods, the northwind blew—the pleasant breath of the Lord of the gods—and turned the hostile fire against Upumme; so it did not set fire to the siege rampart . . . but burnt up his own wall and reduced it to ashes.[84]

Esarhaddon goes on to tell how he defeated the forces of Šubria and brought it back under Assyrian control.

Marduk's involvement is the most arresting feature of this account for readers of the Old Testament. Marduk commanded the north wind to blow against the hostile fire, just as

---

[81]For the translation alternatives, cf. *CAD*, vol. 1, A pt. 1, pp. 77–80 (*abūbu* 1–3). For examples, cf. Grayson, *Assyrian Rulers*, 1:234, 1.ii.17 (Tukulti-Ninurta I); 2:16, 1.ii.78 (Tiglath-pileser I), 2:149, 2.32 (Adad-nārāri II); P. Rost, *Die Keilschrifttexte Tiglat-Pilesers III,* Bd. I (Leipzig: Verlag von Eduard Pfeiffer, 1893), 36, 209 (Tiglath-pileser III).
[82]Borger, *AfO* Beiheft 9, 102–7 (§ 68, Gbr. I–III).
[83]Ibid., 103 (§ 68, Gbr. II:I.21).
[84]Ibid., 104 (§ 68, Gbr. II:II.1–7).

Yahweh "drove the sea back with a strong east wind and turned it into dry land" (Ex 14:21) so that Israel could cross over. Both actions apparently took place during the night. And just as the wind Yahweh brought was characterized as "the blast of your nostrils" (Ex 15:8), the north wind brought by Marduk was called "the pleasant breath of the Lord of the gods." The Assyrian account shows quite simply how an author may characterize one and the same wind both naturalistically (north wind or east wind) and poetically (the blast of the god's nostrils, or his pleasant breath). Such evidence from the ancient Near East goes far to show how unnecessary a source division of Exodus 14 and 15 is on supposed grounds of conflict between these two modes of portrayal. Theologically, the Assyrian account shows how directly the god Marduk became involved in the punishment of a rebellious vassal.

Another example from Esarhaddon's annals shows how the king himself could be theophanically described as he came in battle judgment:

> The king whose march is like a flood-storm,
> whose acts are like a raging lion;
> before him is a storm-demon,
> behind him is a cloud-burst;
> the onset of his battle is mighty;
> a consuming flame,
> an unquenchable fire.[85]

The passage recalls the judgment advent of Yahweh in Psalm 97.

> Clouds and thick darkness surround him;
>   righteousness and justice are the foundation of his throne.
> Fire goes before him
>   and consumes his foes on every side. (vv. 2–3)

Like Yahweh, Esarhaddon is surrounded by storm clouds; like Yahweh, the Assyrian king is preceded by an awesome fire that

---

[85]Ibid., 97 (§ 65, Rs. 12–14). Mann, *Divine Presence,* 64–65, usefully discusses this passage in the context of the divine "vanguard" motif.

consumes his enemies. Just as Yahweh comes to punish the rebellious of the earth, Esarhaddon comes to punish and subdue the insubmissive of all lands. He can do so because he is "the king ... at whose feet [Marduk and the gods] have cast all lands ... who imposes tax and tribute on them all."[86] In other words, all are vassals subject to Esarhaddon and his gods and subject also to covenantal judgment, theophanically portrayed.

Divine Temple Abandonment

Yahweh theophanies occur throughout the Old Testament as part of God's wise and just covenant administration. The saddest of these "personal appearances," however, occurs when God lets Ezekiel watch the Lord's departure from the Jerusalem temple and, soon after, from Jerusalem itself. It is a sign that the covenant is over: "While I watched, the cherubim spread their wings and rose from the ground.... They stopped at the entrance to the east gate of Yahweh's house, and the glory of the God of Israel was above them." (Eze 10:19) "Then the cherubim, with the wheels beside them, spread their wings, and the glory of the God of Israel was above them. The glory of Yahweh went up from within the city and stopped above the mountain east of it" (Eze 11:22–23). The prophet sees the glory of Yahweh, on his chariot throne, depart the Jerusalem temple and ascend above the city. He is borne on the cherubim in cloud and stormy glory as he abandons both city and temple. God's abandonment of his temple, his "house," is a sign that he has forsaken his people because of their sin. He said to Ezekiel in the temple vision, "Son of man, do you see what they are doing–the utterly detestable things the house of Israel is doing here, things that will drive me far from my sanctuary?" (Eze 8:6). This idea, however, is not new to Ezekiel or even to the Old Testament. It is attested earlier in Assyrian epic poetry.[87]

---

[86]Ibid., 97 (§ 65, Rs. 8–11).
[87]For fuller discussion of the Ezekiel theophanies, see chap. 7.

Assyria

An early exemplar of divine temple abandonment appears in the Middle-Assyrian poem the "Tukulti-Ninurta Epic." The poem celebrates among other things the victory of the Assyrian king Tukulti-Ninurta I over his adversary Kashtiliash IV, king of Kassite Babylon. The Kassite king is portrayed as a covenant breaker from a long line of covenant-breakers. His fathers broke covenant with the kings of Assyria, and he has followed in their footsteps. By doing so he has outraged the king of Assyria, who appeals to Shamash, the sun god and overseer of covenants in Mesopotamia. The sun god is supposed to judge between the two kings and grant victory to the one who has kept covenant. That one (as the poem would have it) is Tukulti-Ninurta I, king of Assyria.

The Assyrian king wins the victory. But one cardinal fact that precedes his victory and makes it possible is the behavior of the gods. Angry at the sin of Kashtiliash IV, they forsake the urban temples and thus abandon him to sure defeat:

> . . . impious Cassite king . . .
> Against the covenant-breaker Kashtiliash the gods of heaven [and earth]
> They showed [. . .] against the king of the land and the peop[le . . .]
> They were angry with the overseer, their shepherd, and [. . .]
> The Enlilship of the Lord of the Lands was distressed and [. . .] Nippur,
> So that he did not approach the dwelling of Dur-Kurigalzu [. . .]
> Marduk abandoned his lofty shrine, the city of [. . .]
> He [cu]rsed his beloved city Kar [. . .]
> Sin left Ur, [his] cult center [. . .]
> With Sippar and Larsa Sha[mash . . .]
> Ea [. . .] Eridu, the House of Wisdom [. . .]
> Ishtaran was angry [. . .]
> Anunitu does not approach Akkad [. . .]
> The mistress of Uruk forsook [. . .]
> The gods were wrath [. . .][88]

---

[88] W. G. Lambert, "Three Unpublished Fragments of the Tukulti-Ninurta Epic," *AfO* 18 (Graz, 1957–58), 42–45.

The pantheon was irate against Kashtiliash. To show their wrath the gods and goddesses abandoned their temples and holy cities.[89] One might well ask, *"tantaene animis caelestibus irae?"*[90] The sinful king is called "their shepherd"—the ruler the gods had appointed to take care of their people (cf. Isa 44:28!)—indicating the royal shepherd typology of the ancient Near East.[91] Yet because he has sinned, the gods have abandoned their shepherd. His sin is that he has broken covenant and thus led his people to disaster (as his soliloquy in an earlier portion of the poem indicates).[92]

Later in Assyria Sennacherib tells how the gods abandoned seven unsubmissive cities on the border of Qummuhu. The gods' abandonment implies their disapproval of the foe in favor of Assyria,

> who from days of old, in [the time of] the kings, my fathers,
> were strong and proud, not knowing
> the fear of [Assyrian] rule,—in the time of my rule,
> their gods deserted them
> and left them empty.[93]

Likewise the gods could abandon an individual ruler as a sign of their disapproval, especially if that ruler were a vassal of Assyria and unwisely—even impiously—chose to revolt:

> Kirua, prefect of Illubru,
> a slave, subject to me, whom his gods forsook,

---

[89]Cf. the discussion by P. Machinist, "Literature as Politics: The Tukulti-Ninurta Epic and the Bible," *CBQ* 38 (1976): 458.

[90]Vergil, *Aeneid*, I.11.

[91]See above chap. 3, 97–98.

[92]R. C. Thompson and M. E. L. Mallowen, "The British Museum Excavations at Nineveh, 1931–32," *University of Liverpool Annals of Archaeology and Anthropology* 20 (1933): 71–127. The Cassite king declares, "The (covenant) oath of Shamash oppresses me. . . . I have delivered my people into a ruthless hand, a bondage [unyielding]. Into an inextricable impasse without escape I have [led them]. Punished are my sins before Shamash, the wrongdoing. . . . Who is the god who will rescue my people. . .? (120–21 [Akk.], 125 [Eng.]).

[93]Luckenbill, *Annals of Sennacherib*, 64 (lines 19–24).

> caused the men of Hilakku [Cilicia]
> to revolt, and made ready for battle.[94]

As in the case of Tukulti-Ninurta I and Kashtiliash, so here the theme of divine abandonment is related to that of covenant-breaking, or vassal disloyalty.[95]

Subsequently in Assyria an inscription of Esarhaddon portrays divine abandonment of temples for a period of seventy years because of divine wrath at the sinfulness of the people:

> The Lord of the gods, Marduk, was angry. He planned evil; to wipe out the land, to destroy its inhabitants . . . an evil curse was on his lips.[96]

> The gods and goddesses who dwelt in it [i.e., the temple Esagila] fled like birds and went up to heaven. The protective gods [. . . ran] off and withdrew.[97]

The Assyrian gods and goddesses abandon their temples much as Yahweh abandons his temple before Ezekiel's eyes (see below, chap. 7).

Divine abandonment of temples (and of those unfortunate people in whose land the temples stood) took another form in the ancient Near East. Sometimes the idols, which represented the gods, were removed from their temples.[98] Morton Cogan has noted the significance of this act in the Assyrian realm: "N[eo]A[ssyrian] spoliation of divine images was meant to portray the abandonment of the enemy by his own gods in submission to the superior might of Assyria's god, Ashur."[99]

---

[94]Ibid., 61 (IV.62–65).

[95]The Akkadian $^{am}ardu$ ("slave") is better translated "vassal" in this context.

[96]Borger, *AfO* Beiheft 9, p. 13 (§ 11, Ep. 5, A + B).

[97]Ibid., 14 (§ 11, Ep. 8, A + B).

[98]Hallo and van Dijk, *Exaltation,* 67, in a discussion of the Babylonian recapture of Marduk's statue from Elam by Nebuchadnezzar I (ca. 1124–1103 B.C.), note "the importance attached to the divine statues, their capture and recapture, throughout Mesopotamian history."

[99]Cogan, *Imperialism and Religion: Assyria, Judah and Israel in the Eighth and Seventh Centuries B.C.E.*, 40. As we have noted, the related theme of divine

The theme of divine temple abandonment as a form of covenantal judgment is thus well established in second- and first-millennium Mesopotamia.

Like the Assyrians and other ancient Near Eastern peoples, the Israelites also occasionally took the idols of the foe. For example, when the Philistines had come and arrayed troops in the Valley of Rephaim, David both conquered the foe and took their idols as a token of his triumph:

> David inquired of Yahweh, "Shall I go and attack the Philistines? Will you hand them over to me?"
> Yahweh answered him, "Go, for I will surely hand the Philistines over to you."
> So David went to Baal Perazim, and there he defeated them. . . . The Philistines abandoned their idols there, and David and his men carried them off. (2Sa 5:19–21)

David did not take the idols away to the temple of God to install them there as captive and subordinate gods as a pagan king would have done. Yahweh had said, "You shall have no other gods in my presence" (Ex 20:3, author's trans.), so David burned the Philistine idols, knowing that they were in reality no gods (1Ch 14:12).

CONCLUSION

Attributing human victories and defeats to the action of gods and goddesses was common in the ancient Near East. For example, Inanna's theophany and her exaltation were historically anchored in Sargon's victorious career. The fact that Sargon conquered his foes meant that Inanna was theophanically active, according to the poet. Such a theology recalls biblical theophanies. Hallo goes so far as to draw a parallel between Neb-

---

abandonment occurs in the second millennium "Tukulti-Ninurta Epic." Cogan is mistaken, therefore, when he maintains that "Before the NA period, no conqueror had thought to enlist this thesis [i.e., that of divine abandonment] in justifying his conquests" (21).

uchadnezzar I's recapture of Marduk's statue from Elam and the subsequent exaltation of Marduk, and the Exodus events:

> Since this example brings us well into the second half of the second millennium, it may be worth noting in conclusion the striking parallel that it affords to the "exaltation of Yahweh" at the Exodus, an event datable only a little earlier. The religious history of Israel is almost inexplicable without accepting the historicity of the Exodus, as most Biblical scholars are now inclined to do. But the Exodus gains in historical validity, not only by its continued literary reflection in the "Exodus typology" of later Israelite thought and experience, but also by its direct and intimate bearing on the emergence of Israel's God to an unchallenged supremacy in the eyes of his people. Events at the Reed Sea and God's exaltation are closely related, and this relationship, which deserves further study, can materially help to date the former while strengthening the historical character of the latter.[100]

One key difference emerges, I believe, between the theophanies and exaltations of any pagan deities and the "exaltation of Yahweh" that resulted from the Exodus. The case of Inanna is a good illustration. The Sumerian goddess was exalted by the princess, priestess, and poetess Enheduanna on the foundation of a human military victory (Sargon's), and theophany was attributed to Inanna as a way of accounting for that victory. By contrast Yahweh theophanies occurred and accomplished for Israel a victory it could never have attained on its own, and Yahweh was accordingly—and appropriately—exalted by the prophet, prince, and poet, Moses.

---

[100]Hallo and van Dijk, *Exaltation*, 67–68.

5

Pre-Sinai Theophanies

> Of Man's First Disobedience, and the Fruit
> Of that Forbidden Tree, whose mortal taste
> Brought Death into the World, and all our woe,
> With loss of Eden, till one greater Man
> Restore us, and regain the blissful Seat,
> Sing Heav'nly Muse, that on the secret top
> Of Oreb, or of Sinai, didst inspire
> That Shepherd, who first taught the chosen Seed,
> In the Beginning how the Heav'ns and the Earth
> Rose out of Chaos. . . .
>
> John Milton, *Paradise Lost,* I.1–10

Before discussing pre-Sinai theophanies, one must establish the covenantal context of those theophanies. All Yahweh theophanies do in fact take place in covenantal contexts. The salvation and judgment that occur when God appears thus also take place under an aegis of covenant.

Four pre-Sinai theophanies have clearly Sinaitic characteristics—that is, characteristics of storm theophany. Each of these takes place in a covenantal context. The first is the avian appearance of the Spirit of God in Genesis 1:2; the second is Yahweh God's storm theophany in Genesis 3:8; the third is Yahweh's presence at the Flood (especially as reflected in Ps 29); and the fourth is Abram's theophanic vision of Yahweh in Genesis 15.

Although covenantal elements in Genesis 15 have been noted by several scholars, the passage can still yield more to analysis. The covenantal aspect of the Noahic Flood anticipates the eschaton but also needs to be explored in its own right. The covenant background to Genesis 3:8 and even to Genesis 1:2 (namely, Ge 1:1–2:3) also requires further analysis.

GENESIS 1:1–2:3

A number of scholars have seen a balanced structure in the Creation account. According to this balance, the first three days and the second three are counterposed. S. R. Driver has called the first three "days of preparation" and the next three "days of accomplishment."[1] Derek Kidner has termed the first triad days of "form," the next triad days of "fullness."[2] M. G. Kline sees the first three days as the creation of domains or kingdoms, and the second three as the creation of creature kings to rule over them. Kikawada and Quinn seem to echo Kline's thought when they say, "In the first group [of days] regions are created. . . . In the second group, the corresponding inhabitants of these regions are created."[3] W. I. Dumbrell recognizes "an inner parallelism and progression between days one to three and four to six." He adds that the account "receives its real significance from the addition of the seventh day," by which "the goal of Creation is indicated"—namely, the Sabbath rest of God into which humans have been summoned to participate.[4] Notwithstanding the title of his book, *Covenant and Creation*, Dumbrell discusses the covenantal nature of Genesis 1:1–2:3 only in a very general way.[5] He takes the Noahic renewal of "the mandate given to man in 1:28" as a leading indicator that the Creation account is covenantal in nature, and

---

[1] S. R. Driver, *The Book of Genesis* (London: Methuen, 1904), 2.
[2] D. Kidner, *Genesis* (London: Tyndale, 1967), 46.
[3] Kikawada and Quinn, *Before Abraham Was*, 78.
[4] W. I. Dumbrell, *Covenant and Creation* (Nashville: Nelson, 1984), 34–35.
[5] Ibid., 33, sees the pericope end at Ge 2:4a.

so it is.⁶ But the whole cast of Genesis 1:1–2:3 displays a detailed covenantal form and content.

The Creation account has a second millennium covenant structure that forms the rationale for Yahweh's theophany in Genesis 3:8. A synopsis of the second millennium ancient Near Eastern treaty form sheds light on the legal/literary structure of the Creation narrative:

1 Title/Preamble

This section introduces the words of the great king, or suzerain, e.g.: "These are the words of the Sun(god) Mursilis, the great king, the king of the Hatti land, the valiant, the favorite of the storm god."⁷

2 Historical Prologue

This section tells all the good things that the great king has done for the vassal.⁸

3 Stipulations

This section tells what the vassal must do out of gratitude, in obedience to the great king.⁹

4 Depositing and regular reading of treaty

The treaty, once ratified, was deposited by the suzerain and the vassal in the temples of their respective gods, who participated in the oversight of the treaty (that is, of the kings' obedience to covenant). Each king was supposed to read the treaty regularly in order to remain mindful of its stipulations and so obey them.

---

⁶Ibid., 33.

⁷*ANET*, 3d ed., 203, "Treaty Between Mursilis and Duppi-Tessub of Amurru" ("Preamble").

⁸Ibid., 203–4 ("Historical Introduction").

⁹Ibid., 204–5 ("Future Relations of the Two Countries," "Military Clauses," "Dealings with Foreigners, etc.").

5 Witnesses
Various gods, but also heaven, earth, clouds, mountains, etc.[10]

6 Blessings/Curses
Blessings for obedience, curses for disobedience.[11]

The Creation account (Ge 1:1–2:3) articulates the same international treaty form:

Genesis 1:1–2:3   Analysis

1 Genesis 1:1   Title/Preamble

1:1   "In the beginning God created . . ."

Note that God creates by his word; so ancient Near Eastern treaties were introduced as the "words" of the great king—quite literally, the words by which the suzerain structured the "world" in which the vassal must henceforth live and rule. The analogy makes it clear that God is the Suzerain in what follows.[12]

2 Genesis 1:2–1:29   Historical Prologue

This section tells of God's creative work—all that the Great King has done for the lesser, vassal king and queen.

3 Genesis 1:28, 2:16–17a   Stipulations

1:28   "Be fruitful and increase in number"; "fill the earth and subdue it." "Rule over

---

[10]Ibid., 205 ("Invocation of the Gods").

[11]Ibid., 205 ("Curses and Blessings").

[12]Dumbrell, *Covenant and Creation,* 34, also appropriately sees evidence of God's kingship in the "royal fiat [cf. 'Let there be light!']," which recurs in the pericope. He also sees "man in the image [of God] . . . in terms of a representative but derived kingship role in Gen. 1" (p. 34). For the derivation of kingship from a high god or from heaven in the ancient Near East, cf. chap. 3.

	the fish of the sea and the birds of the air and over every living creature that moves on the ground."
2:16	"You are free to eat from any tree in the garden,"
2:17a	"but you must not eat from the tree of the knowledge of good and evil."

4 Deposition and regular reading

There was no deposition or regular reading because Adam and Eve had no written treaty.

5 **Genesis 1:31; 2:1**	**Witnesses**
a 1:31	"God saw all that he had made, and it was very good."
b 2:1	Implicitly the finished heavens and earth, subsequently called to witness in prophetic literature (Dt 4:26; 31:28; Isa 1:2; Ps 50:4).[13]

6 **Genesis 1:28; 2:3, 17**	**Blessings/Curses**
a 1:28	"God blessed them"
b 2:3	"God blessed the seventh day"
c 2:17b	"for when you eat of it you will surely die."

---

[13] Kline, *Images of the Spirit*, 19–20, understands the Spirit in Ge 1:2 to be "a divine witness to the Covenant of Creation" and argues that this primordial theophany forms the background "for the later use of the rainbow as a sign of God's covenant with the earth (Gen. 9:12ff.)."

Clearly the Genesis 1:1–2:3 Creation account is framed according to the pattern of a second millennium ancient Near Eastern treaty.[14] Its literary/legal form is not the only evidence of its covenantal nature, however. The original Creation covenant is attested elsewhere in the Old Testament. Hosea recognizes its existence: "Like Adam, they have broken the covenant" (Hos 6:7).[15] Jeremiah also alludes to it: "This is what Yahweh says: 'If you can break my covenant with the day and my covenant with the night, so that day and night will not come at their appointed time'" (Jer 33:20, author's trans.); "This is what Yahweh says: 'If I have not established my covenant with day and night and the fixed laws of heaven and earth'" (Jer 33:25)—both clear allusions to the Creation account. Moreover, Jeremiah speaks of Yahweh's "decrees" (חֻקֹּת) that regulate the shining of sun, moon, and stars, using a *terminus technicus* from the realm of covenant (Jer 31:35–36; cf. Ex 12:24; Dt 4:1 and passim).

Even more important are the theological implications of the passage. It shows that, from the beginning, Yahweh has been a God of covenant. Covenant suzerainty and covenant faithfulness are therefore essential attributes of God and are manifest in God's dealing with all Creation. This means that God will remain faithful even though his creatures prove unfaithful. God will not abandon his covenant faithfulness toward what he has made.

When a suzerain made a treaty with a vassal in the ancient Near East, he imposed obligations upon the vassal. Because

---

[14]Cf. Ge 9:8–17 (Noahic re-Creation covenant). Like the covenant structure of Deuteronomy, the structure in Ge 1:1–2:3 has important implications for date, for it indicates a second millennium (i.e., Mosaic) date for the passage.

[15]Isa 24:5, an eschatological judgment passage that indicts humankind for breaking the "everlasting covenant," can only be said with certainty to allude to the first occurrence of that phrase, where it is used to describe the Noahic covenant (Ge 9:16). Since the Noahic covenant is a re-creation covenant, Isaiah's indictment might be seen as reaching back (implicitly) to the original Creation covenant.

those covenantal arrangements were overseen and enforced by the gods—and by their earthly representative, the suzerain—the vassal was supposed to obey them. But the suzerain also had obligations. If a third party attacked the vassal and made an attempt to subvert his throne, the suzerain must then intervene. He must deal with the attacker and restore the vassal to his rightful throne and his kingdom. For example, the Hittite king Muršiliš II says in his treaty with Duppi-Teššub of Amurru:

> When your father died, in accordance with your father's word I did not drop you. Since your father had mentioned to me your name *with great praise*, I sought after you. To be sure, you were sick and ailing, but though you were ailing, I, the Sun[god], put you in the place of your father and took your brothers [and] sisters and the Amurru land in oath for you.[16]

Muršiliš mentions first his treaty with the father of Duppi-Teššub: when Duppi-Teššub's father died, the Hittite saw to it that Duppi-Teššub ascended the throne (according to his father's wish). Moreover, the Hittite suzerain—who in the tradition of Hittite emperors styled himself the "Sun(god)"[17]—had Duppi-Teššub's brothers, sisters, and subjects swear allegiance to Duppi-Teššub as king. By so doing Muršiliš showed his covenant faithfulness to the royal house of Amurru. The suzerain moreover envisioned the possibility that "if anyone should press you hard, Duppi-Teššub, or [if] anyone should revolt against you, [if] you then write to the king of the Hatti land . . . the king of the Hatti land [will dispatch] foot soldiers and charioteers to your aid. . . ."[18] Hittite suzerain-vassal treaties normally contained such provisions. They ensured that the suzerain would aid and restore the vassal in case of attack or revolt.[19]

---

[16] *ANET,* 3d ed., 203–4.

[17] An epithet partly indicating the emperor's semidivine nature, partly exalting him as perspicacious judge in international affairs.

[18] *ANET,* 3d ed., 204.

[19] Cf. E. F. Weidner, *Politische Dokumente aus Kleinasien, Die Staatsverträge in Akkadischer Sprache aus dem Archiv von Boghasköi,* Boghasköi Studien 8–9

The Creation account—being cast in such a covenant form—implies the same principles. If a third party made any effort to subvert the throne of Adam and Eve (the vassal king and queen), Yahweh implicitly committed himself by covenant to intervene and restore his vassal's throne and kingdom. As we know from the biblical narrative, this is exactly what happened. The serpent deceived the woman, and she in turn led the man astray so that they lost their throne and their kingdom. The New Testament perspective on the resultant state of affairs is that "that ancient serpent called the devil or Satan" (Rev 12:9) has become "the prince of this world" (Jn 12:31; 14:30; 16:11)—indeed "the god of this age" (2Co 4:4), having deposed its rightful king and queen. God, however, is committed to the restoration of his vassals to their throne and kingdom. But that also means the restoration of the world which he made for them at the beginning. That is why Old Testament eschatology anticipates not only a renewed humanity (cf. Isa 65:20–24) dwelling in edenic blessedness (v. 25) but also—in a theophanic context—"the new heavens and the new earth that [Yahweh will] make" (Isa 66:22; cf. 65:17; Rev 21:1). That is why—even in the Old Testament—*Endzeit* reflects *Urzeit*.

Consequently one foundational truth of the Creation covenant is that it already implies the Gospel. God has been committed to the salvation of his vassals and "the restoration of all things" from the beginning.

Because the Creation account is cast in a covenantal form, it also gives a rationale for covenantal judgment. Just as the suzerains of the ancient Near East came in covenant judgment against rebellious vassals, Yahweh must come in judgment against his vassals should they rebel. Just as, for example, the Assyrian suzerain came with a dreadful *melammu*—the theophanic aura of the god Aššur who came with him and supposedly unnerved breakaway vassals[20]—so Yahweh came in theophanic glory occasioning fear as he came.

(Leipzig: J. C. Hinrichs, 1923), 20–21 (Suppiluliuma-Mattiwaza), 64–65 (Suppiluliuma-Tette), 72–73 (Suppiluliuma-Aziru).

[20]See above, chap. 4.

Before we examine Genesis 3:8 (that first of the dreadful theophanies), three others require attention. These are the Yahweh theophanies at Genesis 1:2; 1:27–30; and 2:15–17. They are the only three theophanies the Old Testament portrays before human sin. The first of them portrays an actual appearance of God's Spirit in the process of forming the covenantal context—namely, the Creation. The latter two relate no appearance but only God's gracious words to his covenant vassals.

GENESIS 1:2

The first theophany of the Old Testament shows the Spirit of God in a way that anticipates future glory theophanies. We read that "the Spirit of God was hovering over the face of the waters" (רוּחַ אֱלֹהִים מְרַחֶפֶת עַל פְּנֵי הַמָּיִם). Meredith Kline rightly takes this to be anticipatory of theophanies at Sinai and in the wilderness wanderings: "This form of divine presence is to be identified with the glory-cloud epiphany. At the ratification of the old covenant at Sinai, this cloud-pillar form of theophany represented God standing as witness to his covenant with Israel.[21] Kline then sees this Glory-Spirit theophany reappearing at "the ratification of the new covenant at Pentecost, and finally in eschatological judgment."[22] I will say more later about these related theophanies but affirm now the essential correctness of Kline's identifications.

Concerning the nature of the Spirit's primal appearance, he is portrayed as implicitly the formative agent in creation: he is present in power to accomplish the context for the Adamic covenant—namely, the Creation. Quite aside from subsequent analogies that may legitimately be drawn—the glory presence in Abram's vision to initiate covenant, the presence at Sinai to do the same, and the Pentecostal appearance to

---

[21] Kline, *Kingdom Prologue*, 1:13.
[22] Ibid., 13–14.

empower the new covenant community—analogies from the ancient Near East also add force to this portrayal.

G. E. Mendenhall has demonstrated a theological relationship in the ancient Near East that is relevant to Genesis 1:2. Mendenhall himself did not connect the ancient materials with our passage, but he has developed a background whose relevance soon will become apparent. The background has to do with both literary and iconographic representations of the glory theophanies or presence of ancient gods. We have already discussed at some length the *melammu,* or "glory presence," said to be associated with gods in Mesopotamia, especially in Assyrian tradition but also in Babylonian. We noted that the same *melammu* might be possessed by (or attributed to) human kings who were the gods' elect. Mendenhall has now demonstrated that this same *melammu* was represented iconographically as the winged solar disc in Assyria and that a similar conceptual link obtained in Egypt, Ugarit, and throughout the Near East: "This *melammu* is the word label for a most complex conceptualization of divine and royal glory that is realized in the art motif of the winged sun disk."[23]

The identification of glory presence and wings is probably implicit in the very earliest appearance of the winged-disc motif. After all it is the sun—radiant in glory—that appears with wings. The earliest evidence comes apparently from Egypt of the Old Kingdom: from the reign of King Sahu-Re of the Fifth Dynasty (ca. 2550 B.C.).[24] Mendenhall suggests, "At present it seems quite clear that the winged sun disk did not enter into Mesopotamian iconography until well after it had become established in Syrian and Canaanite iconography, probably under Egyptian influence."[25]

---

[23] G. E. Mendenhall, *The Tenth Generation* (Baltimore: Johns Hopkins University Press, 1973), 53. Cf. in general his development of the evidence, 32–68.
[24] Ibid., 34.
[25] Ibid., 36. Cf. H. Frankfort, *Cylinder Seals* (London, 1939), 208–9.

The antiquity of the evidence may point to its origin in fact. Just as extrabiblical storm theophanies actually echo the way God came in stormy glory into the garden in Genesis 3:8 (see below), so extrabiblical portrayals of solar glory on wings may echo the way the Spirit actually did hover over the face of the waters at the Creation. It is significant that the verb רחף in Genesis 1:2 is used of birds. It is used to portray an eagle in Ugaritic.[26] Eagles also were associated with the winged glory in the ancient Near East.[27] In Sumerian iconography the eagle with outstretched wings was identified with the Im-Dugud bird of Ningirsu (the warrior god of Lagash) and as Mendenhall notes, "in Mesopotamia, this is not so much associated with the sky as with a thunderstorm."[28] The winged glory motif in the ancient world was thus associated with glory/storm theophanies, with various nuances according to subsequent cultural development. It may be that the archetypal theophany as portrayed at Genesis 1:2 was the source for these other attributions of winged glory to subsequent gods. If that is so it may indicate a pre-Mosaic date for the revealed portrait of the Spirit at Creation. On such an understanding an account of the work of Creation—including the portrait of the Spirit—was passed down from Adam through many generations to Moses, who then cast the narrative into its present form.[29]

---

[26]Cyrus H. Gordon, *Ugaritic Textbook* [hereafter *UT*] (Rome: Pontificum Institutum Biblicum, 1965), 484. Cf. Gibson, *Canaanite Myths and Legends*, 112–13 (Aqhat 18.iv.20–21, 31–32.

[27]Mendenhall, *Tenth Generation,* 35, 38.

[28]Ibid., 35–36.

[29]This conclusion may but need not contradict the conclusion of Garrett, *Rethinking Genesis,* 193, that Moses received Ge 1:1–2:3 from God as revelation—that it is "visionary and revelatory and ... Moses, the premier prophet of the Old Testament, is the direct author of this material." An alternate understanding of the Spirit portrait would be that God caused the Creation account to include a theophanic description cast in the mold of ancient Near Eastern "winged disc" glory iconography, just as God used a second millennium international treaty form to encode his covenant with Israel.

The avian quality of theophany does not stop with Genesis 1:2. Subsequently in the Old Testament Yahweh identifies himself metaphorically as an eagle when he declares, "You yourselves have seen what I did to Egypt, and how I carried you on eagles' wings and brought you to myself" (Ex 19:4).[30] His words echo an ancient tradition by which divine and royal glory and power were associated with eagle portraits. Compare the following from the annals of Tiglath-pileser I: "[Tiglath-pileser] . . . offspring of Ninurta-apil-ekur, martial sovereign, loved one of the god Aššur, whose wings were spread like an eagle's over his land and who faithfully tended [i.e., as a shepherd] the people of Assyria."[31]

The tone of parental care associated with the Assyrian eagle imagery remarkably parallels the Old Testament in this case.[32] The tone is appropriate in the Exodus because there God was carrying his young (as it were) into a new life after defeating their mutual foe. The defeat of enemies was also often portrayed in terms of warbird theophanies in the ancient Near East.[33]

The New Testament also boasts an avian theophany that builds upon the Old Testament material—namely, the descent of the Spirit of God (= רוּחַ אֱלֹהִים, Ge 1:2) upon Jesus at his baptism, along with a theophanic voice of approbation from heaven (Mt 3:16–17). I will return to this in its place.[34]

---

[30]Cf. Mendenhall, *Tenth Generation*, 61–62.

[31]Grayson, *Assyrian Rulers of the Third and Second Millennia B.C.*, 2:28 (vii. 55–59).

[32]For more warlike comparisons from the Mesopotamian realm, cf. *CAD*, vol. 4, E, pp. 324–25 (erû C).

[33]Cf. Mendenhall, *Tenth Generation*, 48, 53, discussion of Zu the war bird and theophany.

[34]The use of ancient Near Eastern evidence in the above discussion contrasts with the suggestion of B. F. Batto, *Slaying the Dragon* (Louisville: Westminster/John Knox Press, 1992), that "the wind that subdues the water in [Genesis] 8:1 is apparently the same as 'God's wind' that 'hovered over the surface of the water' in 1:2 while God worked his creative transformation upon the Abyss" (p. 87). Likewise, he says of the Reed Sea event that "P is using the wind . . . as he did at Genesis 1:2 and 8:1–2 as the divine

GENESIS 1:27–30 AND 2:15–17

Both of the two remaining primordial theophanies have the same literary structure though with significant omissions.

Formal Element	Genesis 1:27–30
1 Introductory description, third person	1:27–28a Creation of man and woman in God's image. "God blessed them and said to them,"
2 God's utterance of name of addressee	
3 Response of the addressee	
4 God's self-asseveration	
5 His quelling of human fear	
6 Assertion of his gracious presence	
7 The *hieros logos*	1:28b–30a Commands to be fruitful and to rule; provision of plants for food.
8 Inquiry or protest by addressee	
9 Continuation of the *hieros logos*	
10 Concluding description, third person	1:30b "And it was so."

The first encounter between God and humans in the Bible entirely lacks elements 2 through 6 and 8 of the *Gattung*, which so aptly articulates Old Testament theophanies. The missing elements are just the ones that assume a condition in which God

---

sovereign's instrument in the battle against chaos in all its manifestations" (p. 110). Batto relates this wind to the wind that Marduk blew into Tiamat (the sea dragon goddess) to defeat her. However, the avian connotations of רחף in Ge 1:2 preclude such an interpretation for Genesis 1:2. Winds do not "hover" over the deep. Batto's interpretation is a good example of the basic hermeneutical flaw that distorts his work: he uses ancient Near Eastern myth-making as the interpretive key for the OT. By contrast I maintain that the OT data reveal the true archetypes and thus aid in our understanding of the ancient Near Eastern mythological distortions of the same.

is not familiar to mortals. When God appears to prelapsarian man or woman, he is on such familiar terms that no naming is mentioned (element 2), nor any responding (element 3).[35] God does not need to identify himself as though he were an unknown phenomenon (element 4). Nor does he need to quell human fear (element 5). Nor do humans query or protest about what God has said (element 8). The same facts are true of Genesis 2:15–17, which has simply an introduction in the third person (element 1, 2:15–16a), and a *hieros logos* (element 7, 2:16b–17).

The absence of these elements in both cases makes two very important points. Before the Fall man and woman had no dread of God, and God was not unfamiliar to them. So much is clear from the literary form in which these two conversations with God have been reported.[36]

Once the man and woman fall into sin a drastic change takes place. The signal of this change comes in the form of a greatly altered theophany. God is no longer simply there. His appearance no longer assumes easy intercourse with them. Rather it comes in a dreadful form—the storm theophany that becomes standard in the Old Testament from this point on. It is the only form in which God can show any of his glory in the Old Testament world—until he appears in a new way and with a new covenant.

GENESIS 3:8

In Genesis 3:8 we read that Adam and Eve "heard the voice of the Lord God walking in the garden," לְרוּחַ הַיּוֹם (author's trans.). This phrase is a long-standing interpretive crux.

---

[35]The point is simply that the absence of these suggests familiarity, even perhaps some degree of intimacy. At least, there is no sign that the man and woman were uncomfortable in God's presence.

[36]The prelapsarian context encourages such an understanding. Later short forms of the *Gattung* appear for other, literary reasons. Cf. chap. 9.

"In the cool of the day" has been the accepted translation among the major modern versions.[37] But they have only followed an interpretive guess made by the ancient versions. For example, LXX reads "in the afternoon/evening" (i.e., the cooler part of the day, τὸ δειλινόν). The Vulgate similarly renders "in the afternoon breeze" (*ad auram post meridiem*). The translation "in the cool/breeze of the day/afternoon" thus represents only a guess interpreters have made through the centuries about the meaning of this unusual Hebrew expression.

However, some Akkadian evidence sheds light on the meaning of the Hebrew. It has been known for some time that the Akkadian word *ūmu(m)* corresponds to the Hebrew יום, "day."[38] But a second *ūmu* in Akkadian means "storm" and appears often in divine epithets.[39] The god Ninurta is referred to as "the great *storm* [*ūmu rabû*],"[40] the god Aššur is called "the angry *storm* [*ūmu nanduru*],"[41] and the god Bel (Enlil) is identified as the storm in a Babylonian text that reads:

> "Mighty Bel whose utterance is unchangeable,
> He, the *storm* [*ūmu*] destroys the stable, tears up the fold."[42]

This Akkadian *ūmu* also appears to have a Hebrew cognate, a second יום that also means "storm." On the basis of Akkadian, Koehler and Baumgartner have noted this second יום, "Wind, Storm," in the Old Testament.[43] Perhaps the most striking case

---

[37]E.g., NKJV, RSV, NASB, NJB, NJV, NIV.
[38]Soden, *Akkadisches Handwörterbuch*, Lieferung 15 [hereafter *AHw*] (Wiesbaden: Harrassowitz, 1979), 1418–20; cf. BDB, 398.
[39]*AHw*, Lieferung 15:1420.
[40]Tallqvist, *Akkadische Götterepitheta*, 104.
[41]Ibid., 104; cf. 478.
[42]K. D. Macmillan, "Some Cuneiform Tablets Bearing on the Religion of Babylonia and Assyria," in F. Delitzsch and P. Haupt, *Beiträge zur Assyriologie* (Leipzig: J. C. Hinrichs, 1906), 540. Cf. 540–41 for another text in which storm and god are identified.
[43]L. Koehler and W. Baumgartner, *Hebräisches und Aramäisches Handwörterbuch zum alten Testament*, neu bearbeitet von W. Baumgartner (Leiden: E. J. Brill, 1974), 384. They are followed by Wm. Holladay, *A Concise Hebrew and Aramaic Lexicon of the Old Testament* (Grand Rapids: Eerdmans: 1971), 131.

they note is Zephaniah 2:2b: כְּמֹץ עָבַר יוֹם. This phrase has generally been translated "[that] day sweeps on like chaff." In light of the Akkadian evidence, a better translation might be "[that] storm sweeps on like chaff."[44]

Akkadian $ūmu^{II}$ is often used with theophanic overtones. What if the same were true of Hebrew יוֹם^{II}, "storm"? Such an interpretation understands the enigmatic phrase לְרוּחַ הַיּוֹם to mean not "in the cool of the day," but "in the wind of the storm."[45] The storm wind is the advancing presence of Yahweh. He advances in terrible theophany, in judgment, just like the gods Ninurta, Aššur, or Bel in the Akkadian literature.[46]

---

[44]I.e., the storm of coming judgment advances quickly, driving all before it like chaff driven by the wind. Alternately, since the other occurrences of יוֹם in vv. 2c, 3, are probably best to be taken as "day," they may constitute יוֹם in 2b a wordplay. In other words the translation "day," would be retained, but the allusion to יוֹם^{II}, "storm," would be understood. W. Rudolph, *Micha-Nahum-Habakuk-Zephanja*, Kommentar zum Alten Testament [hereafter KAT] XIII, part 2 (Gutersloh: Gerd Mohn), 272, rightly notes that the phrase is a parenthesis to the larger warning of impending judgment. For the phrasing in Zephania (כְּמֹץ עָבַר), cf. Ps 1:4, "*like the chaff* which the wind [רוּחַ] drives away." Cf. also Ps 18:12, "Out of the brightness of his presence clouds *advanced* [עָבְרוּ], with hailstones and bolts of lightning."

[45]The preposition לְ is translated "in." Cf. BDB, 511 (2). U. Cassuto, *A Commentary on the Book of Genesis* (Jerusalem: Magnes, 1961), 152ff., reads רוּחַ as cognate to an Arabic and Ugaritic verb (*rḥ*) denoting action that takes place in the afternoon. His suggestion is unlikely; for better alternatives cf. J. Niehaus, "In the Wind of the Storm: Another Look at Genesis iii 8," *VT* 44, no. 2 (April 1994): 263–67, esp. 266–67, n. 9. J. Calvin, *Commentaries on the First Book of Moses Called Genesis* (Edinburgh: Calvin Translation Society, 1847), 1:160–61, understands the phrase to mean a "gentle breeze" at dawn, but he adds, "I do not doubt that some notable symbol of the presence of God was in that gentle breeze . . . which should vehemently affect the minds of our first parents." M. G. Kline, *Images*, 102–6, interprets the phrase הַיּוֹם לְרוּחַ to mean "as the Spirit of the Day (i.e., of judgment)"–cf. לְרוּחַ מִשְׁפָּט, "as the Spirit of judgment," Isa 28:6a. He is correct in seeing Ge 3:8 as a judgment theophany. But, we would argue, the phrase in question is more a description of God's storm theophany than an explicit, early reference to the "Day" of Yahweh.

[46]Cf. Kline, *Kingdom Prologue*, 2:99: "Adapting the mode of his self-revelation to the judicial purpose of his coming, the Lord approached the judgment-site in the awesome glory of his theophanic Presence. So he ever comes

This understanding of יוֹם affects the translation of other terms in the passage. For example, in the context of such a theophany, the קוֹל of Yahweh that the man and woman hear is no longer merely Yahweh's "voice." It is the "thunder" of his stormy presence. It is the same theophanic "thunder" that later atop Horeb/Sinai struck terror into the Israelites: "When the people saw the thunder [הַקּוֹלֹת] and lightning and heard the trumpet and saw the mountain in smoke, they trembled with fear" (Ex 20:18).

This meaning for Hebrew קוֹל in the Old Testament is well established.[47] Ugaritic *ql* has a range of meanings similar to the Hebrew and is also used of Baal theophanies, for example:

qlh.qdš [.] b[ʿl.y]tn	Ba[al gi]ves forth his holy thunder,
ytny.bʿl.ṣ[ʾat.ṣ]pth	Baal repeats the ex[pression of] his [li]ps,
qlh.q[dš ypr]r.ʾarṣ	His ho[ly] thunder [shatt]ers the earth.[48]

The verb הלך (Hith.), which appears in Genesis 3:8 also has theophanic overtones elsewhere in the Old Testament. It is used of the fiery appearance in Ezekiel's vision: "Fire moved back and forth [מִתְהַלֶּכֶת] among the creatures; it was bright, and lightning flashed out of it" (Eze 1:13). It also appears in the Reed Sea theophany of Psalm 77:

> The waters saw you, O God,
> the waters saw you and writhed;
> the very depths were convulsed.

---

on the day of judgment, the day of the Lord, the day of the covenant servants' accounting before the Face of their Lord. It is that kind of fearful advent that is reported in Genesis 3:8, properly translated and interpreted."

[47] Cf. BDB, 877 (2b).

[48] A. Herdner, *Corpus des Tablettes en Cuneiformes Alphabetiques* (Paris, 1963), 29. For thunder as Yahweh's voice, and other Canaanite and Assyrian parallels, cf. O. Betz, THw 9:276, nn. 17, 18, and literature there cited; cf. J. Jeremias, *Theophanie*, 89.

> The clouds poured down water,
> the skies resounded with thunder [קוֹל];
> your arrows flashed back and forth [יִתְהַלָּכוּ].
> Your thunder [קוֹל רַעַמְךָ] was heard in the whirlwind,
> your lightning lit up the world;
> the earth trembled and quaked. (Ps. 77:16–18)

Here as elsewhere, קוֹל, "thunder," is used theophanically. In this passage the Lord's "arrows" are the lightning flashes that accompany his stormy advance across the sea—an advance that shows God's superiority over the waters and also introduces God's judgment of Pharaoh's effort to recapture Israel.

These Hebrew terms come together to describe the awesome theophany of Yahweh in Genesis 3:8: "Then the man and his wife heard the thunder [קוֹל] of Yahweh God going back and forth [מִתְהַלֵּךְ] in the garden in the wind of the storm [לְרוּחַ הַיּוֹם], and they hid from Yahweh God among the trees of the garden (author's trans.)."

Man and woman are now in a fallen condition and can have only one reaction to the inbreaking of God's glory: they hide out of fear. Adam attributes his fear to his nakedness but perhaps also to the thunder of God's advance: "I heard you in the garden, and I was afraid because I was naked" (Ge 3:10). Adam is indeed both physically and spiritually naked—or perhaps better, exposed.[49] Exposed in all his sinfulness, he cowers before a holy God.[50] Such fear or dread of the holy is henceforth a characteristic of human response in the Old Testament to all theophanies that actually involve the glory of God.

---

[49]BDB, 735.

[50]Cf. Kline, *Kingdom Prologue*, 2:99: "Trumpeting the advent of the divine Presence—at Sinai, at Pentecost, at the parousia of Jesus, at every day of the Lord—is the fearful sound of the voice of the Lord, the thunderclap of the approaching theophanic storm-chariot. It was precisely by this arresting signal that the primal parousia was heralded. Alarmed by this sound of God's coming (v. 8a), the man and his wife sought escape."

THE "GOD OF GLORY" AND THE NOAHIC FLOOD

How did Yahweh appear in the biblical account of the Flood? Did he actually "appear" in a theophanic sense? Certainly God spoke to Noah—warning him of the Flood and instructing him about the ark (Ge 6:13–21). He commanded Noah and his family to enter the ark (7:1–4), and he told Noah when his family and the animals might leave the ark (8:15–17). But it seems that Yahweh's words to Noah did not occur in a theophany. Certainly there was no account of God's glory manifesting itself before Noah. None of the passages states that Yahweh appeared to Noah in any form. Perhaps it is best to take these accounts at face value as words from Yahweh to Noah (*hieroi logoi* in that sense) heard externally or internally—yet not as theophanies.[51]

The Old Testament does teach, however, that Yahweh was gloriously present at the Flood. The storm clouds that play such an important role in that judgment event carry connotations of theophany. Mendenhall has said of the Flood story at Genesis 9:14, "The translation, 'When I bring clouds over the earth . . . ,' is completely inadequate, since it does not convey the sense that the ᶜānān is first and foremost a theophany in the form of a storm-cloud."[52] Kline likewise suggests that "the

---

[51] Kline, ibid., observes that the statement in Ge 7:16b that Yahweh closed the door of the ark after Noah had entered points to some sort of theophany. But it is not clear that God actually appeared in any way at that moment, nor how he "shut him in."

[52] Mendenhall, *Tenth Generation*, 57, n. 58. He goes on to say, "Of course, whether that was still known at the time the present language was fixed is another matter. In light of later uses, it is quite possible that the writer no longer was aware of the original connotations or denotation of the word." The same may hold true of the meaning of יוֹם in Ge 3:8. However, Mendenhall's reservations in this case depend upon his acceptance of documentary results for the analysis and dating of the Flood narrative. The term עָנָן appears in Yahweh theophany at Ex 13:21; 19:9; et al.—that is, in theophanic contexts well within Moses' experience. If Moses penned the Flood narrative, he

thundering storm clouds of the flood may themselves be regarded as an extended manifestation of the Glory-cloud of the Lord God, riding over the earth in judgment."[53] The same term, of course, is used later in theophany, for example, of God's appearance during the Exodus and wilderness wanderings. Kline's explanation may especially remind us of the extended cloud and storm judgment theophany of Ezekiel 1.

The most dramatic expression of Yahweh's storm presence at the Flood is perhaps to be found in Psalm 29. Kline comments, "The psalmist evidently perceived the royal Glory-presence in the phenomena of the flood."[54] Before we study Psalm 29 in its own right, however, it is important to note the ancient Near Eastern background according to which a flood can be a judgment instrument. Such passages in Babylonian and Assyrian hark back to Mesopotamian echoes of the Deluge as a cosmic event.[55] The Gilgamesh Epic declares that "the gods decided to make the Deluge [*abūbu*]" to eliminate humanity.[56] Narām-Sin (2249–2213 B.C.) boasts that he "made the land of Akkad [look] like [after] the Deluge of water that happened at an early time of mankind."[57] Later theophanic Adad is called upon to send destructive floods against those who break covenant with or otherwise resist Assyria.[58]

A fascinating echo of Yahweh's presence at the Flood may occur in the *Enuma Elish*. Tablet IV portrays Marduk as he arms himself for combat against Tiamat the sea dragon goddess:

39 He placed the lightning before him;
40 With a burning flame he filled his body.

---

most likely would have used the term with understanding of its theophanic overtones.

[53]Kline, *Kingdom Prologue*, 2:99; cf. *Images*, 101.
[54]Ibid. Kline goes on to suggest a connection between the theophanic portrayal of the "Glory-Spirit" (רוּחַ) at Ge 1:2 and the "wind" (רוּחַ) at Ge 8:1.
[55]Cf. *CAD*, vol. 1, A, pt. 1, pp. 77–80 (*abūbu* 1–3).
[56]Ibid., vol. 1, A, pt. 1, p. 77 (*abūbu* 1.a).
[57]Ibid., vol. 1, A pt. 1, p. 77 (*abūbu* 1.a).
[58]See above, chap. 4.

....
47 The winds which he had made—the Seven—he set loose,
48 To destroy the heart of Tiamat they rose up behind him.
49 The Lord raised up the flood, his mighty weapon,
50 The storm chariot irresistible and terrible he mounted.
....
58 [With] a frightful halo covering his head,
59 The Lord went forth and followed his course,
60 Toward the enraged Tiamat he set his face.[59]

The parallels to Yahweh theophany are remarkable. Like Yahweh, Marduk comes with "lightning" and "winds" (a perfect number of them—seven). He mounts a "storm chariot" (*narkabta ūmu*—cf. on *ūmu*, above), and has "a frightful halo" (*melammu*; cf. discussion, chap. 4). Most fascinating perhaps is that "the Lord raised up the flood [*abūbu*], his mighty weapon," to bring judgment upon insubordinate Tiamat—who is herself a sea dragon goddess! So he brings a flood and is triumphant over a flood (dragon). One may compare Psalm 29, which portrays Yahweh who brought the Flood (*mabbūl*; cf. Akk. *abūbu*)[60] as judgment weapon but who is also seated above the Flood in triumphant glory.

The Marduk passage forms but one ancient example of flood imagery in divine judgment passages. The use of divine flood as a judgment instrument against rebels—be they gods or mortals—thus seems well-established in the world of the Bible. Psalm 29 appears to be an echo of the same.

---

[59]Cf. Mann, *Divine Presence*, 48–49.

[60]Hebrew *mabbūl* and Akkadian *abūbu* have similar semantic fields but are not cognates, despite their apparent similarity. Cf. Wm. F. Albright, "The-Babylonian Matter in the Predeuteronomic Primeval History (JE) in Gen 1–11," *JBL* 58, pt. 2 (June 1939): 98. KB, 491, derives מַבּוּל from נָבֵל.

Psalm 29 holds an unusual place in the Psalter, not least because of the history of criticism regarding it. H. L. Ginsberg first suggested in 1935 that the hymn might be Phoenician.[61] He argued that the emphasis on Yahweh's "voice" (קוֹל) showed that the poem was originally about the storm god Baal (= Mesopotamian Adad). The presence of Phoenician toponymy (e.g, "Sirion," the Phoenician name for Mount Hermon in v. 6) also argued for a Phoenician provenance. Eleven years later T. H. Gaster adopted and furthered this line of argument.[62] F. M. Cross, in an article on the psalm three years later, believed that Ginsberg had presented "conclusive evidence" that Psalm 29 was a Canaanite Baal hymn.[63] According to Cross, Psalm 29 now took on "rare new importance for the analysis of Canaanite prosodic canons and their influence on Israelite psalmody."[64] Mitchell Dahood in his *Psalms* commentary took a similar view.[65] And, more recently, Cross has reiterated this idea in a discussion that compares Yahweh and Baal theophanies.[66] Such is a brief history of what one may call the "Canaanite hypothesis."

Peter Craigie has pointed out that there are serious objections of genre and content to this hypothesis, as well as problems in the areas of chronology and geography.[67] In fact, the hypothesis appeared at a time when a comparative appreciation of storm theophany language in the ancient Near East was still relatively lacking. It may not be unreasonable to say

---

[61] H. L. Ginsberg, "A Phoenician Hymn in the Psalter," *XIX Congresso Internazionale degli Orientalisti* (Rome, 1935), 472–76; cf. H. L. Ginsberg, "The Rebellion and Death of Baʿlu," *Orientalia* 5 (1936): 108ff.

[62] T. H. Gaster, "Psalm 29," *JQR* 37 (1946–47): 55–65.

[63] F. M. Cross, "Notes on a Canaanite Psalm in the Old Testament," *BASOR* 117 (1950): 19–21.

[64] Ibid., 19.

[65] M. Dahood, *Psalms I,* Anchor Bible (New York: Doubleday,1966), 175ff.

[66] F. M. Cross, *CMHE,* 151–56. Cross maintains that Psalm 29 is "an ancient Baʿal hymn, only slightly modified for use in the early cultus of Yahweh" (p. 152).

[67] P. C. Craigie, *Psalms 1–50* WBC (Waco: Word, 1983), 244ff.

that, had the hypothesis not been suggested, no one would dream of putting it forward today. One might fairly say the same of the Documentary Hypothesis. However, like the Documentary Hypothesis, the "Canaanite Hypothesis" has developed into a tradition that may only reluctantly (if at all) be abandoned by its advocates.

Yet a search for literary parallels between the ancient Near East and the Old Testament may often be fruitful, and so it is in this case. Craigie says the parallels between Baal storm theophany language and the language of Psalm 29 are sufficient "to require some kind of interpretation of the psalm which takes into account the Canaanite/Ugaritic background," without requiring "that the psalm be treated, in its original form, as a Canaanite or Phoenician hymn."[68]

The psalm is an appropriate object of study at this point not only because of the Sinaitic characteristics of the theophany it describes, but also because it alludes to the Flood. The poem reads:

1   Ascribe to Yahweh, sons of El,[69]
    ascribe to Yahweh *glory and might* [כָּבוֹד וָעֹז].

2   Ascribe to Yahweh [the] *glory* [כְּבוֹד][due] his Name,
    bow down to Yahweh who appears[70] in holiness!

3   The *voice* [קוֹל] of Yahweh is above the waters,
    the God of *glory* [כָּבוֹד] *thunders* [הִרְעִים],
    Yahweh is above the mighty waters.

---

[68]Ibid., 244.

[69]D. N. Freedman suggests original *'Eli-m* (El with enclitic mi/a) as the *Vorlage* for MT's אֵלִים ("[the] gods"); cf. Cross, *CMHE*, 152, n. 25. Cf. similarly Dahood, *Psalms 1–50*, 175, n. 1.

[70]For הדרת meaning "apparition, divine visitation," cf. A. Herdner, *Corpus des tablettes en cunéiformes alphabétiques découvertes à Ras Shamra–Ugarit de 1929 à 1939* [hereafter *CTA*] (Paris: Imprimerie Nationale, 1963), 14.3.155:
   krt.yht.whlm   Keret awoke, and [it was] a dream
   ᶜ*bd.il.whdrt*   the servant of El, and [it was] a *visitation*
Cf. Cross, *CMHE*, 152, n. 28.

PRE-SINAI THEOPHANIES

4   The *voice* [קוֹל] of Yahweh in power,
    the *voice* [קוֹל] of Yahweh in *splendor* [הָדָר]!

5   The *voice* [קוֹל] of Yahweh splinters the cedars,
    Yahweh shatters the cedars of the Lebanon!

6   He makes Lebanon skip like a calf,
    and Sirion like a young wild ox.

7   The *voice* [קוֹל] of Yahweh strikes [with] flaming fire
    [לַהֲבוֹת אֵשׁ].

8   The *voice* [קוֹל] of Yahweh makes the desert writhe,
    Yahweh makes the desert of Kadesh[71] writhe.

9   The *voice* [קוֹל] of Yahweh makes the hinds calve.[72]
    He strips the forests bare,
    and in his temple [his] *glory* [כָּבוֹד] appears.[73]

10 Yahweh sat[74] enthroned above the Flood,
    Yahweh sits enthroned as King forever.

11 Yahweh will give strength to his people,
    Yahweh will bless his people with peace.

The presence of elements of Sinaitic theophany is readily apparent. The "glory" of Yahweh that appears at Sinai recurs in verses 1, 2, 3, and 9. The "fire" of Sinaitic theophany is also present (v. 7). The "voice," i.e., "thunder" of Yahweh (קוֹל), so significant at Sinai, is not only prevalent—it contributes in a major way to the structure of the poem, as a simple diagram illustrates:

---

[71]Or perhaps "the holy desert," with Cross, *CMHE*, 154 and n. 37.
[72]Lit., "writhe" (in giving birth).
[73]MT וּבְהֵיכָלוֹ כֻּלּוֹ אֹמֵר כָּבוֹד ("and in his temple all of it is saying glory") is awkward to say the least. We take כֻּלּוֹ as dittography, and אֹמֵר as meaning "to see," stative-passive "to appear," after M. Dahood, "Hebrew-Ugaritic Lexicography I," *Biblica*, 44 (1963): 295ff.
[74]For the translation of יָשַׁב as perfect, cf. F. Delitzsch, *Psalms*, Commentary on the Old Testament, vol. 5 (Grand Rapids: Eerdmans, 1976), 373.

1	הבו	הבו	bicolon
2	השתחוו	הבו	bicolon
3	קול	קול	tricolon
4	קול		bicolon
5	קול		bicolon
6	Hinge verse		bicolon
7	קול		monocolon
8	קול		bicolon
9	קול		tricolon
10	יהוה	יהוה	bicolon
11	יהוה	יהוה	bicolon

The poem has a remarkably symmetrical structure. It opens with two bicola and closes with two bicola. In each pair of bicola a key term is repeated three or four times: "Ascribe" (הבו) at the opening (three times, plus the parallel "bow down"), and "Yahweh" at the end (four times). Just after the first two bicola comes a tricolon; reflecting this, a tricolon comes just before the last two bicola. And a pervasive symmetrical structure is accomplished by the repeated "voice" (קול) of Yahweh.[75]

The poem opens with a call to praise (vv. 1–2) typical of the hymn. The summons is to the "sons of El" apparently meaning the angels, elsewhere called the "sons of Elohim."[76] They are called upon to ascribe glory to Yahweh.

---

[75] The word is repeated seven times, the biblical number of perfection. For the Psalm's reflection of the motif of the seven thunders, attributed to Baal in a Ugaritic text, cf. J. Day, "Echoes of Baal's Seven Thunders and Lightnings in Psalm XXIX and Habakkuk III 9 and the Identity of the Seraphim in Isaiah VI," *VT* 29 (1979): 143ff.

[76] The very phrase "sons of El" might further indicate a Canaanite connection for the poem. Cf. Gibson, *Canaanite Myths and Legends*, 41 (2.i.20–21):

> The gods also had sat down to eat,
> the sons of the Holy one [*bn qdš*] to dine,
> [and] Baal was standing by *El.*

The Ugaritic gods were conceived of as the "sons of El," the "Holy one." Cf.

The body of the poem (vv. 3–9) gives the reasons for such praise, again typical of the hymn *Gattung*. The motivation for praise is twofold. It is partly a roll call of theophanic qualities: in verses 3–4 and 7, Yahweh's *voice/thunder* (קוֹל) in *splendor* (הָדָר), his *glory* (כָּבוֹד), the way he *thunders* (הִרְעִים), e.g., above the mighty waters, and the way his voice strikes with "flaming fire" (לַהֲבוֹת אֵשׁ). The second motive for praise is the awesome effect that Yahweh's coming has on nature: in verses 5–6 and 8–9, Yahweh makes Lebanon "skip like a calf," and his thunderous voice shatters the cedars of Lebanon, makes the desert writhe, and strips the forests bare. His glory appears in his temple, and this is not only a motive for praise but also a transitional statement to the poem's conclusion.

The conclusion celebrates Yahweh in two ways. It extols him as King and sees him as a suzerain who will bless his people and give them peace.

The psalm portrays Yahweh as King (v. 10b), and this praise seems established by the fact that he "sat enthroned above the Flood" (author's trans.). The word here translated "Flood" (מַבּוּל) occurs elsewhere only to describe the Noahic "Flood" (Ge 6:17 et al.).[77] Most commentators have understood the word to have this meaning and make this historical reference.[78]

---

p. 58 (4.iii.14): "the assembly of the sons of El/the gods (*bn. 'ilm*)." The meaning could be "Sons of El" or "sons of the gods," depending on whether *'ilm* stands for "gods" or "El" with enclitic *m*.

[77]Cf. BDB, 550.

[78]E.g., Delitzsch, *Psalms,* 373; A. Maclaren, *The Psalms* (London: Hodder & Stoughton, 1894), 1:278; C. A. Augustus and E. G. Briggs, *The Book of Psalms,* ICC (New York: Scribners, 1906), 1:254–55; D. Kidner, *Psalms 1–72* (Leicester: Tyndale, 1973), 127; Craigie, *Psalms 1–50,* 249. Cross, *CMHE,* 155–56, translates "Flooddragon," but this is part of his effort to see the poem as a progressive victory hymn in which the "Divine Warrior" triumphs over "Sea or the flood-dragon" after the pattern of Ugaritic mythology. Dahood, *Psalms I,* 180, had earlier made the same identification: "The psalmist alludes not to the Flood in the days of Noah, but to the motif of the struggle between Baal, lord of the air and genius of the rain, and Yamm, master of sea and subterranean waters." M. K. Wakeman, *God's Battle With the Monster* (Leiden: E. J. Brill, 1973), 101, sees Yahweh's enthronement over the flood as parallel

The statement that Yahweh "sat enthroned above the Flood" appears to reflect the assertion earlier, in verse 3, that "the thunderous voice of Yahweh is above the *waters*, the God of glory thunders, Yahweh is above the *mighty waters*." Such language reflects the ancient Canaanite concept that Baal, the sky god whose rain brought fecundity and blessing (cf. v. 9, "The *voice/thunder* of Yahweh makes the hinds calve"), was superior to and victorious over Yam, the chaotic sea god who harbored the seven-headed monster, Leviathan, and who may have counted the god of death, Mot, among his allies.[79] Against such a background, Craigie is right to suggest that "in Ps 29:3, the Lord is described not merely as a deity whose thunderous voice is heard, but as one victorious over the chaotic forces symbolized by the 'mighty waters.'"[80] Craigie notes that the su-

---

to El's enthronement amid the channels of the deep and to the Babylonian god Ea's enthronement above Apsu (the subterranean waters that feed the springs and rivers). She hardly makes a case for understanding this flood to be the cosmic flood or world-surrounding heavenly ocean. Hebrew *mabbûl* appears to be used only of the Flood (cf. BDB, 550) and plays no role in the parallelisms from Hebrew and Ugaritic that she cites (all involving *yām*, *tehom*, and *šāmayim*, pp. 100–102). (Cf., however, KB, 491, which also construes *mabbûl* here and in Ge 6:17; 7:6, 7, 10, 17 as the "Himmelsozean.")

[79]Cf. *CTA* 5.1.1–8, in which Mot says to Baal, "Because you smote Lītānu the slippery serpent, [and] made an end of the wriggling serpent, the tyrant with seven heads . . . I myself will crush you in pieces; . . . you must come down into the throat of divine Mot." Translations vary, especially of initial *k* (= Heb. כִּ, translated "Because" above). So *ANET*, 138, "If thou smite Lotan"; A. Caquot, M. Sznycer, and A. Herdner, *Textes Ougaritiques*, Tome 1, *Mythes et Legendes* (Paris: Éditions du Cerf, 1974), 239, "Quand tu frappes Lotan"; Gibson, *Canaanite Myths and Legends,* 68, "for all that you smote Leviathan"; and, in his more popular edition, M. D. Coogan, *Stories from Ancient Canaan* (Philadelphia: Westminster, 1978), 106, "When you killed Lotan." For Ugaritic "Lotan/Lītānu" and Hebrew "Leviathan" (cf. Ps 74:15; Isa 27:1; et al.) see above, chap. 4.

[80]Craigie, *Psalms 1–50*, 247. An older school of thought said that the waters were "the sea of waters floating above the earth in the sky [i.e., the storm clouds]" (Delitzsch, *Psalms*, 370); so also A. F. Kirkpatrick, *The Psalms I–XLI*, Book 1 (Cambridge: Cambridge University Press, 1891), 149: "Hardly the sea . . . but rather the waters collected in the dense masses of storm cloud upon which Jehovah rides." Likewise Maclaren, *Psalms,* 275: "It is better to

periority of Yahweh over the waters was illustrated in the "Song of the Sea."[81] In fact, Psalm 77:20(19) says that Yahweh's path through the Sea of Reeds led "through the mighty waters." Yet the phrase "mighty waters" may also be used of any distress that threatens a godly man (e.g., Ps. 32:6, "At a time of distress, in the rush of mighty waters, they shall not reach him"). In fact, the phrase has a variety of uses in the Old Testament—although the connotation of chaotic forces, with its Canaanite mythological background, predominates.[82] Moreover, as May has noted, Yahweh's superiority over the waters is an important factor in the Creation account of Genesis 1.[83] Yahweh's supremacy over the waters at Creation implies his ongoing supremacy over all waters—and all forces of chaos.

It appears, then, that the "waters" and "mighty waters" of verse 3 allude ultimately back to the watery chaos of Creation and subsequently to other watery threats such as the Reed Sea. If so, the poem's closing allusion to the Flood makes perfect sense. Yahweh at Creation was supreme as he brought order out of watery chaos. But he also sat enthroned above the Flood, which reintroduced primordial chaos as God uncreated the world he had made. In a creative act parallel to God's original Creation, God then caused a new world to emerge from the chaotic waters of the Flood and placed upon it a new humanity—Noah and his family. And God solemnized this act of "new Creation" by establishing a *re-*Creation covenant with Noah (cf. Ge 9:9), which had significant commands and mandates parallel to those of the original Creation covenant (Ge 9:1 // 1:28a; 9:2 // 1:28b; 9:3 // 1:29; and cf. 9:6b // 1:27).

---

take the expression as referring to the super-terrestrial reservoirs or the rain flood stored up in the thunder-clouds." More recently cf. Wakeman, *God's Battle*, 101.

[81] Ibid., 247.

[82] For a fuller discussion of the various uses and implications of this phrase, cf. H. G. May, "Some Cosmic Connotations of *Mayim Rabbim*, 'Many Waters,'" *JBL* 74 (1955): 9–21.

[83] Ibid., 11–12.

Since the poem portrays Yahweh as both Creator God and God of judgment (the Flood), it can also portray him summarily as absolute monarch: "Yahweh sits enthroned as King forever" (v. 10b).[84]

Because Yahweh can be extolled as Suzerain, the second celebration is also possible—namely, that "Yahweh will give strength to his people, Yahweh will bless his people with peace" (v. 11). The God who has "glory and might" (v. 1) as personal attributes can also impart strength to his people. The God whose theophanic glory was superior over chaos at Creation and enables him to be universal Judge over chaotic forces today can assuredly grant his people peace.

Theophany in Psalm 29, therefore, appears to unify and even structure the poem. Moreover, any theological import the poem has is grounded in the theophany it portrays. For it is the theophany that ties together the Creation and the Flood: God appears in holy glory, in effect, as both Creator and Judge.[85]

The statement that "Yahweh sat enthroned above the Flood" does not mean that he appeared that way to Noah. It asserts rather that the Flood was caused by Yahweh's glorious act. In other words Yahweh—"the God of glory"—thundered. But the poem is more than just theological reflection. It extols the God who actually came into history and brought judgment with him (just as Baal was said to have done by Canaanites).[86]

---

[84]For the relation between God as Creator and God as King, see above, chap. 3.

[85]Maclaren, *Psalms,* 275, sees eschatological implications in the theophanic portrayal: "Seven times 'the voice of Jehovah' is heard, like the apocalyptic 'seven thunders before the throne.'"

[86]Cf. the comparison of Pharaoh Akhenaton to Haddu (i.e., Baal) in a letter from the vassal Abdimilki of Tyre: "who utters his thunderous voice [*rigmašu*] in the heavens like Haddu so that the whole land shakes at his his thunderous voice [*rigmašu*],"Knudtzon, *EA,* 147.13–15.

If Psalm 29 connects the Creation and the Flood, it is no accident. God made a covenant at Creation. Adam and Eve broke that covenant. As we have seen, God was committed to restore his vassals and their kingdom. Typologically God made that restoration as he dealt with Noah and Noah's world. God destroyed the old world and made a new one. He destroyed the old humanity and began again with Noah and his family. And God made a new, re-Creation covenant with the new man. In this sense Dumbrell is right in calling Noah a "second Adam."[87] But the new man was really still only an old man. The true new Man–the Son of God–would come later. And with him–and because of him–would come the new humanity and ultimately the new heavens and new earth implied in the Creation covenant.

The same glorious presence that fashioned Creation (cf. laconically Ge 1:2) also fashioned the Flood. When that presence appeared to Adam and Eve after their sin, it was a terrible, stormy presence. Adam heard the awesome "thunderous voice" (קוֹל) of Yahweh–his thunder in theophany–and he hid. That same "thunderous voice" appears in Psalm 29 as the predominant theophanic characteristic of Yahweh who sat enthroned above the Flood. Since the Flood was a judicial event, the poem's theological commentary on the Flood is that Yahweh's glorious, theophanic presence in Noah's day brought judgment. Likewise God's theophanic entrance into the garden of Eden brought judgment for his disobedient vassals Adam and Eve. But not all Sinaitic Yahweh (storm) theophanies bring instant judgment. Genesis 15 portrays such a theophany in a ceremony full of promise.

---

[87]Dumbrell, *Covenant and Creation*, 27.

GENESIS 15—A FLAMING TORCH AND A PROMISE OF SALVATION

Genesis 15 is a complex chapter and may be approached form critically in more ways than one. As noted earlier, the chapter contains four sections that fall nicely into the theophanic *Gattung*.[88] Two of these sections are of special importance as they relate to the passage's Sinaitic theophany: 15:12–16, and 15:17–21. Both illustrate the *Gattung* in a simple form:

	Formal Element	Genesis 15:12–16
1	Introductory description, third person	15:12–13a
7	*Hieros logos*	15:13b–16

The pericope lacks God's self-asseveration (element 4), because that has already occurred at 15:1, 7. It does contain the descent of a "deep sleep" upon Abram into which Yahweh speaks and also—most importantly—appears.

The Hebrew word for Abram's sleep is תַּרְדֵּמָה and is used in the Old Testament in two senses. It can mean a deep but natural sleep: "Slothfulness casts into a *deep sleep* / And an idle person will suffer hunger" (Pr 19:15, author's trans.). But usually it means a deep supernatural sleep: "So Yahweh God caused the man to fall into a *deep sleep*" (Ge 2:21); "[all of Saul's men were] sleeping, because Yahweh had put them into a *deep sleep*" (1Sa 26:12); "Yahweh has brought over you [prophets and seers] a *deep sleep*" (Isa 29:10); and in Job it portrays a time when visions occur to sleepers (Job 4:13; 33:15). The predominant usage of the word suggests that Abram's sleep also is a supernaturally induced "deep sleep." In any case, it is no or-

---

[88]The sections are 15:1–6; 15:7–11; 15:12–16; and 15:17–18. See above, chap. 1.

PRE-SINAI THEOPHANIES

dinary slumber, for as Abram sleeps Yahweh not only speaks to him but also appears.

Before God appears he makes several promises. God's *hieros logos* contains the promise that Abram's descendants will be "strangers in a country not their own" for four hundred years and will return in the fourth generation, at which time Yahweh will punish the land where they sojourn and will also use them to judge the Amorites. Abram himself will live to a "good old age" and die in peace. These are not just promises as one man might make a "promise" to another. They are covenant promises made by a great Suzerain as the theophanic action of God makes clear:

Formal Element		Genesis 15:17–18
1 Introductory description, third person	15:17–18a	
	15:17	Sinaitic theophany
	15:18a	Yahweh makes a covenant with Abram
7 *Hieros logos*	15:18b–21	Yahweh grants land to Abram's seed

The passage contains a key covenant term, Hebrew בְּרִית ("covenant," 15:18). It is the standard Old Testament term for Yahweh's relation with his people. That covenant takes the literary/legal form of a Hittite suzerain-vassal treaty in Deuteronomy especially, but also in the Decalogue. The word itself is attested in some Egyptian contracts as a loan word from Canaan, and in the Ugaritic phrase, '*il brt*–"god of covenant" (like אֵל בְּרִית, Jdg 9:46; cf. בַּעַל בְּרִית, Jdg 8:33; 9:4).[89] Such ev-

---

[89]K. A. Kitchen, "Egypt, Ugarit, Qatna and Covenant," *Ugarit-Forschungen*, Band 11 (Neukirchen-Vluyn: Neukirchener Verlag, 1979), 453–64.

idence makes it quite clear that the term was current in the second millennium despite the contrary contention of some scholars who would use terminological evidence to date Deuteronomy to the seventh century B.C.[90]

Genesis 15 has other elements that show its covenantal nature. Yahweh announces himself in 15:7 according to a standard covenant form: "I am Yahweh, who brought you out of Ur of the Chaldeans." This self-asseveration actually consists of two parts: a royal title ("I am Yahweh"), and a historical prologue ("who brought you out from Ur of the Chaldeans").[91] The same two introductory covenant elements occur at Exodus 20:2 // Deuteronomy 5:6 in the introduction to the Decalogue, which has a similar covenant structure: "I am Yahweh your God" (royal title), "who brought you out of Egypt, out of the land of slavery" (historical prologue). As Kline[92] and Kitchen[93] have shown, the historical prologue (along with other form-critical data) helps to date the covenant. Historical prologues were a standard part of second millennium international treaties but were completely lacking in first-millennium treaties.[94]

If Genesis 15 contains a covenant or treaty, what sort of covenant is it? Moshe Weinfeld has argued,[95] and Gordon Wenham agreed,[96] that the nearest parallel to the covenant form of Genesis 15 is the royal land grant typically made by a king (here, Yahweh) to a man and his descendants (here Abram and his offspring) in perpetuity. The Abrahamic grant promises clearly specified territory (Ge 15:18–21), and this

---

[90] E.g., M. Weinfeld, *Deuteronomy and the Deuteronomic School*, 59ff.
[91] Cf. discussion above at Ge 1.
[92] M. Kline, *Treaty of the Great King*, 27ff.
[93] K. A. Kitchen, *Ancient Orient and Old Testament*, 90–102.
[94] As even Weinfeld admits, *Deuteronomy*, 67.
[95] M. Weinfeld, "The Covenant of Grant in the Old Testament and in the Ancient Near East," *JAOS* 90 (1970), 184, 203.
[96] G. Wenham, *Genesis 1–15* (Waco: Word, 1987), 333.

specificity was an important part of ancient Near Eastern land grants.

But there may be an even more appropriate parallel to the Abrahamic grant in the assertions of ancient kings that their gods granted them specific lands and peoples to conquer. For example, the Assyrian king Tukulti-Ninurta I (1244–1208) made the following claim in his annals:

> At that time, from Tulsina [and] Mount Lashqu, [the region] between the city Shasila [and] the city Mashhat-sharri on the opposite bank of the lower Zab, from Mount Zuqushku [and] Mount Lallar–the district of the extensive land of the Qutu–the entire land of the Lullumu, the land of the Pahpu to the land Kadmuhu [and] all the land of the Shubaru, the entirety of Mount Kashiyari to the border of Nairi [*and*] the border of the land M[akan], to the Euphrates–those regions the great gods allotted to me. All [my] enemies [I brought] under one command.[97]

Such a parallel seems even more appropriate than the royal land grant cited by Weinfeld and Wenham for two reasons. First, it is from a god to a man, as in the case of Yahweh and Abram. Second, it involves conquest, as does the Abrahamic grant (cf. 15:16). If, therefore, God's promise to Abram has a background in ancient Near Eastern land grants as Weinfeld and Wenham argue, it also appears to have a background in the claims of royalty that their gods had granted them lands to possess. The claim in Abram's case is certainly royal in extent. Stretching from the Nile to the Euphrates, it described an imperium rivaling that of Assyria at its height. Only during Solomon's reign do the boundaries of the kingdom seem to have reached the limits (1Ki 5:1 [4:21]), which Yahweh here promises to Abram.

---

[97]E. Weidner, *AfO* 12, 4–5 (IV.25–36). Cf. A. K. Grayson, *ARI*, 1:104 (1.694).

God's promise of land to Abram apparently has two ancient Near Eastern types of "land grant" as a background. But that does not explain the use of covenant animals in the account. Surely a most peculiar thing about Genesis 15 is Yahweh's passage between the animals that Abram has cut up (Ge 15:10). However, such animal rituals are typical of suzerain-vassal treaties. They are used here because, in addition to being a royal land grant, this covenant is a suzerain-vassal treaty between Yahweh and Abram. Such a treaty in the ancient world involved just such a ritual for its ratification.

In those treaties animals were cut up, and the vassal king was required to walk between the parts of the animals. The symbolism was as follows: If the vassal king breaks covenant, may the same fate befall him as befell those animals. The Assyrians took this literally. So Ashurbanipal says of a rebellious vassal named Dunanu, "In Nineveh they [i.e., Ashurbanipal's men] threw Dunanu on a skinning-table and slaughtered him like a lamb."[98] Yahweh also took the ritual literally, as we read later in Israel's history:

> The men who have violated my covenant and have not fulfilled the terms of the covenant they made before me, I will treat like the calf they cut in two and then walked between its pieces. The leaders of Judah and Jerusalem, the court officials, the priests and all the people of the land who walked between the pieces of the calf, I will hand over to their enemies who seek their lives. Their dead bodies will become food for the birds of the air and the beasts of the earth. (Jer 34:18–20)

The fate that awaited a rebellious vassal in the ancient Near East was hardly to be desired. But the astounding fact of Genesis 15—once the covenant ritual is understood—is that Yahweh and not Abram passed between the cut-up pieces. The Suzerain and not the vassal made that dreadful passage. The

---

[98] A. C. Piepkorn, *HPIA,* 74–75 (vi.87–89).

roles are thus in a sense reversed. According to Yahweh's covenant with Abram, it is Yahweh the Suzerain and not Abram the vassal who will bear the punishment for any future transgression of this covenant. Against the ancient Near Eastern background, it is therefore apparent that Gerhard Hasel is mistaken in thinking that the author of Genesis would not have applied the imprecatory significance of this ritual to the participants.[99] In Abram's world the symbolism of Yahweh's passage between the animals spoke for itself. It was clearly an act of self-imprecation. Nor does Gordon Wenham's approach to the ritual leave us with an adequate understanding of it. Wenham takes the passage as a symbolic illustration of Israel's future, in which the animals represent Israel, the birds the nations, and the passage as a whole the protection given to Israel by the Abrahamic covenant.[100] Dumbrell adds little to Wenham's analysis but does note that "in any case, no undertaking is exacted from Abram; God alone is bound."[101] But God is more than bound. If the self-imprecatory aspect of the rite is allowed—as it apparently must be on the ancient Near Eastern evidence—the way is cleared for a proper biblical theological understanding of the pericope. It becomes apparent that—as Kline has argued—the passage of Yahweh's theophanic glory

---

[99] G. Hasel, "The Meaning of the Animal Rite in Gen. 15," *JSOT* 19 (1981): 70.

[100] G. Wenham, "The Symbolism of the Animal Rite in Gen. 15: A Response to G. F. Hasel," *JSOT* 19 (1981): 61–78; *JSOT* 22 (1982), 134–37.

[101] Dumbrell, *Covenant and Creation,* 49.

[102] Kline, *Kingdom Prologue,* 3:39–40, notes that "though the Lord would not undergo the curse of the Genesis 15 oath-ritual as a covenant-breaker," he would still suffer it to sustain the covenant: "that suffering Savior is the Lord of Glory." He further sees the circumstances of the oath ceremony as presaging the sacrificial sufferings of Christ: "the darkness, the sword's violence, the broken flesh, accursed death, abandonment. God's oath-passage was a commitment to the death-passage of Jesus in the gloom of Golgotha. It was a covenant to walk the way of the cross" (p. 40). Kline seems to be the only biblical scholar who has understood this aspect of the pericope.

between those animals foreshadows the cross of Christ, who took on himself the punishment for all covenant infractions of the "sons of Abraham" (cf. Gal 3:29).[102]

Yet more: the animals used in this particular ritual (calf, goat, ram, dove, turtledove) are one of every type that could be used for sacrifice, according to the Torah.[103] This is appropriate for two reasons: It anticipates the requirements of the Law; and since Yahweh walks between them, it anticipates Jesus' fulfillment of the Law—his perfect sacrifice (like a sacrifice of all the possible animals) for our sin.[104]

SUMMARY REMARKS

We have looked at the three pre-Sinai theophanies that have Sinaitic characteristics and have found that each one takes place in a covenantal context. Genesis 3:8 portrays Yahweh's coming in theophanic judgment after Adam and Eve break the Creation covenant. Psalm 29 portrays Yahweh as the God of glory who thundered theophanically at the Flood and sat enthroned above it. As we saw, the psalm is not merely a literary or theological retrospective, but an explication of the fact that Yahweh was theophanically active in history as Judge at the Flood. Mendenhall and Kline have even suggested that the storm clouds of the Flood episode may be understood as an extension of Yahweh's glory cloud as he rode in judgment over the earth. Finally, Yahweh appeared in fire and cloud to cut a covenant with Abram in Genesis 15. It may even be, as Kline

---

[103]Cf. C. F. Keil and F. Delitzsch, *The Pentateuch, Commentary on the Old Testament*, (Grand Rapids: Eerdmans, 1978), 1:213.

[104]Kline, *Kingdom Prologue*, 3:40, similarly relates the animals to Christ's sacrifice when he says, "An indication of the ultimate outworking of God's self-maledictory oath in Messiah's sacrificial death-curse was given in the nature of the animals selected for the Genesis 15 ritual."

[105]Ibid., 38.

has said, that the smoke and fire theophany of Genesis 15 should be seen as "an anticipation of the double-columned cloud-and-fire revelation of the Glory-Spirit at the exodus."[105] Certainly the two theophanic terms of Genesis 15:17 to which Kline draws attention also occur in the Exodus account: "smoke" (עָנָן, Ex 19:9, 16; 13:21; 14:19, 20, 24; et al.) and "fire" (אֵשׁ, Ex 19:18; 13:21, 22; 14:24; et al.). In any case, one major point emerges from these kindred theophanies: if God would appear in glory, he can only do so in one way—a fire and cloud/storm theophany—once humans are in sin. The easy intimacy in which he spoke his first covenant words to the man and woman (Ge 1:28–30) is gone.

Of course God can and does appear anthropomorphically to human beings, as we have noted.[106] The point is that when God comes in glory he must conceal that glory in smoke, cloud, and storm in order to protect sinful humanity from the otherwise devastating effects of it.

God's ultimate desire is to restore the intimacy of the unbroken Creation covenant with humanity. God longs for the restoration of all things. All of his glory-storm theophanies in the Old Testament conduce in some way or other to that end. He appeared in the garden both to judge Adam and Eve and to prevent them from assuming immortality (Ge 3:22), which would have thwarted God's messianic plan (Ge 3:15). He brought the Flood with thunderous voice to judge humanity but also to cleanse the earth for a righteous remnant—a re-Creation act that preserved a chosen line out of which eventually Israel should provide the ethnic and cultural matrix for the Messiah. God appeared to Abram and cut a covenant with him—and ratified the covenant in a self-imprecatory ritual that anticipated what God would do in Jesus Christ. Dramatic as

---

[106]See above, chap. 1.

was that theophanic shadow of things to come, God's appearance at Mount Sinai also prefigured the appearance of Christ both in glory and in his earthly ministry. And in its own way the Sinai theophany makes a case for humanity's dire need of that "prophet like Moses" who was to come.[107]

---

[107]Cf. Dt 18:15; Jn 1:21; 7:40; Acts 3:22–23.

6

The Sinai Theophany

> Last with one midnight stroke all the first-born
> Of Egypt must lie dead. Thus with ten wounds
> The River-dragon tamed at length submits
> To let his sojourners depart. . . .
>
> Such wondrous power God to his Saint will lend,
> Though present in his Angel, who shall go
> Before them in a Cloud, and Pillar of Fire,
> By day a Cloud, by night a Pillar of Fire,
> To guide them in their journey. . . .
>
> God from the mount of Sinai, whose gray top
> Shall tremble, he descending, will himself
> In Thunder, Lightning and loud Trumpet's sound
> Ordain them Laws. . . .
>
> John Milton, *Paradise Lost,* XII.189–92, 200–204, 227–30

SINAI AND EXODUS

Canaanite mythology records how Baal defeated Yam, the sea god, and then had a temple built for himself. The book of Exodus records just such a process. Only here it is Yahweh who shows himself victorious over Rahab, the Nile dragon, and then he has a tabernacle built for himself. Under such an aegis the whole book of Exodus stands.

We saw that Psalm 29 was not only a hymn to Yahweh, but also a reflection of his supremacy over the Flood and over the "mighty waters." Yahweh parallels Baal (and Marduk) in that he, the God of heaven, is victor over the watery forces of chaos. We saw, for example, how his victory over the water monster Leviathan in Isaiah 27:1 echoed with remarkable clarity Baal's victory over Lītānu/Leviathan in Ugaritic myth.[1]

Yahweh's victory over Pharaoh/Egypt is also portrayed as a victory over a water monster–Rahab.[2] Batto observes:

> Egypt [is] an extension of the chaos dragon. In Egyptian belief Pharaoh was the incarnation of their chief god. Israel's theologians inverted this Egyptian "theology" by turning Pharaoh not into the creator god but the Creator's arch foe, the chaos dragon who opposed the Creator's benevolent design.... In a series of spectacular battles Yahweh overwhelms and finally kills Pharaoh-Egypt in the midst of the sea. Through this same battle Israel emerges from out of the midst of the defeated enemy as God's newly-fashioned people, the final "work" of the Creator who brings forth life out of the midst of the unruly sea.[3]

To the extent that the Reed Sea victory echoes Genesis 1, one can see the deliverance/creation of a new people out of/via the chaos waters as a parallel to God's creative act whereby his glory Spirit presence brought orderly creation (cosmos) out of formlessness as he hovered above the deep (Ge 1:2).

The book of Job may reflect on Yahweh's Reed Sea victory when it says, "God does not restrain his anger; even the cohorts of Rahab cowered at his feet" (Job 9:13). The psalmist also recalls that past event as he calls upon Yahweh for present help:

> You rule over the surging sea;
>   when its waves mount up, you still them.
> You crushed Rahab like one of the slain;
>   with your strong arm you scattered your enemies.

---

[1] See above, chap. 4.

[2] For a detailed discussion of Rahab, see M. K. Wakeman, *God's Battle With the Monster*, 56–62, 97.

[3] B. F. Batto, *Slaying the Dragon*, 113. Batto sees the Exodus account as a piece of mythopoeic speculation on the part of the "Priestly Writer."

> The heavens are yours, and yours also the earth;
>> you founded the world and all that is in it.
>>> (Ps 89:10–12[9–11])

Here, Yahweh's victory over Rahab is placed squarely in the context of his supremacy over the waters. The reason for his rule over the sea and his victory over the sea monster is not far to seek: he "founded the world and all that is in it." As Creator he rules both heavens and earth, both the waters above and the waters below (seas).

Rahab is shown to be both a sea monster and a name for Egypt most clearly in Isaiah:

> Was it not you who cut Rahab to pieces,
>> who pierced that monster through?
> Was it not you who dried up the sea,
>> the waters of the great deep,
> who made a road in the depths of the sea
>> so that the redeemed might cross over? (Isa 51:9–10)

Yahweh's victory over Egypt is portrayed in terms of his supremacy over the watery forces of chaos—both the sea and, poetically, Rahab the sea monster, who virtually personifies the sea in the above passage. Nor is Yahweh's supremacy hard won or temporary. Later in Israel's history, Yahweh pronounces Egypt unable to save and calls her "Rahab the Do-Nothing" (Isa 30:7). On the other hand Yahweh's ultimate goal for Rahab is her salvation: "I will record Rahab and Babylon/among those who acknowledge me" (Ps 87:5[4]).[4]

Later reflections on the Exodus clearly regard it poetically as a triumph of Yahweh over the watery forces of chaos. Articulated in terms of Canaanite and Mesopotamian mythology, this theme does not stand alone. Yahweh's triumph also leads to the construction of a temple for himself. We have seen the same

---

[4] Neglect of God's salvific plans for Egypt and Babylon renders Batto's unqualified identification of them as chaos dragon figures one-sided and ultimately simplistic (cf. Batto, *Slaying the Dragon,* 110ff.).

pattern also in Canaanite (Ugaritic) poetry, where Baal's victory over Yam is appropriately followed by the construction of a temple (palace) for him. We saw this pattern earlier in Mesopotamian myth. That such a pattern should appear in the Old Testament is no surprise. The Old Testament is not mythopoeic.[5] But one may say it is mythopoetic if one understands that "in mythopoetic usage the mythic elements have lost their value as operative myths and survive only as literary symbols or images, that is, as mere vestiges of their original mythic function."[6] A good example would be Isaiah's use of the Leviathan figure (Isa 27:1). On such an understanding, the Old Testament sometimes employs elements of myth to portray the *magnalia Dei* among humans. I would argue, however, that in the case of the large pattern involving divine temple/palace construction after theomachy/creation, we are dealing with more than the mythopoetic. The pattern in both Testaments is actually a historical report of what God has done. Since this pattern of divine activity was established at the Creation, it follows that all subsequent occurrences of it are echoes of the original.

The same pattern of theomachy followed by temple construction is, in large, the plan for the book of Exodus. Under this grand plan Yahweh appears in several ways. He appears to Moses both to inaugurate his salvific role in the life of Israel

---

[5] I disagree with Batto, *Slaying the Dragon,* who views the Yahwist and Priestly writer as engaged in mythopoeic enterprise—that is, the creation of myth rather than the transmission of historical events: "Was the intention of biblical writers to present the exodus as a past event, something that happened to their forefathers and foremothers at a particular geographical place at a particular moment in the past? Or was it the biblical writers' intention to explode the exodus into an 'event' that transcends the particularities of time and space, making it the story of every Israelite in every generation? . . . But the exodus that we are dealing with in this case is not the historical event, whatever that may have been, but rather the exodus of tradition. The latter has been thoroughly mythologized and reinterpreted as an 'event' of suprahistorical character through various mythopoeic processes" (103–4; cf. 121).

[6] Batto, *Slaying the Dragon,* 12. The *OED* equates mythopoeic and mythopoetic in meaning.

(Ex 3:1–4:7) and to culminate the establishment of covenant (Ex 19–24). Both of these passages portray theophanies that take place on Mount Sinai. But Yahweh also appears in other ways, as part of his administration of the salvation program that is focused on the Sinaitic covenant. He appears as a pillar of cloud and a pillar of fire to conduct Israel away from Egypt and toward Sinai (Ex 13–14). And he appears at the tents of meeting, both the smaller "tent of meeting" which Moses erects outside the camp (33:7–11) and "the tabernacle, the Tent of Meeting" (40:2), which Yahweh commands, and upon which he descends in glory at its consecration (vv. 34–35). That same shekinah glory leads Israel from then on about the wilderness (vv. 36–38). God also allows Moses to see his glory (33:18–23) and causes his face to shine (34:29–35). As we will see, God's theophanic conduct has eschatological implications.

Subsequent passages further illustrate Yahweh's appearance on Sinai/Horeb (Deuteronomy) and his theophanic covenant administration (Leviticus, Numbers). They will appear in our discussion at appropriate places. But first we turn to the book of Exodus.

Yahweh on Sinai—the Burning Bush

Yahweh first appears on Mount Sinai at a divine appointment with Moses, then shepherd of Midian. In a sense Exodus 1–2 only preface this event. We learn of Israel's agony in Egypt and of Moses' false start at being "ruler and judge" over God's people. When Moses flees to Midian, he learns to be a husband (Ex 2:21), a father (v. 22), and a shepherd (3:1). These are theologically important facts for him, because he now encounters the God who chooses to become a husband (Jer 31:32; Eze 16:1ff.–both reflecting on the Exodus events), a father (Dt 1:31), and a shepherd (Ge 49:24) to his people.

Moses' encounter with Yahweh (Ex 3:1–4:17) has the form of the theophanic *Gattung*, with several *hieroi logoi* and several complaints by Moses:

	Formal Element	**Exodus 3:1–4:17**
1	Introductory description, third person	3:1–4a
2	Deity's utterance of name of mortal addressee	3:4b
3	Response of the addressee	3:4c
4	Deity's self-asseveration	3:5–6
5	Deity's quelling of human fear	
6	Assertion of his gracious presence	3:7–8a
7	The *hieros logos*	3:8b–10
8	Inquiry or protest by the addressee	3:11
9	Continuation of the *hieros logos* with repetition of elements 4, 5, 6, 7, and/or 8:	
	hieros logos	3:12
	protest	3:13
	hieroi logoi	3:14–22
	protest	4:1
	hieroi logoi	4:2–9
	protest	4:10
	hieros logos	4:11–12
	protest	4:13
	hieroi logoi	4:14–17
10	Concluding description, third person	

The passage lacks two of the *Gattung's* possible elements. Yahweh does not quell Moses' fear (element 5). Quite to the contrary, we are told that "Moses hid his face, because he was afraid to look at God" (Ex 3:6). On one hand, it may be that Yahweh does not want Moses to be entirely unafraid; Moses must understand that he is in the presence of a holy God (v. 5). On the other hand, Yahweh does assert his gracious presence: he reassures Moses that he has heard Israel's cry and has "come down to rescue them" (vv. 7–8). Such an assertion should, after all, go far to quell Moses' fear. The passage also lacks a concluding description in the third person. That function is accomplished by the statement in Exodus 4:18, "Then Moses went back to Jethro his father-in-law and said to him, 'Let me go back to my own people in Egypt to see if any of them are still alive'"—a statement that forms a transition between the Sinai theophany and Moses' return to Egypt.

The first Sinai passage is replete with theophanic language. Moses encounters the "angel of Yahweh" (מַלְאַךְ יהוה), who "appears" (יֵרָא) to him "as flames of fire" (בְּלַבַּת־אֵשׁ). The bush is "burning with fire" (בֹּעֵר בָּאֵשׁ) but is "not consumed" (אֵינֶנּוּ אֻכָּל). Yahweh has "come down" (וָאֵרֵד) to rescue Israel.[7]

The "angel of Yahweh" who appears to Moses is identified as God[8] two verses later: "When Yahweh saw that he had gone over to look, God called to him from within the bush, 'Moses! Moses!'" (Ex 3:4). Mendenhall rightly argues that here, as in other Old Testament instances, "*Mal'ak* 'messenger' and *ᶜānān* are two different word labels for the same concept: both refer to the manifestations by which deity becomes functional in human experience."[9] The importance of this observation will become apparent in subsequent "angelic" appearances. Yahweh also appears to Moses "as flames of fire"(3:2).[10] God's fiery theophany is controlled—the bush is not consumed—but it is also unfamiliar, unasked for, and awesome. Moses' response is appropriately one of fear. His reaction is like that of Adam and Eve and of any mortal to the glory of God in the Old Testament. But one reason that God shows up on Mount Sinai is to set in motion a plan of salvation that will undo that fear—undo the separation between God and humanity caused by sin. The proof of God's intention is not only that he appears but also that he reveals more of his nature, for it is ultimately more of his nature that he wants to communicate

---

[7]As Kuntz has noted, the verb, "to come down" (ירד), is often used of Yahweh in theophany in the Old Testament (Kuntz, *The Self-Revelation of God*, 42).

[8]That is, אֱלֹהִים (LXX, κύριος).

[9]Mendenhall, *The Tenth Generation*, 59. Cf. his discussion and ancient Near Eastern backgrounds cited in evidence, pp. 32–66.

[10]Taking the בְּ in בְּלַבַּת־אֵשׁ as the *Beth essentiae* : "as," not "in" (cf. BDB, 88–89; and, more recently, W. H. Gispen, *Exodus* (Grand Rapids: Zondervan, 1982), 51.

to his people. He does this by revealing—or we should say, more profoundly revealing—his known name (3:14).[11]

It is important that the further revelation of God's name comes during a theophany—rather than, say, as part of an interior dialogue with Moses or some other prophet. God's name is a statement of his aseity—of the fact that he is unconditional, essential being. Theophanic radiance and power communicate to the natural senses what it means thus purely *to be*. The same may be said of no lesser being. Now also, for the first time, theophany is directly associated with the fact that God is holy: "Take off your sandals, for the place where you are standing is *holy* ground" (Ex 3:5). Yahweh is not only absolute being; he is holy being.

This same holy being is the one who will judge Egypt (and rescue Israel, Ex 3:8–4:17), whatever the vacillations of his ordained prophet (3:11, 13; 4:1, 10, 13). Also, Yahweh ("HE IS") will one day cause his glory—the emanation of his holiness and his being—to shine upon and transform the face of his servant Moses (34:29–35). Both events have eschatological im-

---

[11]Garrett, *Rethinking Genesis*, 20–21, offers an appealing analysis of Ex 6:2c–3, a long-standing interpretive crux, in which Yahweh further comments on his name. Garret analyzes the structure of the revelation as follows:

    A   אני יהוה
 B וארא אל־אברהם אל־יצחק ואל־יעקב באל שדי
    A' ושמי יהוה
 B' לא נודעתי להם

  A I am Yahweh
  B And I made myself known to Abraham, to Isaac, and to Jacob as El Shaddai.
  A' And my name is Yahweh;
  B' Did I not make myself known to them?

Garrett demonstrates that this interpretation not only reveals the dynamic structure but also makes the best grammatical sense of the passage (cf. p. 21, n. 24). And Andersen has said, "There is no hint in Exodus that Yahweh was a new name revealed first to Moses. On the contrary, the success of his mission depended on the use of the familiar name for validation by the Israelites" (F. I. Andersen, *The Sentence in Biblical Hebrew* [The Hague: Mouton, 1974]), 102.

plications. The judgment of Pharaoh/Egypt/Rahab anticipates the ultimate defeat of Satan—the power behind them and the "chaos monster" par excellence. It also anticipates the eschatological deliverance of God's people. Moses' freedom to stand in God's presence and partake of holy radiance anticipates the day when "the righteous will shine like the sun in the kingdom of their Father" (Mt 13:43).

God's holiness already has implications of judgment. Moses himself is partly judged by God's holy presence, as his fear shows (3:6). Compare 1 John 4:18: "There is no fear in love. But perfect love drives out fear, because fear has to do with punishment." God's purpose for appearing is to overcome that human fear by extending his love and salvation. He does so ultimately by that "prophet" who is both like and greater than Moses. But just now the fiery mode of theophany anticipates the way he will appear to judge Pharaoh and rescue Israel (cf. Ps 29:3 and discussion above, chap. 5). Because God intends salvation, the luminous way he appears to Moses also foreshadows the radiant glory he will impart later.

A Pillar of Cloud, a Pillar of Fire

Exodus 13:21–22 says that Yahweh went before his people by day "in/as a pillar of cloud" (בְּעַמּוּד[הֶ]עָנָן), and by night "in/as a pillar of fire" (בְּעַמּוּד[הָ]אֵשׁ).[12] The same pillar of cloud stood as a barrier between Israel and the army of Egypt who came in pursuit (14:19). As it did so, the cloud (הֶעָנָן) gave darkness (הַחֹשֶׁךְ) to the Egyptians but light (וַיָּאֶר) to the Israelites, so that neither group approached the other all night long (14:20). Apparently the pillar of cloud moved synchronously with the angel of Yahweh (14:19). But we are told that "Yahweh looked down from the pillar of fire and cloud at the Egyptian army" (14:24), a parallel that suggests that here

---

[12]In both phrases the preposition may be taken as *Beth essentiae*, as above, n. 10.

again the "angel of Yahweh" is tantamount to Yahweh in theophany.[13] The phraseology employed suggests the same. Only here (Ex 13:22; 14:19; cf. 13:21) and at the explicitly Yahweh theophany of Exodus 33:7ff. does the phrase "the pillar of cloud" (עַמּוּד הֶעָנָן) occur in the book of Exodus (see Ex 33:9, 10). Elsewhere in the Pentateuch, the phrase occurs only in portrayals of Yahweh (e.g., Nu 12:5; 14:14). The phraseology at Numbers 14:14 is particularly suggestive. Moses tells Yahweh that the surrounding nations have already heard "that you, Yahweh, are with these people, and that you, Yahweh, have been seen face to face, that your cloud stays over them, and that you go before them in/as a pillar of cloud by day and in/as a pillar of fire by night"[14] If the "pillar of cloud" indicated Yahweh in one place, it may do so in another.[15] Moreover, a clear identification is made in Numbers 14:14 between Yahweh, the "cloud," and the "pillar of cloud and . . . of fire." As noted, the same sort of identification between cloud and god has been observed in the ancient Near East. The "cloud" even appears in Ugaritic as a "linguistic surrogate for the proper name of the god, Hadad."[16] The same may be true of other deities, e.g., the goddess Athtart/Athirat.[17]

---

[13]See above, chap. 1.

[14]We may translate "as a pillar of cloud . . . as a pillar of fire," etc., taking ב again as *Beth essentiae*.

[15]See discussion below, 200–201.

[16]Mendenhall, *Tenth Generation,* 55, citing II.AB.viii.14–17:

> . . . wnǵr
> ᶜnn.ilm.al
> tqrb.lbn.ilm
> mt

which Mendenhall renders:

> "Beware, O ᶜnn of the gods;
> do not approach the son of the gods, Mot."

Here the ᶜnn "cloud" of Baal/Hadad is used as tantamount to that god's name.

[17]Cf. C. Gordon, *UT,* 458 (1885. ᶜnn).

THE SINAI THEOPHANY

The angel of Yahweh is perhaps best understood as a theophanic presence of God. He appears to be the same angel who Yahweh later says will lead the people to the Promised Land. The language used to portray that guardian angel also confirms the idea that the angel and Yahweh are one:

> See, I am sending an angel ahead of you to guard you along the way and to bring you to the place I have prepared. Pay attention to him and listen to what he says. Do not rebel against him; he will not forgive your rebellion, since my Name is in him. If you listen carefully to what he says and do all that I say, I will be an enemy to your enemies and will oppose those who oppose you. My angel will go ahead of you and bring you into the land of the Amorites, Hittites, Perizzites, Canaanites, Hivites and Jebusites, and I will wipe them out. (Ex 23:20–23)

Yahweh's angel is that "angel of [God's] presence" who, according to Isaiah, saved Israel from Egypt (Isa 63:9). Isaiah's phraseology recalls Yahweh's promise to Moses, "My Presence will go with you" (Ex 33:14). God made that promise in the context of a Sinai-like theophany at the "tent of meeting" (vv. 7ff.). One may identify "the angel of his presence" and "my Presence" in these two passages. To do so does not violate the spirit of the portrayal of the "angel" of Exodus 23:20–23. This is so for several reasons.

First, I have noted Mendenhall's argument that "*Mal'ak* 'messenger' and ^c*ānān*" can "refer to the manifestations by which deity becomes functional in human experience." Such may be the case for the term "angel" if other data in the context strongly point to its theophanic character.

A further indication that Yahweh and his "angel" may be one is found in the word itself, מַלְאָךְ. The word is routinely translated "angel," yet it can also mean simply "messenger." This means that the "messenger" about whom Yahweh is talking need not be an "angel" in the sense of a created being normally indicated by that term.

Another suggestive fact is the alternation between the third and first person in the passage: "If you listen carefully to what *he* says and do all that *I* say" (Ex 23:22); "*my angel* will go ahead of you . . . and *I* will wipe them out" (v. 23, emphasis mine). This alternation may indicate the unity of Yahweh and his "angel."[18]

An additional consideration is the fact that the angel has authority to pardon or not to pardon sins: "Do not rebel against him; he will not forgive your rebellion" (Ex 23:21). The Pharisees observed when Jesus pronounced a paralytic's sins forgiven, "Who can forgive sins but God alone?" (Mk 2:7).

Also of considerable importance is the rationale that Yahweh gives for the angel's authority to pardon or withhold pardon: "[for] my Name is in him" (Ex 23:21). Roland de Vaux[19] and Gordon Wenham[20] have noted that the phrase "to place one's name" was used in Akkadian to describe a king's placement of a stele with his own name inscribed on it. This indicated at a minimum his possession of the place. But the same phraseology also implied his effective presence there. For example, we find in the Amarna correspondence that Pharaoh "has established his name in the country of Jerusalem for ever."[21] Weinfeld argues, "The old notion of indicating possession by inscribing the name of the possessor, which lies behind the phrase, 'establishing the name,' already implies the extension of one's name and presence."[22] And Abba notes, "The name of God is frequently used as a synonym for God himself."[23] The idea is a very ancient one. We find the "name" of

---

[18]It could also be just a stylistic variant of the sort noted elsewhere. But it is striking and at least suggestive in the context.
[19]R. de Vaux, "Bulletin," *RB* 73 (1966): 449.
[20]Wenham, "Deuteronomy and the Central Sanctuary," *TB* 22 (1971): 113–14.
[21]*EA* 287:60–61.
[22]Weinfeld, *Deuteronomy and the Deuteronomic School,* 194.
[23]R. Abba, "Name," in *The Interpreter's Dictionary of the Bible,* ed. G. A. Buttrick (New York: Abingdon, 1962), 3:502.

Enlil capable of producing theophanic disruptions of nature in a Sumerian lament:

> When your name rests over the mountains, the sky itself trembles;
> The sky itself trembles, the earth itself shivers.
> When it rests over the mountains of Elam,
> When it rests over the horizon,
> When it rests over the "foundation of the earth,"
> When it rests over the farthest reaches of the earth,
> When it rests over the surface of the earth,
> When it rests over the awe-inspiring mountains,
> When it rests over the high mountains,
> When it rests over the powerful (?) mountains,
> When it rests over the mountains and over the wide sky,
> the sky itself [trembles.][24]

The Sumerian poet extols the theophanic glory of Enlil's "name" in a way not so remote from that of Asaph:

> We give thanks to you, O God,
> we give thanks, for your Name is near;
> men tell of your wonderful deeds.
> You say, "I choose the appointed time;
> it is I who judge uprightly.
> When the earth and all its people quake,
> it is I who hold its pillars firm." (Ps 75:1-3)

And again,

> As fire consumes the forest
> or a flame sets the mountains ablaze,
> so pursue them with your tempest
> and terrify them with your storm.
> Cover their faces with shame
> so that men will seek your Name, O Yahweh.
> . . . .

---

[24]R. Kutscher, *Oh Angry Sea, The History of a Sumerian Congregational Lament* (New Haven: Yale University Press, 1975), 145-46 (st. V:62-72). Cf. similarly 146-47 (sts. VII:92-98; IX:119-125). For the various names attributed to Enlil and dates of the same, cf. 47-51.

> Let them know that you, whose Name is Yahweh,
> that you alone are the Most High over all the earth.
> (Ps 83:14–18)

Both Mesopotamian and Old Testament data reflect an ancient tradition whereby storm theophany and earthquake are associated with a divine name. Moreover, the equation of a god with his name is fundamental to this tradition. Gibson has observed the same in Ugaritic. Astarte rebukes Baal, "interestingly using the title, 'the Name,' an example of a religious fastidiousness usually thought in biblical circles to be a mark of advanced theological awareness and therefore of late development."[25] Now Ugaritic as well as prior Mesopotamian evidence shows that a god's "name" could be used as an ontological equivalent to the god himself. What this means for our understanding of Exodus 23:21 is that God's "angel" is one who contains God's essential character because Yahweh's "Name" is in him. Such a statement is next to saying that the angel is God himself.

A final indicator of the oneness of Yahweh and his "angel" is the way the angel's authority is commended: "Pay attention to him and listen to what he says [שְׁמַע בְּקֹלוֹ]" (23:21). The Hebrew idiom (שְׁמַע בְּקֹלוֹ) usually translated "listen to" is actually a *terminus technicus* of covenantal literature. It means in effect "to obey" and is used routinely vis-à-vis Yahweh in his covenant dealings with Israel. In other words, it is normally Yahweh's "voice" that Israel must "obey"—but now it is the voice of Yahweh's "angel." The covenantal background of the phrase thus implies an identity of Yahweh and the angel. The same phraseology is echoed later, when Moses describes the prophet to come: "Yahweh your God will raise up for you a prophet like me from among your own brothers. You must listen to him [אֵלָיו תִּשְׁמָעוּן]" (Dt 18:15). The prophet to come is identified as Christ in Acts 3:22–23. The Horeb/Sinai theophany shows the

---

[25] Gibson, *Canaanite Myths and Legends*, 4, n. 6.

need for such a prophet, who must be God himself (and as such, must be obeyed).

Language used to portray the guardian angel of Exodus 23 strongly indicates that the angel and Yahweh are one. If the angel of Exodus 23 is the angel who parallels Yahweh in the Exodus 13:21–22 account, and who also guards Israel from the approaching Egyptian army, one may call the pillar of cloud and pillar of fire a theophany indeed. It is not just an angel. It is a messenger of God and God himself. It is God in glory theophany, a theophany awesome to the people and dreadful to her foes—a theophany not unlike the one the Israelites encounter atop Mount Sinai.

Yahweh on Sinai—Thunder and Lightning

Yahweh tells Moses to consecrate the people for two days because on the third day "I am going to come to you in a dense cloud" (בְּעַב הֶעָנָן, Ex 19:9). Yahweh's coming is portrayed with theophanic language: e.g., "thunder" (קֹלֹת, 19:16), "lightning" (בְּרָקִים, 19:16), "thick cloud" (עָנָן כָּבֵד, 19:16), "smoke" (עָשָׁן, 19:18), and "fire" (אֵשׁ, 19:18). Some phrases are used now for the first time: "a very loud trumpet blast" (חָזָק קֹל שֹׁפָר, 19:16), "the smoke billowed up" (וַיַּעַל עֲשָׁנוֹ, 19:18), "like smoke from a furnace" (כְּעֶשֶׁן הַכִּבְשָׁן, 19:18), "the whole mountain trembled violently" (וַיֶּחֱרַד כָּל־הָהָר מְאֹד, 19:18). A subsequent account in Exodus 20 echoes these descriptions: "thunder" (הַקּוֹלֹת, 20:18), "lightning" (הַלַּפִּידִם, 20:18), "the trumpet" (קֹל הַשֹּׁפָר, 20:18), "the mountain in smoke" (הָהָר עָשֵׁן, 20:18), and "thick darkness" (הָעֲרָפֶל, 20:21).

Among all these terms there is only one comparison: "The smoke billowed up ... like smoke from a furnace" (וַיַּעַל עֲשָׁנוֹ כְּעֶשֶׁן הַכִּבְשָׁן, Ex 19:18). The furnace simile is more pregnant than it appears, for it occurs only one other time in the Bible, as a description of the destruction of Sodom and Gomorrah: "[Abraham] looked, ... and dense smoke [was] rising from the land, like smoke from a furnace" (הָאָרֶץ כְּקִיטֹר הַכִּבְשָׁן)

עָלָה קִיטֹר, Ge 19:28). The parallel of key terms (עָלָה, הַכִּבְשָׁן) is unmistakable and far from accidental. Yahweh came in judgment upon Sodom and Gomorrah and brought their destruction. That may be why the term קִיטֹר is used instead of עָשָׁן, since it belongs to the word group קטר, normally used of sacrifices and burnt offerings. The word suggests that Sodom and Gomorrah were a sacrifice for Yahweh. But now on Mount Sinai the situation is more complex. God is about to give the law and enter into covenant with Israel. Although he graciously brings the law, however, the law also inevitably implies judgment. This truth, brought out more clearly in the New Testament, is adumbrated here by the reuse of an otherwise unique simile. Interestingly, the only other two uses of the word "furnace" are in Exodus 9, where Moses and Aaron upon Yahweh's command take "handfuls of soot from a furnace" and toss them into the air, causing festering boils to appear on the Egyptians—as a part of God's judgment on them (Ex 9:8, 10).

The account of Yahweh's appearance takes the form of the theophanic *Gattung:*

	Formal Element	**Exodus 19:16–20:17**
1	Introductory description, third person	19:16–21a
2	Deity's utterance of name of (mortal) addressee	
3	Response of the addressee	
4	Deity's self-asseveration	
5	His quelling of human fear	
6	Assertion of his gracious presence	
7	The *hieros logos*	19:21b–22
8	Inquiry or protest by the addressee	19:23
9	Continuation of the *hieros logos* with repetition of elements 4, 5, 6, 7, and/or 8:	
	hieros logos	19:24
	hieroi logoi	20:1–17
10	Concluding description, third person	

Several comments are in order. Elements 2–4 are lacking because Yahweh has already appeared to Moses and spoken with him on various occasions as a preparation for the Sinai event. So there is no need at this juncture for God to utter Moses' name and for Moses to respond to it (elements 2 and 3), or for Yahweh to assert who he is (element 4). Elements 5–6 are lacking, just as they were in Yahweh's original theophany to Moses (Ex 3:1–4:17) and perhaps for the same reasons. On the one hand, it may be that Yahweh does not want Israel to be entirely unafraid. The people must understand that they are in the presence of a holy God and thus have been called upon to "consecrate" themselves (19:10–11) and to limit their approach to the mountain (vv. 12–13). On the other hand, Yahweh has already asserted his gracious presence: he has told Moses that he wants to make Israel "a kingdom of priests and a holy nation" (v. 6). Such an assertion should go far to quell any fear. The passage also lacks a concluding description in the third person (element 10). That function is accomplished by the account of the people's fear and Moses' quelling of it (Ex 18–21), which is a parenthesis in the extended account of God's giving of the Law to Moses (20:1–31:18).

Yahweh on Sinai—A Communion Meal

Exodus 24 records a communion meal that may well have been a regular way of consummating a covenant.[26] Abimelech of Gerar had such a meal with Isaac as they formed a covenant (Ge 26:26–31). Laban and Jacob also made a covenant that included a meal (31:44–54). Moses and Aaron, Nadab and Abihu, and the seventy elders of Israel ascended Mount Sinai and came into the presence of Yahweh—their covenant Suzerain—and had a meal. But God's revelation was not complete. They saw only his feet and what was under his

---

[26]D. J. McCarthy, "Three Covenants in Genesis," *CBQ* 26 (1964): 179–89, has suggested that the meal was a symbol of the covenant, a sort of acted sign.

feet: "Under his feet was something like a pavement made of sapphire, clear as the sky itself" (24:10). Cassuto notes that the term לְבֵנָה, translated "pavement," literally means "brick," so a paved work of sapphire stone is indicated.[27] The description is echoed and amplified later in Ezekiel 1:2. Upon Mount Sinai God did not "raise his hand" against the Israelite leaders. Rather, "they saw God, and they ate and drank" (וַיֹּאכְלוּ וַיִּשְׁתּוּ, 24:11 = Ge 26:30). Their meal was a covenant sign in accordance with earlier practice, but it was also more: a type of the eschatological banquet (cf. Isa 24:6–8) and a type of the Last Supper as well.[28] On those occasions God's revelation would be more complete.

After this communion meal, Moses ascended the mountain again to receive the tablets of stone upon which Yahweh had inscribed the laws. Yahweh was on the mountaintop as before:

> When Moses went up on the mountain, the cloud [הֶעָנָן] covered it, and the glory of Yahweh [כְּבוֹד יהוה] settled on Mount Sinai. For six days the cloud covered the mountain, and on the seventh day Yahweh called to Moses from within the cloud. To the Israelites the glory of Yahweh looked like a consuming fire [אֵשׁ אֹכֶלֶת] on top of the mountain. Then Moses entered the cloud as he went on up the mountain. And he stayed on the mountain forty days and forty nights. (Ex 24:15–18)

The account is rich in numerical symbolism and typology. With regard to the former, it echoes to the Genesis Creation account. The theophanic cloud—God's Holy Spirit glory presence—covers the mountain for six days, just as the Spirit of God moved in creation for six days (Ge 1:2–31). On the seventh day Yahweh calls to Moses. The six-day period and the seventh-day calling of Moses were meant to communicate sym-

---

[27]U. Cassuto, *A Commentary on the Book of Exodus*, trans. I. Abrahams (Jerusalem: Magnes, 1967), 314.

[28]Cassuto, ibid., 315, suggests that "perhaps there is an allusion here to the fact that Aaron and his sons and the elders did not attain to the spiritual level of Moses . . . for during the forty days of his stay on Mount Sinai 'he neither ate bread nor drank water.'"

bolically to Israel the reality of the new creation which Yahweh was accomplishing by the Exodus events and the Mosaic covenant. The new creation was liberated Israel. The connection is not eisegetical. Isaiah later portrayed Yahweh both as Israel's Creator and as the one who led them out of Egypt:

> "I am Yahweh, your Holy One,
>   Israel's Creator, your King."
> This is what Yahweh says—
>   he who made a way through the sea,
>   a path through the mighty waters,
> who drew out the chariots and horses,
>   the army and reinforcements together,
> and they lay there, never to rise again,
>   extinguished, snuffed out like a wick.
>
> (Isa 43:15–17)

Yahweh is Israel's Creator. He is also Israel's Redeemer. The two are fundamentally linked. Yahweh's six-day session atop Mount Sinai symbolizes his work of new creation—a redeemed Israel in covenantal relationship with himself.[29]

The passage also has typological importance. The seventh-day call of Moses implies that Moses will lead the people into God's Sabbath rest. Moses failed to do this (cf. Heb 4:5–6). But as a type of the one to come, he foreshadows that Prophet who will mediate a new covenant and lead God's people into the Sabbath rest of God (vv. 9–11). Moses' sojourn on Sinai is also typological. Moses stayed on the mountain forty days and

---

[29] Batto, *Slaying the Dragon,* 120, offers the following account of the passage in question: "There can be no doubt that the Priestly Writer intends this scene to parallel the opening scene in Genesis with six days of active creation and a seventh day in which God ceased his activity and 'rested.' By implication the Creator completed a new work during the six days when the glory of Yahweh shrouded the mountaintop. This new work is the 'model' that the Creator revealed to Moses during the next forty days." By "model" Batto refers to the tabernacle pattern. It is more likely, however, that the six days are symbolic. Certainly there is nothing in the text to suggest that Yahweh spent six days working on the "model" that he subsequently gave to Moses.

forty nights while God told him how to prepare the tabernacle/temple of God (Ex 25:1–31:18). I have already noted the importance of divine temple/palace building after the defeat of a foe in the ancient world. It is not just a mythological pattern. Ancient kings routinely built or renovated temples after their own victorious campaigns—as Assyrian tradition amply attests. On the mythic plane, a god had his palace built so that he could rest after his battles. Now Yahweh commands a tabernacle as God's place of rest, analogous to the ancient Near Eastern pattern we have already seen. The pattern strongly suggests that Yahweh's "rest" in Genesis 2:2 echoes the ancient Near Eastern pattern—or better, that the ancient pattern echoes what archetypally happened (Yahweh's "rest" after Creation) but in terms of a mythical theomachy between sky god and sea monster/chaos dragon (e.g., Marduk versus Tiamat, Baal versus Yam) followed by temple/palace construction once the god had "rest" from his enemies round about. Moses spent forty days and nights atop Sinai as Yahweh gave him the tabernacle pattern. His experience foreshadows that of Jesus, who likewise spent forty days and nights in the wilderness as a preparation for his ministry, which was to inaugurate the work of building God's temple, the church. Jesus had to defeat the serpent, the chaos dragon Satan, before he could build that temple. He continues to "undo the devil's works" and to build his church until both labors are consummated eschatologically.

Yahweh at the First "Tent of Meeting"

Before Moses constructed the "Tent of Meeting," he constructed a "tent of meeting" (Ex 33:7a). This was a provisional tent at which Moses or "anyone inquiring of the Lord" (v. 7b) could seek God. Yahweh appeared for such audiences:

> As Moses went into the tent, the pillar of cloud would come down and stay at the entrance, while Yahweh spoke with Moses. Whenever the people saw the pillar of cloud standing at the entrance to the tent, they all stood and wor-

shiped, each at the entrance to his tent. Yahweh would speak to Moses face to face, as a man speaks with his friend. (Ex 33:9–11)

Yahweh's cloud theophany recalls the angel/Yahweh theophany of Exodus 13 and 14. Only there (Ex 13:22; 14:19; cf. 13:21) and here (Ex 33:9, 10) does the phrase "the pillar of cloud" (עַמּוּד הֶעָנָן) occur in the book of Exodus. The pillar of cloud and of fire is clearly identified with Yahweh at Numbers 14:14, as we have noted. The same appears to be true here.

The passage portrays an important parallel. Just as Yahweh stands at the entrance to his tent ("the pillar of cloud would come down and stay at the entrance," Ex 33:9), so the people stand "each at the entrance of his tent" (33:10). The parallel is fortified by the use of wordplay: עַמּוּד ("pillar"), עָמַד ("would stand"), and עֹמֵד ("standing") in 33:9–10. During the desert wanderings, a man's tent was his home. Now as Yahweh stands at the entrance to his tent, he affirms that his tent is also an acceptable home for him as he shares the desert wanderings of his people.

In fact, the tabernacle idea is an ancient one. Ugaritic poetry tells us that El, supreme god of the Canaanite pantheon, lived in a tent:

> They set face
> Toward El at the sources of the Two Rivers,
> In the midst of the pools of the Double-Deep.
> They entered the tent(s) of El and went into
> The tent-shrine of the King, Father of Years. [30]

The other gods of Canaan also lived in tents:

> *tity.ilm.l'ahlhm* "The gods returned to their tents,
> *dr il.lmšknthm* the race of El to their habitations"[31]

---

[30]See above, chap. 4.
[31]See above, chap. 4.

The idea that a god should inhabit a tent was thus an old one even in the days of Moses. It perhaps goes back to those faraway days when nomadic man imagined gods who were only man writ large. As man lived in a tent, so his god must live in a tent. Now Yahweh does appear at a tent. As though to endorse an old idea, he approves of Moses' tent by coming down (ירד) to it. So he takes his stand among his people.

The tent theophany is also an affirmation of solidarity: as the Israelites stand at the entrances of their tents and worship Yahweh, he stands at the entrance of his tent and receives their worship. He also speaks with Moses. The "tent of meeting" is thus above all a place at which Yahweh communicates with—"meets with"—his people. The same facts are also true of the "Tent of Meeting" that Yahweh commands Moses to construct.

Yahweh at the Second "Tent of Meeting"

Once Moses has completed the "Tent of Meeting" Yahweh appears above it and fills it much as he had done at the provisional "tent of meeting": "Then the cloud covered the Tent of Meeting, and the glory of Yahweh filled the tabernacle. Moses could not enter the Tent of Meeting because the cloud had settled upon it, and the glory of Yahweh filled the tabernacle" (Ex 40:34–35). Yahweh's theophany at his tabernacle is the crowning event of the book of Exodus. Yahweh has achieved victory over the Nile dragon (Rahab, Pharaoh/Egypt), the watery forces of chaos. He has won himself a people and established himself a house. The people are his household, and the tabernacle is his house. He now enters that house, and his entrance is described, if not in poetry, then certainly in parallelistic prose:

a	b	c
וַיְכַס	הֶעָנָן	אֶת־אֹהֶל מוֹעֵד
Then covered	the cloud	the Tent of Meeting,

THE SINAI THEOPHANY

b'	a'	c'
וּכְבוֹד יהוה	מָלֵא	אֶת־הַמִּשְׁכָּן
and the glory of Yahweh	filled	the tabernacle.

The verse that follows is also parallelistic. It says that Moses could not enter the tent of meeting because,

a	b	c
שָׁכַן	עָלָיו	הֶעָנָן
had settled	upon it	the cloud

c'	a'	b'
וּכְבוֹד יהוה	מָלֵא	אֶת־הַמִּשְׁכָּן
and the glory of Yahweh	filled	the tabernacle.

The poetic parallelism now celebrates God's descent upon and investment in his earthly tabernacle, just as poetic parallelism celebrated the creation of male and female in God's image at Genesis 1:27. A theological connection is to be made, if only because God also descends upon and fills a new humanity at Pentecost—that new humanity, the church, a temple of living stones being created anew in the image of its Creator.[32]

Israel Keeps in Step

God made himself present with Israel not only to give them laws. He came and dwelt among them. One consequence of that occupation was that Israel must move as God moves:

> In all the travels of the Israelites, whenever the cloud lifted from above the tabernacle, they would set out; but if the cloud did not lift, they did not set out—until the day it lifted. So the cloud of Yahweh was over the tabernacle by day, and fire was in the cloud by night, in the sight of all the house of Israel during all their travels. (Ex 40:36–38)

---

[32] As we will see, a connection is also to be made with God's investment in the Solomonic temple. That event, like Yahweh's descent upon the "Tent of Meeting," is a type of Pentecost and of what goes on today when a person receives authority to become a child of God.

The closing words of the book of Exodus communicate one of God's abiding purposes: that his people should follow him. During the wilderness wanderings, he accomplished this purpose by appearing among them in theophanic glory so that they could learn to follow that glory from place to place. The theophany is described in a way that recalls the "angel of Yahweh/Yahweh" in Exodus 13 and 14. There a pillar of cloud by day and a pillar of fire by night led the people. Here a cloud of Yahweh by day and fire in the cloud by night lead the people. The slight differences of phrasing may be accounted for by the fact that Yahweh then stood above the people (cf. Ex 14:24, "Yahweh looked down from the pillar of fire and cloud"), whereas now he is tabernacled among them. The result is that he no longer appears standing on pillars of cloud and fire. The glory presence has now settled upon and entered into the tabernacle. Later, however, in the wilderness wanderings, we read that Yahweh "came down in the pillar of cloud [and] . . . stood at the entrance to the Tent" (Nu 12:5). He came in that way to rebuke Aaron and Miriam. Moses also says of Yahweh that "you go before [the people] in a pillar of cloud by day and a pillar of fire by night" (Nu 14:14). Moreover, what is said of the pillar of cloud and fire–namely, that it descends upon the Tent; that it leads the people by day and night–is also said of the cloud itself, both in the above passage and at, e.g., Numbers 9:15–23; 10:11–13, 33–34. It seems safe to say, therefore, that the "cloud" is synonymous with the "pillar of cloud," and the "fire . . . in the cloud" is the same as the "pillar of fire" in all of these accounts. These are the phrases used to portray Yahweh in theophany as he leads his people through the wilderness.[33] In days to come, that same Glory-Spirit presence would settle upon and enter the church–each member of which is a temple of the Holy Spirit–and seek to lead God's people in a more

---

[33]Kline even sees the pillars of cloud and fire as Yahweh's feet along the journey.

intimate way. So the apostle Paul could urge, "Since we live by the Spirit, let us keep in step with the Spirit" (Gal 5:25).

The role of theophany in the book of Exodus is thus unified and purposeful. Yahweh appears in order to save his people. He saves them by doing battle with Pharaoh/Egypt, characterized elsewhere as Rahab the chaotic dragon. Yahweh achieves victory over this foe and redeems his people. His work of salvation is carried out and portrayed in ways that echo the original Creation; in a sense, Israel is his new creation. Yahweh structures his relationship with his new creation (Israel) by way of a covenant. This may echo the fact that the original Creation account also has a covenantal structure. Just as Yahweh's theophany was essential to establish the original Creation and its covenant (cf. Ge 1:2), his theophany is central to the establishment of the Mosaic covenant. Worship and a temple/tabernacle are a part of that covenant, and Yahweh provides a pattern for the latter and laws for the former. Once the tabernacle is constructed, Yahweh appears in glory above it and stands before it. This behavior on his part shows and assures the people that Yahweh does truly intend to be their God and dwell among them. Then Yahweh in this Sinaitic form of theophany leads the people across the desert toward the Promised Land.

Other passages further illustrate Yahweh's appearance on Sinai/Horeb (Deuteronomy) and his theophanic covenant administration (Leviticus, Numbers). I have suggested the importance of these accounts, but now let us explore them in more detail.

THE LEVITICUS AND NUMBERS ACCOUNTS

The accounts of theophany in the books of Leviticus and Numbers may be studied together. In fact, Leviticus has only one account that tells how Yahweh's fire consumed the offerings at the outset of the priestly ministry of Aaron and his sons.

This event is logically subsumed under the category of Yahweh's ongoing appearances at the Tent of Meeting.

Theophany and Tabernacle Ministry

In addition to Yahweh's regular appearance as a cloud/pillar of cloud/fire above the tabernacle to lead the people from place to place, he also appears at the tabernacle to receive priestly ministry and to talk with Moses. Although such activity may be taken to be routine, as implied by the descriptions of theophany at the Tent that we have already noted, two passages illustrate it especially. One is the account of Yahweh's conversation after the list of offerings for the dedication of the altar (Nu 7:89); the other is the account of Yahweh's consumption of the burnt offering and the fat portions on the altar when Aaron and his sons begin their ministry (Lev 9:23–24).

The account of Yahweh's conversation is brief and notable for its use of theophanic "voice" (קוֹל). We read that "when Moses entered the Tent of Meeting to speak with Yahweh, he heard the voice speaking to him from between the two cherubim above the atonement cover on the ark of the Testimony. And he spoke with him" (Nu 7:89). In this short account we are probably to understand the "voice" as an audible voice, but not necessarily as theophanic "thunder." The statement may be taken as a portrayal of what happened at the dedication of the altar but more probably as a description of the way Yahweh generally spoke with Moses in the tabernacle.

The other theophany mentioned is the account of Yahweh's consumption of the burnt offering and the fat portions on the altar when Aaron and his sons begin their ministry (Lev 9:23–24). This account begins with Moses' warning that "today Yahweh will appear [יֵרָא, Niph., also at 9:6, 23] to you" (Lev 9:4). Moses also commands appropriate sacrifices "so that the glory of Yahweh [כְּבוֹד יהוה] may appear to you" (v. 6). Once the sacrifices are arranged, we read that in fulfillment "the glory of Yahweh appeared to all the people" (v. 23). The promised theophany took a dramatic form: "Fire came out from the presence of Yahweh and consumed the burnt offering and the fat portions on the altar. And when all the people saw it, they shouted for joy and fell facedown" (v. 24).

The phraseology used here becomes characteristic of other theophanies, e.g., when Yahweh's fire consumes Nadab and Abihu for their presumption. In both cases we read, "And fire came out from the presence of Yahweh and consumed . . ." (וַתֵּצֵא אֵשׁ מִלִּפְנֵי יהוה וַתֹּאכַל), Lev 9:24; 10:2).[34] Later in the Old Testament, divine fire consumes the offerings of Manoah and his wife (Jdg 13:15ff.), the offerings at Solomon's temple dedication (2Ch 7:1ff.), and the offering of Elijah on Mount Carmel (1Ki 18:38ff.). On each occasion the worshipers fall to the ground and praise God, as they do here.[35] It is noteworthy that they both shout and fall to the ground. That is, they respond to Yahweh with both their voices and their bodies. As Wenham rightly observes, "These episodes involve a total response of man to God . . . God's greatness and holiness cannot be

---

[34]M. Noth, *Leviticus*, trans. J. E. Anderson (London: SCM Press, 1965), 81–82, believes that "the account given in v. 24a of fire from Yahweh going out from the Presence and consuming the sacrifice and its parts on the altar must be a later addition." He attributes it to P and says it derives from "the fire element in the appearance of Yahweh (cf. Ex. 24:17a)." Given the frequent association of fire and deity in the ancient Near East, Noth's statement is naive at best. Noth also believes the account is inconsistent with the fact that fire had already consumed at least some of the offerings (cf. vv. 10a, 13b, 14b, 17aß, 20b). He says that "assuming that the divine fire only hastened and completed a burning that was already in progress . . . would have been far too modest a role for the divine fire" (p. 82). But there is no need to see inconsistency here. As G. J. Wenham, *The Book of Leviticus*, NICOT (Grand Rapids: Eerdmans, 1979), 150, notes, "It would take some time to burn all the animals mentioned in this chapter, and the process was incomplete when God dramatically demonstrated his acceptance of them by burning them up completely."

[35]The verb translated "shouted" (רנן) is often used in the OT coupled with other words expressing praise and joy at God's ways and works (e.g., Isa 49:13; Jer 31:7; Pss 20:6[5]; 33:1; 35:27; 59:17[16]; 95:1).

ignored; he must be acknowledged by our whole being. Nothing less is adequate."[36]

Theophany and Judgment

Yahweh had to appear in judgment a number of times during the wilderness wanderings—a fact that prefigured sadly the history of his chosen people. Just as he had come in power to deliver his people, so he came in power to judge them when necessary. The same pattern obtained throughout Israel's history. Several passages stand out as chief in this category during the wilderness period: Yahweh's dealing with Nadab and Abihu at Leviticus 10, his punitive fire at Numbers 11, his rebuke of Aaron and Miriam at Numbers 12, his theophany at the people's rebellion at Numbers 14, and his judgment upon the Korahite rebellion at Numbers 16.

Nadab and Abihu

Nadab and Abihu, Aaron's sons, behaved with presumption toward Yahweh. They offered "strange fire" (אֵשׁ זָרָה), that is, unauthorized fire, contrary to God's command.[37] Ironically God then came to them with fire of his own: "Fire came out from the presence of Yahweh and consumed them" (אוֹתָם

---

[36] Wenham, *Leviticus*, 150.

[37] Noth, *Leviticus*, 84, strangely says that Nadab and Abihu were guilty of "bringing down 'strange fire' from Yahweh (v. 1bα)." He also suggests that the offering of incense might itself have been part of their guilt (p. 85). Exodus 30:9 does prohibit "strange incense," which, however, is to be understood as "an incense-offering that was not commanded in the law," as noted by C. F. Keil and F. Delitzsch, *Commentary on the Old Testament, Vol. 1, The Pentateuch* (Grand Rapids: Eerdmans, 1978), 350. As Wenham, *Leviticus*, 155, notes, the sense in both cases seems to be of an unauthorized offering. Odd as the phrase may be in Leviticus 10:1, it is sufficiently clarified by what is stated next: it was fire that Yahweh had not commanded of them. Cf. further J. C. H. Laughlin, "The 'Strange Fire' of Nadab and Abihu," *JBL* 95 (1976): 559–65.

וַתֵּצֵא אֵשׁ מִלִּפְנֵי יהוה וַתֹּאכַל, Lev 10:2). Moses later refers to this event as "the burning which Yahweh burnt" (אֲשֶׁר שָׂרַף יהוה הַשְּׂרֵפָה, Lev 10:6). The same phrase (verb with cognate accusative) is used of funerary burnings, e.g., 2 Chronicles 16:14, "They laid him [Asa] on a bier covered with spices and various blended perfumes, and they made a huge fire in his honor [lit., burned for him a very great burning, וַיִּשְׂרְפוּ־לוֹ שְׂרֵפָה גְדוֹלָה] (author's trans.)." Burning of bodies was not an acceptable funeral practice in Israel, although it was used for people who committed certain sexual sins (Lev 20:14; 21:9), for Achan (Jos 7:15, 25), and for Saul and Jonathan (1Sa 31:12).[38]

The holy conflagration that consumes the sons of Aaron is the first example of Yahweh theophany in judgment against his own people. It illustrates, however, the warning that was voiced on Mount Sinai, that the people must not approach too near Yahweh lest he "break out" against them and consume them (Ex 19:24). Indeed, even the priests must not approach Yahweh unless they have consecrated themselves, or else he will "break out" against them, too (v. 22). The point made by those warnings was that Yahweh is a holy God, not to be trifled with. Fallen man may not approach him carelessly. Even his own priests must be consecrated before they approach him. Nadab and Abihu, who acted in sin by filling their censers with unauthorized fire for Yahweh, suffered the penalty that God had warned about on Mount Sinai: he did indeed "break out" against them. God's holy fire "consumed" (וַתֹּאכַל) the presumptuous. Such a warning and such an event are at least part of the background for the statement that "Yahweh your God is a consuming fire" (אֵשׁ אֹכְלָה, Dt 4:24; cf. Ex 24:17). Calvin rightly observes:

> If we reflect how holy a thing God's worship is, the enormity of the punishment will by no means offend us. Besides, it was necessary that their religion should be sanc-

---

[38] See further, Niehaus, *Amos*, 1:444 (Am 6:10).

tioned at its very commencement; for if God had suffered the sons of Aaron to transgress with impunity, they would have afterwards carelessly neglected the whole law. This, therefore, was the reason for such great severity, that the priests should anxiously watch against all profanation.[39]

The same observations apply to God's severe treatment of Ananias and Sapphira in the early days of the new covenant community (Ac 5:1–11).

Taberah[40]

The holy fire that consumed the priests could also consume the people. We do not know exactly what caused the people to grumble, only that they "complained about their hardships in Yahweh's hearing" (Nu 11:1a, author's trans.). As a result of their complaint, Yahweh's anger was aroused. Then "fire from Yahweh burned among them and consumed some of the outskirts of the camp. When the people cried out to Moses, he prayed to Yahweh and the fire died down. So that place was called Taberah, because fire from Yahweh had burned among them" (vv. 1b–3).

The account's phraseology recalls God's judgment on the sons of Aaron. Fire from Yahweh (אֵשׁ יהוה, 11:1b, so 11:3; cf. אֵשׁ מִלִּפְנֵי יהוה, 10:2) burned and consumed (תִּבְעַר ... וַתֹּאכַל, 11:1, cf. וַתֹּאכַל, 10:2). Because Yahweh's fire burned (בער)

---

[39]J. Calvin, *Commentaries on the Last Four Books of Moses* (Grand Rapids: Eerdmans), 3:431.

[40]The location of Taberah is not known, but the place was obviously named after what Yahweh did there. I cannot agree with P. J. Budd, *Numbers*, WBC (Waco: Word, 1984), 5:120, who says that "the story is the continuation of the Yahwist's account of Israel's journey from Sinai to the land . . . [the] name–'burning'–evidently suggested to the author a site for a story of disaffection. . . . The expression of Israel's fear and doubt may reflect the attitude of those who sought security in foreign alliances." There is no proof of the aetiology he suggests and no need to search for a historical anchorage of wilderness events in the later history of Israel.

among them, the place was named "Burning" (תַּבְעֵרָה). The etymology is legitimate and not the ground of a false aetiology.[41] Just as Yahweh judged the priests and did not hesitate to burn up Aaron's own sons, so he judges the people. God shows the gravity of sin by sending theophanic fire to consume the sinner. Such a theophany forms the background of the command, "You shall burn (וּבִעַרְתָּ) the evil [one] out of your midst" (NIV, "You must purge the evil from among you"; Dt 13:(6)5; 17:7, 12; 19:13, 19; 21:21; et al.). Just as God has "burned the evil" from the midst of his people, so his people must learn to do. Such "burning" was essential in the face of the idolatrous Canaanite context they would be entering. It has a New Testament analogy in the Lord's command to expel the unrepentant brother (Mt 18:15–17; 1Co 5:1–5).

Aaron and Miriam

Miriam and Aaron appear to have been destined, among other things, to prove that being made a prophet or a priest by God is no guarantee of one's character. When they criticize Moses for having a Cushite wife, they do not fail to remind their audience of their own qualifications: "Has Yahweh spoken only through Moses? Hasn't he also spoken through us?" (Nu 12:2). As a contrast to their presumption, the author tells us that Moses was "more humble than anyone else on the face of the earth" (v. 3). Yahweh's reaction to their presumption is to appear: "Yahweh came down [וַיֵּרֶד] in a pillar of cloud [עָנָן עַמּוּד]; he stood [וַיַּעֲמֹד] at the entrance to the Tent and sum-

---

[41]BDB, 128–29, derives תַּבְעֵרָה from בער, "to burn." M. Noth, *Numbers*, trans. J. D. Martin (Philadelphia: Westminster, 1968), 84, suggests that the biblical derivation is secondary, and that we should "regard it as derived from the root *bʿr* = 'to remove' (perhaps also 'to graze') or as connected with the Arabic *baʿr* = 'dung,' 'dirt.'" In this way he can claim that a secondary and mistaken etymology is "the basis of the whole passage." His suggestion, however, is quite arbitrary.

moned Aaron and Miriam" (v. 5). There follows a brief discourse that forever distinguishes the role of Moses among the prophets:

> When a prophet of Yahweh is among you,
> I reveal myself to him in visions,
> I speak to him in dreams.
> But this is not true of my servant Moses;
>   he is faithful in all my house.
> With him I speak face to face,
>   clearly and not in riddles;
>   he sees the form of Yahweh.
> Why then were you not afraid
>   to speak against my servant Moses? (Nu 12:6–8)

Moses as covenant mediator sees Yahweh in a way that no one else does. He has an unparalleled exposure to the divine glory.[42] So he anticipates Christ, who can speak of "the glory I had with you before the world began" (Jn 17:5). Parallelism can also be seen in the way God affirms the commands of these two prophets. Yahweh comes among his people to judge those who oppose his covenant mediator, Moses. In the same way, God will come eschatologically to judge those who oppose his Prophet Jesus. At the eschaton, however, God and his Prophet will be one—God the Son. If God shows himself a severe judge during the wilderness wanderings, that is still only a foreshadowing of the severity of eternal punishment. The form of Yahweh's judgment in the case of Aaron and Miriam is not so severe, however. They are not destroyed as Aaron's sons had been. We read, "The anger of Yahweh burned against them, and he left them. When the cloud lifted from above the Tent, there stood Miriam—leprous, like snow" (Nu 12:9–10).[43]

---

[42]Moses' exposure to God's glory still has severe limits, as Ex 33:12–23 makes clear.

[43]Aaron is not affected, although he declares his solidarity with Miriam (12:11). At Aaron's request, Moses intercedes with Yahweh, who commands that Miriam be confined for seven days outside the camp, after which she

THE SINAI THEOPHANY

"If Only We Had Died in Egypt!"

Such is the cry of Israel once they hear the report of the twelve spies. They even plan to stone those who advocate conquering the land (Nu 14:10). At that point we are told that "the glory of Yahweh [כְּבוֹד יהוה] appeared [נִרְאָה] at the Tent of Meeting to all the Israelites" (v. 10). This is another way of saying that Yahweh came to the tabernacle entrance as before, in a cloud/pillar of cloud. Moses' intercessory prayer reminds Yahweh, "Your cloud stays [עֹמֵד] over them, and ... you go before them in a pillar [עַמֻּד] of cloud by day and a pillar [עַמֻּד] of fire by night" (v. 14). The theophany is aptly described as the "glory" of Yahweh. Yahweh himself uses the word. He refers to "my glory and the miraculous signs I performed in Egypt" (v. 22). And as a way of rebuking the people's lack of trust in God's ability to conquer the Canaanites, he avers that "the glory of Yahweh fills the whole earth" (v. 21). The phrase forms the background for the psalmist's prayer, "May the whole earth be filled with his glory" (Ps 72:19), and the seraphs' declaration, "The whole earth is full of his glory" (Isa 6:3). If Yahweh's glory fills the earth, he is certainly a match for any human army! The passage even contains an apparent allusion to the theomachy involved in the conquest. Joshua and Caleb encourage the people that the Canaanites' "protection is gone, but Yahweh is with us" (14:9). The expression translated "their protection is gone" (סָר צִלָּם מֵעֲלֵיהֶם) indicates the withdrawal of any protection the Canaanite gods might have afforded their worshipers against the advance of Yahweh and Israel.[44] The phrase סוּר מֵעַל is used of the turning away of

---

can be brought back (12:14b). This tacitly implies that she has been cured, since a person cleansed of leprosy could be fully accepted only after a seven-day waiting period (Lev 14:2ff.). The word translated "leprous" (מְצֹרַעַת) probably covered a range of skin diseases, as at Nu 5:2.

[44]So L. E. Binns, *The Book of Numbers* (London: Methuen, 1927), 92; Noth, *Numbers*, 108; J. Sturdy, *Numbers* (Cambridge: Cambridge University Press, 1972), 100.

divine presence at Judges 16:20 (shorn Samson did not know that "Yahweh had left him") and 1 Samuel 28:15 (rebellious Saul laments that "God has turned away from me"). The noun צֵל is often used of God's protective presence in the Old Testament (e.g., Pss 17:8; 36:8[7]; 57:2[1]; 63:8[7]; 91:1; Isa 49:2).[45] These two lines of evidence converge in Numbers 14:9 to indicate the departure of the Canaanite gods from their tutelary role of the Canaanites as Yahweh advances against them in theomachy on Israel's behalf (cf. Jos 10:42). In the fullness of time Jesus did the same: "Having disarmed the powers and authorities, he made a public spectacle of them, triumphing over them by the cross" (Col 2:15). By so doing he cleared the way for the impartation of his Holy Spirit and the victorious advance of his church. Paul could declare, "If God is for us, who can be against us?" (Ro 8:31).

The Korahite Rebellion

Korah, Dathan, and Abiram come before Moses with a claim of false equality, just as Aaron and Miriam had done before them. Now, however, the case is far more severe. Not only these three men, but a group of 250 "well-known community leaders" come against Moses and Aaron with this complaint: "The whole community is holy, every one of them, and Yahweh is with them. Why then do you set yourselves above the assembly of Yahweh?" (Nu 16:3). One form their challenge takes is the ironic charge that Moses and Aaron have brought the people up "out of a land flowing with milk and honey" (v. 13) but have not yet brought the people "into a land flowing with milk and honey" (v. 14).

---

[45] It can also be used of the protection afforded by human kings and rulers, e.g., Abimelech (Jdg 9:15), Egypt (Isa 30:2.3), and Assyria (Eze 31:6). By extension the same figure of speech, used of the Great King (Yahweh) and human kings, could also be used of pagan gods who were considered to be "kings." Cf. above, chap. 3.

Yahweh's answer to their challenge is to appear as before: "When Korah had gathered all his followers ... at the entrance to the Tent of Meeting, the glory of Yahweh appeared [יהוה וַיֵּרָא כְבוֹד] to the entire assembly" (Nu 16:19; cf. 14:10). Yahweh causes the earth to open up and swallow Korah, Dathan, Abiram, and all their households and possessions (Ex 16:32).[46] Not only so, but "fire came out from Yahweh and consumed [אֵשׁ יָצְאָה מֵאֵת יהוה וַתֹּאכַל; cf. Lev 9:24; 10:2] the 250 men" who allied themselves under Korah's leadership. These are subsequently referred to as "those who had been burned up" (הַשְּׂרֻפִים, Nu 16:39).

God's judgment on them is not unlike that which later befalls Achan and his household, who were burned (שׂרף, Jos 7:25) after being stoned. We are told that "Achan son of Zerah, the silver, the robe, the gold wedge, his sons and daughters, his cattle, donkeys and sheep, his tent and all that he had" were taken to the Valley of Achor and destroyed (vv. 24–26). The total destruction of both sinner and household is a mode of covenantal punishment well-attested both in the Bible and in the ancient Near East. Assyrian kings often reported the capture and exile of covenant-breaking vassal kings and their households. Tiglath-pileser I reported that Kadmuhu land was in revolt and had "withheld tax and tribute from Aššur my Lord."[47] The suzerain reconquered them and punitively destroyed their cities. He said of their king, Kili-Teshub, "His wives, his sons, the offspring of his loins, his clan, copper kettles, five bronze bathtubs, together with their gods, gold and silver, the best of their property, I carried off."[48] A remarkable

---

[46]Quite possibly Ex 15:12 ("You stretched out your right hand and the earth swallowed [בלע, as at Nu 16:32] them." On this understanding, אָז at Ex 15:1 would not mean "then," but "that being the case." In other words, Ex 15 was not sung by Moses and the Israelites immediately after the Reed Sea crossing but later–although as a result of what Yahweh did at the Reed Sea.

[47]Grayson, *Assyrian Rulers of the Third and Second Millennia B.C.*, 2:14 (A.0.87.1.i.90–91).

[48]Ibid., 15 (A.0.87.ii.28–32). Cf. p. 15 (A.0.87.ii.47–48); p. 22 (A.0.87. v.17–18).

parallel exists between this passage and God's dealing with his rebellious vassals. Both concern relations between a suzerain and his vassal, and both entail punishment of a rebellious vassal and his entire household. Such practice is well attested among the Assyrian kings, both before and after Tiglath-pileser I.[49] Tukulti-Ninurta II declared of a Nairi king, "His sons, his daughters, his wives, the property of his palace, I carried away."[50] Tiglath-pileser III said of one Ursanika, "Himself, his wife, his sons and daughters, his gods I carried away."[51] Similar treatment of rebellious kings is attested by Sargon II,[52] Sennacherib,[53] Esarhaddon,[54] and Ashurbanipal.[55] The same rationale applies in all of these cases. The conquered kings whose households and goods—and sometimes gods—are taken were vassals, bound by covenant to the Assyrian suzerain. As the Assyrian yoke was onerous, the vassal(s) strove to throw it off. They withheld both fealty and tribute from the Assyrian emperor. In Assyrian parlance they "withheld tax and tribute from Aššur my Lord." As a result, the Assyrian suzerain was authorized to treat those covenant vassals

---

[49] E.g., Adad-nirari I; cf. E. F. Weidner, "Die Kämpfe Adadniraris I. gegen Ḫanigalbat," *AfO* 5 (Berlin, 1928–29): 90 (Text A.48–52).

[50] W. Schramm, "Die Annalen des Assyrischen Königs Tukulti-Ninurta II," *BO* 27, no. 3/4 (May-July 1970): 148 (v. 3); cf. more recently Grayson, *Assyrian Rulers*, 2:171 (A.0.100.5.3). This inscription of the king's "annals" contains a pervasive shifting between first and third person singular, which is brought out more effectively in Schramm's translation. The shift can hardly be explained except as a stylistic phenomenon. Cf. J. Sperber, "Der Personenwechsel in der Bibel," *ZA* 21 (1918/19): 23–33.

[51] Rost, *Die Keilschrifttexte Tiglat-Pilesers III.*, Bd. I, p. 8 (40–41).

[52] Thureau-Dangin, *Une Relation de la Huitième Campagne de Sargon*, 52 (348).

[53] Luckenbill, *The Annals of Sennacherib*, 34 (46–48).

[54] Borger, *AfO* Beiheft 9, p. 48 (§ 27 Ep. 5.74–77).

[55] Ashurbanipal declared of the rebel Dunanu: "His wife, his sons, his daughters, his concubines, his singers, male and female—I led forth and counted as spoil. Silver, gold, the treasure of his palace—I brought forth and counted as spoil. The officials who stood before him, [his] smiths, his quartermasters—[I led forth] and counted as spoil" (Piepkorn, *HPIA*, 70 [vi.27–32]).

as spoil—as plunder taken in payment for the debt of covenant-breaking. Sometimes death was the penalty of disobedience. Tukulti-Ninurta I boasts that he burned a whole city of rebellious vassals alive.[56] The Old Testament contains many parallels to this mode of punishment, of which the Korahite example is perhaps the most dramatic.[57]

THE DEUTERONOMIC ACCOUNTS

In the book of Deuteronomy, Moses mentions the Horeb/Sinai events several times as part of the grand historical review by which he exhorts the people before they cross the Jordan to conquer the land. The word "deuteronomic" is simply an adjective and does not imply subscription to the hypothesis of Noth and his followers regarding a supposed "Deuteronomistic History."[58] Moses' purpose is to encourage the people to obey Yahweh, to be faithful to their God. It is appropriate, given that purpose, that he remind them not only of their deliverance from Egypt, but also of the awesome theophany they experienced at Horeb/Sinai. He does this in three passages: Deuteronomy 4:1–40; 5:1–33; and 9:7–21.

The Standard of Revelation

Moses first recalls to popular cognizance the unprecedented way in which Yahweh revealed himself to Israel.

---

[56] Grayson, *Assyrian Rulers*, 1:236 (A.0.78.1.iii.44).

[57] E.g., 1Ki 14:7–11; 16:1–4, 11–13; 21:20–24; Ezr 6:11; Da 6:24 (the destruction of the lawbreaker's house here implies the destruction of his household); Est 8:11; 9:5–10. Cf. Mt 18:23–25!

[58] E.g., M. Noth, *Überlieferungsgeschichtliche Studien,* 2d ed. (Tübingen: Max Niemeyer Verlag, 1957); 1–110, trans. into English by J. Doull, J. Barton, et al. as *The Deuteronomistic History,* JSOT Supplement Series 15 (Sheffield: JSOT Press, 1981). Noth's hypothesis appears quite arbitrary in light of the literary realities of the ancient Near East. I believe that it will, in time, become a curious relic in the history of scholarship, like the Documentary Hypothesis and some other imaginary constructs still employed in Old Testament studies.

According to Moses, no other nation has their gods near them as Israel has Yahweh whenever they pray to him (Dt 4:7). He recalls the grand Yahweh theophany that came before the lawgiving: "You came near and stood at the foot of the mountain while it blazed with fire to the very heavens, with black clouds and deep darkness. Then Yahweh spoke to you out of the fire. You heard the sound of words but saw no form; there was only a voice" (Dt 4:11–12).

The deuteronomic phraseology parallels that of the Exodus accounts. The "mountain blazes with fire" (הָהָר בֹּעֵר בָּאֵשׁ; cf. Ex 19:18; 24:17; and the phrasing at Taberah, Nu 11:1b–3). There is "darkness" (חֹשֶׁךְ; cf. the "darkness" Yahweh's theophany causes for the Egyptian army, Ex 14:20), "smoke" (עָשָׁן; cf. Ex 19:18), and "deep darkness" (עֲרָפֶל; cf. Ex 19:16). They also heard a "thunderous voice" (קוֹל; cf. Ex 19:16). The awesome nature of Yahweh's theophany constitutes a polemic against idolatry. As part of that polemic, Moses reminds the people that they saw no "form" (תְּמוּנָה), although they did hear Yahweh's voice (Dt 4:12). Since audition was paramount in that theophany, the people should obey what they have heard from God, but not make any image of him (Dt 4:15–20). Much later Jesus would allude to this statement of Moses to show the Jews of his day how deficient they were in their knowledge of God. God's people in Moses' day at least heard Yahweh's voice, although they did not see his form. But Jesus tells his hearers, "You have never heard his voice nor seen his form" (Jn 5:37).[59]

Not only was Yahweh's theophany a special revelation to Israel; what Yahweh has done is utterly unique:

> Ask now about the former days, long before your time, from the day God created man on the earth; ask from one end of the heavens to the other. Has anything so great as this ever happened, or has anything like it ever been heard of? Has any other people heard the voice of God speak-

---

[59]See below, chap. 9.

ing out of fire, as you have, and lived? Has any god ever tried to take for himself one nation out of another nation, by testings, by miraculous signs and wonders, by war, by a mighty hand and an outstretched arm, or by great and awesome deeds, like all the things Yahweh your God did for you in Egypt before your very eyes? (Dt 4:32–34)

The phrases of Moses' address echo the Exodus experience: God's "thunderous voice" and his "fire"; and his miraculous deliverance of Israel "by signs and wonders" (וּבְמוֹפְתִים בְּאֹתֹת; cf. Ex 3:7). Of particular interest is the deuteronomic phrase "by a mighty hand and an outstretched arm" (נְטוּיָה בְּיָד חֲזָקָה וּבִזְרוֹעַ, 4:34; cf. Ex 3:19; 13:19). The phrase has an Egyptian background. At Karnak, Raamses II (ca. 1290–1224 B.C.) is portrayed aiming an arrow at a town as his chariot horses trample defeated enemies. A vanquished captain looks back at him. The explanatory legend reads, "The fear of him is like [that of] Ba‘al in the foreign lands, valiant without his equal whose hand is outstretched."[60] Another figure shows a fort with the inscription, "Town which the strong arm of Pharaoh, L. P. H., captured."[61] The "outstretched hand" and "strong arm" are part of pharaonic typology in war against the foe but also apparently in action on behalf of a vassal. Earlier, in the Amarna correspondence, Abdi-Hepa of Jerusalem writes to Pharaoh: "The mighty hand of the king has led me into the house of my father"–in other words, Pharaoh has secured the hereditary throne for his vassal (cf. the similar action of the Hittite suzerain for his vassal, above, chap. 3).[62] The phraseology of a "hand outstretched" and a "strong arm" are thus apparently, as Weinfeld notes, part of "Egyptian royal typology."[63] The irony of the deuteronomic usage becomes im-

---

[60] G. A. Gaballa, "Minor War Scenes of Ramesses II at Karnak," *JEA* 55 (1969): 86–87 (Fig. 5A).
[61] Ibid., 86–87 (Fig. 5C).
[62] *EA* 286:12–13.
[63] Weinfeld, *Deuteronomy*, 329.

mediately apparent. According to Moses, it is Yahweh and not Pharaoh who really has the "strong hand" and "outstretched arm." The reversal of the traditional phrasing (Pharaoh has an "outstretched hand" and a "strong arm," but Yahweh has a "strong hand and an outstretched arm") may even be meant to underscore the irony. Just as Pharaoh could use his strong arm and outstretched hand to do battle with the foe and establish his vassal, so Yahweh could use his strong hand and outstretched arm to do the same. And in Israel's case, Yahweh used his arm and hand against Pharaoh himself.

Moses not only reminds the people of the glory theophany they saw at Horeb/Sinai. He also structures his argument in a way that should bring confidence in their God. The sequence of key ideas may be diagrammed as follows:

1 God created man upon the earth (4:32)
2 God appeared at Horeb/Sinai (4:33)
3 God took Israel out of Egypt (4:34)

This sequence of ideas is no accident. Here and elsewhere God's ability to save is mentioned in the context of the fact that he is the Creator (e.g., Pss 121, 135). Psalm 136 connects God as Creator (vv. 5–9) with the God of the Exodus (vv. 10–22) most clearly. Moses explains that God's purpose in such self-revelation is that Israel may know him: "You were shown these things so that you might know that Yahweh is God; besides him there is no other" (Dt 4:35). But the knowledge of God always brings salvation, because God is life itself. So in the New Testament John could echo Moses and declare of Jesus' miraculous signs recorded in his book, "These are written that you may believe that Jesus is the Christ, the Son of God, and that by believing you may have life in his name" (Jn 20:31).

The Lawgiving

The deuteronomic account of God's lawgiving parallels and adds information to the earlier account in the book of Exodus. Moses begins by reminding the people that Yahweh made a covenant under which they are accountable (Dt 5:1-3). He tells them that "Yahweh spoke to you face to face out of the fire on the mountain" (v. 4). The phrase "face to face" (פָּנִים בְּפָנִים) emphasizes the facticity of the event and the personal nature of God's involvement with Israel; it does not mean that the people actually saw God's face.[64] The phrase used to portray Israel's experience of God at the mountain (פָּנִים בְּפָנִים) is not quite the same as that used of God's speaking to Moses (פָּנִים אֶל פָּנִים, Ex 33:11; cf. Ge 32:31; Dt 34:10). The latter, as Keil and Delitzsch note, "expresses the very confidential relation in which the Lord spoke to Moses as one friend to another; whereas the former simply notes the directness with which Jehovah spoke to the people."[65] Of course, not even Moses literally saw Yahweh's face—which no one can see and live (Ex 33:20). In any case, the people's reaction showed that they were not on easy terms of intimacy with God. In fact, they showed an appropriate human fear of Yahweh's holy presence: Moses had to stand between God and the people because they were afraid of the fire (Dt 5:5). Moses' purpose in recalling all of this is probably to reawaken in the people a due sense of Yahweh's holiness and goodness and of their own obligation to God.

After Moses recalls the people's encounter with Yahweh at the mountain, he recounts the commands that Yahweh has given. The larger pericope, Deuteronomy 5:1-33, involves a good deal of parallel structure:

---

[64]Cf. C. F. Keil and F. Delitzsch, *Biblical Commentary on the Old Testament, The Pentateuch*, vol. 3, trans. J. Martin (Grand Rapids: Eerdmans, 1978), 320; P. Buis and J. Leclercq, *Le Deutéronome* (Paris: Librarie Lecoffre, 1963), 63; P. C. Craigie, *The Book of Deuteronomy*, NICOT (Grand Rapids: Eerdmans, 1976), 148. Buis and Leclercq cite a similar observation by Augustine (*Le Deutéronome*, 63).

[65]Keil and Delitzsch, *Commentary*, 3:320.

5:1–5 Theme
    5:1–3   Summons to hear laws of the covenant
    5:4   Yahweh spoke out of the fire
    5:5   Moses describes the people's fear

5:6–27 Theme
    5:6–21   Laws of the covenant
    5:22   Yahweh spoke out of the fire
    5:23–27 Moses describes the people's fear

The parallels are obvious and purposeful. Much has been written about the repetitive phraseology of Deuteronomy, and it has been generally recognized that the purpose of such a style is to achieve emphasis on the key themes that are repeated. The same purpose is evident here, as the key themes are stated in a brief introduction (Dt 5:1–5) then expanded upon and repeated in the body of the passage (vv. 6–27).

The body of the passage includes the Decalogue (5:6–21) and a further account of the people's encounter with Yahweh at the mountain (vv. 22–27). The account repeats the theophanic terms used in 5:1–5.[66] The people's reaction is one of fear—but of an appropriate fear. They know they are in the presence of a holy God and dare not prolong the experience lest they be consumed. So their reluctance, far from being a faithless shrinking back (Heb 10:39), receives God's approval (Dt 5:28–29). A proper human fear of God is an abiding fact, not only in the Old Testament, but even in the New. But in the New, God reveals an unexpected way of dealing with it.

---

[66] Again we find the theophanic terms of Horeb/Sinai. The people heard Yahweh's "voice" (קוֹל) out of "the fire, the cloud and the deep darkness" (הָאֵשׁ הֶעָנָן וְהָעֲרָפֶל). Amid the "darkness" (חֹשֶׁךְ) "the mountain was ablaze with fire" (הָהָר בֹּעֵר בָּאֵשׁ). The leading men know that Yahweh has shown them his "glory and his majesty" (אֶת־כְּבֹדוֹ וְאֶת־גָּדְלוֹ). They fear that "this great fire will consume us" (כִּי תֹאכְלֵנוּ הָאֵשׁ הַגְּדֹלָה הַזֹּאת).

"A Prophet Like Me"

At the end of his career Moses addresses a people who are about to cross over Jordan and conquer the Promised Land. In a way, he is speaking to a different people: a generation that was under twenty when God declared that those over twenty would not see the land flowing with milk and honey—that their bodies would fall in the desert (Nu 14:29–30). Yet again, Moses is speaking to the same people: those under twenty who had seen the *magnalia dei* but had not been counted among the rebellious (v. 31).

Consequently Moses is able to remind the people of what they have seen. He recalls the awesome Horeb theophany in order to give a rationale for a new prophet whom Yahweh will one day raise up. The passage in Deuteronomy 18 deserves attention not only for its mention of the Horeb/Sinai theophany, but also for the way it uses that historic event. The structure of the prophecy is important to its message:

A Yahweh your God will raise up for you a prophet like me from among your own brothers. You must listen to him.

B For this is what you asked of Yahweh your God at Horeb on the day of the assembly when you said, "Let us not hear the voice of Yahweh our God nor see this great fire anymore, or we will die."

A' Yahweh said to me: "What they say is good. I will raise up for them a prophet like you from among their brothers; I will put my words in his mouth, and he will tell them everything I command him. If anyone does not listen to my words that the prophet speaks in my name, I myself will call him to account" (Dt 18:15–19).

Moses' prophecy includes a final comment on the Horeb/Sinai event that supplies new information. We learn more about Yahweh's response (18:15–19; cf. 5:28–31). That response is pregnant with meaning. So that the reader may better appreciate it, I reiterate the reason for Israel's words to Moses: they are motivated by fear of a holy God. God knows this, and that is why he approves of their fear: "Everything they said was good. Oh, that their hearts would be inclined to fear me and keep all my commands always" (Dt 5:28b–29). And yet, although God approves their fear, that fear does present a problem. The problem at Horeb/Sinai is the same problem that Adam and Eve had with God once they had sinned. God could no longer appear in his glory without also concealing himself in a storm. And if that storm-cloud theophany was awesome, even frightening, the full revelation of his glory would have been even worse—fatal, in fact. As Yahweh warned Moses, "You cannot see my face, for no one may see me and live" (Ex 33:20). The people were right to say, "Do not have God speak to us or we will die" (Ex 20:19), and again, "What mortal man has ever heard the voice of the living God speaking out of the fire, as we have, and survived?" (Dt 5:26). The people knew that sinful humans cannot endure the presence of a holy God.

This is the Old Testament dilemma. God wants to reveal himself to humanity, and humanity needs to have a revelation of God. God's presence is our life, as the Aaronic blessing well shows. But in the Old Testament that presence must be partly an absence. The self-revelation of God must also be a self-concealment of God.

God himself now produces the solution: there must be another prophet, like Moses, who can mediate between God and the people. But this prophet, to be like Moses, must be a covenant mediator between God and all the people, just as Moses was. If this is so—and it is—it must imply a new covenant. Moreover, the new prophet will be more than a prophet and more than a man, because he is identified in the New Testament as Christ (Ac 3:22–23).

Moses' prophecy concerning the prophet to come adumbrates this truth by its very literary structure. The passage begins with a statement by Moses that Yahweh will raise up another prophet like him, and the people must obey him (= A). The sole reason he gives for this coming prophet is the way the people feared God at Horeb/Sinai (= B). Moses then recalls Yahweh's words to him, which again promise the prophet to come and warn that people must obey God's words, which the prophet speaks in his name (= A'). The structure can be diagramed in a way that clearly brings out its implications:

A The prophet
B Horeb/Sinai theophany
A' The prophet

This simple literary structure is eloquent in stating that the prophet (A, A') would in days to come actually contain the theophanic glory of God (B)–the A elements here bracketing the B. And this is just what humanity needs–God among us–but even more, a Man who can contain the glory of God so that the glory of God can fill all people. Thus Jesus can say, "Anyone who has seen me has seen the Father" (Jn 14:9), and again, "The Father is in me" (v. 10), and "It is the Father, living in me, who is doing his work" (v. 10). In fact, this is why Jesus can do great works of deliverance just as Yahweh did for Israel in Egypt, and why both these latter and those former works are described as the "glory" of God (e.g., Nu 14:22; Jn 11:40; et al.). In a parallel way, Jesus can also speak of "my glory" (Jn 17:24). Even of his followers' works Jesus can say, "I will do whatever you ask in my name, so that the Son may bring glory to the Father" (Jn 14:13). Jesus expected his followers to do the same works that he did (v. 12), because they would contain the same glory presence that he contained: "I have given them the glory that you gave me, that they may be one as we are one: I in them and you in me" (Jn 17:22–23a). Jesus portrays a more intimate relationship with God than even Moses experienced. Yet we can see that Moses' experience of God anticipated that Christian relationship.

Moses' Radiant Face

Deuteronomy closes with an account of Moses' death (Dt 34) and offers an encomium on the prophet: "Moses was a hundred and twenty years old when he died, yet his eyes were not weak nor his strength gone" (v. 7). The reason for Moses' remarkable vitality apparently lay in his relationship with God.

Moses not only saw the glory of God, he displayed it, and at first unawares. The relevant passage (Ex 34:29–32) deserves attention because of its importance for biblical anthropology:

> When Moses came down from Mount Sinai with the two tablets of the Testimony in his hands, he was not aware that his face was radiant because he had spoken with Yahweh. When Aaron and all the Israelites saw Moses, his face was radiant, and they were afraid to come near him. But Moses called to them; so Aaron and all the leaders of the community came back to him, and he spoke to them. Afterward all the Israelites came near him, and he gave them all the commands Yahweh had given him on Mount Sinai.

Several facts make this account parallel to an account of a theophany. First, Moses appears on the scene with theophanic glory—his "radiant face" (קָרַן עוֹר פָּנָיו, Ex 34:29, 30).[67] When

---

[67]Batto, *Slaying the Dragon,* 124, follows L. Bailey, "Horns of Moses," *IDB-Sup,* 419–20, in thinking that "horns sprouted from Moses' forehead," a metaphor for divinity in ancient Near Eastern iconography. The idea more often seems to be associated with assertions of prowess in war, however. The idea of taking "horns" to oneself as an assertion of military strength, although disputed by J. Wellhausen, *Skizzen und Vorarbeiten,* vol. 5: *Die kleinen Propheten übersetzt, mit Noten* (Berlin: Reimer, 1893) p. 86, is well-illustrated by the prophet Zedekiah, who encouraged Ahab by a lying spirit (1Ki 22:19–23) to a fatal attack on Aram: "Now Zedekiah son of Kenaanah had made iron *horns* [du., "*a pair of horns*"], and he declared, 'This is what the Lord says: "With these you will gore the Arameans until they are destroyed"'" (1Ki 22:11). Micah prophesies a future military victory for Jerusalem in these terms: "Rise and thresh, O daughter of Zion, / for I will give you *horns* of

Aaron and all the people see this apparition, they react in fear—just as the Israelites reacted at Sinai and just as Moses himself reacted at the burning bush when he hid his face "because he was afraid to look at God" (Ex 3:6). Like God, however, Moses quells the fear of the people by calling to them—a signal that it is only he, and they need not be afraid (cf. Mt 14:25–27). The leaders and the people respond by returning to Moses, and then he, like God, gives them the commands that God had given to him.

This "theophanic" account does more than make Moses parallel to God—although, within limits, it certainly does that. It adumbrates what God intends for all humanity. In that regard the veil assumes some importance. Moses wore a veil to cover the radiance of his face when he was before the people, but when Moses turned to go before God, "he removed the veil until he came out" (Ex 34:34). Moses' removal of the veil meant that he was exposed to God's glory when he was in God's presence. His experience of God's glory presence is a vivid illustration of the Aaronic blessing:

> [May] Yahweh make his face shine upon you
> and be gracious to you;
> [May] Yahweh turn his face toward you
> and give you peace. (Nu 6:25–26)

---

iron; / I will give you hoofs of bronze, / and you will break to pieces many nations" (Mic 4:13–14). The Hebrew use of "horn" as a symbol for strength, especially military strength (an idea derivative from the might of beasts that have horns) is well-attested, e.g., Dt 33:17; 2Sa 22:3 ("the horn of my salvation"); Pss 75:5–6, 11(4–5, 10), 89:18(17). Cf. Ashurbanipal's claim that his goddess "Ninlil, the lordly Wild-Cow, the most heroic among the goddesses who rivals in rank [only] with Anu and Enlil, was butting my enemies with her mighty horns" (Maximilian Streck, *Assurbanipal und die letzten Assyrischen Könige bis zum Untegrange Nineveh's* [Leipzig: J. C. Hinrichs, 1916], II, 78–79 [ll. 75–78]; cf. *ANET*, p. 300). In view of the Bible's own understanding of Moses' experience (e.g., 1Co 3:12–18), it is better to follow the traditional understanding that "horns of light"—i.e., divinely imparted radiance—is intended by the unusual Hebrew phrase. Cf. my discussion of the *melammu* imparted to ancient kings, above, chap. 3.

The ancient Near Eastern background of this idea is clear. The face of a god radiated light and life to those fortunate enough to gaze upon it. Among pagans such an experience was only claimed—and that rarely—by kings.[68] Aaron's blessing expresses the hope that Yahweh will cause his luminous, life-giving face to shine upon all of God's people. If God does turn his face toward someone, the result will be "peace" (שָׁלוֹם)—that is, the wholeness that is the "abundant life" that only God can provide (cf. Jn 10:10b).

Moses' experience illustrates this idea. He spent some forty years frequently in God's radiant, life-giving presence. It may be for this reason that we read, "Moses was a hundred and twenty years old when he died, yet his eyes were not weak nor his strength gone" (Dt 34:7). Moses' frequent exposure to God's "shining face" imparted extraordinary vitality to the prophet. Moses' experience, however, was unique among God's people: "Since then, no prophet has risen in Israel like Moses, whom Yahweh knew face to face" (v. 10).

If the unparalleled nature of Moses' exposure to God was a glory, it was also a problem of the order we have already discussed. The problem was that God wanted all people to receive light and life from himself. For reasons already noted, this could not happen under the Old Testament regime. It could only come as a result of the person and work of Christ. Because of that incarnation, death, and resurrection—and in particular because of the impartation of the Holy Spirit—the situation has now changed. Consequently Paul is able to portray the new situation in terms of the Mosaic veil:

> Whenever anyone turns to the Lord, the veil is taken away. Now the Lord is the Spirit, and where the Spirit of the Lord is, there is freedom. And we, who with unveiled faces all reflect the Lord's glory, are being transformed

---

[68]Cf. above, chap. 4, and examples there cited.

> into his likeness with ever-increasing glory, which comes from the Lord, who is the Spirit. (2Co 3:16–18)

Because of what Christ has done, the encounter between God and people can be far more intimate than it was under the old covenant. When someone turns to the Lord under the new covenant, the veil is taken away and that person can be exposed to God's glory as Moses was. Yet the new covenant person who encounters God is not exactly exposed to him as Moses was. Paul's analogy describes a new work of the glory Spirit—within one's body, which is a "temple of the Holy Spirit" (1Co 6:19), rather than an outer work such as Moses experienced in the tabernacle. Our faces do not shine with an external radiance but with an internal radiance because we "are being transformed into [the] likeness" of God who is himself luminous and radiates glory. That is the work of "the Lord, who is the Spirit" in each Christian.

7

Post-Sinai Theophanies:

Theophanies Demonstrating Sinai Theophany Characteristics in Historical Books and Prophetical Accounts

> The vivid, florid, turgid sky,
>   The drenching thunder rolling by,
>
> The morning deluged still by night,
>   The clouds tumultuously bright
>
> And the feeling heavy in cold chords
>   Struggling toward impassioned choirs,
>
> Crying among the clouds, enraged
>   By gold antagonists in air–
>
> I know my lazy, leaden twang
>   Is like the reason in a storm;
>
> And yet it brings the storm to bear.
>   Wallace Stevens, "The Man With the Blue Guitar," 8.1–9

Yahweh theophanies occur both before and after the events of Sinai. God's appearances in the Old Testament are an ongoing part of his wise and just covenant administration. So it is no surprise that Joshua, Gideon, Manoah, Solomon, Elijah, and Isaiah were allowed to experience theophanies evocative of what happened on Mount Sinai and during the wilderness wanderings. God appeared in a similar way to Ezekiel as his glory departed from the Jerusalem temple. But as he departed, God will return. So the eschatological theophany of Yahweh is normally portrayed in Sinaitic terms—although, in fact, this storm-cloud theophany predates Sinai, as we have seen. All of these portrayals, both the historical and the prophetical, can be understood properly and *seriatim* under the aegis of God's covenant with Israel.

HISTORICAL BOOKS

Joshua

The book of Joshua early establishes Joshua as the true successor to Moses. The Jordan parts for Joshua, as the Sea of Reeds parted for Moses. God hardens the hearts of the Canaanites (Jos 11:20) so that he can destroy them by Joshua's hand, just as he hardened Pharaoh's heart (Ex 4:21; 7:3, 13, 14, 22; et al.) in order to destroy him by Moses' hand. Joshua also experiences a theophany parallel in some respects to the theophany Moses first experienced at Mount Sinai. When Joshua was before Jericho, the "commander of Yahweh's army" appeared to him. The passage (Jos 5:13–15) is structured according to the theophanic *Gattung*:

	Formal Element	Joshua 5:13–15
1	Introductory description, third person	5:13a
3	Response of the addressee	5:13b
4	Deity's self-asseveration	5:14a
8	Inquiry or protest by the addressee	5:14b
7	The *hieros logos*	5:15a
10	Concluding description, third person	5:15b

The angel does not address Joshua first but vice-versa. So there is no "Deity's utterance of the name of the (mortal) addressee" (element 2). Joshua's bold approach to such an angelic visitor is apparently accounted for by the fact that the angel appears as a man with a drawn sword—naturally prompting the question, "Are you for us or for our enemies?" (Jos 5:13). Joshua's question is his "response" (element 3), not to anything the angel has said but to the situation that suddenly confronts him. The angel's answer to Joshua is pregnant with meaning: "Neither, but as commander of the army of Yahweh I have now come" (5:14). The form of his statement (עַתָּה בָאתִי, "now I have come") is that of an official visit (cf. וְעַתָּה אֲשֶׁר בָּאתִי, 2Sa 14:15), used also of a theophany at Daniel 9:23 (וַאֲנִי בָאתִי, Gabriel to Daniel). The angel's response (his self-asseveration, element 4) does not negate the reality that he is there for Joshua and Israel; it is a statement that he is not a man who might be on one side or the other of the impending battle. No, he has come as "commander of the army of Yahweh." Yahweh's "army" is his heavenly host of warrior angels.[1] Joshua's response to this unexpected statement is an appropriate reverence—especially in light of the fact that the angel says nothing exactly to "quell human fear" (element 5) or to "assert his gracious presence" (element 6). On the other hand, what he has already said may go far to quell Joshua's fear. The appearance of God's angel—indeed the commander of God's army—before strong Jericho should afford some sense of God's gracious presence! Surely Yahweh would be with Joshua, just as he was with Moses (Jos 1:5). The angel's *hieros logos* to him would encourage Joshua along these lines. It makes radically clear the parallel between Joshua's experience of theophany at Jericho and Moses' at Sinai. As Yahweh's angel commanded Moses, the angel now commands Joshua: "Take off your sandals, for the place where you are standing is holy" (Jos 5:15a, cf. Ex 3:5). God gave Moses this command just before the Exodus.

---

[1]Cf. J. Gray, ed., *Joshua, Judges and Ruth,* Century Bible (London: Nelson, 1967), 74; M. H. Woudstra, *The Book of Joshua,* NICOT (Grand Rapids: Eerdmans, 1981), 105.

He gives Joshua the same command now, just before the Conquest. The clear parallel to the first Sinai theophany not only affirms Joshua as true successor to Moses, although it certainly does that, it also shows Yahweh's ongoing covenantal—even theophanic—action on behalf of his people.[2]

Gideon

Gideon's experience of Yahweh—or of his angel, or of both—does not begin as a glory theophany. At first it seems to be one of those anthropomorphic angelic appearances such as Abraham experienced (cf. Ge 18:1ff.). "The angel of Yahweh came and sat down under the oak in Ophrah" beside Gideon, who was busy threshing wheat (Jdg 6:11). At the outset of this encounter there is symbolism that adds to its depth: Gideon is "threshing" (חבט) wheat. The verb is used elsewhere four times in the Old Testament. Twice it portrays ordinary harvesting (Dt 24:20; Ru 2:17). But it also portrays God's redemptive judgment upon Israel (Isa 28:27) and his salvific harvesting of them: "In that day Yahweh will *thresh* from the flowing Euphrates to the Wadi of Egypt, and you, O Israelites, will be gathered up one by one" (Isa 27:12). From its metaphorical usage a picture of a saving harvest emerges. It is at least poetically just (in light of such usage) that God finds Gideon threshing, because God will use him to bring a harvest of redemption for Israel out of the hands of Midian.

---

[2]M. Noth, *Das Buch Josua*, Handbuch zum Alten Testament, 7 (Tübingen: J. C. B. Mohr, 1953), 23, unnecessarily attributes the origin of this theophany to a respect for the holiness of the area that stems from the earlier Canaanite period. The suggestion is ad hoc and seeks to locate the pericope in an ancient tradition partly to explain its brevity and apparently fragmentary nature. It is not so fragmentary as one might think, however. For example, it does not lack an indication of the purpose of the theophany (p. 23) if one understands the warlike character of the commander's self-asseveration as an adequate indication of the purpose of his coming. Any contemporary of Joshua would have taken this as a sign that Yahweh and his heavenly armies would be waging war for Israel against Jericho.

Although Gideon's encounter with Yahweh/the angel of Yahweh does not begin dramatically, it takes the form of the theophanic *Gattung*. It falls properly into two parts: Gideon's encounter with God by the oak tree (Jdg 6:11–18) and the account of his offering to Yahweh (vv. 19–24). Taken together, the parts form a narrative whole; one flows naturally from the other. But each half also lends itself to separate analysis:

Formal Element	Judges 6:11–18
1 Introductory description, third person	6:11–12a
2 Deity's utterance of name of addressee	6:12b
3 Response of the addressee	6:13
6 Assertion of his gracious presence	6:12b, 14b, 18b
7 The *hieros logos*	6:14a
8 Inquiry or protest by addressee	6:15
9 Continuation of the *hieros logos*	6:16
8 Inquiry by addressee	6:17–18a

The first half of the account portrays Gideon's encounter with and commission by Yahweh. There is terminological ambivalence. We are told that "the angel of Yahweh" came to him (Jdg 6:11–12), but also that "Yahweh turned to him and said ..." (v. 14). This recalls Moses' dialogue at the burning bush with "the angel of Yahweh," who was also called "Yahweh."[3] The theophanic fire in both accounts is another parallel, although Gideon's encounter with God begins in a more pedestrian way than did Moses'.

The angel/Yahweh appears to Gideon and hails him as "mighty/resourceful warrior" (גִּבּוֹר הֶחָיִל, Jdg 6:12b).[4] The salutation functions as a divine naming in the passage: God has al-

---

[3] Ex 3:2 ("the angel of Yahweh"); 3:4 ("Yahweh").

[4] As Gray, *Joshua, Judges, and Ruth*, 297, notes, the Hebrew is "a technical term for a freeman of substance or land whose status made him liable for military service," but it also has a moral connotation along the lines of "gentleman." The Greek ἥρως ("hero") is not a bad equivalent.

ready determined what Gideon shall be and addresses him accordingly.⁵ However, since the angel seems to be a man, Gideon is bold to address him as such.⁶ He expresses doubt that Yahweh is with Israel anymore (v. 13). Even after God's commission Gideon expresses reluctance to take it up. His diffidence seems endemic to the character of those whom God chooses to be prophets. Like Moses before him (Ex 4:1, 10, 13) and others after him (Jer 1:6; Jnh 1:3ff.), Gideon mistrusts his ability to do what God asks of him (Jdg 6:15).⁷ Yahweh reassures Gideon, "I will be with you [אֶהְיֶה עִמָּךְ, 6:16]," just as he reassured Moses (כִּי־אֶהְיֶה עִמָּךְ, Ex 3:12; cf. Mt 28:19–20). As awareness grows in Gideon that he may actually be talking with God, he asks for a sign. We recall that God gave Moses a sign to bolster his faith (Ex 3:12; cf. 4:1ff.) A number of Mosaic/Exodus parallels are thus established, and the first half of the narrative draws to a close (Jdg 6:17–18).

The second half of the passage gives Gideon the sort of dramatic confirmation he either needs or inwardly desires. God produces supernatural fire and disappears:

---

⁵Cf. C. F. Keil and F. Delitzsch, *The Book of Judges. Commentary on the Old Testament in Ten Volumes* (Grand Rapids: Eerdmans, 1978), 2:331: "This address contained the promise that the Lord would be with Gideon, and that he would prove himself a mighty hero through the strength of the Lord. This promise was to be a guarantee to him of strength and victory in his conflict with the Midianites."

⁶Gray, *Joshua, Judges, and Ruth,* 296, sees this account as a spiritualizing of something human; of the angel he says, "The angel, or bearer of God's message, was here in human form and was not immediately recognized by Gideon. Doubtless human associates who raised scruples and were instrumental in nerving a man's holy resolve were so understood, and the encounter with the angel of the Lord might even be the personification of a man's spiritual conflict when faced by what he recognized as a divine challenge."

⁷Cf. A. E. Cundall and L. Morris, *Judges & Ruth* (London: Tyndale, 1968). Cundall suggests, "It is when a man is fully conscious of his own weakness and the difficulties of the situation that the Lord can take and use him" (p. 105). Gideon's reluctance may not be entirely negative!

Formal Element	**Judges 6:19–24**
1 Introductory description, third person	6:19–22a
3 Response of the addressee	6:22b
5 His quelling of human fear	6:23
10 Concluding description, third person	6:24

Gideon prepares an offering before Yahweh at the oak (Jdg 6:19). But "the angel of God" tells him to place it on a rock.[8] The theophanic act that now occurs further recalls the Exodus. Just as Moses worked wonders with his staff, the angel of God has a staff (מִשְׁעֶנֶת) with which he works a wonder: as his staff touches the offering, fire comes from the rock and consumes the meat and the bread (וַתַּעַל הָאֵשׁ ... וַתֹּאכַל, Jdg 6:21).[9] God's fire conveys an approval of Gideon's offering, just as it did at the ordination of Aaron and his sons (וַתֵּצֵא אֵשׁ ... וַתֹּאכַל, Lev 9:24).[10] Once Gideon's offering is consumed, the "angel of Yahweh" promptly "disappears" (הָלַךְ מֵעֵינָיו, Jdg 6:22).[11] As the sequel shows, this does not mean that God has gone.

Gideon's response to Yahweh's theophany is like that of Israel at Mount Sinai. They said, "Do not have God speak to us, or we will die" (Ex 20:19). Gideon—like Adam and Eve, Moses,

---

[8]When Moses met Yahweh at the burning bush that "angel of Yahweh" was also called "God" (Ex 3:5). In Gideon's case, the angel is now also called "the angel of God" (Jdg 6:20). As elsewhere in the OT, the terms appear to be somewhat interchangeable.

[9]Gideon's angel uses a מִשְׁעֶנֶת, whereas Moses uses a מַטֶּה, Ex 4:2ff. Usage elsewhere suggests some interchangeability of these terms, e.g., Ps 23:5(4), where we read, "Your rod [שֵׁבֶט] and your staff [מִשְׁעֶנֶת] they comfort me." In addition to this parallelistic usage, we find מַטֶּה // שֵׁבֶט in Isa 10:15. Cf. BDB, 986–87.

[10]For other examples of a miracle given as a confirmatory sign, cf. Ex 4:8ff.; 7:8ff.; Dt 13:2ff.; 1Chr 21:26; Isa 38:7.

[11]The expression is a *hapax legomenon*, but cf. Ge 31:40 ("sleep departed [נדד] from my eyes"); Pr 3:21 ("let them [sound judgment and discernment] not depart[לוז] from your eyes"; similarly 4:21); and Eze 10:19, where the cherubim and the glory of Yahweh "went up from the earth as I watched" (וַיֵּרוֹמּוּ מִן־הָאָרֶץ לְעֵינַי).

and Israel before him—is afraid because he has seen God. He says, "Ah, Sovereign Yahweh! I have seen the angel of Yahweh face to face!" (Jdg 6:22). He assumes that he must die as a result (v. 23). But just as Moses quelled the fear of the people (Ex 20:20), Yahweh quells Gideon's fear: "Peace! Do not be afraid. You are not going to die" (Jdg 6:23). So Gideon responds in classic fashion to the theophany he has experienced. He builds an altar to Yahweh and names it after that final word of encouragement: "Yahweh is peace" (6:24).[12] As the pericope closes we see that Gideon, who doubted that God was still with Israel (6:13), suddenly found him; and Yahweh, who already had a plan for Gideon, made him a savior.[13]

Manoah

In what one may call the Manoah theophany, Manoah was not the one to whom the "angel of Yahweh" (Jdg 13:3) or the "angel of God" (v. 9) first appeared. The angel came to make a birth announcement to Manoah's wife (who remains

---

[12]For the pattern of altar-building after a theophany, cf. Ge 12:7; 26:24–25; 35:7; Ex 17:15. M. Kline, *Treaty of the Great King,* 81–82, notes an essential connection between altars and theophanies:

> Significant changes in the nature of theophany from era to era required corresponding changes with respect to the altar. Thus, during the days of the patriarchs altars were frequently erected at the various sites where God appeared, but there was not a continuing central altar until there was a continuing revelation of the presence of God in the form of the Shekinah glory tabernacling in the midst of Israel. This form of theophany began in the Mosaic era, and the covenant stipulations given at Sinai, though they did not exclude altars at other places where God might record his name, were concerned primarily with the continuing central or official altar which would be associated with this abiding Shekinah theophany.

[13]Cf. Jdg 3:9, 15, where the title "savior" (מוֹשִׁיעַ) is applied to judges.

nameless). That announcement has a classic form: "You are sterile and childless, but you are going to conceive and have a son" (v. 3). His words recall Yahweh's promise to Sarai that, although she was worn out and as good as dead, she would have a son: "And behold, a son to Sarah" (Ge 18:10, author's trans.). It also prefigures Isaiah's promise of a son who would be born to a virgin: "The virgin will be with child and will give birth to a son, and will call him Immanuel" (Isa 7:14). There is a Ugaritic background for this formula. A poem celebrating the successful marriage of the lunar goddess Nikkal (i.e., Sumerian Ningal) and the moon god Yarih (cf. Heb. יָרֵחַ, "moon") also prophesies the birth of a son to the moon goddess: "Behold, a virgin [i.e., the moon goddess] shall bear a son."[14] The resemblance of Isaiah 7:14 to the older Ugaritic verse is particularly striking: "*The virgin* will be with child and *will give birth to a son.*" The phraseology in both cases is identical.[15] The promise to Manoah's wife is exactly the same with the exception of "virgin" (עַלְמָה) because she was not one.

The formula in question was apparently used only for unusually important births. The parallelism of phrasing is striking:

Ugaritic	*hl glmt tld b[n]*
Genesis 18:10	וְהִנֵּה־בֵן לְשָׂרָה
Judges 13:3	אַתְּ־עֲקָרָה וְלֹא יָלַדְתְּ וְהָרִית וְיָלַדְתְּ בֵּן הִנֵּה־נָא
Isaiah 7:14	הִנֵּה הָעַלְמָה הָרָה וְיֹלֶדֶת בֵּן

Ugaritic *hl* is a functional equivalent to Hebrew הִנֵּה and emphasizes the sentence it introduces.[16] All four announcements do announce significant births: one the birth of a god (Ugaritic), one the birth of a child of promise (Isaac), one the

---

[14]J. C. L. Gibson, *Cananite Myths and Legends,* 128 (24.7).
[15]For further discussion, see chap. 9.
[16]Cf. C. Gordon, *UT,* 109 (12.7).

birth of a "savior" (Samson), and one the birth of the Savior who is also the Son of God (Isaiah's messianic prophecy).[17] Each announcement contains nuances appropriate to its particular subject: in Ugaritic, the virgin moon goddess will bear a son; although she is past the age of childbearing, Sarah will bear a son (Ge 18:11);[18] like Nikkal, the virgin of Isaiah's prophecy will "be pregnant and bear a son"; although she is barren and has not been pregnant or born a son, Manoah's wife will "bear a son." In each case the birth is improbable—hence somewhat miraculous—given the condition of the mother-to-be (past menopause, barren, or simultaneously virgin and pregnant).[19]

The fact that the Old Testament phraseology echoes the Ugaritic deserves special comment: We can hardly do better at this point than to quote what Edward J. Young has said about the Isaiah announcement:

---

[17]A. D. H. Mayes, *Israel in the Period of the Judges*, Studies in Biblical Theology, 2d ser. 59 (Naperville: Alec R. Allenson, 1974), 78, states the case rather imperfectly when he contends, "These Samson stories tell of no great victory achieved by Israel over their enemies, nor is Samson said to have been raised up by Yahweh in order to deliver Israel from oppression in the same way that this is related of the other charismatic deliverers." In Jdg 13:5 Manoah's wife is told that the son to be born will be a Nazirite who will "begin the deliverance of Israel from the hands of the Philistines," as he did (cf. Jdg 15; 16:22–30). Keil and Delitzsch, *Commentary on the OT*, 2:400–401, more aptly comment:

> Samson was to exhibit to his age generally a picture on the one hand of the strength which the people of God might acquire to overcome their strongest foes through faithful submission to the Lord their God; and on the other hand the weakness into which they had sunk through unfaithfulness to the covenant and intercourse with the heathen. And it is in this typical character of Samson and his deeds that we find the head and flower of the institution of judge in Israel.

[18]Details of Sarah's condition are also included, but in the narrative rather than in the birth announcement formula, e.g., Ge 18:11–14.

[19]Compare the birth announcements to Zechariah (Lk 1:5–25) and Mary (vv. 26–38). See discussion, chap. 9.

This does not mean that Isaiah is simply taking over a phrase that was common in the ancient Orient; it does mean, however, than because of the solemnity and importance of the announcement which he was to make, Isaiah did take over as much of this ancient formula as suited his purpose. His reason for so doing was to attract attention to the announcement itself. If Ahaz and the others who were present were at all familiar with this formula, they would immediately realize that an announcement of supreme importance was about to be made. Isaiah is not going to declare the birth of just any child, but of a significant Child.[20]

The same may be said *mutatis mutandis* of the announcement to Manoah's wife: the formula was used to let her know that God was promising an unusual child. The theophany itself would suggest that, but the traditional formula was employed to add formal weight to the declaration.

But it is not at all clear that Manoah's wife understood that she had seen an angel. After her first encounter with him she goes to her husband and reports that "a man of God came to me. He looked like an angel of God, very awesome" (13:6). The phrasing she employs, "a man of God" (אִישׁ הָאֱלֹהִים), suggests that she imagines she saw a prophet, since this term is routinely used elsewhere for God's prophets.[21] The angel's glory was not entirely lost on her, however, for she also likens this "man" to an angel of God, and portrays him in a way elsewhere used of God himself, "very awesome" (נוֹרָא מְאֹד).[22] Manoah consequently prays that Yahweh would send the "man of God" to show them how the child must be taught (v. 8). When the angel comes in answer to Manoah's prayer, Manoah's wife still refers to the angel as "the man who appeared to me the other day" (v. 10). Soon after we are told that

---

[20] E. J. Young, *The Book of Isaiah* (Grand Rapids: Eerdmans, 1965), 1:285.
[21] E.g., 1Sa 2:27; 9:6, 7, 8, 10; 1Ki 12:22; 13:1ff.; 20:28; et al.
[22] For "awesome/terrible" (נוֹרָא) descriptive of God, cf. Ex 15:11; Dt 7:21; 10:17; Ps 47:3(2); et al.

"Manoah did not realize that it was the angel of Yahweh" (v. 16). He and his wife remain unaware of the angel's identity until Manoah offers sacrifice.

Just before that offering Manoah asks the angel's name, "so that we may honor you when your word comes true" (13:17). The angel's reply probably suggests his deity. He says, "Why do you ask my name? It is wonderful" (פֶּלִאי, 13:18). The angel may be saying, "My name is beyond understanding" (cf. NIV). But his words may also be a divine asseveration: "My Name is Wonderful." "Wonderful" occurs as part of a divine title at Isaiah 9:6: "Wonderful Counselor/Wonder-Counselor" (פֶּלֶא יוֹעֵץ). The term at Judges 13:18, פֶּלִאי,[23] is a byform of the more common פֶּלֶא and occurs elsewhere only at Psalm 139:6, where it describes God's knowledge, which is too "wonderful" for the psalmist. In both cases (Jdg 13:18; Ps 139:6) פֶּלִאי portrays something of God. The more common פֶּלֶא is likewise used only of God's works or (in Isa 9:6) of his Messiah.[24] On the basis of these facts it appears that the angel's words to Manoah are not meant to put him off by avowing the mystery of his name. It is a divine asseveration that he is "Wonder"–perhaps that same "Wonder" later promised through Isaiah. Such an understanding in no way diminishes the mysteriousness of his name. The Name of God may be revealed but never fathomed (cf. Ex 3:13–14). On this understanding it is appropriate that the "angel of Yahweh" is also called Yahweh in the passage (13:16) and that Manoah later exclaims, "We have seen God!" (v. 22).

The name given by the angel also has overtones of salvation. The same root, פלא, is used of Yahweh's saving works at the Exodus:

> Who among the gods is like you, Yahweh?
> Who is like you–

---

[23] Probably to be corrected to פֶּלִאי.
[24] E.g., Ex 15:11; Pss 77:12, 15(11, 14); 78:12; 89:6(5); Isa 25:1; et al.

majestic in holiness,
awesome in glory,
working *wonders*? (Ex 15:11, emphasis mine)

The poem portrays Yahweh as "awesome" (נוֹרָא), just like the "man of God" who appears to Manoah's wife. The term is also applied to Yahweh's presence during the Exodus and wilderness wanderings (e.g., Dt 7:21; 10:17; 28:58). But more important is the allusion to the "wonders" God worked. Such wonders included the parting of the Reed Sea and Israel's safe passage across, the overwhelming of Pharaoh's army, and Israel's theophanic conduct by a pillar of cloud and of fire. In short, פלא not only has an abundant theophanic background; it also evokes the awesome salvation worked by Yahweh at the Exodus when he appeared in glory as at Mount Sinai.[25]

A similar glory now appears to Manoah and his wife. When Manoah made his sacrifice to Yahweh upon a rock, "Yahweh did a *wonder* [מַפְלִא לַעֲשׂוֹת] . . . as the flame blazed up from the altar toward heaven, the angel of Yahweh ascended in the flame" (Jdg 13:19–20a, author's translation). The combination of flame and supernatural ascent terrified Manoah and his wife so that they "fell with their faces to the ground" (וַיִּפְּלוּ עַל־פְּנֵיהֶם אָרְצָה, 13:20b). The people did the same when Yahweh's fire consumed the offerings at Aaron's ordination (וַיִּפְּלוּ עַל־פְּנֵיהֶם, Lev 9:24) and also when theophanic fire consumed Elijah's offering on Mount Carmel (וַיִּפְּלוּ עַל־פְּנֵיהֶם, 1Ki 18:39; 1Chr 21:16). That fear is a familiar human result of the glory theophanies of Yahweh. So is Manoah's statement, "We are doomed to die! We have seen God!" (Jdg 13:22; cf. 6:22–23 and discussion above). Manoah, like those who have gone before, fully expects to die after seeing something of God's glory. But Manoah's wife, with uncommon good sense, calms his fears: "If Yahweh had meant to kill us, he would not have . . . shown us all these things or

---

[25]Cf. Young, *Isaiah,* 1:334. The word first occurs at Ex 15:11.

now told us this" (13:23). Her role is like that of Moses, who had to reassure Israel at Mount Sinai, "Do not be afraid. God has come to test you" (Ex 20:20). Both are able to see God's saving purpose in an otherwise devastating theophany.

Solomon

When Yahweh publicly appears at the dedication of the Solomonic temple, his theophany is placed squarely in the context of the Horeb/Sinai covenant:

> The priests then brought the ark of Yahweh's covenant to its place in the inner sanctuary of the temple.... There was nothing in the ark except the two stone tablets that Moses had placed in it at Horeb, where Yahweh made a covenant with the Israelites after they came out of Egypt.
> When the priests withdrew from the Holy Place, the cloud filled the temple of Yahweh. And the priests could not perform their service because of the cloud, for the glory of Yahweh filled his temple.
> Then Solomon said, "Yahweh has said that he would dwell in a dark cloud; I have indeed built a magnificent temple for you, a place for you to dwell forever." (1Ki 8:6–13 // 2Ch 5:13b–6:1)

The passage recalls Yahweh's theophany at the completion of the Tent of Meeting. There we read, "Moses could not [וְלֹא־יָכֹל] enter the Tent of Meeting because the cloud [הֶעָנָן] had settled upon it, and the glory of Yahweh filled [וּכְבוֹד יהוה מָלֵא] the tabernacle" (Ex 40:35). Here we read, "The priests could not [לֹא־יָכְלוּ] perform their service because of the cloud [הֶעָנָן], for the glory of Yahweh filled [מָלֵא כְבוֹד־יהוה] his temple" (1Ki 8:11).[26] Yahweh's session in his tabernacle and temple antici-

---

[26] J. Gray, *I & II Kings*, 2d ed. (Philadelphia: Westminster, 1970), 210, believes that "the miracle of the cloud, the symbol of the glory of Yahweh and his presence in the sanctuary, is influenced by the tradition eventually expressed in Ex. 33.9ff.; 40.34ff." He further suggests that the "poetic fragment ...'Yahweh has said that he would dwell in thick darkness'... may retain [a] tradition expressed in P." Such an approach inevitably entails inversions of

pates his descent upon New Testament believers at Pentecost, when he begins to make them tabernacles (cf. 2Co 5:1, 4; 2Pe 1:13–14) or temples (1Co 6:19) of his Holy Spirit. Solomon's statement that Yahweh dwells in a "thick cloud" (עֲרָפֶל, 8:12) echoes the way he appeared atop Mount Sinai (Ex 20:21; Dt 4:11; 5:22). The same term is used in the Psalms to portray Yahweh's theophany (Pss 18:10[9]; 97:2) and in the Prophets to portray his judgment (Joel 2:2; Eze 34:12; Zep 1:15) with eschatological implications. The phrase translated "magnificent temple" (בֵּית זְבֻל, 8:13) may also be rendered "royal house." The term זְבֻל, occurs in Ugaritic with the meaning, "prince": zbl // ṭpṭ ("judge").[27] The verbal noun שֶׁבֶת ("to dwell/dwelling"), parallel to "royal house," may be taken as "throne" (cf. יוֹשֵׁב, "he who sits enthroned," Ps 2:4; Am 1:5).[28] Yahweh's temple is a royal dwelling because he is the Great King. It is appropriate that the portrayal of his theophanic session in Solomon's temple is both couched in terms of the Mosaic covenant (cf. אֲרוֹן בְּרִית־יְהוָה, 8:6; cf. also 8:9, which is rich in evocations of the Exodus and Sinai: "the two stone tablets that Moses had placed in it at Horeb, where Yahweh made a covenant with the Israelites after they came out of Egypt") and explicated in terms of the Davidic covenant (e.g., 8:15ff., echoing 2Sa 7), which culminated in great David's greater Son. From a biblical theological standpoint, then, the passage looks both backward to Sinai and forward to the work of Christ.

---

chronology; cf. Wellhausen's youthful a priori conviction that the Prophets must have preceded the Law, *Prolegomena to the History of Ancient Israel* (Gloucester: Peter Smith, 1973), 3: "I learned through Ritschl that Karl Heinrich Graf placed the Law later than the Prophets, and, almost without knowing his reasons for the hypothesis, I was prepared to accept it."

[27]Cf. Gibson, *Canaanite Myths and Legends*, 38 (2.iii.16), "prince Yam" (i.e., Sea) // "judge Nahar (i.e., River)." Cf. Gordon, *UT*, 393 (815).

[28]Cf. Niehaus, *Amos*, 1:339, 342.

PROPHETICAL BOOKS

Elijah

Elijah's encounter with God on Horeb parallels in many ways Moses' encounter with God in Exodus 33–34. A simple outline may help us to appreciate the parallels:

Theme	**Exodus // 1 Kings**
God commands Moses to prepare for theophany	Exodus 33:19–34:3
God commands Elijah to prepare for theophany	1 Kings 19:11a
God appears to Moses	Exodus 34:5–7
God appears to Elijah	1 Kings 19:11b–13
Moses asks God to be "with us"	Exodus 34:8–9
Elijah complains, "I am the only one left"	1 Kings 19:14
God makes covenant, intends destruction of idolaters and idols	Exodus 34:10 Exodus 34:11–14
God intends anointing of leaders to destroy idolaters,	1 Kings 19:15–17
notes seven thousand covenant faithful	1 Kings 19:18

Differences can be found between the two events. Moses asks God to appear before him and "show me your glory" (Ex 33:18). God agrees and also uses the occasion to fashion another set of tablets to replace those broken by Moses (Ex 32:19). Elijah, on the other hand, does not request a theophany; rather, God speaks to him and, apparently unexpectedly, tells him to prepare for one. The emphasis in Moses' encounter with God seems to be the articulation of God's "Name" along with its implications for the covenant he is making with Israel (Ex 33:19; 34:5-7). A number of covenant stipulations also follow (Ex 34:11-26). None of these acts is replicated in Elijah's encounter with God—and with good reason. Elijah's Israel had long had the covenant, and God's covenant stipulations were always before them. But they had broken covenant. Specifically, they had disobeyed God's command to destroy idolatrous apparatus (Ex 34:13) and to abstain from heterodox worship (v. 14), or the making of foreign alliances—unavoidably involving other gods as covenant witnesses (v. 12). Thus God must later command Elijah to anoint those who will destroy the idolaters who arose in Israel (1Ki 19:15-17). God's commission to Elijah is a good illustration of his retributive justice. For as Israel had made alliances with foreign kings (cf. 16:29-33),[29] so Elijah was commanded to anoint a foreign king to punish Israel (Hazael of Aram, 19:15); as Israel's kings had been idolaters (from Jeroboam I onward), so Elijah was to anoint a king over Israel to destroy them (Jehu, 19:16);[30] as Israel had tolerated false prophets (e.g., 18:19; 22:6ff.), so Elijah would anoint Elisha a true prophet to "put to death any who escape the sword of Jehu" (19:17).[31]

---

[29] The evidence is strong that Ahab had a treaty with "Ethbaal king of the Sidonians" (1Ki 16:31). Ahab not only married Ethbaal's daughter Jezebel, but also adopted his gods (Baal, Asherah). Neither act was uncommon for treaty partners.

[30] As Wm. E. Barnes, *The First Book of the Kings* (Cambridge: Cambridge University Press, 1911), 158-59, notes, Elijah apparently did not anoint either Hazael (whom Elisha told that he would become king but did not anoint, 2Ki 8:7-15) or Jehu (who was anointed by Elisha, 9:3). He comments that Elijah's "courage, though great, was spasmodic. He shrank from anointing Hazael and from anointing Jehu."

[31] J. R. Lumby, *The First Book of the Kings* (Cambridge: Cambridge University Press, 1890), 203, believes that no actual anointing took place, apparently because it is not actually reported. Textual silence is perhaps an ambiguous witness. But it is possible in these cases of anointing that, as Gray, *Joshua, Judges, and Ruth,* 411, says, the way in which the commands were fulfilled "suggests that the verb *māšaḥ* here means 'to set apart,' which was the real significance of the rite of anointing." Cf. already Barnes, *First Kings,* 203:

The two prophets also show differences in perspective appropriate to their unequal situations. Moses asks God to be "with us" when he and the people embark upon the Conquest (Ex 34:8–9). Yahweh promises not only that he will be with them, but that he "will do wonders never before done in any nation in all the world" (v. 10). By contrast, Elijah complains, "I am the only one left" (1Ki 19:14) in a nation of blatant idolaters whose queen is out to destroy him (v. 2). Whereas Moses can envision Yahweh at one with the people, leading them into the Promised Land, Elijah believes that he alone stands with and for God in that same land. But just as God had commanded covenant faithfulness to and through Moses (Ex 34:11ff.), so he can inform Elijah that "Yet I reserve seven thousand in Israel—all whose knees have not bowed down to Baal and all whose mouths have not kissed him" (1Ki 19:18). The historical irony involved in Yahweh's theophany to Elijah does not preclude his covenant faithfulness toward his people.

Just as structural parallels exist between the Mosaic and Elijan accounts, so do terminological ones, as well as terminological echoes of other Mosaic encounters with God. Moses asks to see God's "glory" (כָּבוֹד, Ex 33:18), and God says that he will cause all of his "goodness" (כָּל־טוּבִי, 33:19) to pass (עבר, 33:19; 34:6) in front of him. In the account of the actual theophany, the emphasis is on Yahweh's "name" (33:19; 34:6) as noted. The Elijan theophany echoes these terms. As he did with Moses, Yahweh is going to "pass" (עבר) by Elijah (1Ki 19:11). As Moses hid his face from Yahweh, so Elijah hides his face in his cloak (Ex 3:6; 1Ki 19:13). The passage also recalls Yahweh's appearance upon Mount Sinai above the people in Exodus 19 and the following chapters. Elijah experiences "a great and powerful wind" (רוּחַ גְּדוֹלָה וְחָזָק, 1Ki 19:11b), "an

---

"Hence 'anoint' in the text becomes equivalent to 'point them out as the anointed ones'"; and earlier, Keil and Delitzsch, *Commentary on the OT,* 3:260: "Consequently מָשַׁח must be taken figuratively here, as in Judg. ix.8, as denoting divine consecration to the regal and prophetic offices."

earthquake" (רַעַשׁ; 19:11c; cf. Ex 19:18), a "fire" (אֵשׁ, 19:12a; cf. Ex 19:18), and "a roaring thunderous voice" (קוֹל דְּמָמָה דַקָּה; 19:12b; cf. Ex 19:16). The latter phrase is still routinely translated "a still small voice" (KJV), "a gentle whisper" (NIV), or the like. The very appearance of "voice" (קוֹל) in a theophanic context should warn us against such a translation. This word routinely carries connotations of thunderous divine speaking both in the Old Testament and in the ancient world. J. Lust has ably demonstrated a more appropriate rendering, "a roaring, thunderous sound" or the like, with illuminating discussions of דְּמָמָה (root דמם[II], "to roar") and דַקָּה ("crushing," rather than "fine, thin").[32] The repeated statement that Yahweh was "not in" the wind, the earthquake, or the fire, is rightly understood to mean "not yet": Yahweh is "not yet" in any of these cosmic phenomena. Rather, they precede and announce his coming, just as they did on Mount Sinai (Ex 19:16–19).[33] In both cases the storm wind, fire, and so on precede the "thunderous voice"—that actual articulation of Yahweh, as opposed to the natural disturbance his coming creates.

Another aspect of the Elijah account that deserves attention is its parallel structure. The structure of the second half of the account mirrors that of the first half:

Theme	**1 Kings 19:9b–18**
Yahweh's word: "What are you doing here, Elijah?"	19:9b
Yahweh's word: "What are you doing here, Elijah?"	19:13b
Elijah's reply: "I have been very zealous. . . . I alone am left. . . ."	19:10

---

[32]J. Lust, "A Gentle Breeze or a Roaring, Thunderous Sound?" *VT* 25 (1975): 110–15.
[33]Ibid., 114.

Elijah's reply: "I have been very zealous. . . . I alone am left. . . ."	19:14
Yahweh theophany	19:11b–13a
Yahweh commands out of theophany	19:15–18

The parallels are remarkable. Yahweh asks exactly the same question in verses 9b and 13b, and Elijah's response both times is exactly the same. The final parallel is actually an expansion, or an expounding: first Yahweh appears, then he gives the word for which he chose to appear. The parallels can hardly avoid notice and are no doubt emphatic. Yahweh is persistent in his questioning, and Elijah is pertinacious in his complaint. But Yahweh has appeared not only to answer his complaint (and indeed correct it), but also to command a national corrective—judgment on the idolaters. Yahweh repeats his question ("What are you doing here, Elijah?" 19:9, 13) to impress upon Elijah that God has called him here (cf. v. 11) and has a purpose for him. As Barnes suggests, a parallel may be seen in Jesus' later threefold questioning of Peter, "Do you love me?"[34] The same Lord who was to command his shepherd, "Feed my sheep," must now sadly command his prophet to annihilate idolaters.

Isaiah

Theophany marked Isaiah's calling, a theophany that recalls both Mount Sinai and Yahweh's occupation of Solomon's temple at its consecration.[35] The account of Isaiah's ordination

---

[34] Barnes, *First Kings,* 158: "The Divine question is repeated in order that the divine lesson may be repeated and impressed upon the prophet. Cf. our Lord's threefold question to St. Peter, 'Lovest thou me' (John xxi.15, 16, 17)."

[35] Young, *The Book of Isaiah,* 1:236, recognizes the visionary quality of Isaiah's experience and perhaps correctly declares, "Inasmuch, then, as it was a vision, it is beside the point to seek to determine whether the palace described was either the earthly Temple or the heavenly. For that matter, we

contains terms evocative of both past events and also follows essentially the theophanic *Gattung*:

Formal Element	Isaiah 6:1–13
1 Introductory description, third person	6:1–4
3 Response of the addressee	6:5
5 His quelling of human fear	6:6–7
7 The *hieros logos*	6:8a
8 Inquiry or protest by addressee	6:8b
9 Continuation of the *hieros logos*	6:9–10
8 Inquiry by addressee	6:11a
9 Continuation of the *hieros logos*	6:11b–13

Here again, certain elements are lacking. There is no utterance by God of Isaiah's name (element 2). Nor does Yahweh assert who he is (element 4). He also does not promise to be with Isaiah (element 6), although the divine commission may be understood to entail Yahweh's ongoing accompaniment and empowerment. And there is also no concluding third person description (element 10), but that is not unusual in theophanic or other narratives.

Due to the nature of this particular theophany, there are also slight variations on the *Gattung*. Isaiah's initial "response" (element 3) is not a response to Yahweh's words, but to his dreadfully holy appearance. God himself does not quell

---

have no means of knowing where Isaiah was when the vision came to him. He may have been in the Temple, but he may also have been in his own home." G. A. Smith, *The Book of Isaiah* (London: Hodder and Stoughton, 1897), 1:62, imagines that Isaiah saw "Jehovah's own heavenly *palace* (ver. 1—not *temple*); only Isaiah describes it in terms of the Jerusalem temple which was its symbol." Of course, Hebrew הֵיכָל, which derives by way of Akkadian *ekallu* from Sumerian *E.GAL* ("big house") can mean either "palace" or "temple," and a god's earthly "temple" imaged forth his heavenly "palace," as I have noted. Wherever Isaiah saw the Lord, Young is certainly correct in observing that "Isaiah did not see God because he was more spiritually attuned than others; he saw God because God had revealed Himself to him" (*Isaiah*, 1:237).

Isaiah's fear (element 5), but one of the seraphs around his throne touches his lips with a burning coal from the altar and assures him that his guilt is removed and his sin atoned for. Isaiah's "protest" (element 8), which we may also call a "response," is also unusual: he "protests" that he is available.

The terms used to portray Yahweh are few, but they recall both Mount Sinai and subsequent theophanies. The angels chant a praise to Yahweh, whose "glory" (כָּבוֹד, Isa 6:3; cf. Ex 24:16; 1Ki 8:11) fills the whole earth. We read that the temple "was filled with smoke" (יִמָּלֵא עָשָׁן, Isa 6:4, cf. Ex 40:34–35; 1Ki 8:10) and that the doorposts and "thresholds shook" (יָנֻעוּ ... הַסִּפִּים, Isa 6:4). The phraseology resembles Amos 9:1, where Amos sees the Lord standing in judgment above the altar at Samaria and commanding, "Strike the [capital] so that the thresholds shake [וְיִרְעֲשׁוּ הַסִּפִּים]."[36] It also anticipates Isaiah 24:20, which portrays the earth (which, if not God's temple, is at least his footstool, Mt 5:35) shaken by Yahweh in judgment theophany (נוֹעַ תָּנוּעַ אֶרֶץ). It is appropriate that such phraseology should relate Yahweh's temple theophany to Isaiah and other judgment theophanies, because all of God's judgment intrusions into history foreshadow his eschatological return, when he will remove "what can be shaken—that is, created things—so that what cannot be shaken may remain" (Heb 12:27).[37]

Granted its eschatological implications, there is also a clear terminological parallel between this account and the account of the original temple dedication. The parallel is no accident. Yahweh appeared in Solomon's day to seal his promise to David that his son would sit upon his throne and build the Yahweh temple, and that Yahweh would cause his name to dwell there (cf. 2Sa 7:12–13). But Yahweh now appears in judg-

---

[36]For further discussion cf. Niehaus, *Amos*, 1:478–79.
[37]Cf. below, chap. 9.

ment glory. Yes, his name still inhabits the temple—although even that must one day end. But he has come now to command unalterable judgment upon his people (Isa 6:9–13).

One fact in the portrayal that may indicate a judgment presence is the unusual appearance of Yahweh upon his throne. Isaiah says, "I saw Yahweh seated on a throne, high and exalted" (Isa 6:1). The verb "seated" (יֹשֵׁב, present participle) is the same form used in Psalm 2:4 where Yahweh is portrayed as "enthroned" and about to judge the nations, and also in Psalm 29:10 where he "sits enthroned" above the judgment waters of the Flood.[38] The terms "high and lifted up" (רָם וְנִשָּׂא) form an ironic allusion since the same terms occur elsewhere of all that will come under God's judgment (Isa 2:12, 13). In other words, it is only Yahweh who should—and shall—be "high and lifted up." Yahweh is exalted on his "throne" (כִּסֵּא). His lofty location may echo the account of the covenant communion meal at Exodus 24, where the elders of Israel saw the God of Israel. There we read, "Under his feet was something like a pavement made of sapphire, clear as the sky itself" (Ex 24:10). Given the resemblance of this description to Ezekiel's later vision of Yahweh on his throne (see below), it may be that the elders of Israel "ate and drank" (Ex 24:11) in the presence of Yahweh enthroned, with his feet resting upon the ethereal pavement. Whether or not they saw him enthroned, the Exodus account assumes the background of a cardinal idea: that the holy presence of Yahweh among humans normally implies judgment unless God takes steps to protect and reassure the one(s) to whom he appears. So we read that, although they saw God in an awesome theophany, "God did not raise his hand" against them (Ex 24:11). Isaiah likewise sees God, and the moment he does, he is judged by that holy presence: "Woe to me!

---

[38] See above, chap. 5. Cf. also Am 1:5, 8. As Young, *Isaiah*, 1:237, notes, "The word is also employed of the Lord when He sits as king or judge."

... I am ruined! For I am a man of unclean lips..." (Isa 6:5).[39] God reassures Isaiah by causing Isaiah's lips to be cleansed (6:6–7). The purification of Isaiah's lips involves a metonomy whereby the lips represent the inner man. As Smith has noted, "The lips are, as it were, the blossom of a man."[40] Or, as Jesus chose to explicate Isaiah 29:13, "'These people honor me with their lips, but their hearts are far from me'... Listen and understand. What goes into a man's mouth does not make him 'unclean,' but what comes out of his mouth, that is what makes him 'unclean'" (Mt 15:8a, 10b–11). Because Isaiah is "a man of unclean lips" who dwells among "a people of unclean lips," he must have his lips cleansed—his inner man sanctified—before he can speak for God.

God's holy judgment theophany judges sin in Isaiah and deals with it by judgment fire. The same idea may account for the presence of seraphim in this passage—their only occurrence in the Old Testament. The root שרף ("to burn"), suggests an expurgative function. It occurs with this sense elsewhere in the Old Testament. For instance, Moses commands the people to put to the sword and "burn" (שרף) any town of people who counseled them to follow other gods (Dt 13:17[16]). When Josiah smashed the Asherah poles and idols in Jerusalem, he also "burned [שרף] the bones of the priests on their altars, and so he purged [יְטַהֵר] Judah and Jerusalem" (2Ch 34:5). The root שרף occurs in a purgative sense in both the Law and history. We find the same in extrabiblical materials. In fact, a Middle-Assyrian course on demon exorcism is entitled "Šurpu" (i.e., "Burning," from the Akkadian cognate root *šarāpu*, "to burn"), as a metaphor for the expulsion of unwanted spirits

---

[39]The seraphim's declaration, "Holy, holy, holy is the Lord Almighty" (6:3), verbally affirms that holy Presence that devastated Isaiah. Isaiah needed—God's people always seem to need—a fresh revelation of God's holiness. As Smith, *Isaiah*, 67, so rightly observes, "The Trisagion rings, and has need to ring, for ever down the Church."

[40]Smith, *Isaiah*, 70.

from people.⁴¹ The Old Testament use of שׂרף in judgment passages also recalls the phrase "You must burn [בער, NIV 'purge'] the evil from among you," which occurs in the larger context of the deuteronomic command to "burn" (שׂרף) the heterodox just noted (see Dt 13:6[5]).⁴²

Although the presence of the seraphs remains essentially mysterious, such a background of usage for the root שׂרף does suggest the compatibility of these angels with the theophanic judgment commission that Isaiah receives as a result of his unexpected and initially devastating encounter with Yahweh.⁴³ The unique mission of one of them to remove Isaiah's guilt and sin by a burning coal from the altar is also quite compatible with this tentative ontology.⁴⁴

Ezekiel

Ezekiel's visions of Yahweh are beyond doubt the most bizarre in the Bible. If in some ways they are difficult to explicate, that may be because a man was using human words to

---

⁴¹E. Reiner, *Šurpu, A Collection of Sumerian and Akkadian Incantations, AfO* Behieft 11 (Graz, 1958). Cf. *AHw* 3:1185.

⁴²Cf. chap. 6, 214–17.

⁴³As Young, *Isaiah*, 1:238–39, notes, "It is true that in the ancient Near East two figures were often present with the deity as his special tutelary deities." The seraphim, however, are not an accommodation to ancient Near Eastern religious imagery, but part of a true revelatory vision to Isaiah. As Young rightly comments, "It must also be remembered that the pagan religious of antiquity were degenerations from the true, and indeed were imitative of it" (p. 239). Cf. H. Ringren, *Word and Wisdom* (Lund: Häkan Ohlssons Boktryckeri, 1947), 11ff.

⁴⁴Cf. already Keil and Delitzsch, *Commentary on the OT,* 7:197: "The seraph, therefore, did here what his name denotes: he burned up or burned away (*comburit*). He did this, however, not by virtue of his own fiery nature, but by means of the divine fire which he had taken from the heavenly altar." They further suggest that the seraphim "were the vehicles and media of the fire of divine love, just as the cherubim in Ezekiel are vehicles and media of divine wrath," and compare the seraphim's use of purgative "fire of love from the altar" with the cherub who "takes the fire of wrath from the throne-chariot" in Eze 10:6–7.

describe the indescribable. It may be assumed that only God can fully describe himself. What Ezekiel saw, however, resonates strongly with earlier Sinaitic theophanies and is a more thorough articulation of the stormy presence of God. Against that background his vision can be understood.

As regards Ezekiel's visions by Kebar and after, one fact is paramount: what he saw was disastrous. Yahweh appears in an awesome storm theophany as covenant judge. He also appeared as covenant judge to Adam and Eve, and if they saw anything like what Ezekiel saw (and the storm theophany of Ge 3:8 laconically suggests that they did), their fear was well grounded.

When Yahweh appeared in stormy glory atop Mount Sinai, he also took care to protect the people from the devastating effects of his holy presence. He had come to cut a covenant with them, to reveal himself and his ways to a chosen people (סְגֻלָּה). He had appeared at the tent of meeting and at the Tent of Meeting and finally at the Solomonic temple, and every such visitation indicated his abiding intention to be available at God's place of worship for his people. Now, however, he comes in theophanic judgment. The revelation of his glory portends not covenant blessings but covenant curses—disaster for his people, who have long broken their covenant. As he visited and filled his tent, tabernacle, and temple with his glory, he will now depart his temple as a sign of disapprobation of a sinful people.

The Chariot Throne

Ezekiel is astounded to see "an immense cloud with flashing lightning and surrounded by brilliant light" approach out of the north (Eze 1:4). A theophany is underway, and it is significant that it comes out of the north. The north is elsewhere named symbolically as God's abode (e.g., Ps 48:2; Isa 14:13). The cloud from the north actually conceals Yahweh on his chariot throne. What Ezekiel first sees is a "windstorm" (סְעָרָה, 1:4), the same term used when Yahweh's "chariot of fire" comes down and takes up Elijah (2Ki 2:11).⁴⁵ The other terms employed are all characteristic of Old Testament theophanies: "cloud" (עָנָן), "flashing lightning (אֵשׁ מִתְלַקַּחַת), and "fire" (אֵשׁ). The chariot throne presence that approaches is probably the same that Daniel later sees in a night vision:

> His throne was flaming with fire,
> and its wheels were all ablaze.
> A river of fire was flowing,
> coming out from before him. (Da 7:9–10)

Whereas Daniel has a dream vision, Ezekiel apparently sees Yahweh's awesome chariot throne approach with his physical eyes.⁴⁶

There follows a description of the "four living creatures" (Eze 1:5–14) who are associated with the wheels of the chariot throne (vv. 15–21). Ezekiel's account of the creatures (later identified as cherubim, 10:1ff.) is as thorough as it is unusual:

> In appearance their form was that of a man, but each of them had four faces and four wings. Their legs were straight; their feet were like those of a calf and gleamed like burnished bronze. Under their wings on their four sides they had the hands of a man. All four of them had faces and wings, and their wings touched one another. . . .
> Their faces looked like this: Each of the four had the face of a man, and on the right side each had the face of a lion, and on the left the face of an ox; each also had the face of an eagle. (1:5b–10)

---

⁴⁵The phrasing in Ezekiel is רוּחַ סְעָרָה; I take the latter as an appositive, i.e., "a wind, [namely] a stormwind." Of course, the chariot that takes up Elijah cannot automatically be identified with Yahweh's chariot throne here. We note simply the parallel stormwind of the two theophanies.

⁴⁶It is fascinating that among the plans that David gave to Solomon for the Temple, "He also gave him the plan for the chariot, that is, the cherubim of gold that spread their wings and shelter the ark of the covenant of Yahweh" (1Ch 28:18). Peter C. Craigie, *Ezekiel* (Philadelphia: Westminster, 1983), 11, concludes from the latter that "the ark itself was called a chariot"–an attractive idea, but one that hardly derives from the text.

Ezekiel's portrayal anticipates the "four living creatures" with lion, ox, eagle, and human faces about God's throne in John's vision (Rev 4:6b–8). Similar creatures are attested from the ancient Near East as throne bearers or guardians of temple or palace thresholds. Eichrodt remarks, "The half-human, half-bestial shape and attributes load them with all the powers of both species, and express how awe-inspiring such guardians of holy things must be."[47] The creatures are at once remarkably similar to and different from those ancient Near Eastern quadrupeds that combine the characteristics of two species, "the serpent-griffons, and lion-men or ox-men of Babylonia or Assyria."[48] The similarity has been understood in terms of provenance. For instance, I. G. Matthews has explained Ezekiel's imagery in terms of the Babylonian pantheon:

> The four living creatures . . . were the common symbols throughout Babylonia for four of their chief deities. . . . The bull colossus, with ox-face, was the symbol of Marduk; that with the lion-face was Nergal, the god of the underworld and of plague; that of the eagle was Ninib, god of the chase and of war; while the human face represented Nabu, the announcer or revealer. . . . These four were chief in their pantheon at this time, and may be considered as representing all the gods of that empire.[49]

---

[47] W. Eichrodt, *Ezekiel, A Commentary,* trans. Cosslett Quin (Philadelphia: Westminster, 1975), 55.

[48] Ibid., 55.

[49] I. G. Matthews, *Ezekiel,* American Commentary on the Old Testament 21 (Chicago: American Baptist Publication Society, 1939), 5. "Ninib" is Ninurta. Wm. H. Brownlee, *Ezekiel 1–19,* WBC 28 (Waco: Word Books, 1986), 151, notes that "in Mesopotamia, winged bulls guarded the entrances to temples and palaces, and were called 'cherubs.'" D. Stuart, *Ezekiel,* The Communicator's Commentary 18 (Dallas: Word, 1989), 32, does not see the cherubim with reference to Mesopotamian iconography. Instead he comments, "These were traditionally the four most impressive of the land and air animals: man, chief over all; the lion, chief of the wild animals; the ox, chief of the domesticated animals; and the eagle, chief of the birds of the air. Intelligence, strength, ferocity, freedom, etc. were all wrapped up in one of these special angelic creatures."

Matthews' comparison is illuminating. It may be that God revealed himself and his cherubim in a way that would be intelligible to Ezekiel in his Babylonian setting. Or it may be that Ezekiel saw what really was, and that Mesopotamian religion had dimly and derivatively reflected the same. After all, Adam and Eve had seen cherubim at the entrance to Eden (Ge 3:24). Our first parents' account of the cherubim's appearance may have been passed down and eventually formed a basis for pagan conceptions of deity.

The way in which the creatures are associated with the throne suggests another idea—namely, comparison with some other ancient Near Eastern throne bearers.[50] Phoenician iconography, for example, shows two winged creatures who uphold the seat of Astarte. A cherub-throne of Ishtar on the Assyrian rock-relief of Maltaia displays a similar arrangement.[51] By contrast, however, the living creatures of Ezekiel's vision are portrayed in a way that recalls Sinai and similar theophanies: like "burning coals of fire or like torches" (כְּגַחֲלֵי־אֵשׁ בֹּעֲרוֹת ... הַלַּפִּדִים, 1:13). We read that "fire moved back and forth" among them, and the motion is described using the same verb (מִתְהַלֶּכֶת) intriguingly used to describe the motion of the "thunderous voice of Yahweh God" in the garden at Genesis 3:8.

Ezekiel's portrayal of the throne itself recalls Yahweh's appearance to Moses and the elders on Mount Sinai (Ex 24). Ezekiel sees an "expanse" (רָקִיעַ, 1:22, 23, 25, 26) above which is something "like a throne of sapphire" (כְּמַרְאֵה אֶבֶן־סַפִּיר דְּמוּת כִּסֵּא, 1:26). Moses and the elders saw something "like a pavement of sapphire" (כְּמַעֲשֵׂה לִבְנַת הַסַּפִּיר, Ex 24:10). Moses and the elders saw the sapphire pavement beneath Yahweh's feet; Ezekiel sees a throne of sapphire above the expanse.

---

[50]Stuart, *Ezekiel*, 31–32, observes that "cherubim are sometimes likened to the 'animals' of the angelic creation.... In the Bible, they are often depicted as God's beasts of burden, as it were, the creatures that draw His divine chariot."
[51]Eichrodt, *Ezekiel*, 56.

There is similarity enough to suggest that Ezekiel saw a throne theophany of Yahweh not unlike that seen by Moses and the elders on Mount Sinai, or by Isaiah at the temple.

What comes next is the first portrayal of God in full-blown anthropomorphic glory. We are told that Moses and the elders of Israel "saw" God above the pavement, and that Isaiah "saw" Yahweh "high and lifted up" above the altar of the temple. But only now do we have a description of God's form. Just as the storm theophany and throne descriptions have more detail in Ezekiel than before, so does the portrayal of God.

The first manifestation of God himself is a theophanic "thunderous voice" (קוֹל, 1:25). The thunderous nature of God's "voice" is not simply assumed from an analogous theophany at Mount Sinai. It is indicated by the account of the four creatures that prefaces Ezekiel's vision of God: "I heard the sound [קוֹל] of their wings, like the roar [קוֹל] of many waters, like the thunderous voice [קוֹל] of Shaddai . . . a sound [קוֹל] of a great storm, like the tumult [קוֹל] of an army" (1:24; cf. 10:5, author's translation). The phraseology, moreover, sadly anticipates the disastrous judgment Yahweh intends. The phrase "sound of a great storm" (קוֹל הֲמֻלָּה) occurs elsewhere only at Jeremiah 11:16 (also the only other occurrence of הֲמֻלָּה), where it characterizes Yahweh's judgment on Judah. The combination of "roar" (קוֹל) and "many waters" (מַיִם רַבִּים) recalls the portrayal of Yahweh enthroned above the judgment waters of the Flood (Ps 29:3, 10).[52] The sound of the creatures' wings is like that of an army, and God will bring an army against Judah. Against such an ominous background, Ezekiel hears Yahweh's "thunderous voice."

Above the throne there is "a *likeness/figure* like that of a *man*" (דְּמוּת כְּמַרְאֵה אָדָם, 1:26). Ezekiel's vision affirms Moses' ancient portrayal of God, who said, "Let us make *man* in our

---

[52] Ps 29:3 (קוֹל יהוה עַל־הַמָּיִם . . . יהוה עַל־מַיִם רַבִּים) especially seems to be echoed here. See discussion above, chap. 5.

image, in our *likeness/figure*" (אָדָם בְּצַלְמֵנוּ כִּדְמוּתֵנוּ, Ge 1:26; cf. 5:1). It is remarkable—and a sign of God's progressive revelation—that Ezekiel does see a "form," an appearance of God.[53] His vision contrasts with events at Horeb/Sinai, about which Moses warned the people: "You saw no form [תְּמוּנָה] of any kind the day Yahweh spoke to you at Horeb out of the fire. Therefore . . . do not become corrupt and make for yourselves an idol" (Dt 4:15–16). The portrayal of God's form is unlike anything prior in the Old Testament and anticipates the accounts of Daniel in his night vision and of John in Revelation:

> I saw that from what appeared to be his waist up he looked like glowing metal, as if full of fire, and that from there down he looked like fire; and brilliant light surrounded him. Like the appearance of a rainbow in the clouds on a rainy day, so was the radiance around him. (Eze 1:27–28)

The account has familiar theophanic language ("fire," "clouds"), but also terms uncommon for a theophany: "glowing metal" (עֵין חַשְׁמַל, cf. 1:4), "rainbow" (הַקֶּשֶׁת), and "brilliant light" (הַנֹּגַהּ, cf. 1:4, 13; 10:4).[54] Craigie may be correct when he sees a connection between this theophany and the Noahic rainbow:

> The rainbow recalls the ancient covenant God made with humans following the flood. . . . For the Christian reader of the Old Testament, there is a breadth here to Ezekiel's vision. He was a Hebrew prophet. . . . Yet he sees a vision

---

[53]There appears to be some interchangeability of the terms "likeness/figure" (דְּמוּת), "image" (צֶלֶם), and "form" (תְּמוּנָה). The first two occur together parallelistically, as noted. Solomon made the sea with "figures (דְּמוּת) of bulls" below the rim (2Ch 4:3), but Moses warned the people not to make any "statue-form" (תְּמוּנַת כָּל־סָמֶל), that is, any idol, of "any animal on earth" (Dt 4:16–17).

[54]The term נֹגַהּ is not exactly a common theophanic term, but it does occur in other theophanic descriptions: 2Sa 22:13; Ps 18:13(12); Isa 4:5; Hab 3:4.

of God who cares not only for his chosen people, Israel, but also for the totality of the world.[55]

Such an understanding of Ezekiel's vision contains Gospel implications. It may also hark back to the Flood and imply that the covenantal rainbow of Genesis 9 was actually theophanic in character.[56] Both the Noahic rainbow and the rainbow of Ezekiel's vision in turn anticipate the rainbow throne of God in Revelation 4:3. Mendenhall has noted that Mesopotamian iconography also portrays a god's "bow" hung in the air as a sign that the god has stopped warring. In a relief of Aššur-naṣir-pal II, for instance, the bow of the god in the winged sun disc is in the stance of the rainbow of Genesis 9.[57] The Assyrian symbolism says that the god has won victory over his foes (i.e., the foes of Assyria) and so brought peace to his people.[58] Likewise, God, during the Flood, won a victory against his enemies and brought peace—in fact, a new covenant—to his people, the Noahic remnant. The same bow also had another symbolism in Assyria, however: that of the god en route to war. Mendenhall comments:

> The bow of the king, and also that of Aššur's *melammū* . . ., is drawn and firing at the enemy. It is a most graphic description of the ancient Assyrian "*Blitzkrieg,*" complete with storm troops and the raining down of fire . . . that must end in the "perpetual victory over all enemies."[59]

The biblical data make it clear that the "bow" is part of true theophany, perhaps especially associated with God's (chariot)throne. Apparently it can relate either to God's peaceful coming (Ge 9, comparable to Aššur's bow suspended after battle) or to God's coming in judgment (Eze 1; Rev 4, compa-

---

[55] Craigie, *Ezekiel*, 13.
[56] Cf. Kline, *Images of the Spirit*, 19–20.
[57] Mendenhall, *The Tenth Generation*, 47.
[58] Ibid., 47.
[59] Ibid., 45.

rable to Aššur's "*Blitzkrieg*"). The Mesopotamian data appear to reflect these aspects of theophany in a polytheistic context.⁶⁰

On the basis of past theophanies, Ezekiel's reaction to what he sees is predictable. The awesome appearance that was "the likeness of the glory of Yahweh" (דְּמוּת כְּבוֹד־יהוה)⁶¹ causes the prophet to "fall facedown" (וָאֶפֹּל עַל־פָּנַי, 1:28; cf. 3:23; 43:3; 44:4)—just as Israel did when theophanic fire consumed the ordination sacrifices of Aaron and his sons (Lev 9:24), as Joshua did at the Jericho theophany (Jos 5:14), as Manoah and his wife did at the angel's fiery ascent (Jdg 13:20b), as the people did when theophanic fire consumed Elijah's offering on Mount Carmel (1Ki 18:39), and as John will when the Son of Man appears to him in glory (Rev 1:17).

Ezekiel's prostration before the glory of Yahweh concludes the first chapter of the book. It also concludes the introduction of a long theophanic passage (1:1–3:15) which can be diagramed as follows:

Formal Element	**Ezekiel 1:1–3:15**
1 Introductory description, third person	1:1–1:28
2 Deity's utterance of name of addressee	2:1
3 Response of the addressee	2:2
7 The *hieros logos*	2:3–3:11
10 Concluding description, third person	3:12–15

---

⁶⁰Mendenhall, *Tenth Generation,* 47–48, unfortunately thinks the derivation flows in the other direction, with the result that the Flood account becomes unhistorical: "The Flood Story of Genesis 6–9 is a parable based upon this age-old heathen 'theology.'. . . The undrawn bow of the Assyrian triumph becomes a symbol, then . . . of the determination that never again can the evil and chaos of mankind provoke God into returning the world to chaos (i.e., the Flood) as a just punishment."

⁶¹As Matthews, *Ezekiel,* 5, suggests, the emphasis of such terms as "likeness" and "appearance" implies the inadequacy of human language to portray the spiritual realm with visual accuracy: "So far as possible, Yahweh was removed from the material and conceived of as a spiritual being. . . . This is an effort to describe the indescribable."

The passage contains typical elements of the theophanic *Gattung* but also gives a peculiar twist to some of them. God does not exactly call Ezekiel by name (element 2), yet he gives him a name, or a title, which is at once common to all humanity and is also messianic: "Son of man."[62] God does not exactly assert who he is (element 4)–that apparently was affirmed already by the throne theophany. And when God quells Ezekiel's fear, he does so with an irony reminiscent of Jeremiah (Jer 1:8, 17). God does not remove the man's fear of his own dreadful theophany; rather, he commands Ezekiel not to be afraid of man (Eze 2:6; 3:9). God reassured Jeremiah, "Today I have made you a fortified city, an iron pillar and a bronze wall to stand against the whole land" (Jer 1:18). So God reassures Ezekiel that "I will make you as unyielding and hardened as they are. I will make your forehead like the hardest stone, harder than flint" (Eze 3:8–9). That reassurance–along with the command to speak the words that God gives him (2:7; 3:4)–are couched within the *hieros logos* (element 7) and function as an "assertion of God's gracious presence" (element 6).

God's Spirit concludes Ezekiel's first theophanic encounter: "Then the Spirit [רוּחַ][63] lifted me up [נשׂא][64] ... and took me away"[65] (Eze 3:12, 14). Ezekiel's unusual conveyance is anticipated by Obadiah, who complains to Elijah, "I don't know where the Spirit [רוּחַ] of Yahweh may carry [נשׂא][66] you when I leave you" (1Ki 18:12), and by the prophets at Jericho who tell Elisha, "Perhaps the Spirit [רוּחַ] of Yahweh has picked [נשׂא][67] him [Elijah] up and set him down on some mountain or in some valley" (2Ki 2:16). It is later echoed by the account

---

[62]For a good brief discussion of the messianic title, "Son of man," cf. L. Morris, *The Gospel According to John*, NICNT (Grand Rapids: Eerdmans, 1971), 172–73.
[63]LXX: πνεῦμα.
[64]LXX: ἐξῆρέν.
[65]LXX: ἀνέλαβέν.
[66]LXX: ἀρεῖ.
[67]LXX: ἦρεν.

of Philip at the Ethiopian eunuch's baptism: "When they came up out of the water, the Spirit [πνεῦμα] of the Lord suddenly took Philip away [ἥρπασεν]" (Ac 8:39).

Once the Spirit sets Ezekiel down, the prophet does what any child of God must do after such a theophany—he praises God: "Blessed be the glory of Yahweh [כְּבוֹד-יהוה] in his [dwelling]place!" (Eze 3:12, author's translation). He comes among the exiles at "Tel Aviv." The latter is probably best understood from the common Akkadian phrase *til abūbi,* meaning "ruin heap [left by] a flood/the Flood." It is not a town or city name (nor simply Heb. "hill of wheat").[68] Here, by the Kebar River (Akk. *nar Kabari*, a navigable channel of the Euphrates),[69] he sits "among them for seven days—overwhelmed" (3:15). The prophet's reaction is hardly a surprise. The theophany he saw surpasses in awesomeness and detail any other in the Old Testament. Although it is introduced as a visionary account, it is far from a dream vision or such visions as people can have when their eyes are closed in prayer or meditation. Perhaps it is what some today would call an "open" vision. In any event, it was real—*awfully* real, in the original sense of that word.

It may be that what Ezekiel saw was in fact a microcosmic revelation of Yahweh as God of the cosmos. Several factors indicate this. The word for the "expanse" beneath God's throne (רָקִיעַ, Eze 1:22) is the same used to portray the "firmament" God made to separate the upper and lower waters (Ge 1:6) above which God is enthroned.[70] The four living creatures may stand for the earth's four quarters—an indication of the universal sway of the Great King. Their four faces and wings may suggest the same.[71] Mesopotamian kings from the

---

[68]Cf. *CAD*, vol. 1, pt. 1, p. 78 (abūbu 1b). Apparently the exiles had found some ruin heap and settled there.

[69]Eichrodt, *Ezekiel,* 52.

[70]Cf. Ps 29:3, on the understanding that the מַיִם רַבִּים there indicate the cosmic flood. Cf. discussion at chap. 5.

[71]Cf. Eichrodt, *Ezekiel,* 58.

third millennium had styled themselves rulers of the "four quarters" as a way of claiming universal sway.⁷² The God-man on the throne is surrounded by a radiance like "a rainbow in the clouds on a rainy day" (Eze 1:28). As noted, Ezekiel's rainbow theophany is evocative of the rainbow God gave as covenant sign to Noah after the Flood (Ge 9:12ff.). Such an apparition could strongly suggest God's ongoing covenant faithfulness to the world he had created out of water and rinsed clean by the Flood. He would continue faithful to the cosmos he had made. But that must be small consolation to his own people, against whom he now comes in theophanic judgment.

We have seen how God's appearance to the prophet also recalls theophanies of the Mosaic period. The quality of Ezekiel's vision may say something about his humility—another Mosaic quality. We know little about his background except that he was a priest, the son of a certain Buzi (Eze 1:3). We know that God appeared to him and ordained him as a prophet during the fifth year of Jehoiachin's exile (v. 2). But no ordinary man has such visions as Ezekiel had. His dynamic experience of God is probably second only to that of Moses, at least among the prophets of the Mosaic covenant; and we read of Moses that he "was a very humble man, more humble than anyone else on the face of the earth" (Nu 12:3).

*In the Valley*⁷³

After Ezekiel's recovery (which takes seven days), Yahweh appears to him again: "And the glory [כָּבוֹד] of Yahweh was standing there, like the glory I had seen by the Kebar River, and I fell facedown [וָאֶפֹּל עַל־פָּנָי]" (Eze 3:23). The terms of the portrayal are those of the prior theophany, with

---

⁷²*CAD*, 8:331–33 (*kibrātu*).

⁷³As Craigie, *Ezekiel*, 25, notes, the word בִּקְעָה here denotes "valley," not "plain" (RSV, NIV), and occurs again in Ezekiel's book only at 37:1 (the valley of dry bones), where he has another similar vision of God's glory. Craigie speculates that the valley of 3:22 and the valley of 37:1 may be one and the same.

the additional fact that the glory "was standing [עמד] there," a phrase evocative of those times during the Exodus and wilderness wanderings when the "pillar" (עמוד) of cloud/fire "stood" (עמד), e.g., between Israel and Pharaoh's army (Ex 14:19), or before the tent of meeting (Ex 33:10).

Significantly, God's one act in this encounter is to make his prophet stand: "Then the Spirit came into me and caused me to stand [וַתַּעֲמִדֵנִי] upon my feet" (Eze 3:24, author's translation; cf. 2:2). The account suggests a doctrine made clear in the New Testament—namely, that Old Testament believers did not have the Spirit in the way that New Testament believers do: "I will ask the Father, and he will give you another Counselor to be with you forever—the Spirit of truth . . . you know him, for he lives with you and will be in you" (Jn 14:16–17). This Spirit "came into" (וַתָּבֹא־בִ) Ezekiel and empowered him to stand for God.[74]

A Man of Fire

Ezekiel has a third Kebar-like theophany at his own home. There—with the elders of Judah before him—"the hand of the Sovereign Yahweh came upon [him]" (Eze 8:1; cf. 3:14,

---

[74]Stuart, *Ezekiel*, 50, notes an element of graciousness in this: "God was still accepting him and would deal with him as an approved servant. (For a sovereign to invite a suppliant to stand meant that he at least was willing to do business with him.)"

[75]Matthews, *Ezekiel*, 29, rightly rejects the notion that "fell upon me, lends itself to the interpretation that the prophet was a psychopathic case," while noting that "many other features in the book have been so interpreted." As he says, "If God chooses an erratic personality as the medium of his message, it in no way discredits that message" (p. xxii). He rejects the idea that Ezekiel was "erratic," however. But the solution he adopts to account for the unusual in Ezekiel is hardly more satisfactory: "The solution to the problem was arrived at from an entirely different angle. Instead of a dual personality, literary criticism has arrived at dual authorship. The strange physical activities, the dumbness, the visions and hallucinations, all those features that have been interpreted as the results of mental infirmity, are the literary product of a Babylonian editor of the prophetic roll" (p. xxii). But hypotheses of

22).[75] A theophany before the prophet and the elders seems to echo the communion meal that Moses and the elders shared in God's presence (Ex 24), although the others in Ezekiel's house may not have shared in God's revelation to the prophet. He saw "a figure that appeared like fire [אֵשׁ]" (Eze 8:2, author's translation).[76] The man is apparently the same one Ezekiel saw on the chariot throne: "From what appeared to be his waist down he was like fire, and from there up his appearance was as bright as glowing metal" (8:2; cf. 1:27 and the "man whose appearance was like bronze"–apparently an angel–who conducts the prophet around the eschatological temple, 40:3).

The throne man extends "a semblance of a hand" (יָד תַּבְנִית) and takes the prophet by the hair of his head (Eze 8:3).[77] Another way of saying this, perhaps, is that "the Spirit lifted me up [וַתִּשָּׂא אֹתִי רוּחַ, 8:3; cf. 3:12; 11:1; 37:1; 40:1b–2; 43:5] between earth and heaven and in visions of God he took me to Jerusalem" (8:3).[78]

---

dual personality or dual authorship are only ways of avoiding the idea that God could really reveal himself in the ways that Ezekiel reports. After all, why shouldn't the phenomena and the acts of God's kingdom be outlandish? "There are more things in heaven and earth.... Than are dreamt of in your philosophy" (*Hamlet*, I.v.166–67).

[76]Or, with LXX, "like a man [ἀνδρός, i.e., אִישׁ]."

[77]The word "semblance" (תַּבְנִית) is used for everything from the tabernacle pattern (Ex 25:9) and altar and temple patterns (Jos 22:28; 2Ki 16:10; 1Ch 28:11, 12, 18, 19) to idolatrous representations of animals (Dt 4:16–18; Ps 106:20; Eze 8:10) or of man (Isa 44:13).

[78]Brownlee, *Ezekiel 1–19*, 129, comments,

> One may wonder whether 'between earth and sky' was an editorial insertion ... but we have in any case a sense of levitation on the part of the prophet in other passages, and most notably in 3:12–15, where almost every scholar agrees that the prophet travelled physically from the plain of his vision to Tel-abib. It is interesting that in the story of Bel and the Dragon contained (at vv 33–39) among the additions to Daniel, Habakkuk is considered as making a round trip from Palestine to Babylon, where he delivered a bowl of soup to Daniel at the lions' den. In this context, the trip is wholly objective, in the flesh.

God takes Ezekiel to see the idol at the inner court of the temple, where he also sees "the glory of the God of Israel, as in the vision I had seen in the plain" (Eze 8:4). How ironic that Ezekiel now sees God's glory in the temple—that same glory that filled the temple during Solomon's dedication of it. For Yahweh is there in theophany not to show Ezekiel how he dwells there (faithful to the Davidic promises of long ago) but to show him the cause that will drive him "far from [his] sanctuary" (v. 6)—namely, Israel's sin. Ezekiel is about to witness not only the sin that causes Yahweh to leave but also the departure itself. We will now consider that departure and try to understand the rationale for it.

Temple Abandonment

Once the tabernacle was completed Yahweh came to inhabit it in Sinaitic glory (Ex 33:9–10). When the Solomonic temple was completed he did the same (1Ki 8:1–11). Even so, God's presence in the temple was not a guarantee that he would always stay there. Jeremiah had to make that point to those who had misunderstood the promises of God:

> You trust in deceptive words to no avail. Will you steal, murder, commit adultery, swear falsely, burn incense to Baal, and go after other gods that you have not known, and then come and stand before me in this house, which is called by my Name, and say, "We are delivered!"—only to go on doing all these abominations? Has this house, which is called by my Name, become a den of robbers in your eyes? I Myself have seen it, says Yahweh. Go now to my place that was in Shiloh, where I made my Name dwell at first, and see what I did to it for the wickedness of my people Israel. And now, because you have done all these things, says Yahweh, and when I spoke to you persistently you did not listen, and when I called you, you did not answer, therefore I will do to the house which is called by my Name, and in which you trust, and to the place which I gave to you and to your fathers, as I did to Shiloh. And

> I will cast you out of my sight, as I cast out all your kinsmen, all the offspring of Ephraim. (Jer 7:8–15 RSV)

God's people seriously misunderstood the "Name" theology involved in the original Davidic covenant (2Sa 7:13; cf. 1Ki 8:29). Yahweh plans to abandon his temple because of the sin of his people. As in Mesopotamian examples, divine abandonment of the temple means a parallel abandonment of the holy city: Yahweh will do both to his "house" (temple) and to "the place which I gave you" (Jerusalem) as he did to Shiloh. Such abandonment results in military defeat, foreign rule, and exile, just as it does in pagan examples.[79]

Yahweh's temple abandonment is a major theme in Ezekiel's oracles of doom. Yahweh will abandon his temple because of national sin and in particular because his house has been polluted:

> Their beautiful ornament they used for vainglory, and they made their abominable images and their detestable things of it; therefore I will make it an unclean thing to them. And I will give it into the hands of foreigners for a prey, and to the wicked of the earth for a spoil; and they shall profane it. I will turn my face from them, that they may profane my precious place; robbers shall enter and profane it, and make a desolation. (Eze 7:20–22 RSV)

God's judgment is ironic. Jeremiah said that people had made God's temple a den of robbers (פָּרִצִים, Jer 7:11; cf. Jesus' later accusation, Mt 21:13). But now—as a judgment on Judah's sin—pagan robbers (פָּרִיצִים, Eze 7:22) will profane that temple. God will make the punishment fit the crime. Worse, Yahweh will turn his face away from his people with all the implications of that act. Not only will God be unavailable in the temple, he will also turn away the very source of national and personal life.

---

[79]Cf. discussion above, chap. 4.

God's judgment may seem harsh, but the prophet can understand its justice because God allows him to see some idolatrous abominations as they are committed in the temple. Yahweh says, "Son of man, do you see what they are doing, the great abominations that the house of Israel are committing here, to drive me far from my sanctuary?" (Eze 8:6 RSV). Why is the judgment on idolatry so great? Because idolatry is a "walking after [הלך אחרי] other gods"–that is, adoption of other gods as covenant lords (cf. Israel "walking after" idols, 11:21; 20:16). The idiom appears in Akkadian *alāku arki*, where it is used of vassal kings "walking after" (= in vassaldom to) a great king or suzerain. An extract from a letter of Itun-Asdu to King Zimri-lim (1782–1759 B.C.) of Mari illustrates the concept:

24 There is no king who is strong (enough) for himself
25 10–15 kings walk after Hammurapi, king (lit. "man") of Babylon
26 likewise after Rim-[S]in king of Larsa
27 likewise after Ibalpil king of Eshnunna
28 likewise after Amutpil king of Qatanim
29 20 kings walk after Iarimlim king of Iamh[a]d[80]

As the Mari document makes clear, "walking after" a great king means being that king's vassal. The Deuteronomic reproach also lodged by Ezekiel against Israel is that they have tended to "walk after" idols (other gods)–i.e., become their vassals–and so refused Yahweh as covenant God. God warned Israel through Moses that they would be cursed "if you do not obey the commands of Yahweh your God, and turn away from the way which I am commanding you today to walk after other gods whom you have not known" (Dt 11:28, author's trans.). But that is just what Israel has done. For such a renunciation of

---

[80]G. Dossin, "Les Archives Epistolaire du Palais de Mari," *Syria* (1938), 117 (ll. 24–29).

his covenant, Yahweh will abandon his sanctuary. God allows his prophet to see that very act of abandonment.

Yahweh's departure begins as his theophanic glory interrupts its session above the cherubim and moves to the temple threshold: "Now the glory of the God of Israel went up from above the cherubim, where it had been, and moved to the threshold of the temple" (Eze 9:3). The cherubim are those living creatures Ezekiel saw before, but the phrasing evokes the statuesque representations of them in the Mosaic tabernacle and later in the Solomonic temple, above whom Yahweh's throne was supposed to rest (1Sa 4:4; 2Sa 6:2; 2Ki 19:14ff.; Pss 80:2[1]; 99:1).

Before Yahweh's glory departs, he commands judgment in a remarkable passage:

> Then I heard him call out in a loud voice, "Bring the guards of the city here, each with a weapon in his hand." And I saw six men coming . . . each with a deadly weapon in his hand. With them was a man clothed in linen who had a writing kit at his side. They came in and stood beside the bronze altar. (Eze 9:1-2)

The six "men" are angelic warriors whom we may or may not imagine to be of gigantic size.[81] They are surely of gigantic power—supernatural power to destroy people at a blow, much like the "Destroyer" of the Exodus (Ex 12:23) or the "angel [who] stretched out his hand to destroy" Jerusalem as he brought God's punishment upon David (2Sa 24:16-17). The Davidic example may be symbolic. When Yahweh stopped the angel from his destructive work, "the angel of Yahweh was then at the threshing floor of Araunah the Jebusite" (2Sa 24:16). In David's day God's compassion made judgment stop at the future temple site (cf. 2Sa 24:18-25; 2Ch 3:1-2). But now God's judgment begins at the temple: he commands those warrior angels to "begin at my sanctuary" (Eze 9:6). Judgment begins at the house—indeed, at the household—of God (see below).

---

[81]Cf. Eichrodt, *Ezekiel*, 129.

The angels, or "guards of the city," whom Yahweh commands are a small troop of seven—six warriors bearing arms and one scribal angel clothed in linen and carrying a writing kit.[82] Each of the six may have carried a special weapon of his own, just as the Assyrian/Babylonian gods each had his own peculiar weapon: Hadad the storm god wielded the lightning bolt and ax; Marduk the supreme god used the bow and net; Sin the moon god bore the crescent-shaped scimitar, and so on. The total number of the troop, seven, has astral connotations: it echoes the seven planetary gods of Mesopotamian myth, including even Nabu, the secretary of the Babylonian pantheon.[83] Note also the image of seven demons working in association, which was a widespread idea in Babylon (and cf. Mt 12:43–45).[84] The sevenfoldness may also suggest completeness: a perfect judgment because a divine judgment is about to take place.

As noted, the seventh angel carries not a weapon but a writing kit–probably a reed pen and ink in a wooden case

---

[82]Stuart, *Ezekiel*, 92–93, notes of the seventh angel that "his dress is linen, typical of angels not on bloody assignments (e.g., Ezek. 10:6–7; Dan. 12:6–7), indicating his heavenly origin (cf. Ezek. 44:17–18; Rev. 18:8, 14)."

[83]Cf. H. Gunkel, "Der Schreiberengel Nabu im Alten Testament und im Judentum," *Archiv für Religionswissenschaft* 1 (1898): 294ff.

[84]Scholarly speculation about these "men" has varied widely. Brownlee, *Ezekiel 1–19*, 143–44, provides a concise overview:

> Gunkel saw in the seven divine agents a derivation from the mythology of the seven planets, whom the pagans regarded as gods. The "man" with the writing case was a reflection of the scribal god Nabu (or Nebo), a close associate of Bel (or Marduk). Other scholars have suggested, because of their destructive role, a well-known heptad of demons.... Yet the seven "men" in Ezekiel have as their function the punishment of apostasy, and the "man" clothed in linen has the duty of safeguarding the righteous, which does not seem demonic. The Hebrew word used for "writing case" (קסת) is an Egyptian loan word. Whatever analogies one may find for these "men," they are angel-warriors who wreak judgment at Jerusalem, starting with the temple.

along with parchment or papyrus in his girdle.[85] God gives him an unusual job—to go throughout the city and put a "mark" on the foreheads of those who grieve over Israel's sin (Eze 9:4) and who are to be spared (v. 6). The mark was a *tau* (the last letter of the Hebrew alphabet) and took the shape of a sloping cross. God marks his people now just as he used a mark of blood to protect his faithful during the Passover (Ex 12:7ff.). The location of the mark—the forehead—is symbolic of a consecration of the mind and will of the person to God and anticipates the "seal" placed on the heads of the 144,000 (Rev 7:2–3), also called the "name" of the Father and the Lamb (Rev 14:1). The mark of the Beast (which is also his "name" or "the number of his name") on the forehead of his subjects indicates the same (Rev 13:16–17).[86] The shape of the mark may be symbolic. The Greeks who borrowed the Semitic alphabet wrote *tau* as an upright cross (it was a sloping cross in the Hebrew of the sixth century B.C.). Several church fathers saw an allusion to the cross of Christ in this mark.[87] Others have held this view, and it should not be renounced out of hand as naive or unscholarly.[88] It is remarkable, after all, that the only letter in the Hebrew alphabet that bears such a resemblance was chosen by God long before any human could have known its eventual significance.[89]

---

[85]Cf. Eichrodt, *Ezekiel*, 130.

[86]The mark of the beast will be applied either to the forehead or to the right hand (Rev 13:16). The latter apparently indicates action, so that, as regards both volition and action, everyone on earth must be subject to the beast and render him homage in both thought and deed.

[87]Cf. Brownlee, *Ezekiel 1–19*, 145.

[88]Cf. Craigie, *Ezekiel*, 68. Keil and Delitzsch, *Commentary on the OT,* vol. 9, *Ezekiel, Daniel*, 129, remark, "There is something remarkable in this coincidence to the thoughtful observer of the ways of God, whose counsel has carefully considered all beforehand."

[89]Stuart, *Ezekiel*, 93, rightly notes, "Some commentators have suggested that this signified Christ or the cross, but in Ezekiel's day, it merely signified an 'X,' nothing more."

The cross marks those who are being saved, but otherwise God's planned destruction is total. God now enacts a principle articulated before the Conquest—that if his people adopted the ways and worship of the nations, God would turn about and treat them just as he had treated those nations (Dt 8:19-20). Just as he had driven nations out before Israel, he would drive Israel out before the nations. God's judgment begins at the temple (his "house") with the elders in front of it (Eze 9:6). Yahweh's holy war against his own people begins with those who are (or should be) senior in knowledge of him. They have had the greatest advantage but have squandered it. God's action here illustrates the biblical principle that "from everyone who has been given much, much will be demanded; and from the one who has been entrusted with much, much more will be asked"(Lk 12:48). Peter warned more broadly that "it is time for judgment to begin with the family of God; and if it begins with us, what will the outcome be for those who do not obey the gospel of God?"(1Pe 4:17). God is generous in his gifts but also calls to account those who receive them, and he judges those who abuse them.

God's judgment takes the form of apocalyptic fiery coals scattered abroad by the "man clothed in linen" who thus emerges not only as a scribe but as an executive secretary who both records the saved and carries out God's judgment (Eze 10:2). In the midst of another throne vision like that of 1:26, Yahweh commands the "man" to collect the coals from among the cherubim under his throne and scatter them over Jerusalem (10:2). The cherubim help the man by handing him the coals (vv. 6-7), and there follows an account of the wheels and the cherubs, their motion and their appearance (vv. 9-17), echoing that in 1:4-21. At this point Ezekiel becomes aware that what he saw under the throne by Kebar were these same cherubim (10:15, 20-22). The one astonishing new fact in the account is that the cherubim and the wheels are "full of eyes"

(v. 12).⁹⁰ Monstrous as it may seem, this is either an accurate visual rendering of a heavenly reality or a symbolic element of the vision indicative of perspicuous knowledge.

The account is sadly ironic. As God's judgment unfolded against his people "a cloud filled [הֶעָנָן מָלֵא] the inner court. Then the glory of Yahweh rose from above the cherubim and moved to the threshold of the temple. The cloud filled the temple [וַיִּמָּלֵא הַבַּיִת אֶת־הֶעָנָן], and the court was full of the radiance of the glory of Yahweh [מָלְאָה אֶת־נֹגַהּ כְּבוֹד יהוה]" (Eze 10:3–4). The phraseology echoes Exodus 40:34–35, where Yahweh's glory so filled the Tent of Meeting that Moses could not enter. It also recalls 1 Kings 8:10–11, where the cloud, the glory of Yahweh, so filled the temple that the priests could not perform their duties.⁹¹ In those days Yahweh came in cloudy glory to visit approbation upon his tabernacle/temple. He came to bring the greatest possible covenant blessing–his own presence. Now by contrast his glory cloud and radiance fill the place because he has come to loose judgment. Not only so, he has chosen to abandon his temple and people. He has come to bring the greatest of all covenant curses–the absence of God.

Yahweh departs from his house in stages. He has already moved from above the cherubim to the threshold (Eze 9:3; 10:4). On both occasions his motion is followed by commands to the "man in linen" (9:3–4; 10:6). God appears to be standing there (עמד, 10:6) to issue commands as he moves gradually toward the exit. At last "the glory of Yahweh departed from over the threshold of the temple and stopped (עמד) above the cherubim" (10:18). Yahweh is now back on his chariot throne and about to depart. The cherubim spread their wings and lift the throne to the east gate of Yahweh's "house," with Yahweh's glory above them (v. 19). Then "the cherubim lifted up their

---

⁹⁰Cf. 1:18, where we read of the throne wheels that "all four rims were full of eyes all around."

⁹¹Cf. discussion above, pp. 243–44.

wings, with the wheels beside them; and the glory of the God of Israel was over them. And the glory of Yahweh went up from the midst of the city, and stood [עמד] upon the mountain which is on the east side of the city" (11:22–23 RSV). So God departs from his earthly home.

A more total disaster is hardly possible. The removal of God's glory means the removal of his effective presence and protection for his people. The use of the verb עמד, "to stand," throughout (Eze 10:6, 18; 11:23) is most ironic. It recalls the wilderness wanderings when Yahweh "stood" at the door of his tent and all the men of Israel did likewise (Ex 33:7–11). The parallel is no accident. Man is made in God's image, and both dwell in tents or houses. Humans even dwell in "earthly tabernacles"—that is, bodies (2Co 5:1–4; 2Pe 1:13–14). The same parallel appears in Ezekiel. The foreign robbers who despoil Yahweh's "house" (Eze 7:21)[92] will also despoil the "houses" of his people (7:23–24). As God abandons his "house," the people—conquered and uprooted—will be forced to abandon their houses as well.

Excursus: Temple Abandonment and Personal Abandonment

Yahweh's temple abandonment has an Old Testament analog: his abandonment of an individual. If Yahweh could abandon his temple, he could also abandon a person. The temple symbolism of that act becomes clearer in the New Testament. But the analogy in the Old Testament between individual and temple is clear enough when we consider both in relation to God's Spirit. The cases of Saul and David are illustrative.

Just as Yahweh comes in theophany to the tabernacle and the temple, so the Spirit of Yahweh comes upon his chosen

---

[92]For Yahweh's temple as his "house," cf. 8:14; 9:3ff.; et al.

kings, Saul and David. Samuel declares of Saul among the prophets: "The Spirit of Yahweh will come upon you in power, and you will prophesy with them; and you will be changed into a different person. Once these signs are fulfilled, do whatever your hand finds to do, for God is with you" (1Sa 10:6–7). Samuel's word comes to pass almost immediately: "As Saul turned to leave Samuel, God changed Saul's heart, and all these signs were fulfilled that day" (v. 9).

When Samuel anointed David the Spirit of Yahweh also came upon him: "So Samuel took the horn of oil and anointed him in the presence of his brothers, and from that day on the Spirit of Yahweh came upon David in power" (1Sa 16:13).

As Saul waxed rebellious he lost God's favor and the Spirit of Yahweh left him because of his sin: "Now the Spirit of Yahweh had departed from Saul, and an evil spirit from Yahweh tormented him" (1Sa 16:14; cf. 18:10–12). The Spirit of Yahweh departed from Saul because he had disobeyed his covenant God, just as the glory of Yahweh departed from his temple and holy city because Israel had disobeyed her covenant God.

Because of what happened to Saul, David (after his sin with Bathsheba) very reasonably prayed, "Do not cast me from your presence or take your Holy Spirit from me" (Ps 51:11). Just as Yahweh's glory presence came upon the tabernacle and the temple, so his Spirit came upon his anointed kings, Saul and David. And just as his glory-Spirit departed from his temple and holy city, so his Holy Spirit departed from Saul—and so, David feared, might depart from Saul's successor.

Yahweh's departure was caused by sin in both these cases, both national (Israel) and individual (Saul). The result of God's departure was possession by a force hostile to God and his people. In the case of the temple and Jerusalem, the hostile force was Babylon, and the people were taken into bondage. In Saul's case, the hostile force was an evil spirit, and the king was deranged (i.e., taken into bondage by an evil spirit). In both cases the Lord turned away from his rebellious servant (from Israel, Eze 7:22 ["I will turn my face away from them"]; from Saul, 1Sa 28:15 ["and God has turned away from me"]) with mortal consequences. God's abandonment of rebellious vassals lies at the heart of theodicy. As I have shown, it appears in the area of common grace as well as in the special revelation of the Old Testament. It appears more fully in the New Testament, as we shall see.

God's Glory Returns to the Temple

Like Isaiah before him, the prophet Ezekiel offers consolation to God's people. Yahweh has abandoned his temple, but he will return. The idea that gods and goddesses returned to their abandoned temples was well understood in the ancient Near East. They would not harbor their wrath against their people forever. The man "whose appearance was like bronze" (Eze 40:3)—an angel, as noted above—brought Ezekiel to the east gate of the temple. From that vantage point he was able to see Yahweh's return:

> I saw the glory of the God of Israel coming from the east. His voice was like the roar of rushing waters, and the land was radiant with his glory. The vision I saw was like the vision I had seen when he came to destroy the city and like the visions I had seen by the Kebar River, and I fell facedown. The glory of Yahweh entered the temple through the gate facing east. Then the Spirit lifted me up and brought me into the inner court, and the glory of Yahweh filled the temple. (43:2–5).

The phraseology echoes the prophet's portrayals of those earlier visions to which he alludes. Yahweh's "voice" (קוֹל, Eze 43:2 = 1:28) was like the "roar of rushing waters" (מַיִם רַבִּים כְּקוֹל, 43:2 = 1:24). The "glory of Yahweh" (כְּבוֹד יהוה, 43:4 = 1:28) comes again. The prophet's reaction is the same as before: "I fell facedown" (וָאֶפֹּל אֶל־פָּנָי, 43:3; 44:4 = וָאֶפֹּל עַל־פָּנַי,

1:28; 3:23).⁹³ Again the Spirit transports the prophet (רוּחַ + נָשָׂא, 43:5 = 3:12; 8:3; 11:1).⁹⁴ Yahweh's return must have been as encouraging as it was awesome. The most encouraging phenomenon of all, however, was not the theophany but the fact that "the glory of Yahweh filled the temple" (כְּבוֹד־יהוה הַבָּיִת מָלֵא; cf. 44:4). The phraseology repeats that used to portray Yahweh's session in his tabernacle (Ex 40:34–35) and temple (1Ki 8:10–11; 2Ch 5:13–14; 7:1–2). It portends the restoration of all things–that day when, as John wrote, there will be no "temple in the city, because the Lord God Almighty and the Lamb are its temple. The city does not need the sun or the moon to shine on it, for the glory of God gives it light, and the Lamb is its lamp" (Rev 21:22–23).

---

⁹³His reaction to theophany is to be distinguished from his similar prostration in supplication at 9:8; 11:13.

⁹⁴Cf. also 37:1; 40:1b–2.

8

Memory, Imagination, and Eschatology:
Sinai-like Theophanies in the Psalms and Prophets

> The water's going out to sea
> And there's a great moon calling me;
> But there's a great sun calls the moon,
> And all God's bells will carol soon
> For joy and glory and delight
> Of someone coming home tonight.
>
> John Masefield, "The Everlasting Mercy"

God's descent upon Mount Sinai was a formative event in the life of Israel. On that occasion God's people saw not only an awful revelation of God's glory but an equally awful revelation of their own sin. God's appearance defined them categorically—just as his appearance to postlapsarian Adam and Eve had defined our first parents—as sinful human beings. Even so God did not appear to judge them but to save them. And it was his saving purpose and saving acts that Israel remembered and celebrated long after. God's Sinaitic appearance, also, set the stage for subsequent portrayals of his glorious inbreaking, be it in lament or eschatology. For example, the poets and prophets who celebrated Yahweh's theophanic warfare against Pharaoh and the gods of Egypt also urged God to act again in days of crisis (lament genre). David and others even portrayed particular acts of salvation—as enjoyed or anticipated by an individual—in terms that evoked the Sinai theophany (as the Psalms illustrate especially well). The prophets also warned, however, that God would come in Sinaitic glory to judge Israel and the nations. And both the Psalms and the Prophets cast God's greatest possible act of salvation, his eschatological invasion of history and judgment of all nations, in terms of Sinai-like theophany. In fact, all Old Testament "theophanies" that are Sinaitic yet do not portray actual contemporary appearances of God, fall into one of these three categories: evocative recollections of the *magdalia Dei* of the Exodus and wilderness wanderings; imaginative portrayals of God's Sinai-like coming (to save the suppliant, or to judge Israel and the nations); and eschatological portrayals of God's return to judge the nations and save his people.

EVOCATIVE RECOLLECTIONS OF THE MAGNALIA DEI

One could well say that the events of the Exodus and/or Sinai were scarcely past before Israelite poetry began to celebrate them. Exodus 15 is certainly one example. Early in the poetry of Israel comes another, the "Song of Deborah" (Jdg 5:2–31), which vividly portrays Yahweh's intervention for his people:

> O Yahweh, when you went out from Seir,
>   when you marched from the land of Edom,
> the earth shook, the heavens poured,
>   the clouds poured down water.
> The mountains quaked before Yahweh, the One of Sinai
>   before Yahweh, the God of Israel. (Jdg 5:4–5)

After Deborah's song both the Psalms and the Prophets are rich in evocations of God's great acts of salvation wrought during the Exodus and the wilderness wanderings. Yahweh's theophanic parting of the Reed Sea forms a part of such recollections. But God's global command of many waters at the Flood is also an object of celebration and contributes to the portrait of Yahweh as supreme over watery chaos, not only in his battle against Rahab/Egypt (cf. Ps 89:11[10]; Isa 51:9–10), but also as Judge of the wicked and even as Creator.

A fairly standard overall pattern can be seen in such literary evocations of theophany:

1 Potential or real enemies are mentioned
2 Yahweh's past theophany is recalled
3 A renewal of such intervention is called for
4 God's redemption is assured

The above pattern may be said to represent special cases of the larger, so-called "lament" pattern:

1 Address to God   (a cry of distress or ascription of praise)
2 Complaint   (threat of enemies, drought, famine, etc.)
3 Confession of trust   (expression of confidence in God despite troubles)
4 Petition   (appeal to God to intervene)
5 Words of assurance   (reassurance that God will intervene)
6 Vow of praise   (vow to praise God for deliverance)[1]

The general correspondence is clear. The chief point of special differentiation is the evocation of past theophany as a ground for future hope. Such evocations are fairly common in the Psalms and the Prophets.

---

[1] Cf. the handy (but nontechnical) introduction by B. W. Anderson, *Out of the Depths* (Philadelphia: Westminster, 1983), 76–77.

The Psalms

Although it is impossible to discuss every psalm in detail, we can look closely at a few, and note the location of relevant material in others.

Psalm 68

One of the more powerful evocations of the God of Sinai is this Davidic poem. Perhaps composed for the cult (cf. vv. 25–28[24–27]), it begins with an invocation of God with theophanic overtones ("as wax melts before the fire, may the wicked perish before God," 68:3[2]), and invites us to "extol him who rides on the clouds" (68:5[4], cf. Ps 18:10[9]).[2] There follows a vivid portrayal of the "One of Sinai":

> [8] When you went out before your people, O God,
>   when you marched through the wasteland,
> [9] the earth shook [רעש],
>   the heavens poured down rain,
>   before God, the One of Sinai,
>   before God, the God of Israel.

At this point the psalm clearly echoes the "Song of Deborah" (cf. Jdg 5:4–6). After portraying God's victory over his enemies, the poem goes on to taunt the mountains of Bashan for being envious of Mount Zion:

> [17] Why gaze in envy, O rugged mountains,[3]
>   at the mountain where God chooses to reign,
>   where Yahweh himself will dwell forever?
> [18] The chariots of God are tens of thousands
>   and thousands of thousands;
>   Yahweh has come from Sinai into his sanctuary.

---

[2] The phrase, "rider on the clouds" (רֹכֵב בָּעֲרָבוֹת) echoes the Ugaritic epithet of Baal, *rkb ʿrpt*. Cf. J. C. L. Gibson, *Canaanite Myths and Legends*, 43 (2.iv.8).

[3] Of Bashan, cf. v 16.

The passage illustrates a well-established ancient Near Eastern theme: that of the god who (builds and) enters his sanctuary/palace after the rout of his enemies. But it also illustrates an important fact: that the so-called Sinai theology and the so-called Zion theology are closely related. The one follows upon the other here exactly as in Exodus 15:17. One builds upon the other, for the whole theological structure demands that the palace/temple building take place after a god's victory over his foes. It follows that there really is no "Zion theology" separable from a "Sinai theology," or vice-versa—except so far as the theologian may choose to study the one or the other in separation for a time in order to discover its particular emphases. To speak of a "Zion theology" that somehow arose separately from a "Sinai theology" is meaningless and actually is impossible from an ancient Near Eastern point of view.[4]

The poem closes with a promise that Egypt and Cush will submit to God and with a summons to all nations to praise God:

[33] Sing to God, O kingdoms of the earth,
   sing praise to Yahweh,
[34] to him who rides the ancient skies above [רֹכֵב בִּשְׁמֵי שְׁמֵי־קֶדֶם],
   who thunders [יִתֵּן בְּקוֹלוֹ] with mighty voice [קוֹל עֹז].
[35] Proclaim the power of God,
   whose majesty [גַּאֲוָתוֹ] is over Israel,
   whose power is in the skies.
[36] You are awesome [נוֹרָא], O God, in your sanctuary....

The poem includes many theophanic terms that appear in Sinaitic theophanies. For instance, the poet declares that "the earth shook" (רעש; cf. Jdg 5:4, "The mountains *quaked* [רעש] before the One of Sinai"; cf. further Joel 2:10; 3:16[4:16]; Na 1:5). Yahweh "thunders" (יִתֵּן בְּקוֹלוֹ) with "mighty voice" (קוֹל עֹז), in the same idiom we have seen at Ugarit and at Sinai

---

[4]So, e.g., J. K. Kuntz, *The Self-Revelation of God,* 196, is not quite right to say that in Psalm 50 "the Sinaitic theophanic tradition . . . has been transferred to Zion."

(cf. Ex 19:16, 19). The poet would "proclaim the power of God" who "rides the ancient skies above" (רֹכֵב בִּשְׁמֵי שְׁמֵי־קֶדֶם) and whose "majesty [גַּאֲוָתוֹ] is over Israel," just as Moses proclaimed God's power in Baal-like terms ("the rider of the heavens") that would have been especially vivid after Sinai:

> There is no one like the God of Jeshurun,
> who rides on the heavens [רֹכֵב שָׁמַיִם] to help you
> and on the clouds in his majesty [גַּאֲוָתוֹ]. (Dt 33:26)

Finally, we read that Yahweh is "awesome [נוֹרָא]," a term often used of him as God of the "signs and wonders" of the Exodus and Conquest (cf. Ex 15:11; Dt 7:21; 10:17; 28:58).

The overall pattern of the poem is standard in literary evocations of theophany: potential or real enemies are mentioned (element 1: 68:2–3[1–2]); Yahweh's past theophany is recalled (element 2: 68:8–19[7–18]); a renewal of such intervention is called for (element 3: 68:29, 31[28, 30]); and God's redemption is assured (element 4: 68:22–24[21–23]), even to the point of anticipating a nearly eschatological glory (68:30[29]), especially in the final call on all nations to praise Yahweh (68:33–36[32–35]). Because the poem is a hymn, it naturally is interspersed with praise to God (68:5–7[4–6], 20–21[19–20], 27[26], 33–36[32–35]).

Exodus and Heilsgeschichte in Other Psalms

Events of the Exodus, including Sinai and the Reed Sea event, stand out in various psalms as components of salvation history. Some Psalms recall those events extensively. Psalm 78, a great salvation history poem that concludes with a celebration of the Davidic election, devotes considerable space to the days of Moses (vv. 1–54). Psalm 81:1–7 recalls them as part of an appeal for godliness, and reminds the people that "in your distress you called and I rescued you, I answered you out of a thundercloud" (v. 8[9]). Psalm 105, a hymn, reviews those days

(vv. 23–45) after an invitation to praise Yahweh and a celebration of the Abrahamic covenant; we are reminded among other things that Yahweh "spread out a cloud as a covering, and a fire to give light at night" (105:39; cf. 78:14). Psalm 106:7–33 recalls them in the context of a lament (cf. vv. 6, 47)– with some emphasis on the Reed Sea event (vv. 7b–12, 22).

Some Psalms, when they recall the events of those days, seem to emphasize Yahweh's sovereignty not only over the Reed Sea but over the waters generally. Such are Psalms 66:6; 77:13–15; and 89:9–12. Noteworthy in Psalms 77 and 89 is the connection made between Yahweh as both Redeemer (77:12–15; 89:9–10) and Creator (77:16–17; 89:11–12), for which see below. All of Psalm 114 briefly recalls Yahweh's power over the waters: both the sea (114:3a, 5a), the Jordan (114:3b, 5b), and the water of Meribah (114:8), as well as the mountains and hills (114:4, 6). The psalm calls upon the earth to "tremble" (חול; 114:7; cf. Ps 29:8, where the celebration of Yahweh over the waters [vv. 4, 11] also declares, "The voice of Yahweh *shakes* [חול] the desert; Yahweh *shakes* the Desert of Kadesh/holy desert").

Particularly interesting is the connection between Yahweh as Creator and Yahweh as the Redeemer of the Exodus. This connection is made in Psalms 77 and 89 (see above) and stands out in Psalms 135 and 136 as well:

	Psalm 77	Psalm 89	Psalm 135	Psalm 136
Yahweh as Creator	77:16–17	89:11–12	135:6–7	136:5–9
Yahweh as Redeemer	77:12–15	89:9–10	135:8–12	136:10–24

Especially vivid in Psalm 135 is the celebration of Yahweh as the one who Baal-like "sends lightning with the rain and brings out the wind from his storehouses" (v. 7). Canaanite Baal was identified with these natural phenomena, but Yahweh is sovereign over them. Because he is Suzerain over all nature as its Creator, Yahweh also has power to save as no other god can. So the recollection of his saving acts in Egypt (vv. 8–10; cf. 136:10–15) and against Sihon and Og (vv. 11–12; cf. 136:17–22) is followed logically by a sarcastic polemic against the "idols of the nations" that are not gods and so cannot save (vv. 15–18). In the same way, Psalm 74 makes a connection between Yahweh as the victor over Leviathan (v. 14), as miraculous maker of fountains (v. 15a) and drier of rivers (v. 15b), and Yahweh as Creator (vv. 16–17), who "established the sun and the moon" (v. 16b). Psalm 89 celebrates Yahweh as one who "rules over the surging sea" (v. 9) and who "crushed Rahab" (v. 10),[5] but also as the one who "founded the world and all that is in it" (v. 11). All of these poems make the point that Yahweh has the capacity to save people because he created all things including people. The poems contain clear allusions back to Genesis 1, where the Spirit of God hovered over the waters, able to draw from their chaos an order within which humans might live.

Other Psalms allude briefly to the days and events of Moses (e.g., 95:7b–11; 103:6–7) or in a very general way to them (e.g., 44:1–3; 111:2–6; 145:3–7)–that is, without specific personal or place names but with allusive phraseology such as: "It was not by their sword that they won the land . . . it was your right hand, your arm, and the light of your face, for you loved them" (44:3; cf. Ex 15:6; Nu 6:25); "He has shown his people the power of his works, giving them the lands of other nations" (111:6; cf. Ge 15:7; Ex 13:5; 34:10–11; et al.); and "awesome works" (145:6; cf. Dt 10:21). Such passages presuppose the more detailed accounts of God's theophanic activity, his "signs and wonders," "pillars of cloud and of fire," parting of the waters, lawgiving, defeat of Sihon and Og (and the larger Conquest), and so on, found elsewhere.

---

[5] I.e., Egypt; cf. 87:5[4].

The Prophets

It is beyond the scope of this work to consider minutely every case of Sinaitic theophany in the Prophets. But study shows that the general categories of historical recollection are the same as in the Psalms. And just as *Heilsgeschichte* formed a basis for appeal to Yahweh for aid in the Psalms, past events also sometimes introduce an appeal for God to renew his saving acts in the Prophets.

Habakkuk 3

The prayer in Habakkuk 3 was also intended to be used as a song in the cult, according to the colophon: "For the director of music. On my stringed instruments" (v. 19). Much like a hymn, the poem opens and closes with praise to Yahweh. Craigie comments, "The passage has many similarities to the biblical psalms."[6] In other respects it conforms to the pattern already noted:

1	Potential or real enemies are mentioned (implied)	3:2b
2	Yahweh's past theophany is recalled	3:2a.3–15
3	A renewal of such intervention is called for	3:2b
4	God's redemption is assured	3:16

As in all matters of *Gattung*, there are varieties to the pattern. The enemies (Babylon) are not mentioned by name (although they have been the subject of most of the foregoing prophecy) but are implied in 3:2b, where Yahweh is called upon to help against them:

> Yahweh, I have heard of your fame;
> I stand in awe of your deeds, O Yahweh.

---

[6]P. C. Craigie, *Twelve Prophets* (Philadelphia: Westminster, 1985), 2:101. Similarities include the title verse (3:1), musical notations (3:19b), and the term *selah* (3:3, 9, 13). F. F. Bruce, *Habakkuk*, in *The Minor Prophets*, vol. 2, ed. T. E. McComiskey (Grand Rapids: Baker, 1993), 837 (cf. p. 878), calls the section "The Psalm of Habakkuk."

> Renew them in our day,
>> in our time make them known;
>> in wrath remember mercy. (3:2)[7]

Habakkuk has heard the fame of Yahweh's saving deeds of the Exodus and Conquest (described theophanically in 3:3–15), and he stands in "awe" of them.[8] Such a historical recollection should offer some ground of hope, even though God has made it clear that he is about to judge his people. Yet God does not exactly assure his people of "redemption" (although the imperfect of בוא at 3:3 may point in this direction; see below). Rather he consoles them that "the day of calamity" will also come upon "the nation invading us" (3:16).

Habakkuk's long theophanic portrayal of Yahweh recalls the Exodus and God's mighty triumph over Pharaoh. It begins with lines reminiscent of those days:

> God came from Teman [אֱלוֹהַ מִתֵּימָן יָבוֹא],[9]
>> the Holy One from Mount Paran. (3:3)

This introduction recalls Moses' celebratory words:

> Yahweh came from Sinai [יהוה מִסִּינַי בָּא]
>> and dawned over them from Seir;
>> he shone forth from Mount Paran. (Dt 33:2)

The parallels of geography (Teman corresponding to Seir; Mount Paran) and phraseology create an allusion not only to

---

[7]G. A. Smith, *The Book of the Twelve Prophets* (New York: A. C. Armstrong and Son, 1898), 2:150, n.1, notes that רֹגֶז in 3:2 does not mean wrath, "but either roar and noise of thunder (Job xxxvii.2) and of horsehoofs (xxxix.24), or the raging of the wicked (iii.7) or the commotion of fear (iii.26; Isa. xiv.3)." The interpretation "wrath" is still appropriate, however, because Yahweh's stormy advent is a judgment intrusion in which his wrath is in fact unleashed against his foes (cf. 152, n. 5).

[8]Cf. Craigie, *Twelve Prophets*, 2:102: "The principle substance of the psalm (verses 3–15) alludes to the Hebrew experience of God in the Exodus, at Mount Sinai, and during the period of wilderness wandering."

[9]The term אֱלוֹהַ occurs for the first time at Dt 32:15. There it is used to portray Yahweh as Creator of Israel; here it shows him as God of the whole world.

the Sinai theophany and God's mighty victory over Egypt, but also to the lawgiving of Sinai.[10] That same law (1:4) is the reason why God must now judge his people.

The poem continues with stock theophanic phraseology, some of it allusive to the Exodus. God's "glory [הוֹד] covered the heavens" (3:3; cf. Nu 27:20; Job 37:22; 39:20; Ps 8:2[1]). Habakkuk celebrates God's "splendor" (נֹגַהּ, cf. 2Sa 22:13; Isa 4:5; Eze 1:4, 13, 27, 28; 10:4) and "power" (עֹז, cf. Ex 15:2,13; Ps 29:1) when "rays flashed from his hand" (קַרְנַיִם מִיָּדוֹ, 3:4; cf. Ex 34:29, 30, 35).[11]

When Yahweh comes his theophanic presence produces natural upheaval, first in the earth and the mountains (3:6):

---

[10]C. F. Keil and F. Delitzsch, *Commentary on the Old Testament in Ten Volumes* (Grand Rapids: Eerdmans, 1978), vol. 10, *The Twelve Minor Prophets*, 97, comment:

> As the Lord God once came down to His people at Sinai, when they had been redeemed out of Egypt, to establish the covenant of His grace with them, and make them into a kingdom of God, so will He appear in the time to come in the terrible glory of His omnipotence, to liberate them from the bondage of the power of the world, and dash to pieces the wicked who seek to destroy the poor. . . . As Moses depicts the appearance of the Lord at Sinai as a light shining from Seir and Paran, so does Habakkuk also make the Holy One appear thence in His glory.

Keil and Delitzsch take the shift from the perfect of בוֹא (Dt 33:2) to the imperfect here as an indication that "he is about to describe not a past, but a future revelation of the glory of the Lord" (10:97). C. E. Armerding, *Habakkuk*, in *Daniel–Minor Prophets*, EBC, vol. 7 (Grand Rapids: Zondervan, 1985), 525, more cautiously and perhaps more appropriately comment: "Habakkuk's omission of the focal term 'Sinai' admits a certain imprecision to the allusion: it recalls, not the exact details of a past event, but the dynamics of that event as an analogy for another revelation of God's presence and power."

[11]Cf. KD, 10:99–100, for a discussion of the allusion to Exodus 34 and the solar comparison of God. Bruce, *Habakkuk*, 882, translates 3:4a: "The brightness beneath him is like the light" and relates it to the pavement beneath Yahweh's throne at Exodus 24:10 and comments, "God himself is the center of his glory; the spreading of his radiance throughout heaven and earth is compared to the rays of the sun, diffusing its light far and wide."

> He stood [עָמַד], and shook [מֹדֶד] the earth;[12]
>   he looked, and made the nations tremble.
> The ancient mountains crumbled
>   and the age-old hills collapsed.

God's theophanic appearance causes that "upheaval of nature" noted by Jeremias and evocative of what God did at Sinai, when the mountain "trembled violently" (Ex 19:18) and "the mountains quaked before Yahweh, the One of Sinai" (Jdg 5:5). Yahweh comes to take his stand, and the term "stood" (עָמַד) may recall the language of the Exodus and wilderness wanderings, including the pillar (עַמּוּד) of cloud and of fire by which God led his people. Yahweh's appearance "causes the earth to shake" (יְמֹדֶד אֶרֶץ), just as "O Yahweh, when you went out from Seir . . . the earth shook [אֶרֶץ רָעָשָׁה]" (Jdg 5:4). Yahweh "looks and makes the nations tremble" (רָאָה וַיַּתֵּר גּוֹיִם) just as he "looked down from the pillar [עַמּוּד] of fire and cloud at the Egyptian army and threw it into confusion [וַיַּשְׁקֵף . . . וַיָּהָם]" (Ex 14:24). Likewise his wondrous acts at the Reed Sea cast the nations into fear and despair (שָׁמְעוּ עַמִּים יִרְגָּזוּן, Ex 15:14; cf. vv. 15–16). The conceptual and phraseological echoes of the Exodus and Sinai are clear. As Yahweh once came in cloudy glory at Sinai and made the mountains shake, so now he comes and makes the mountains crumble. As his theophany and wonders made the nations quake, so now "when God moves from Teman to the Red Sea, the nations on both sides of it [namely, Cushan and Midian, 3:7] are filled with terror."[13] In Moses' day a report of Yahweh's appearance was able to cause such anguish; but God's eschatological theophany (2:3) will accomplish the same on a much grander scale.[14]

---

[12]I follow Keil and Delitzsch, *Commentary*, 10:101, who understand יְמֹדֶד here as the *Poel* of מוד = מוט, "to set in a reeling motion" // "make . . . tremble" (יַתֵּר).

[13]Ibid., 102.

[14]Not all interpreters have seen the passage as eschatological. Saint Augustine, *The City of God*, trans. M. Dodds (New York: Random House, 1950), 637ff. (= 18.32), understood Habakkuk 3 to foreshadow the work of Christ

Habakkuk's evocation of past deliverance continues as he celebrates Yahweh's glory over the waters in a way that evokes his miracle at the Reed Sea (3:8–11):

> Were you angry with the rivers [נְהָרִים], O Yahweh?
>   Was your wrath against the streams?
> Did you rage against the sea [יָם]
>   when you rode with your horses [כִּי תִרְכַּב סוּסֶיךָ]
>   and your chariots of salvation [מַרְכְּבֹתֶיךָ יְשׁוּעָה]?[15]
> You uncovered your bow,
>   you called for many arrows.
> You split the earth with rivers;
>   the mountains saw you and writhed [חִיל].
> Torrents of water swept by;
>   the deep roared [נָתַן תְּהוֹם קוֹלוֹ]
>   and lifted its waves on high.
> Sun and moon stood still [שֶׁמֶשׁ יָרֵחַ עָמַד] in the heavens
>   at the glint [אוֹר] of your flying arrows,
>   at the lightning of your flashing spear [לְנֹגַהּ בְּרַק חֲנִיתֶךָ].

The language is evocative of the Reed Sea event and also of the Jordan crossing by Joshua and Israel. The poet asks rhetorically whether Yahweh was angry with the "rivers" (נְהָרִים, 3:8a; cf. Ps 66:6, "He turned the sea [יָם] into dry land, they passed through the water [נָהָר] on foot"; cf. also Ps 114:3, 5). He

---

and the church. Cf. his interpretation of 3:2, "'O Lord, I have heard of thy hearing, and was afraid: O Lord, I have considered thy works, and was greatly afraid.' What is this but the inexpressible admiration of the foreknown, new, and sudden salvation of men?" Or of 3:8b: "'For Thou shalt mount upon Thy horses, and Thy riding shall be salvation'; that is, Thine evangelists shall carry Thee, for they are guided by Thee, and Thy gospel is salvation to them that believe in Thee'" (p. 638); Smith, *Twelve Prophets,* 2:157, is noncommittal himself but notes that "Calvin's more sober and accurate learning interpreted it of God's guidance of Israel from the time of the Egyptian plagues to the days of Joshua and Gideon." Cf. J. Calvin, *Commentaries on the Twelve Minor Prophets,* trans. J. Owen (Edinburgh: Calvin Translation Society, 1848), 4:132ff.

[15]Keil and Delitzsch, *Commentary,* 10:103–4, note, "*Yᵉshûʿâh* signifies salvation, even in this case, and not victory . . . because *yᵉshûʿâh* is interpreted in ver. 13 by לְהוֹשִׁיעַ. By describing the chariots of God as chariots of salvation, the prophet points at the outset to the fact that the riding of God has for its object the salvation or deliverance of his people."

asks whether Yahweh raged against the "sea" (יָם, 3:8b; cf. Ex 10:19; 14:16ff.; 15:1ff.), and tells us that the "deep" (תְּהוֹם, 3:10; cf. Ex 15:5, 8) "roared" (קוֹלוֹ ... נָתַן, 3:10), a phrase often used in theophanies (cf. above, chap. 5).[16] As Keil and Delitzsch note, these allusions to the past also look forward. On such an understanding the rivers may indicate the rivers of earth generally and the sea may also connote "the world sea" with God's eschatological advent in view.[17] The portrayal of Yahweh's judgment intrusion is partly ironic: he comes "riding horses and chariots" (כִּי תִרְכַּב סוּסֶיךָ ... מַרְכְּבֹתֶיךָ) in Habakkuk's recasting of the Reed Sea conflict (3:8b), although originally it was Pharaoh whose "horses and chariots and riders" (וּפָרָשָׁיו פַּרְעֹה סוּס רֶכֶב פַּרְעֹה, Ex 14:9, 23; 15:19; cf. סוּס וְרֹכְבוֹ, 15:1, 21; מַרְכְּבֹת, 15:4) were cast into the sea. Habakkuk's imagery also recalls the theophany at Elijah's assumption when a "chariot of fire and horses of fire" (רֶכֶב־אֵשׁ וְסוּסֵי אֵשׁ, 2Ki 2:11) appeared and Elisha cried out, "My father! My father! The chariots and horsemen of Israel" (רֶכֶב יִשְׂרָאֵל וּפָרָשָׁיו, 2Ki 2:12; cf. Ex 14:9). Yahweh may come to judge, but he also comes on chariots of "salvation" (יְשׁוּעָה, 3:8). Moses could rejoice in God's salvific act and sing that "Yahweh has become my salvation" (יְשׁוּעָה, Ex 15:2). Just as Yahweh came to save Israel from Egypt, he now comes at the eschaton to save his people.

In addition to its historical and eschatological aspects, the portrayal here is exactly that of a Baal theophany.[18] Yahweh rode through the contrary waters, victorious with his horses

---

[16]Cf. also Ps 93:3.

[17]KD 10:103. They further remark, "It is true that this description rests upon the two facts of the miraculous dividing of the Red Sea and of the Jordan . . . but it rises far above these to a description of God as Judge of the world, who can smite in His wrath not only the sea of the world, but all the rivers of the earth."

[18]As Bruce, *Habakkuk,* 886 observes, "Yahweh's campaign against the enemies of his people is depicted in terms reminiscent of the conflict with chaos in Semitic mythology—Marduk's victory over Ti'amat (the subterranean deep) in the *Babylonian Genesis,* for example, or Baal's victory over Yam (the unruly sea) in Ugaritic lore."

and chariots. He called for bow and arrows, and his arrows and spears are the lightning bolts that he hurled down against the foe. Baal appears similarly in Canaanite iconography with a spear that is a lightning bolt.[19] Even the sun and moon must stand still "at the lightning of your flashing spear." The phraseology is apt to Baal and also portrays in a theophanic way God's intervention at Aijalon (שֶׁמֶשׁ יָרֵחַ עָמָד, 3:11; cf. וַיִּדֹּם הַשֶּׁמֶשׁ וְיָרֵחַ עָמָד, Jos 10:13). We also read that in the midst of Yahweh's supremacy over the waters "the mountains saw you and writhed [חיל]" (3:10). The earth also "writhes" at Yahweh's coming in the Psalms. Psalm 114 reviews Yahweh's power over the waters (the sea, vv. 3a, 5a; the Jordan, vv. 3b, 5b; the water of Meribah, v. 8) and over the mountains and hills (vv. 4, 6) and then commands the earth to "tremble" (חול, v. 7). Psalm 29 celebrates Yahweh's supremacy over the waters (vv. 4, 11) and then declares, "The voice of Yahweh *shakes* [חיל] the desert, Yahweh *shakes* the Desert of Kadesh/[holy desert]" (29:8). The concept has deep roots in ancient Near Eastern theophany, as is illustrated by the Akkadian cognate *ḫâlu*. For example, the storm god Adad (or Hadad, also a name of Baal)[20] is the one "at whose thundering [*ša ina rigim pîšu*, lit., "at the voice/thunder of whose mouth"][21] the fields tremble, the plain shakes [*iḫillu*]."[22] And in what may be called a "name theology" ac-

---

[19]Cf. the figure of Baal in J. B. Pritchard, *The Ancient Near East in Pictures* (Princeton: Princeton University Press, 1954), 168 (fig. 460), the so-called "Baal au foudre," where Baal "stands on what appear to be mountains, brandishes a club in his right hand, and holds in his left a lance with point resting on the ground and the upper part extending upward in the form of a tree or stylized lightning" (p. 307). The figure was found west of the great temple at Ras Shamra (ancient Ugarit) in 1932, and has been dated anywhere from 1900 to 1500 B.C. For a clearer reproduction of the same, see J. D. Douglas, ed., *The Illustrated Bible Dictionary* (Leicester: Inter-Varsity Press, 1980), 1:153. The club presumably represents thunder, as the lance does lightning.

[20]Hadad (Akk. Adad) is the personal name of Baal, and apparently means "thunderer." Cf. Gibson, *Canaanite Myths and Legends*, 5, n. 4.

[21]Cf. above, chap. 4.

[22]*CAD,* vol. 6 (H), p. 55 (*ḫâlu* B); cf. vol. 13 (Q), p. 213 (*qerbetu* 2.e).

count, we read "he pronounces your awe-inspiring name in heaven and the earth shakes [*iḫal*]."[23]

Habakkuk has portrayed an eschatological advent of God in terms evocative of the Reed Sea and Jordan events. The God who worked so powerfully in the past could easily come again to deliver his people. Yet, although he hopes for salvation, Habakkuk's reaction at the end is one of fear:

> I heard and my heart pounded,
>   my lips quivered at the sound [קוֹל];
> decay crept into my bones,
>   and my legs trembled [וְתַחְתַּי אֶרְגָּז]. (3:16)

Habakkuk's account of himself recalls how Yahweh comes theophanically. The prophet "trembles" (רגז), echoing how Yahweh comes amid "tumult/wrath" (רֹגֶז, 3:2). No doubt that theophanic tumult made him tremble just as did the "sound" (קוֹל, 3:15) of Yahweh's advent. Calvin astutely comments that Habakkuk "had already said at the beginning, 'Lord, I have heard thy voice; I feared.' He now repeats the same thing."[24] Habakkuk shows an altogether appropriate fear of the holy God who can come in such power and glory–the

---

[23] *CAD*, vol. 6 (H), p. 55 (*ḫalu* B).

[24] Calvin, *Minor Prophets*, 4:169. Because he takes the content of Habakkuk's poem to refer to God's guidance from the Exodus into the Promised Land, Calvin believes that

> those interpreters are mistaken ... who connect the verb, 'I have heard,' with the last verse, as though the Prophet had said that he had conceived dread from those evidences of God's power: for the Prophet had no occasion to fear in regarding God as armed with unexpected power for the salvation of his people; there was no reason for such a thing. Hence these two things do not agree together. (p. 169)

But if, as I maintain, the passage is eschatological, Habakkuk's reaction is quite understandable. God's glory presence normally produces fear even when he comes to bless, as we have seen (cf. Ex 20:18–19). Divine judgment messengers can provoke dread on the part of God's prophets even when their message is ultimately one of salvation (e.g., Da 10:7; Rev 1:17) as it is here.

same fear shown by our first parents and by God's people at the foot of Sinai.

Other Examples From the Prophets

In general, the Prophets do not dwell as extensively as the Psalms on such historical reminiscences. The nature of their concern may account for the difference. The Psalms tend to celebrate what God has done in the past or recall it as a basis for some present appeal for help. The same can occur in the Prophets. But the historical concern of the Prophets is more often that of the covenant lawsuit *genre*: the people's own record of sins. When they recall the *magnalia* of the Exodus and wilderness wanderings, it is to encourage the people that God is able to do great works for them again and even plans to do so in the future. In other words, evocations of the *magdalia Dei* tend to occur in words of consolation.

Lament Context in the Prophets

Sometimes a prophet recalls God's deliverance during the Exodus and bases a present appeal for mercy on it. An outstanding example is Isaiah 63:7–14, the longest such evocation in the Prophets. Isaiah recalls how "the angel of his presence" (v. 9a; cf. Ex 33:14) saved Israel, how he "lifted them up and carried them" (v. 9b; cf. Dt 1:31), how he sent his "glorious arm of power" and "divided the waters before them" (v. 12; cf. Ex 15:6–8), and "led them through the depths" (v. 13; cf. Ex 14:22; 15:16–17; Ps 106:9).[25] Upon this basis the appeal for God to act now is built (63:15–19a). It continues with language evocative of Sinai in 63:19b–64:11 (64:1–12):

> [63:19b] Oh, that you would rend the heavens [שָׁמַיִם] and come down [ירד],

---

[25]Isaiah also recalls how they "rebelled" (מָרוּ, 63:10; cf. Nu 20:24; 27:14)—a minor note in his overall appeal for God's action in his own day.

> that the mountains would tremble [הָרִים נָזֹלּוּ] before you!
>
> [64:1] As when fire [אֵשׁ] sets twigs ablaze
> and causes water to boil,
> come down [ירד] to make your name [שִׁמְךָ] known to your enemies
> and cause the nations quake before you [מִפָּנֶיךָ גוֹיִם יִרְגָּזוּ]!
>
> [64:2] For when you did awesome things [נוֹרָאוֹת] that we did not expect,
> you came down [ירד], and the mountains trembled [הָרִים נָזֹלּוּ] before you.

God's theophanic descent upon Sinai is evoked as a ground for some similar descent now. The poet asks Yahweh to "rend the heavens" (שָׁמַיִם, 63:19b; cf. Dt 4:11) and "come down" (ירד, 63:19b; 64:1, 2; cf. Ex 19:9, 18) so that the "mountains tremble" (הָרִים נָזֹלּוּ, 63:19b; 64:2; cf. Ex 19:18; Hab 3:6). He asks for theophanic "fire" (אֵשׁ, 64:1; cf. Ex 19:18; Dt 4:11). He calls upon Yahweh to make his "name" (שֵׁם) known among his enemies (64:1; cf. Ex 9:16; 15:3; and the Deuteronomic emphasis on Yahweh's name, Dt 12:5 and passim). He wants Yahweh to come so that "the nations quake" (גוֹיִם יִרְגָּזוּן; cf. עַמִּים יִרְגָּזוּן, Ex 15:14; וַיִּתֵּר גּוֹיִם, Hab 3:6). He recalls how Yahweh did "awesome things" (נוֹרָאוֹת, 64:2, cf. Ex 15:11; Dt 10:21) and hopes that he will again.

The passage is a lament and includes the elements noted above:

1	Potential or real enemies are mentioned	63:18b–19
2	Yahweh's past theophany is recalled	63:7–14; 64:3
3	A renewal of such intervention is called for	63:15–17; 64:1–12
4	God's redemption is assured	

The one thing lacking, of course, is a promise of redemption. It does not come until Isaiah 65:8–10, 13ff. after further covenant lawsuit material (65:1–7, 11–12), replete with indictments (65:1–5) and judgment announcements (65:6–7, 11–12).

In Words of Consolation

Isaiah recalled the "days of old" as part of a lament. Far more often the prophets evoked the Sinai and Exodus events as a basis for future consolation. Yahweh, who waged theophanic warfare against Pharaoh and the gods of Egypt, could and would act again to save his people. Often his action was portrayed in theophanic terms evocative of Moses' day.

Isaiah abounds in these pregnant evocations. In 43:16–17 he recalls the Reed Sea event and follows it with a promise of a new thing: God will make "streams in the wasteland" (v. 19) to "give drink to my people" (v. 20). The God who was able to dry up the Reed Sea will now make water spring in the desert. He can do this because he has already done it: "They did not thirst when he led them through the deserts; he made water flow for them from the rock; he split the rock and water gushed out" (48:21; cf. Nu 20:1–13; Dt 8:15b). Both of these thematically coordinated promises have to do with a future deliverance from Babylon (43:14; 48:20). The association of Babylon with the Reed Sea—and of the Babylonian exodus with the Egyptian—is made complete a few chapters later (51:9–11):

> 9 Awake, awake! Clothe yourself with strength [עֹז],
> O arm [זְרוֹעַ] of Yahweh;
> awake, as in days gone by,
> as in generations of old.
> Was it not you who cut Rahab to pieces,
> who pierced that monster through?
> 10 Was it not you who dried up [חרב] the sea [יָם],
> the waters of the great deep [תְּהוֹם רַבָּה],
> who made a road in the depths of the sea [יָם]
> so that the redeemed [גְּאוּלִים] might cross over [עבר]?
> 11 The ransomed of Yahweh will return.
> They will enter Zion with singing;
> everlasting joy will crown their heads.

MEMORY, IMAGINATION, AND ESCHATOLOGY

> Gladness and joy will overtake them,
> and sorrow and sighing will flee away.

Isaiah calls upon Yahweh to arm himself with "strength" (עֹז, 51:9; cf. Ex 15:2, 13). He calls upon Yahweh's "arm" (זְרוֹעַ, cf. Ex 15:16) for deliverance. After all, Yahweh "dried up" the "sea" (חרב, יָם, 51:10; cf. Ps 106:9, "He rebuked the Reed Sea, and it dried up"). He dried up the "waters of the great deep" (תְּהוֹם רַבָּה, 51:10; cf. Ge 7:11; Ex 15:5.8; Am 7:4). He made a way in the sea so that the "redeemed" (גְּאוּלִים, 51:10; cf. Ex 15:13) might "cross over" (עבר, 51:10; cf. Ex 15:16). Just as Yahweh parted the Reed Sea and led the people across to "the mountain of [his] inheritance" (Ex 15:17), so he will deliver them again and return them to Mount Zion (51:11). Rahab in the passage is the sea monster (cf. Job 9:13; Ps 89:10) emblematic of Egypt, which the prophet also calls "Rahab the Do-Nothing" (Isa 30:7).[26] As Isaiah recalls the Reed Sea event, he also evokes a mythical theme: Yahweh's supremacy over the chaotic waters. Ultimately the chaos dragon (Rahab) is emblematic of "that ancient serpent the Devil" who is the source of all chaos (Rev 12:9). His goal is to uncreate, and he represents uncreation. In such a context it is natural that God's capacity as Savior (51:12–13b–14, 16a, c) is once again related to the fact that he is the Creator (51:13a, 15, 16b). God is supreme over the chaotic waters, and so he is able to save:

> For I am Yahweh your God
>   who churns up the sea so that its waves roar–
>   Yahweh of hosts/armies is his name.
> I have put my words in your mouth
>   and covered you with the shadow of my hand–
> I who set the heavens in place,
>   who laid the foundations of the earth,
>   and who say to Zion, "You are my people" (Isa 51:15–16)

---

[26]Other passages in Isaiah that deal with Yahweh's supremacy over the waters are: 44:27; 50:2; 51:15 (all recalling the Reed Sea); 54:9 (Noah); and 57:20 (comparing the wicked to the sea).

The waters are merely a creation of God; the one who gave Israel safe conduct through them can also save his people in the end.

Elsewhere in the Prophets specific recall of the *magnalia Dei* against Egypt is sparse. Hosea briefly assumes the Exodus theme but without direct theophanic references (e.g., Hos 12:13; 13:4–5). Amos mentions the plagues Yahweh sends to Israel as warning judgments and likens them to those he sent against Egypt (Am 4:10). Micah promises future wonders like the ones Yahweh showed "in the days when you came out of Egypt" (Mic 7:15). Jeremiah, commanded by God to buy a field as a sign of God's plan to restore the people after exile, prays for confirmation. His prayer notes that God, as Creator, can do anything, and he recalls the "signs and wonders" of the Exodus and Conquest (Jer 32:17–23). Zechariah mentions what Yahweh did in Moses' day as a foreshadowing of what God would do eschatologically: he would recall his people from Egypt and Assyria, and they would "pass through the sea of trouble . . . and all the depths of the Nile will dry up" (Zec 10:10–11; cf. Ex 15:16; Ps 106:9; Isa 51:10). The day will come when "Yahweh will shield those who live in Jerusalem, so that the feeblest among them will be like David, and the house of David will be like God, like the Angel of Yahweh going before them" (Zec 12:8). The "Angel of Yahweh" recalls the "Angel" of Exodus 23:20–22–that theophanic presence who fought Yahweh's battles (cf. Zec 12:9). The allusion to the Davidic covenant ("the house of David will be like God," cf. 2Sa 7:14; Ps 2:7) looks forward to what God ultimately provided in Christ ("To those who believed in his name, he gave the right to become children of God," Jn 1:12). Zechariah's evocation of the "Angel" of the Exodus thus occurs in a prophetic adumbration of an even greater salvation God has planned.

Our study so far shows that the theophanies of the Exodus and/or Sinai were scarcely past before Israelite poetry began to celebrate them. Exodus 15 is one early example, as in the

"Song of Deborah" (Jdg 5:2–31). As we have seen, evocations of these theophanies also took place in lament contexts and in words of consolation. Sometimes, and especially in the latter, those contexts have eschatological overtones. In addition to evocations of the past, the Old Testament presents ahistorical, imaginative theophanic portrayals of God's coming in lament and consolation that also adumbrate the eschaton.

IMAGINATIVE PORTRAYALS OF GOD'S SINAI-LIKE COMING

When David portrays Yahweh in stormy glory routing his foes (Ps 18), his portrait is a purely literary creation. But even that artistic portrayal (and others like it) arises on the ground of Yahweh's covenant relationship with his people to whom he more than once actually appeared in such a way. Every such portrayal can and should be understood under the aegis of God's covenantal self-disclosure—that is, against a background of actual theophanies that occurred as part of God's covenant administration.

The Psalms

Theophanic portrayals of this purely imaginative sort are abundant in the Psalms and especially in laments. It is not hard to see why. God had appeared long ago and had done awesome deeds of salvation. What better way to portray him now—when the individual or the nation calls upon him to bare his arm once again and save with his mighty hand? One may call these portrayals "judgment intrusions" because they have Yahweh appear not only in the same theophanic glory as before but also in the same glory he will show when he comes to judge the earth. The examples of such portraits are too numerous for detailed treatment of them all. But close examination of a few can illustrate the main points.

GOD AT SINAI

Psalm 18:5–20 (4–19)

David cries to God for help in this lament which is highly evocative of Yahweh's theophany on Sinai. The poem also contains echoes of Canaanite poetry not least of which is a parallel between the powers of death and the powers of the chaotic sea—the "many waters."

5 The cords of death [מָוֶת] entangled me;
the torrents of destruction overwhelmed me.
6 The cords of the grave coiled around me;
the snares of death [מוֹקְשֵׁי מָוֶת] confronted me.
7 In my distress I called to Yahweh;
I cried to my God for help.
From his temple he heard my voice;
my cry came before him, into his ears.

8 The earth trembled [געש] and quaked [רעש],
and the foundations of the mountains shook [רגז];
they trembled [געש] because he was angry.
9 Smoke [עָשָׁן] rose from his nostrils;
consuming fire [אֵשׁ...תֹּאכֵל] came from his mouth,
burning coals [גֶּחָלִים] blazed [בער] out of it.
10 He parted the heavens [שָׁמַיִם] and came down [ירד];
dark clouds [עֲרָפֶל] were under his feet.
11 He mounted the cherubim [כְּרוּב] and flew;
he soared on the wings of the wind [רוּחַ].
12 He made darkness [חֹשֶׁךְ] his covering, his canopy around
him— the dark rain [חֶשְׁכַת־מַיִם] clouds of the sky [עָבֵי שְׁחָקִים].
13 Out of the brightness [נֹגַהּ] of his presence [his] clouds [עָבָיו]
advanced,
with hailstones [בָּרָד] and bolts of lightning [וְגַחֲלֵי־אֵשׁ].
14 Yahweh thundered [רעם] from heaven;
the voice of the Most High resounded [עֶלְיוֹן יִתֵּן קֹלוֹ].
15 He shot his arrows [חִצָּיו] and scattered the enemies,
great bolts of lightning [בְּרָקִים רָב] and routed them.
16 The valleys of the sea [אֲפִיקֵי מַיִם] were exposed[27]
and the foundations of the earth laid bare
at your rebuke, O Yahweh,
at the blast of breath from your nostrils [נִשְׁמַת רוּחַ אַפֶּךָ].

17 He reached down from on high and took hold of me;
 he drew me out of [great]/many waters [מַיִם רַבִּים].
18 He rescued me from my powerful enemy,
 from my foes, who were too strong for me.
19 They confronted me in the day of my disaster,
 but Yahweh was my support.
20 He brought me out into a spacious place;
 he rescued me because he delighted in me.

David's cry for help in some measure replicates the Exodus/Sinai experience. As in the days of Egyptian bondage, God's chosen one is under attack unto death. The poem abounds in language evocative of the Mount Sinai theophany: "smoke" (עָשָׁן, 18:9[8]; cf. Ex 19:18), "consuming fire" (תֹּאכֵל ... אֵשׁ, 18:9[8]; cf. Ex 19:18; Dt 4:25) that "blazed" (בָּעַר, 18:9[8]; cf. Dt 4:11) as Yahweh "came down" (יָרַד, 18:10[9]; cf. Ex 19:18) amid "clouds" (עָב, 18:12, 13[11, 12]; cf. Ex 19:9); "dark clouds" (עֲרָפֶל, 18:10[9]; cf. Dt 4:11); the "foundations of the mountains shook"(מוֹסְדֵי הָרִים יִרְגָּזוּ, 18:8[7]; cf. "the whole mountain trembled" [וַיֶּחֱרַד כָּל־הָהָר], Ex 19:18). Yahweh's onslaught is described in terms that also anticipate the open visions of Ezekiel: "Out of the brightness [נֹגַהּ] of his presence clouds [עָב] advanced" (18:13[12]; cf. Eze 1:4) as Yahweh rode the "cherubim" (כְּרוּב, 18:11[10]; cf. Eze 9:3; 10:15). His attack on the foe is reminiscent of the "hailstones" (בָּרָד, 18:13[12]) by which he slaughtered Joshua's foes at Aijalon (Jos 10:11). The foundations of the earth are laid bare at the "blast of the breath from your nostrils" (נִשְׁמַת רוּחַ אַפֶּךָ, 18:16[15]; cf. רוּחַ אַפֶּךָ, Ex 15:8) in a clear evocation of the Reed Sea event. Yahweh also drew David "out of great/many waters" (מַיִם רַבִּים)—phraseology that recalls both the Reed Sea event and the Flood theophany (cf. Ex 15:10; Ps 29:3).[28]

The poem also echoes Ugaritic mythology. Death is a menace that engulfs its victim, and it is closely associated with

---

[27]Cf. Vergil, *Aeneid*, 1.102–7.
[28]For discussion of the Flood and Ps 29, see chap. 5.

watery chaos: "The cords of death [מָוֶת] entangled me; the torrents of destruction [נַחֲלֵי בְלִיַּעַל, 18:5–6(4–5)] overwhelmed me." In Ugaritic myth Death (the god Mot) and the watery powers of chaos are associated. As we have noted, the deadly sea monster Leviathan is one of Mot's friends.[29] Opposed to those powers is the sky god, Baal. When Yahweh comes to rescue, he does so in a Baal-like theophany. He "thunders [רעם] from heaven" (cf. Ps 29:3), and his heavenly voice is portrayed in a phrase that could have been lifted right out of a Ugaritic poem: "The voice of the Most High resounded [עֶלְיוֹן יִתֵּן קֹלוֹ, 18:14(13)]." "He shot his arrows [חִצָּיו] and scattered the enemies, great bolts of lightning [בְּרָקִים רָב] and routed them" (18:15[14]; cf. Ex 19:16). The Ugaritic parallels are striking. Baal also is described as "the Most High" (cf. "the rain of Baal" // "the rain of the Most High" [mṭr bʿl // mṭr ʿly]).[30] Baal often "gives voice" (ytn ql) in theophany.[31] And just as they do in David's poem, Baal's "voice" and his "lightning" come together: "Now . . . Baal may appoint a time . . . for the sounding of his voice [tn.qlh] in the clouds, for him to release his lightnings [brqm] on the earth."[32] As we have noted, Baal's triumph over Mot (Death) and his watery allies parallels Marduk's over Tiamat, the chaotic sea-dragon goddess in Babylonian myth. Yahweh is like Baal/Marduk in the Psalm. He triumphs over both death and the chaotic watery threat as he descends in theophanic glory to save the suppliant. David employs the classic phraseology of ancient Near Eastern storm theophany, simultaneously evocative of what Yahweh actually did at Sinai, at the Reed Sea, and at Aijalon, to portray Yahweh's hoped-for descent to save.

---

[29] See above, chap. 4; cf. Gibson, *Canaanite Myths and Legends,* 68 (5.i.1ff.).

[30] Gibson, *Canaanite Myths and Legends,* 98 (16.iii.5–6). The Ugaritic term is from the same root as the Hebrew and has the same meaning: ʿly (Heb. עלה), "to go up." Cf. C. Gordon, *UT,* 456 (19.1855).

[31] See above, chap. 4.

[32] Gibson, *Canaanite Myths and Legends,* 60–61 (4.v.68–71).

In Other Psalms

The storm theophany elements apparent in Psalm 18 also appear more or less extensively in other portrayals of Yahweh's theophanic judgment intrusion in the Psalms. Sometimes Baal-like theophanic elements are mentioned, such as God's "arrows."[33] In Psalm 144 David again calls upon Yahweh to part the heavens and "come down" (ירד), to send forth "lightning" (בָּרָק), to shoot his "arrows" (חֵץ), and to rescue him from the "mighty waters" (מַיִם רַבִּים), i.e., from the "hands of foreigners" (vv. 5–7).

Sometimes God's "fire" and/or "burning coals" are evoked, echoing the fiery theophanies of the Exodus.[34] Or the "Angel of Yahweh" is envisioned, who might save again as he did in days of old (e.g., Pss 34:8[7], 35:5–6). The psalmists evoke Yahweh's "Name," which he explained to Moses on Mount Sinai.[35] And they portray Yahweh or his deeds as "awesome" (נוֹרָא), a term applied to them by Moses (Ex 15:11; Dt 7:21).[36] The poets are also concerned for and exult in Yahweh's "glory," which he revealed in such splendor at Mount Sinai.[37] In his glorious state, Yahweh is seated on the "cherubim" (e.g., Pss 80:2[1]; 99:1; cf. Ge 3:24; Ex 25:18ff.; Eze 9:3; et al.). And when he comes to judge and to save, natural disasters—earthquakes, melting of the earth, smoking of mountains—may occur at his advance (e.g., Pss 46:7[6]; 60:3[2]; 144:5), just as Mount Sinai/Horeb shook severely at his descent (Ex 19:18), and again when he appeared there to Elijah (1Ki 19:11–13).

Sometimes with a phrase that recalls Exodus 15:6, Yahweh's "right hand" (יָמִין) is portrayed as the instrument of

---

[33]E.g., Pss 7:13–14(12–13); 38:3(2); 64:8(7); 120:4.
[34]E.g., Pss 50:1–3ff.; 68:3(2); 79:5; 89:47(46); 120:4; 140:11(10).
[35]E.g., Pss 8:2, 10(1, 9); 75:2(1); 79:9; 99:3.
[36]E.g., Pss 47:3(2); 66:3, 5; 99:3.
[37]E.g., Pss 57:6, 12(5, 11); 63:3(2); 66:2–5; 72:19; 79:9; 85:9; 113:4; 138:5.

judgment and salvation.³⁸ As he had saved the Israelites before, "in the years of the right hand of the Most High" (Ps 77:11[10]), and brought them "to the hill country his right hand had taken" (Ps 78:54), so he could save again. The image is ultimately applied to the king as a type of the Messiah to come: "Let your right hand display awesome deeds" (Ps 45:5[4]); "Watch over this vine, the root your right hand has planted, the son [of man] you have raised up for yourself" (Ps 80:15–16[14–15]).³⁹

The Psalms portray Yahweh theophanies artistically, in ways that recall the Exodus and Sinai events. Such portrayals often occur in lament contexts, where the poet calls for God's help on the personal or national level. The poetic pleas arise on the ground of Yahweh's covenant relationship with his people, to whom he more than once actually appeared in such a way. I therefore repeat that every such portrayal can and should be understood under the aegis of God's covenantal self-disclosure—that is, against a background of actual theophanies that occurred as part of God's covenant administration. Such an understanding is not only historically appropriate; it also preserves these theophanic passages from being understood as merely human invention, whether arising from the cult or elsewhere.⁴⁰

In the Prophets

One finds in the Prophets, as in the Psalms, a variety of theophanic terms evocative of the Exodus and Sinai experiences. Many of the Sinaitic terms are applied imaginatively to the desired or anticipated salvation of God, just as in the

---

³⁸E.g., Pss 20:6; 21:8; 48:10; 89:14(13); 108:6; 118:15–16; 138:7.
³⁹See below for a discussion of the "son of man" typology.
⁴⁰For a discussion of the historicity issue vis-à-vis the traditio-historical approach involving cultic source attribution see above, chap. 2.

Psalms. By far the majority of such echoes appear in the book of Isaiah, with scattered examples also in Hosea, Joel, Amos, Micah, and Nahum.

Isaiah

Perhaps the most powerful example of judgment intrusion theophany in Isaiah comes in an oracle against Assyria (Isa 30:27–33) that has definite eschatological overtones:[41]

27 See, the Name [שֵׁם] of Yahweh comes from afar,
   with burning anger [בֹּעֵר אַפּוֹ] and dense clouds of smoke [וְכֹבֶד מַשָּׂאָה];
   his lips are full of wrath,
   and his tongue is a consuming fire [אֵשׁ אֹכָלֶת].
28 His breath [רוּחוֹ] is like a rushing torrent,
   rising up to the neck.
   He shakes the nations in the sieve of destruction; . . .
30 Yahweh will cause men to hear his majestic voice [הוֹד קוֹלוֹ]
   and will make them see his arm [זְרוֹעוֹ] coming down
   with raging anger and consuming fire [לַהַב אֵשׁ אוֹכֵלָה],
   with cloudburst, thunderstorm and hail [אֶבֶן בָּרָד].
31 The voice [קוֹל] of Yahweh will shatter [יֵחַת] Assyria.

The Baal-theophany aspects of the passage are obvious, as are the evocations of the Mount Sinai and Exodus experiences. The "Name of Yahweh," which God began most fully to reveal to Moses on Mount Sinai, is here virtually hypostasized—or at least substituted for Yahweh himself.[42] His name comes with "burning anger" (בֹּעֵר אַפּוֹ, 30:27; cf. Ex 3:2; Nu 11:1.3; Dt 4:11) and with "dense clouds of smoke" (וְכֹבֶד מַשָּׂאָה, 30:27; cf. עָנָן כָּבֵד, Ex 19:16). Yahweh's tongue is a "consuming fire" (אֵשׁ אֹכָלֶת, 30:27; cf. v. 30; Dt 4:25). His "breath" (רוּחוֹ) is like a rushing torrent, rising up to the neck (30:30)—a statement that may echo the Reed Sea event ("You blew with your breath [רוּחַ] and the sea covered them," Ex 15:10). Yahweh will cause

---

[41] Cf. 30:23–26.

[42] For similar exaltation of a divine "Name" in the ancient Near East, see chap. 6.

men to hear his "majestic voice" (הוֹד קוֹלוֹ, 30:30; cf. Job 37:22; 39:20) and see his arm (זְרוֹעוֹ, 30:30; cf. Ex 6:6; 5:16) coming to save. God will come theophanically with cloudburst, thunderstorm, and "hail" (אֶבֶן בָּרָד, 30:30; cf. Joshua at Aijalon, Jos 10:11). As in Psalm 29, the voice alone of Yahweh is sufficient to "shatter" things: "The voice of Yahweh shatters [שׁבר] the cedars" (Ps 29:5); "The voice of Yahweh will shatter [יֵחַת, root חתת] Assyria" (Isa 30:31).[43]

Other judgment intrusions in Isaiah that may be called Sinaitic appear throughout the book with similar frequency in both halves: fifteen times in chapters 1–39 (i.e., roughly seven per twenty chapters), and six times in chapters 40–66.[44] Perhaps the glory Isaiah saw at his calling prepared him in a special way for future revelations of God's glory. The same may be said *mutatis mutandis* of his great precursor, Moses.

Isaiah's portrayals of Yahweh in Sinaitic judgment/salvation intrusion have a variety of emphases similar to what we find in the Psalms. Sometimes the earth-shattering or earthquake-like nature of the theophany is stressed.[45] Sometimes the fiery aspect of his judgment is paramount.[46] Yahweh's supremacy over the waters is also evoked, reminiscent of his command at the Reed Sea (e.g., Isa 10:26; 17:12–24; 27:1; 59:19). The stormy or thunderous nature of God's advent can work both judgment and salvation.[47] And the "glory" of Yah-

---

[43] The two terms (שׁבר and חתת) appear parallelistically in Jer 17:18, where the prophet calls upon Yahweh to let his persecutors "be shattered/terrified" (יֵחַתּוּ), and even "shattered with double shattering" (מִשְׁנֶה שִׁבָּרוֹן שָׁבְרֵם).

[44] In the first half of Isaiah: 2:19–20; 5:25; 6:1–7; 10:16–17, 26; 13:9–13; 17:12–14; 26:10–11; 28:2; 29:6; 30:27, 30, 31, 33; 31:9; 33:3; 35:2; in the second half: 42:25; 43:7; 48:11; 58:8; 59:19; 64:1–3. Distinctly eschatological Yahweh theophanies have the following distribution: three in the first half of the book (4:4–6; 19:1–25; 24:14–23); five in the second half (27:1; 40:5; 60:1–3, 13, 19–20; 66:15–16; 66:17–24).

[45] E.g., Isaiah 2:19–21; 5:25; 29:6; 30:28; 64:1–3.

[46] E.g., 10:16–17; 26:10–11; 30:27; 31:9; 42:25.

[47] E.g., 28:2; 29:6; 30:30; 33:3.

weh is often salvific, as it was at Mount Sinai and during the Exodus.[48]

Other Prophets

Yahweh's Sinaitic judgment/salvation intrusions occur infrequently in other prophets. When they do occur, the emphases are those that we have already seen in the Psalms and in Isaiah. Hosea, for example, warns the Israelites that "a whirlwind [רוּחַ] will sweep them away" (Hos 4:19). However, the "fire" that Yahweh threatens to send against Israel ("I will send fire upon their cities," 8:14) is not theophanic fire, but only the fire of human attackers—although brought by God.[49]

Joel anticipates the Day of Yahweh as a day of "darkness" (חֹשֶׁךְ, 2:2; cf. Ex 14:20; Dt 4:11; 5:20[23]) and "gloom" (וַאֲפֵלָה, 2:2; cf. Ex 10:22), a day of "clouds and blackness" (עָנָן וַעֲרָפֶל, 2:2; cf. Ex 20:21; Dt 4:11, 5:22). A great army of locusts (a metaphor for Assyrian or Babylonian armies) will invade—an army brought by Yahweh: "Yahweh thunders [נָתַן קוֹלוֹ] at the head of his army" (2:11).[50]

Amos, too, portrays Yahweh's theophanic thunder ("Yahweh roars [שָׁאָג] from Zion and thunders [יִתֵּן קוֹלוֹ] from Jerusalem," Am 1:2; cf. Joel 4:16[3:16]); and he warns that Yahweh will sweep through the house of Joseph "like a fire" (אֵשׁ) that will "devour" (אָכַל; 5:6; cf. Dt 4:25). He also warns of the "darkness" (חֹשֶׁךְ) of the "day of Yahweh" (5:18–20) and anticipates a devastating theophanic appearance of Yahweh, who "touches the earth and it melts" (מוּג, 9:5; cf. Ps 46:7[6]; Na 1:5).

---

[48]E.g., 35:2; 40:5; 43:7; 48:11; 58:8; 59:19; 60:1, 2; 66:18–19.

[49]For the phraseology here, "I will send fire upon their cities that will consume their fortresses," cf. Niehaus, *Amos*, 1:339ff. (Am 1:4ff.).

[50]For the Assyrian or Babylonian identification of the locust army, cf. D. Stuart, *Hosea-Jonah*, WBC (Waco: Word, 1987), 250.

Micah describes a similar theophanic disaster at slightly greater length, as Yahweh comes to punish "Jacob's transgression": "Yahweh . . . comes down [ירד]. . . . The mountains melt beneath him, and the valleys split apart, like wax before the fire [אשׁ]" (Mic 1:3–4).

A longer but similarly evocative passage occurs early in Nahum, as Yahweh's catastrophic descent upon Nineveh is envisaged. He comes down in the "whirlwind" (סוּפָה, 1:3; cf. Ps 83:15[16]; Isa 66:15) and the "storm" (שְׂעָרָה, 1:3; cf. Job 9:17),[51] and in "clouds" (עָנָן, 1:3; cf. Ex 19:16). He rebukes the sea and it "dries up" (יבשׁ, 1:4; cf. Jos 2:10; 4:23; Ps 74:15; Isa 44:27), and the rivers "run dry" (חרב, 1:4; cf. Ps 106:9; Isa 44:27). The mountains "quake" (רעשׁ, 1:5; cf. Jdg 5:4; Ps 18:8) before him, and the hills melt (מוּג, 1:5; cf. Am 9:5). The earth trembles at his presence as he pours out his wrath like "fire" (אשׁ) and shatters "rocks" (הַצֻּרִים, 1:6; cf. Ex 17:6; Ps 78:15; 1Ki 19:11b) before him. As in the Psalms and Isaiah, Yahweh's judgment against contemporary nations (e.g., Assyria) and against his own people are portrayed in theophanic terms both evocative of Exodus-Sinai and anticipatory of the eschaton. But God's purpose is never exclusively judgmental. The God who comes to judge also comes to save. The God who comes with fiery devastation also comes with the light of life.

Excursus: *The Light of God's Countenance*

As we have seen (chaps. 3, 6), the association of fire and theophany is not accidental. According to the Old Testament, God is not only indestructible life, but also powerful light. The two qualities are inextricably associated. The outstanding Old Testament example is Moses. Exodus 33:11 tells us that, "Yahweh used to speak to Moses face to face, as a man speaks to

---

[51]Cf. the related theophanic term סְעָרָה, "whirlwind," 2Ki 2:1, 11; Isa 29:6; Eze 1:4.

his friend," and in the closing comments of Deuteronomy we read, "There has not arisen a prophet since in Israel like Moses, whom Yahweh knew face to face." (Dt 34:10 RSV). When Moses entered God's luminous presence, he became imbued somehow with divine effulgence. When he left God's presence, his face shone with God's glory (Ex 34:29–30, 34–35). And when he died, we are told, "Moses was a hundred and twenty years old ... yet his eyes were not weak nor his strength gone" (Dt 34:7). We have observed that the cause of Moses' ongoing vigor—even at the age of 120—was quite probably his ongoing relationship with the God who often called him into that luminous, revitalizing presence.

As part of the ancient Near Eastern background, we recall that Samsuiluna (1749–1712 B.C.), son of Hammurapi, was supposedly, like Moses, privileged to speak with deity face to face. Enlil, the supreme god, sent two lesser deities, Zababa and Ishtar, with a message to Samsuiluna. Zababa and Ishtar "lifted their radiant, life-giving faces [*bu-ni-šu-nu ša ba-la-ṭim*] towards Samsuiluna ... and they spoke to him with glee"(ll. 62–9).[52] This parallel with Moses' experience shows how accessible such an idea might well have been to Moses' contemporaries.

As the parallel suggests, Moses not only spoke face to face with God; he also took on a portion of God's life. In the light of this observation, we noted implications of the Aaronic blessing of Numbers 6:22–27:

> May Yahweh bless you and keep you.
> May Yahweh make his face to shine upon you,
> and be gracious to you.
> May Yahweh lift up his countenance upon you,
> and give you wholeness ["peace," i.e., שָׁלוֹם].

---

[52]E. Sollberger, "Samsu-iluna's Bilingual Inscriptions C and D," *RA* 63, no. 1 (1969), 29–43.

Aaron's blessing calls upon Yahweh to make his face shine upon his people, and the consequence of that event will be wholeness, *shalom*. Then comes a notable commentary by God upon the blessing itself: "So shall they put my Name upon the people of Israel, and I will bless them" (Nu 6:27). In other words, when Aaron and his sons ask Yahweh to make his face to shine upon his people, they will also be invoking God's name upon them, and that will result in his blessing. Yahweh's blessing upon the people and the radiance of his face toward them are parallel and thus to a considerable extent equivalent. Not only so. To call God's name upon them is to invoke upon them something of Yahweh's own character—since, as is well known, the name is tantamount to the character. Just as Moses reflected some of God's nature as a result of his self-revelation to Moses, so the people can reflect some of God's nature—his "Name"—when he "makes his face to shine upon" them.

Such divine self-disclosure is not meant only to bless God's people. It is meant also to accomplish their victory/salvation, and to extend God's revealed authority among the nations. This is made clear from Psalm 67:1–3, which opens with a very explicit allusion to the Aaronic blessing:

> May God be gracious to us and bless us
> and make his face to shine upon us,
> that your way may be known on earth,
> your salvation among all nations.
>
> May the peoples praise you, O God;
> may all the peoples praise you.

And the poem concludes with the affirmation (v. 7):

> God has blessed us;
> let all the ends of the earth fear him.

The poet affirms an important soteriological point. When Yahweh's face illuminates his people, the result should be a manifestation of God's salvation among the nations. When Yahweh makes his face shine upon them, that luminous act should not only endow them with some of his own nature, it should also produce a witness of—an extension of—God's authority across the earth. In the words of the psalmist, "God has blessed us; let all the ends of the earth fear him!" The obedience of the servant (namely, Israel) to whom God has revealed himself ought to provide that testimony and produce that result.

Similarly, when Enlil, the supreme god, sent two lesser deities, Zababa and Ishtar, with a message to King Samsuiluna, that high god commissioned Samsuiluna to conquer various foes, to build the wall of Kish (the holy city) higher than it was before, and to enhance the city's temple complex. All these tasks were meant to make the divine authority more manifest than before, in addition to being an honor and a blessing to the king and his people. A god's blessing was never without a purpose in the ancient Near East—namely, to make manifest the authority of the god, so that others may fear (i.e., worship) him. So it was in Israel. And the blessing was portrayed as a revelation of divine countenance, the "radiant, life-giving faces" of Zababa and Ishtar, just as it is in the Aaronic blessing and in Psalm 67.

That association of life and God's radiant face runs throughout the Psalms. It mostly appears in supplications, either of the personal or of the national form: "Let the light of your face shine upon us, Yahweh" (4:7[6]); "Let your face shine on your servant" (31:17[16]); "May God be gracious to us and bless us and make his face shine upon us" (67:2[1]); "Restore us, O God; make your face shine upon us, that we may be saved" (80:4, 7, 19[3, 6, 18]); "Make your face shine upon your servant and teach me your decrees" (119:135).[53]

A contrary condition occurs when God turns his face away, or hides it, from his people. Adam's son Cain first artic-

---

[53] For passages similar in idea, cf. Pss 11:7(6); 13:4(3) ("Look on me" // "Give light to my eyes"); 17:16(15); 34:6(5) ("Those who look to him are radiant"); 36:10(9); 37:7(6); 43:3; 56:14(13); 97:11; 112:4.

ulates the idea: "Today you are driving me away from [lit., "from (upon) the face of," מֵעַל פְּנֵי] the land, and I will be hidden from your presence [lit., "from your face," מִפָּנֶיךָ]" (Ge 4:14). Cain's complaint implies that separation from God's "face" is as fatal as separation from the life-giving land. The parallelism (which in Hebrew has the added elegance and impact of chiasmus) emphasizes the point:

a	b
Today you are driving me	from the face of the land
b'	**a'**
and from your face	I will be hidden

No worse calamity could befall one than to be hidden from God's face or to have God hide his face from oneself. So a Deuteronomic counterpart to the Aaronic blessing says that when the people break covenant and forsake God, "I will hide my face from them, and they will be destroyed.... I will certainly hide my face" (Dt 31:17, 18), and again, "I will hide my face from them ... and see what their end will be; for they are a perverse generation, children who are unfaithful" (Dt 32:20).

Cain's punishment provides the ultimate background to this idea. God's storm-theophany in Genesis 3:8, which like all storm theophanies is both a self-revelation to and a self-concealment from fallen humanity, is a foundational illustration of the same idea. But the proximate background for Israel was the warning—or set of warnings—given in Deuteronomy. Those warnings form the covenantal context from which the same notion then springs up in the Psalms and in the Prophets.

Like its counterpart (the cry for God's face to shine upon them), the psalmists' appeal for God to cease his turning away, or not to turn away his face, comes in both personal and national forms. On one hand, David cries, "How long will you hide your face from me?" (Ps 13:2[1]); "Do not hide your face from me" (27:10[9]); "Why do you hide your face and forget our misery and oppression?" (44:25[24]); "Do not hide your face from me when I am in distress" (102:3[2]). Or the psalmist may recall, "When you hid your face, I was dismayed" (30:8[7]). On the other hand, Yahweh can also be celebrated because "he has not hidden his face from him [the afflicted one]" (22:25[24]).[54]

Among the prophets, Isaiah portrays God's judgment as a hiding of his face, e.g., "I punished him, and hid my face in anger" (Isa 57:17), and especially,

> No one calls on your Name
>   or strives to lay hold of you;
> for you have hidden your face from us
>   and made us waste away because of our sins.
>
>   (Isa 64:7)

God is the light of life, but no one may grab hold of him—lay hold on that life—unless God's luminous face shines upon him. Salvation comes from God alone. So later the apostle wrote, "In him was life, and that life was the light of men" (Jn 1:4); "The true light that gives light to every man was coming into the world" (v. 9); "To all who received him . . . he gave authority to become children of God" (v. 12). And consummately, "For God, who said, 'Let light shine out of darkness,' made his light shine in our hearts to give us the light of the knowledge of the glory of God in the face of Christ" (2Co 4:6). The idea of salvation tantamount to the favorable revelation of God's luminous face not only emerges, then, in ancient Near Eastern theology, but also courses through the Old Testament and into the New.

---

[54]For a similar idea, cf. Ps 89:47(46). By contrast, cf. Ps 39:14(13), "Look away from me, that I may rejoice again before I depart and am no more"– a very Job-like lament that scrutiny from God means death to mortal man (cf. Job 7:19; Ps 90:8–9).

Our study so far shows that the Old Testament presents ahistorical, imaginative theophanic portrayals of God's coming, in both lament and consolation. When David portrays Yahweh in stormy glory routing his foes (Ps 18), his portrait is a purely literary creation. But even that artistic portrayal (and others like it) arises on the ground that Yahweh more than once actually appeared in such a way. Each such portrayal can and should be understood against a background of actual theophanies that occurred as part of God's covenant administration. All of them, therefore—from David's stormy, Baalistic vision of Yahweh in Psalm 18, to Isaiah's lament that God has "hidden [his] face from us" (Isa 64:7)—in one way or another, directly or indirectly, adumbrate God's ultimate parousia.

ESCHATOLOGICAL PORTRAYALS OF GOD'S RETURN

Yahweh's eschatological theophanies are normally Sinaitic in character—although the storm-cloud theophany as an actual event antedates Sinai, as we have seen. God appeared in stormy glory—a glory partly concealed by storm—when Adam and Eve first sinned. In their fallen condition they could not endure a full revelation of God's glory. On that day God came to judge their sin, but also to promise a savior. At the Parousia he comes again to judge all sin and to save. His latter advent is like his former: he comes on clouds, with fire and storm, in glory. God's eschatological return is portrayed in such "Sinaitic" terms more often in the Prophets (particularly in Isaiah and Daniel, but also in Joel, Zephaniah, Haggai, Zechariah, and Malachi) than in the Psalms.

Psalms

Indisputable Sinaitic eschatological theophanies are few in the Psalms. Messianic psalms provide some of the clearest candidates. The conclusion of Psalm 2 (a psalm applied to Christ in Ac 4:25–26) warns kings and rulers that Yahweh's wrath can momentarily "flare up" (בער, 2:12; cf. Ex 3:2; Dt 4:11). Psalm 110 anticipates the day when the messianic royal priest (vv. 2, 4; cf. Heb 5:6; 7:17, 21) will march forth arrayed in "holy majesty" (הַדְרֵי קֹדֶשׁ, 110:3; cf. Pss 29:4; 96:6; 1Ch 16:27; Isa 2:10, 19, 21). Psalm 72 concludes with a broad eschatological hope: "Praise be to his glorious Name [שֵׁם כְּבוֹדוֹ] forever; may the whole earth be filled with his glory" [כְּבוֹדוֹ יִמָּלֵא, 72:19; cf. Ex 40:34, 35; 1Ki 8:11; Isa 6:3]. Some other examples may be said to have eschatological overtones but are not simply or even primarily eschatological (e.g., Pss 11:4–7; 97:1–6; 99:1–3). It is therefore to the Prophets that we most naturally turn for the major eschatological examples.

The Prophets

Isaiah

Isaiah abounds in eschatological visions of judgment and glory that both recall and surpass what Yahweh did at Mount Sinai. Eight passages stand out in this regard: 4:4–6 (Yahweh's Sinaitic session on Mount Zion); 13:9–13 (a worldwide, implicitly eschatological judgment, set in the midst of an oracle against Babylon); 19:1–25 (eschatological redemption of Egypt and Assyria); 24:14–23 (eschatological judgment of the universe); 40:5 (Yahweh's glory revealed to all humanity); 60:1–20 (Yahweh's glory comes to Israel; Yahweh replaces the sun and moon as light for his people); 66:15–16 (fiery eschatological judgment); and 66:17–24 (God's glory among the nations; new heavens and a new earth). Of these passages, Isaiah 4:4–6 best illustrates the Sinaitic nature of God's eschatological descent upon Mount Zion, and Isaiah 24:14–23 best shows the theophanic involvement by which *Endzeit* may be said to reflect *Urzeit*.

Isaiah 4:4–6

These verses are part of a larger eschatological vision (4:2–6) in which the messianic "Branch" (4:2; cf. 11:1) will be involved in the ultimate fruition and holiness of God's people.

> Yahweh will wash away the filth of the women of Zion; he will cleanse the bloodstains from Jerusalem by a Spirit of judgment and a Spirit of fire. Then Yahweh will create over all of Mount Zion and over those who assemble there a cloud of smoke by day and a glow of flaming fire by night; over all the Glory will be a canopy. It will be a shelter and shade from the heat of the day, and a refuge and a hiding place from the storm and rain. (4:4–6)

Isaiah portrays an eschatological advent of Yahweh's "Spirit" (רוּחַ, 4:4; cf. Ge 3:8; Ex 15:8) of "fire" (אֵשׁ, 4:4; cf. Ge 15:17; Ex 19:18), that will both judge the people and wash away their sins. Afterward, Yahweh will create a "cloud of smoke by day" (עָנָן יוֹמָם וְעָשָׁן, 4:5; cf. Ex 13:21, 22; 14:19; 19:16, 18) and a "glow of flaming fire by night" (וְנֹגַהּ אֵשׁ לֶהָבָה לָיְלָה, 4:5; cf. Ex 13:21, 22; 14:24; 19:18; Ps 29:7; Eze 1:4). God will provide a canopy that will be a "shelter" (סֻכָּה, 4:6)—a term used elsewhere for Yahweh's tabernacle (Ps 27:5) and for clouds as a temporary enclosure of Yahweh in storm (Ps 18:12; Job 36:29).[55] The canopy will cover Yahweh's "glory" (כָּבוֹד, 4:5; cf. Ex 24:16) as he dwells among his people. Yahweh's session upon Mount Zion echoes the way he settled upon Mount Sinai. That echo is deliberate and meaningful. Just as Yahweh came down on Sinai and made a covenant with his people, so he will come again at the end. At that second advent he will perform covenantal judgment and take up permanent residence on Zion. So he will fulfill the yearnings and hopes of the old covenant, that God's "tabernacle" (σκηνή) would be

---

[55] Cf. BDB, 697.

among men and that he would "tabernacle" (σκηνώσει) among them (Rev 21:3; cf. Jn 1:14).[56]

Isaiah 24:14–23

A profound vision of final judgment, this chapter also concludes with Yahweh's "glory" established among his people. It opens with a vision of worldwide devastation brought about because of humanity's sin (24:1-13): they have broken "the everlasting covenant" (24:5). This latter term (as noted earlier) recalls penultimately the Noahic covenant and ultimately the Adamic covenant.

After that apocalyptic vision, the prophet is alerted to the advent of Yahweh's "majesty" (גָּאוֹן, 24:14; cf. Ex 15:7), and from the ends of the earth people sing, "Glory to the Righteous One" (צַדִּיק, 24:16; cf. Ex 9:27). But Isaiah cannot yet exult in that advent. He is grieved by the awful judgment that must first befall the world. He first expresses that judgment spectacle in a riddle (*raz*, 24:16b–18b):[57]

16b   And I said: My secret, for me; my secret, for me!
16c   Woe to the treacherous—they deal treacherously;
       the treacherous deal most treacherously!
17a   *paḥad wāpaḥat wāpāḥ*
17b   against you, inhabitant of the earth.
18a   And he who flees from the sound of dread [*paḥad*][58]
       will fall into the pit [*paḥat*],
18b   and he who comes up from amid the pit [*paḥat*]

---

[56] As C. Anderson Scott, *Revelation* (Edinburgh: T. C. & E. C. Jack), 288, notes, the word σκηνή in Rev 21:3 is the same used in the LXX for the tabernacle in the wilderness.

[57] For the *rāz-pᵉšar* (riddle–interpretation) aspect of this pericope, see J. Niehaus, "*RĀZ–PᴱŠAR*, in Isaiah XXIV," *VT* 31, n. 3 (1981): 376–77. On this understanding, רָזִי in 24:16b is not a *hapax legomenon* from the root רזה, "to be lean" (so RSV, "I pine away, I pine away!"), but "my secret," from the Aram. רָז. Because alliteration and assonance play a significant role in the passage the Hebrew of alliterated terms is transliterated.

[58] Or perhaps, "terrible thunder" (קוֹל הַפַּחַד).

will be taken in the cage [*pāḥ*];
18c for the windows [אֲרֻבּוֹת] are opened from on high,
and the foundations of the earth quake [רעש].

The judgment to come deliberately echoes the Noahic flood: "the windows [אֲרֻבּוֹת] are opened from on high" (24:18c); cf. "the windows/floodgates [אֲרֻבּוֹת] of the heavens were opened" (Ge 7:11). The reason is that the eschatological judgment will destroy the world and produce a new heavens and new earth (Isa 65:17; 66:22), just as the Noahic judgment destroyed the world that then was and produced a "new" world. At God's judgment advent the earth also "quakes" (רעש, 24:18c; cf. Jdg 5:4; Pss 18:8[7]; 68:9[8]; Isa 13:13), just as the heavens and earth do in Joel's eschatological portrait (Joel 4:16[3:16]).

The storm and earthquake indicated in Isaiah 24:18c introduce a further portrayal of natural tumult. The earth is broken up, split asunder, and thoroughly shaken (24:19). It reels like a drunkard and falls under the weight of its sin (v. 20). The cause of this natural tumult is the theophanic advent of God in final judgment. Isaiah makes a remarkable statement:

21 In that day Yahweh will punish
the host of heaven in heaven
and the kings of earth on the earth.
22 They will be herded together
like prisoners bound in a dungeon;
they will be shut up in prison
and be punished after many days.
23 The moon will be abashed and the sun will be ashamed
for Yahweh of Hosts will reign
on Mount Zion and in Jerusalem,
and before its elders—Glory!

Yahweh has authority to judge all things in heaven and earth because he created heaven and earth and is God of both (Isa 37:16; 45:18). The magnitude of the "Judge of all the earth" (Ge 18:25) portrayed now is apparent in the fact that even the moon (הַלְּבָנָה, lit., "the white/pale one") and the sun (הַחַמָּה, lit.

"the hot one") will be ashamed before him. The language echoes that of Isaiah 13:10, where the sun and moon and stars will be darkened at the eschatological advent of the Judge (cf. Joel 2:10; 3:4[2:31]). But the relative "shame" of sun and moon here is not so much at the judgment advent as it is before the glory-presence of God. The final word (כָּבוֹד) simply means Yahweh's "Glory," and should be translated as such–i.e., nominally, not adverbially.[59]

The grand conclusion—that the sun and moon will be ashamed before the Glory, and that the Glory will be before the elders—is further developed later in the book. God himself will be the light of his people:

> The sun will no more be your light by day,
>   nor will the brightness of the moon shine on you,
> for Yahweh will be your everlasting light,
>   and your God will be your glory. (60:19)

God will become his people's light. The adumbration of that astonishing fact appeared on the theological horizon when God plagued Egypt with darkness, but "the children of Israel had light" (Ex 10:23). Once they had left Egypt, God guided them with "light from the fire all night" (Ps 78:14). It was "your right hand . . . and the light of your face" that brought Israel out of Egypt and conquered the nations for them (Ps 44:4[3]). Moreover, the light of Yahweh's countenance is the life of those who behold it (cf. above; Ps 4:7[6]). But if such things may be said of God's light in Old Testament experience, where his glory must always be shrouded in "thick darkness," how much more may it be so in the age to come, that when sin is eradicated and all barriers between God and humans removed, the city of God's people will "not need the sun or the moon to shine on it, for the glory of God gives it light, and the Lamb is its lamp" (Rev 21:23).

---

[59]Cf. RSV: "He will manifest his glory," as opposed to "gloriously," NIV.

Daniel

Daniel's book contains two glory theophanies: the chariot-throne appearance of God at 7:9–10, and the angelic revelation at 10:1–12:13. The former is an eschatological vision, and the latter is an actual theophany with eschatological revelation. Both relate back to God's throne appearance on Mount Sinai and forward to John's revelation of Christ at Patmos.

Daniel 7:9–10

We have already seen how Ezekiel's vision of God upon his chariot throne marked an advance in God's self-revelation over what the elders had seen during their communion meal on Mount Sinai. The same may be said of Daniel's vision of the "Ancient of Days" upon his chariot throne:

> Thrones were set in place,
>   and the Ancient of Days took his seat.
> His clothing was as white as snow;
>   the hair of his head was white like wool.
> His throne was flaming with fire,
>   and its wheels were all ablaze.
> A river of fire was flowing,
>   coming out from before him.
> Thousands upon thousands attended him;
>   ten thousand times ten thousand stood before him.
>
> (Da 7:9–10)

Daniel does not experience an open vision as Ezekiel did. His vision comes to him in a dream (7:1–14). An interpretation (vv. 15–27), given by "one of those standing there" (vv. 16–17) follows the dream. It is understood that Daniel's dream shows world empires–imaged forth as beasts–and that the divine session portrayed in 7:9–10 both judges and destroys the last of those world empires (represented by its king, the "little horn," 7:8, 11, 24b–26). Our purpose is not to add to the debate as to what world powers the beasts represent, but to consider the theophany—the throne presence of God—vouchsafed to Daniel.⁶⁰

Daniel's throne-vision adds substantially to what has gone before. Moses and the elders sat beneath God's throne and ate and drank. They saw only God's feet and under his feet a pavement of sapphire (Ex 24:10–11). Ezekiel saw a whole figure "like that of a man" who looked like glowing metal from his waist up and like fire from his waist down, surrounded by brilliant light and seated upon a chariot throne (Eze 1:26–27). Daniel sees more than any of those. His vision of God is perhaps the most "human" glory theophany yet portrayed in the Old Testament. He sees one whom he calls the "Ancient of Days" (עַתִּיק יוֹמִין, 7:9). The same phrase occurs in the Syriac of Wisdom of Solomon ii.10 for "an old man," and in Ecclesiasticus xxv.4 (in the plural) for "elders." Keil is so impressed with the humanity of the portrayal that he says, "Although God is meant, yet Daniel does not see the everlasting God, but an old man, or a man of grey hairs, in whose majestic form God makes himself visible (cf. Eze 1:26)."⁶¹ Since God modulates his theophanies out of consideration for human frailty, this is probably true. The ancient's clothing was "white as snow," symbolizing purity (cf. Ps 51:7; Isa 1:18). His hair was "white like wool"—possibly another indication of purity.⁶² The same is true of the Lord Christ in John's vision (Rev 1:14).⁶³

---

⁶⁰For dispensational approaches, see A. C. Gaebelein, *The Prophet Daniel* (Grand Rapids: Kregel, 1955); J. F. Walvoord, *Daniel* (Chicago: Moody, 1971). For a covenant-theology approach, see E. J. Young, *The Prophecy of Daniel* (Grand Rapids: Eerdmans, 1949). For a more liberal approach, see S. R. Driver, *The Book of Daniel* (Cambridge: Cambridge University Press, 1922).

⁶¹KD, 9:230.

⁶²As Driver, *Daniel*, 85, notes, "The white hair would have the same symbolism [i.e., of purity], though this would be natural independently [i.e., of any purity] in an aged man."

⁶³The resemblance between the two portrayals is striking. Compare Da 7:9: καὶ τὸ τρίχωμα τῆς κεφαλῆς αὐτοῦ ὡσεὶ ἔριον λευκὸν καθαρόν and Rev 1:14: ἡ δὲ κεφαλὴ αὐτοῦ καὶ αἱ τρίχες λευκαὶ ὡς ἔριον λευκόν.

Like Ezekiel's fiery man, Daniel's Ancient of Days is seated on a chariot throne. Daniel's vision portrays the throne and its wheels as flaming with fire, which goes beyond what Ezekiel saw. Since fire in such visions can be an attribute of divine life and is always an attribute of divine power, it would seem that the throne itself and its wheels have those attributes. We recall that the wheels of Ezekiel's vision had rims that were "full of eyes all around" (Eze 1:18), suggestive of divine omniscience. A river of fire flows out from before the enthroned figure (7:10a)–probably a picture of God's judgment flowing forth to consume his enemies, as in Psalm 97:

> Yahweh reigns, let the earth be glad;
> let the distant shores rejoice.
>
> Clouds and thick darkness surround him;
> righteousness and justice are the foundation of his throne.
> Fire goes before him
> and consumes his foes on every side. (vv. 1–3)

Keil remarks, "The fire which engirds with flame the throne of God pours itself forth as a stream from God into the world, consuming all that is sinful and hostile to God in the world, and rendering the people and kingdom of God glorious."[64]

That glory becomes more apparent as Daniel sees "one like a son of man, coming with the clouds of heaven" (Da 7:13). The phrase "son of man" can indicate simply a human being or humanity (Ps 8:5[4]). Both Ezekiel (Eze 2:1; et al.) and Daniel (Da 8:17; et al.) are addressed as "son of man"–to emphasize their humanity when angels speak to them. The phrase also came to be a messianic title, however, in part because of its appearance at Daniel 7:13.[65] Understandably, then, Jesus refers to himself as the "Son of Man" (Jn 3:13; et al.) And just as Daniel saw one like a son of man coming with the clouds of heaven to

---

[64]KD, 9:230.
[65]Cf. S. Mowinckel, *He That Cometh*, trans. G. W. Anderson (Nashville: Abingdon, 1954), 346–50 (= chap. 10).

receive "authority, glory, and sovereign power" (7:14), so Jesus prophesied, "In the future you will see the Son of Man sitting at the right hand of the Mighty One and coming on the clouds of heaven" (Mt 26:64). Daniel saw the Son of Man coming with the clouds (i.e., a theophanic vision) to receive dominion from God. Jesus said the Son of Man would come on the clouds (in theophanic glory) to establish that dominion at the eschaton. In both cases the clouds are theophanic attributes—as so often in Old Testament and ancient Near Eastern theophanies. The result in Daniel's vision will be that "the sovereignty, power and greatness of the kingdoms under the whole heaven will be handed over to the saints, the people of the Most High. His kingdom will be an everlasting kingdom, and all rulers will worship and obey him" (7:27). John later affirms the same. He hears voices in heaven at the eschaton that declare,

> The kingdom of the world has become the kingdom of our Lord and of his Christ,
> and he will *reign as king for ever and ever.*
> (Rev 11:15, emphasis mine)

God's servants will reign with God in theophanic glory: "They will not need the light of a lamp or the light of the sun, for the Lord God will give them light. And they will *reign as kings for ever and ever*" (Rev 22:5, emphasis mine). John's revelation reaffirms the royal rule that God's saints will exercise subordinate to God himself according to Daniel 7:27.

Daniel 10:1–12:13

An unnamed angel appears to Daniel in a manner evocative of Ezekiel's open vision by the River Kebar:

> On the twenty-fourth day of the first month, as I was standing on the bank of the great river, the Tigris, I looked up and there before me was a man dressed in linen, with a belt of the finest gold around his waist. His body was like chrysolite, his face like lightning, his eyes like flaming torches, his arms and legs like the gleam of burnished

bronze, and his voice like the sound of a multitude. (Da 10:4–6)

Daniel's description harks back to pentateuchal theophanies and also anticipates the revelation of Christ to John on Patmos. It also recalls some of the terminology of Ezekiel's open vision by the River Kebar. The "man" Daniel sees is clothed in "linen" and has a "belt of finest gold" around his waist (cf. Rev 1:13b). His body was like "chrysolite" (תַרְשִׁישׁ, cf. Eze 1:16; 10:9). His "face was like lightning" (וּפָנָיו כְּמַרְאֵה בָרָק, cf. Ex 19:16; Dt 32:41; Eze 1:13; Rev 1:16b).[66] His eyes were like "flaming torches" (לַפִּידֵי אֵשׁ, cf. Ge 15:17; Ex 20:18; Eze 1:13). His arms and legs were like the gleam of burnished "bronze" (נְחֹשֶׁת, cf. Eze 1:7; 40:3; Rev 1:15). And his voice was like the "sound of a multitude" (קוֹל הָמוֹן, cf. a voice "like the sound of rushing waters," Rev 1:15; cf. Eze 1:24).

Daniel's vision adds important detail to earlier theophanies. It shows more clearly a combination of human form and glory presence—after all, the glorious figure he sees is a "man"—a combination that finds ultimate expression in the figure of the glorified Christ who appears to John.[67]

---

[66]Cf. also 2 Sa 22:15; Pss 18:15(14); 77:19(18); 97:4; 144:6; Hab 1:13; Zec 9:14.

[67]Here again there is a remarkable parallel between the portrayals of Daniel and John. Compare the following:
Daniel 10:6
καὶ οἱ ὀφθαλμοὶ αὐτοῦ ὡσεὶ λαμπάδες πυρός
Revelation 1:14
καὶ οἱ ὀφθαλμοὶ αὐτοῦ ὡσεὶ φλὸξ πυρός
Daniel 10:6
αὐτοῦ καὶ οἱ πόδες ὡσεὶ χαλκὸς ἐξαστράπτων
Revelation 1:14
καὶ οἱ πόδες αὐτοῦ ὅμοιοι χαλκολιβάνῳ
Daniel 10:6
καὶ φωνὴ λαλιᾶς αὐτοῦ ὡσεὶ φωνὴ θορύβου
Revelation 1:14
καὶ ἡ φωνὴ αὐτοῦ ὡς φωνὴ ὑδάτων πολλῶν

The angel who thus appears to Daniel carries *hieroi logoi* from God. Understood from a form-critical point of view, the whole passage 10:1–12:13 has the form of the theophanic *Gattung*, much of it taken up with the *hieroi logoi* of the supernatural visitant:

1	Introductory description in the third person	10:1–10
2	Deity's utterance of the name of the (mortal) addressee	10:11a
3	Response of the addressee	10:11b
4	Deity's self-asseveration	10:12b
5	His quelling of human fear	10:12a
6	Assertion of his gracious presence	10:12b–14
1	Further description in the third person	10:15–16a
8	Inquiry or protest by the addressee	10:16b–17
7+9	*Hieros logos* and continuation of the same	10:20–12:4
	with repetition of element 5	10:18–19
1	Further description in the third person	12:5–6a
	and conversation between two angels	12:6b–7
8	Inquiry or protest by the addressee	12:8
9	Continuation of the *hieros logos;* conclusion	12:9–13

The passage has some minor variations on the form. For instance, it includes a conversation between the "man" and one of two other supernatural visitants (12:6b–7). And it lacks element 10, the "concluding description in the third person." But the overall structure is clearly that of the *Gattung*. Perhaps the most important part of the long *hieros logos* comes near the end, where Daniel has a glimpse of the resurrection glory to come: "Those who are wise will shine like the brightness of the heavens, and those who lead many to righteousness, like the stars for ever and ever" (12:3). The "brightness" (זֹהַר, 12:3) of that resurrection glory recalls the "brightness" of the "man" who appeared to Ezekiel, "as bright as glowing metal" from the waist up (Eze 8:2). The word appears only in these passages in the Old Testament and apparently indicates the glorious destiny of the righteous ones, who will "shine . . . like the stars" in the presence of God (cf. Mt 13:43). In place of a concluding description in the third person, the supernatural messenger gives a word of encouragement to Daniel (12:13).

Other Prophets

Eschatological theophanies of the Sinai type are relatively few and brief in the other prophetical books. They appear in Joel, Zephaniah, Haggai, Zechariah, and Malachi.

Joel's eschatology is notable for an explicit promise of the Spirit, which appears adjoined to a prophecy that has yet to be fulfilled completely (2:28–32):

> 28 And afterward,
>   I will pour out my Spirit on all people.
>   Your sons and daughters will prophesy,
>   your old men will dream dreams,
>   your young men will see visions.
> 29 Even on my servants, both men and women,
>   I will pour out my Spirit in those days.
> 30 I will show wonders in the heavens
>   and on the earth,
>   blood and fire and billows of smoke.
> 31 The sun will be turned to darkness
>   and the moon to blood
>   before the coming of the great and dreadful day of Yahweh.

Joel's prophecy was of signal importance for the embryonic church. Peter applied it to the supernatural donation of human tongues on the Day of Pentecost (Ac 2:16–21). Implicit in that comparison is an equation of Joel 2:31 (the sun turned to darkness, the moon to blood) with what happened on Golgotha: "It was now about the sixth hour, and darkness came over the whole land until the ninth hour, for the sun stopped shining" (Lk 23:44–45). Matthew adds that when Jesus died, "The earth shook and the rocks split" (Mt 27:51), familiar features of Old Testament judgment theophanies. Such an application is true, but it does not exhaust the fulfillment of Joel 2:31, nor is it meant to. The day has not come when God may be said to have shown "wonders in the heavens and on the earth," involving "blood and fire and billows of smoke" on the cosmic level. If the sun was temporarily darkened at the Crucifixion, we may expect a more catastrophic and eschatological darkening of sun and moon "before the coming of the great and dreadful day of Yahweh." It seems best, therefore, to see Joel 2:28–29 and 2:30–32 as two related prophecies juxtaposed or, better, "telescoped" together: the former portraying what happened at Pentecost as well as the ongoing dispensation of the Spirit in the church age, the latter portraying what happened at the Crucifixion—to be sure—but also what will happen on a cosmic scale at the eschaton.

Joel also prophesied an eschatological judgment of all nations when "the sun and moon will be darkened and the stars no longer shine" (Joel 4:15[3:15]). The cause (cf. Isaiah 13:10) will be a Sinaitic judgment theophany of Yahweh: "Yahweh will roar [שׁאג] from Zion and thunder [יתן קולו] from Jerusalem; the earth and the heavens will tremble [רעשׁ]" (Joel 4:16[3:16]). The ultimate goal, however, will be Yahweh's session in Zion (4:21[3:21]).

Jeremiah also anticipates a judgment of all nations, including his own land. The oracle is not eschatological, although it is couched in terms that adumbrate the eschaton (cf. especially Jer 25:31). "Yahweh will roar [שׁאג] from on high" and "lift his voice" (יתן קולו) from his holy dwelling (v. 30); he will shout against all who inhabit the earth and bring judgment against all humankind (v. 31).[68] Another judgment passage with eschatological overtones is Jeremiah 30:23–24. There we are

---

[68]The resemblance of Jer 25:30 to Joel 4:16 (3:16) is obvious. It is probably another case of dependence, since Jeremiah characteristically alludes to and borrows from other prophets (including Moses!) Cf. J. Niehaus, "*RĀZ-PᴱŠAR*, in Isaiah XXIV," 378, n. 6.

told that the "storm of Yahweh" (סַעֲרַת יהוה; cf. 2Ki 2:1, 11; Job 38:1; 40:6; Eze 1:4) will burst out in wrath, a "driving and swirling wind" (סַעַר מִתְגּוֹרֵר, cf. Ps 83:16[15]) on the heads of the wicked (30:23).

Zephaniah also portrays the "Great Day of Yahweh" (Zep 1:14), "a day of darkness and gloom, a day of clouds and blackness" (v. 15 = Joel 2:2). His advent will be such that "in the fire [אֵשׁ] of his jealousy the whole world will be consumed [אכל]" (v. 18). The "storm" [יוֹם] of his coming will "sweep on like chaff" (2:2).[69] Before a promise of restoration, Zephaniah again portrays God's wrath: "In the fire [אֵשׁ] of my jealousy the whole world will be consumed [אכל]" (3:8, a first-person variant of 1:18).

Haggai characterizes Yahweh's advent, not in terms of fire, but in terms of earthquake: "In a little while I will once more shake [רעשׁ] the heavens and the earth, the sea [יָם] and the dry land [חָרָבָה]" (Hag 2:6). The wording not only echoes other Sinaitic theophanies; it also recalls the Creation account, in which God created the heavens and the earth and separated the sea (יַמִּים) from the dry land (יַבָּשָׁה, Ge 1:9–10). Haggai's allusion to the original Creation is appropriate, on the understanding that *Endzeit = Urzeit*. The author of Hebrews also, appropriately, relates this prophecy to Sinai and to God's final judgment: "At that time [i.e., at Sinai] his voice shook the earth, but now he has promised, 'Once more I will shake not only the earth but also the heavens.' The words 'once more' indicate the removing of what can be shaken–that is, created things–so that what cannot be shaken may remain" (Heb 12:26–27). Eschatology is related to the Mount Sinai event because of a contrast between the dreadful theophany that accompanied the Mosaic dispensation (Heb 12:18–21) and the free access to God and his joyous ones that accompanies the new covenant (vv. 22–24). We are told that God's "voice" once

---

[69]For the translation "storm" for יוֹם, cf. above, chap. 5.

shook the earth, in the days of Sinai, because that voice implied judgment on sinful man. When God shakes the earth again, it will be in final judgment of fallen humanity. By contrast, God's kingdom and those who are in it cannot be "shaken" (12:28), but God should still be worshiped with reverence and awe, because "our God is a consuming fire" (12:29; cf. Ex 24:17; Dt 4:25).

In Zechariah's eschatological visions, Yahweh's return partakes of both a fire that refines (Zec 13:9) and an earthquake-like split in the Mount of Olives (14:3–5). He will advance stormlike, "his arrow [חִצּוֹ; cf. Ps 18:15(14); Hab 3:11] will flash like lightning [בָּרָק; cf. Ex 19:16; Ps 18:15(14)]," and he will "march in the storms [סַעֲרוֹת; cf. 2 Ki 2:1, 11; Eze 1:4] of the south" (9:14). Yahweh's ultimate promise is that "I myself will be a wall of fire around it . . . and I will be its glory within" (2:5; cf. Isa 4:5–6; 24:23).

Malachi, the last prophet of the Old Testament, foretells clearly that "the Lord [אָדוֹן, cf. Ex 23:17; Dt 10:17] you are seeking will come to his temple; the messenger of the covenant, whom you desire, will come" (Mal 3:1). But he raises the question, "Who can endure the day of his coming," because he will be like a refiner's "fire" (אֵשׁ) (3:2). That day itself, according to Malachi 3:19(4:1), will "burn" (בער, cf. Ex 3:2; Dt 4:11, 5:23[20]) like a "furnace" (תַּנּוּר, cf. Ge 15:17; Isa 31:9).

CONCLUSION

All Old Testament "theophanies" that are Sinaitic, yet do not portray actual contemporary appearances of God, fall into one of three major categories: evocative recollections of the *magdalia Dei* of the Exodus and wilderness wanderings; imaginative portrayals of God's Sinaitic judgment and salvation intrusions; and eschatological portrayals of God's return to judge the nations and save his people. The poets and prophets recall what Yahweh has done as an encouragement about what he may yet do. They portray God's contemporary action in terms evocative of the old theophanies. And they anticipate his eschatological advent in the same stormy way. Their portrayals echo the way God actually showed up in days past. They also adumbrate in one way or another the manner of his return. That return is most fully taught and portrayed in the pages of a new and better covenant, to which we now turn.

9

Sinai Theophany: The New Testament and Beyond

New Covenant Fulfillment of the Implications of the Sinai Theophanies

The vision of the universe which she had begun to see in the last few minutes had a curiously stormy quality about it. It was bright, darting, and overpowering. Old Testament imagery of eyes and wheels for the first time in her life took on some possibility of meaning.... She had come into a world, or into a Person, or into the presence of a Person. Something expectant, patient, inexorable, met her with no veil or protection between.... This demand which now pressed upon her was not, even by analogy, like any other demand. It was the origin of all right demands and contained them. In its light you could understand them.... There was nothing, and never had been anything, like this. And now there was nothing except this. Yet also, everything had been like this; only by being like this had anything existed.

C. S. Lewis, *That Hideous Strength*

What is that sound high in the air
Murmur of maternal lamentation
Who are those hooded hordes swarming
Over endless plains, stumbling in cracked earth

> Ringed by the flat horizon only
> What is the city over the mountains
> Cracks and reforms and bursts in the violet air
> Falling towers
> Jerusalem Athens Alexandria
> Vienna London
> Unreal. . . .
>
> T. S. Eliot, "The Waste Land," 367–77

The Sinai story does not stop with the Old Testament any more than the Mosaic Law concludes God's revelation to his people. The New Testament picks up the theme of Sinai and the theophanies that occurred there and makes them a significant part of its theology. The gospel of that one who fulfills the Law may in fact be called a "Tale of Three Mountains"—the Mount of the Beatitudes, the mount of the Transfiguration, and the mount of the Crucifixion—all of which look back to Mount Sinai, and all of which surpass it. In this chapter I will explore the significance of these "mountains" and their relation to Mount Sinai, as well as other New Testament uses of the Sinai motif. I will also show how New Testament theophanies in the Gospels and elsewhere parallel form-critically the Old Testament glory theophanies. I will take an especially close look at Jesus' eschatological discourse. Such theophanies contribute in a major way to the structure of Revelation, where God shows that ultimate theophany for which all creation longs.

ALLUSIONS TO SINAI: THE GOSPEL ACCOUNTS

The Mount of the Beatitudes

Jesus stands as a new and better Moses when he teaches the disciples from the "mountainside" (Mt 5:1–2) at the outset of his ministry. As Moses spent years in Midian, where he fled from Pharaoh and learned to be a shepherd, Jesus spent forty days in the wilderness, where he confronted the Devil and showed that he was trustworthy enough to be called "the good

Shepherd." As Moses gave the Torah (God's teaching, instruction) from Mount Sinai (where God had given it to him), so Jesus gave God's teaching from the mountainside.[1] And since Jesus was himself God in the flesh, the prophecy began to be fulfilled which said, "All your children will be taught by Yahweh" (Isa 54:13).

Not only did God's teaching occur at a mountain in both cases. Jesus makes it clear that he stands in Moses' place by the way he handles the Law. He begins by informing the people that he has come not to abolish the Law and the Prophets, but to fulfill them (Mt 5:17). He then deliberately takes up laws from the Decalogue–the first recorded laws of the Book of the Covenant–and magisterially recasts them, e.g., "You have heard[2] that it was said to the people long ago, 'Do not murder, and anyone who murders will be subject to judgment.' But I tell you that anyone who is angry with his brother will be subject to judgment . . ." (5:21–22). Jesus takes up the sixth commandment and extends its implications for those who will hear. He handles other Mosaic laws in the same fashion, contrasting what was "said/said to people long ago" (5:27, 31, 33, 38, 43) with the adversative, "But I tell you" (5:28, 32, 34, 39, 44). In this way Jesus contrasts what God said through Moses with what God now says through himself. The contrast does not es-

---

[1] R. H. Gundry, *Matthew* (Grand Rapids: Eerdmans, 1982), 66, notes, "Because it falls between the ascent of Jesus up the mountain and his descent, the sermon gains the connotation of law, related to the Mosaic law, which was also issued from a mountain. Indeed, ἀνέβη occurs frequently in the LXX for Moses' going up Mount Sinai to receive the law for promulgation. So also does the phrase εἰς τὸ ὄρος." Cf. E. Hatch and H. A. Redpath, *Concordance to the Septuagint* (Graz: Akademische Druk-W. Verlangsanstant, 1954), s.v. ἀναβαίνω and ὄρος.

[2] With regard to Jesus' introductory "You have heard," W. C. Allen, *Gospel According to St. Matthew*, ICC (Edinburgh: T. & T. Clark, 1912), 47, plausibly notes that "we might have expected, 'It is written in the law,' or, 'Ye have read in the law' . . . but here the audience presupposed is one of unlearned people (cf. 7:28)." Hence Jesus' references are to the Mosaic Law as mediated to the people of his day by Israel's teachers.

tablish any contradictions. Rather Jesus shows the deeper meaning of the Mosaic Law and also shows how impossible it is for sinful humans to fulfill that Law. His discourse treats of murder (the sixth commandment, Ex 20:13; Mt 5:21–26), adultery (the seventh commandment, Ex 20:14; Mt 5:27–30), and other Mosaic laws: divorce (Dt 24:1; Mt 5:31–32), keeping oaths (Nu 30:2; cf. Lev 5:4; Mt 5:33–37), the *lex talionis* (Ex 21:24; Lev 24:20; Dt 19:21; Mt 5:38–42), and love for neighbor (Lev 19:18; Mt 5:43–48). Jesus chooses not from the Decalogue only, but from the whole corpus of the Mosaic legislation—both apodictic and casuistic—to show that his authority over the Law is complete.[3] Like the book of Deuteronomy, this is a sort of "second law."[4] But whereas Moses' review of the Law exhorts the people to obedience before the conquest of Canaan, Jesus' review of the Law shows us that we cannot be perfectly obedient and must rely on him to fulfill the Law for us. That is why he began the discourse with the statement, "Do not think that I have come to abolish the Law or the Prophets; I have not come to abolish them but to fulfill them" (Mt 5:17).

The Mount of Transfiguration

Jesus came to fulfill not the Law only, but also the Prophets. He can say this because both spoke of him. It is appropriate, then, that his superiority to both should be illustrated in a most convincing way. This happens at the Transfiguration mount (Mt 17:1–8):

> After six days Jesus took with him Peter, James and John the brother of James, and led them up a high mountain by themselves. There he was transfigured before them. His face shone like the sun, and his clothes became as white as the light. Just then there appeared before them Moses and Elijah, talking with Jesus.

---

[3] R. H. Gundry, *Matthew*, says, "Here the portrayal of Jesus as the greater Moses attains its greatest clarity" (p. 78).
[4] Cf. Dt 17:18 (LXX).

> Peter said to Jesus, "Lord, it is good for us to be here. If you wish, I will put up three shelters—one for you, one for Moses and one for Elijah."
>
> While he was still speaking, a bright cloud enveloped them, and a voice from the cloud said, "This is my Son, whom I love; with him I am well pleased. Listen to him!"
>
> When the disciples heard this, they fell facedown to the ground, terrified. But Jesus came and touched them. "Get up," he said. "Don't be afraid." When they looked up, they saw no one except Jesus.

If the Sermon on the Mount gave a restatement of the Sinaitic Law, the transfiguration mount shows us the Sinaitic glory. And this is exactly its purpose. The tale of this second gospel "mountain" is that God's glory appears to Jesus just as it did to Moses.[5] Yet the passage has far more to tell. At the beginning, Jesus takes Peter, James, and John with him, just as Moses took Aaron, Nadab, and Abihu up Mount Sinai for a time of communion with God (Ex 24:9–11).[6] Like Moses, Jesus reflects the glory of God's presence, his face shining like the sun and his clothes as white as the light. As a cloud came down on Mount Sinai with flashes of light, so a "bright cloud" comes down on Jesus and the disciples. As Yahweh's "voice/thunder" sounded atop Mount Sinai, so God's "voice/thunder" speaks to Jesus. And the voice here is very likely that same "thunderous voice" that terrified Adam and Eve in Eden and all Israel at the foot of Mount Sinai, for we read that "When the disciples heard this, they fell facedown to the ground, terrified" (Mt 17:6).

Now something happens that shows why—against the backdrop of Israel's terrifying experience of Yahweh at Horeb (Sinai)—God promised another prophet like Moses (Dt 18). At

---

[5]Cf. Gundry, *Matthew,* 342: "Matthew's repeated paralleling of Moses and Jesus . . . justifies the supposition that he looks on 'the high mountain' as a new Sinai and on Jesus' going up it after six days as a repetition of Moses' going up Sinai after six days, i.e., on the seventh (Exod 24:16). Both times the cloud of divine glory covered the mountain."

[6]Moses also took the seventy elders of Israel, whereas Jesus did not take his seventy disciples.

Mount Sinai the people stood in dread of that theophany (that theophanic "thunderous voice") of a holy God—just as Elijah had when he encountered that same theophany later at Horeb/Sinai (Ex 20:18–20; 1Ki 19:13; cf. Mt 17:3). But now God is here in the flesh, to comfort and encourage from the dread of that theophanic Majesty: "'Get up,' he said. 'Don't be afraid'" (Mt 17:7). As Moses allayed the fear of the people, Jesus allays the fear of the disciples. But it is also true in the Old Testament that human fear is allayed in theophany by God himself. So it is now—only by God in the flesh. The Sinai/Transfiguration parallels may be diagramed as follows:

Parallel event	Exodus	Matthew
Prophet and disciples ascend mount	24:9	17:1
Prophet reflects God's glory	34:29ff.	17:2
Cloud envelops Prophet	24:15	17:5
God's thunderous voice	19:16–19	17:5
Human fear of theophanic voice	20:18–19	17:6
Prophet quells human fear	20:20	17:7

The passage on the Mount of Transfiguration clearly draws together typical Mosaic events, all of which occurred at Mount Sinai. Like the Sermon on the Mount, the Transfiguration is meant to recall God's revelation to Moses on Mount Sinai. The Sermon on the Mount recalls the Mosaic lawgiving. The Transfiguration recalls the Mosaic transfiguration. The Sermon on the Mount shows the hopelessness of fulfilling the Law. The Transfiguration shows the glory God will give to his chosen ones. It shows how the glory of God that briefly transfigured Moses and Jesus will one day transfigure all people who are found in Christ, who fulfills the Law for them. It also shows how Jesus brought God's glory to earth and mediated it as Good Shepherd to his followers: "Get up. . . . Don't be afraid!" (Mt 17:17).

This theophanic narrative also makes another point: Jesus is superior to Moses and Elijah—who together represent the Law and the Prophets. Both of these prophets appear with

Jesus during the Transfiguration. Moses received the Law from God and gave it to the nation. Jesus redefined the Law with authority, not only in the Sermon on the Mount, but throughout his career. Elijah was the Old Testament prophet par excellence in the signs and wonders that he did (at least of a healing kind), which extended even to raising the dead.[7] Jesus far surpassed Elijah in these, just as he surpassed Moses in his authoritative handling of the Law.[8] The superiority of Jesus to these two Old Testament prophets—each the supreme Old Testament example of his kind—is made clear in the passage by God himself. For in the presence of Moses and Elijah, God directs attention to neither of them but to the "Son, whom I love," and says, "Listen to him!" Both the Sermon on the Mount and the Transfiguration on the "Mount" thus affirm Jesus' superiority over the Law and the Prophets that he has come to fulfill.

The Mount of the Crucifixion

On the first New Testament mount, Jesus showed how impossible it was for anyone but the Son to fulfill the Law. On the second, he showed a glimpse of what glory awaits those

---

[7] Gundry, *Matthew,* 343, comments that "the failure of Elijah to appear among the writing prophets" militates "against Moses' standing for the OT law and Elijah's standing for the OT prophets." The criterion he applies is narrow and misses the point. The biblical-theological significance of Elijah is not that he failed to write a book but that he anticipates Christ as a prophet of word and power. J.H. Stek, "Elijah," *ISBE* (Grand Rapids: Eerdman, 1982), 2:67, also rightly sees an implied succession in the appearance of Moses and Elijah to Jesus: "As fellow servants in God's mission, they were speaking with the last Joshua/Elisha, who would finish their work and lead Israel into God's promised 'rest.'"

[8] Cf. the discussion by J. Niehaus, "Old Testament Foundations," in *The Kindgom and the Power,* eds. G. Greig and K. Springer (Ventura: Regal, 1993), 41–53. Later, in Rev 11:3–13, God has "two witnesses" who recall Moses and Elijah. Like Elijah they have power to "shut up the sky so that it will not rain during the time they are prophesying" (11:6a; cf. 1Ki 17:1). Like Moses they

who put their faith in the Son to fulfill that Law for them. On the third, he laid down his life to pay for those very ones.

Just as those first two "mountains" alluded to events of Sinai, so does this third (Mt 27:45–56). More will be said later about the theophanic aspects of the Crucifixion, especially with regard to form criticism. We note here that it contains key elements of an Old Testament theophany. In particular the darkness (Mt 27:45) and earthquake (v. 51) echo the "dark cloud" (Ex 19:16) above Sinai and the "violent trembling" of that mountain (v. 18) as God descended upon it. We noted that God's advent at Sinai was a judgment upon sinful Israel even though he graciously brought the Law. So now God unleashes a theophanic *"Aufruhr der Natur"* as his Son lays down his life to pay the penalty of disobedience to that Law—although he himself knew no sin.

Jesus' death on the cross fulfills a promise made in another Old Testament theophany. When Yahweh in flaming glory passed between the cut up pieces that Abram placed opposite each other, he invoked upon himself the penalty of any future covenant breaking by a member of that covenant (Ge 15:17–18). Since all of God's children are children of Abraham, the Son's crucifixion accomplishes what was symbolized in that dreadful passage.[9]

ALLUSIONS TO SINAI: THE LETTERS

"Now Hagar Stands for Mount Sinai in Arabia ..."

The apostle Paul's use of the Sinai idea is a logical development of what Jesus had already taught. Jesus showed how impossible it was for sinful humans to fulfill the Sinaitic Law and so be saved. Paul further argues that the Law can only

---

have power to "turn the waters into blood and to strike the earth with every kind of plague as often as they want" (11:6b; cf. Ex 7:14–12:30). Both of them, like Jesus, are resurrected in Jerusalem after being gloated over by the nations (11:9–11) and go "up to heaven in a cloud" (11:12; cf. 2Ki 2:11; Ac 1:9).

[9]Cf. the discussion above, chap. 5.

mean bondage because, although it shows us our sin (Ro 3:20), it has no power to deliver us from it (7:7–25). He develops this idea in a figure of speech, a well-known metaphor in the book of Galatians:

> These things may be taken figuratively, for the women [Hagar and Sarah] represent two covenants. One covenant is from Mount Sinai and bears children who are to be slaves: This is Hagar. Now Hagar stands for Mount Sinai in Arabia and corresponds to the present city of Jerusalem, because she is in slavery with her children. But the Jerusalem that is above is free, and she is our mother. (4:24–26)

Paul's argument rests on a concatenation of carefully drawn correspondences that may be diagramed as follows:

Hagar = (slave woman)	Mount Sinai =	city of Jerusalem =	Law
[Sarah] = (free woman)		Jerusalem above =	Promise

The Law brings slavery as noted above, whereas the Promise brings freedom because Christ has fulfilled the Law for us and has given the Spirit so that we in turn can begin to fulfill the Law. So Paul asks, "Did you receive the Spirit by observing the law, or by believing what you heard?" (Ga 3:2). The powers of the age to come are ours, but not because we observe the Law: "Does God give you his Spirit and work miracles among you because you observe the law, or because you believe what you heard?" (v. 5). The glory of the new covenant is that God imparts that Spirit whose glory shook Mount Sinai to the humblest *believer* in Jesus Christ—both for kingdom work and for eternal life.

"A Mountain That Can Be Touched"

Paul chooses Mount Sinai as a key element in his metaphorical argument just because the Law (to which the

Galatians were so foolishly reverting) was given at Sinai. The Law brought bondage because it defined sin without giving the power to conquer sin. By contrast, partakers of the new covenant are no longer slaves to sin and are citizens of the "Jerusalem that is above." The same contrast between Mount Sinai and the "heavenly Jerusalem"—and between the partakers of the corresponding covenants—is drawn by the author of Hebrews:

> You have not come to a mountain that can be touched and that is burning with fire; to darkness, gloom and storm; to a trumpet blast or to such a voice speaking words that those who heard it begged that no further word be spoken to them, because they could not bear what was commanded: "If even an animal touches the mountain, it must be stoned." The sight was so terrifying that Moses said, "I am trembling with fear."
>
> But you have come to Mount Zion, to the heavenly Jerusalem, the city of the living God. You have come to thousands upon thousands of angels in joyful assembly, to the church of the firstborn, whose names are written in heaven. You have come to God, the judge of all men, to the spirits of righteous men made perfect, to Jesus the mediator of a new covenant, and to the sprinkled blood that speaks a better word than the blood of Abel. (12:18–24)

The author of Hebrews draws a vivid contrast between the theophany at Mount Sinai and the theophanic presence of God at Mount Zion—in the "heavenly Jerusalem."[10] There God cloaked himself in "fire . . . darkness, gloom and storm," and spoke with "a trumpet blast" and a terrifying, thunderous "voice speaking words." God at Sinai revealed himself, but also partly concealed himself in stormy glory, just as he had

---

[10]Cf. F. F. Bruce, *The Epistle to the Hebrews* (Grand Rapids: Eerdmans, 1964), 372–75, for a good discussion of the background of the "heavenly Jerusalem idea" in the OT, the *Apocalypse of Baruch,* and in Paul. Cf. the heavenly temple archetype and discussion at chap. 3.

done after our first parents' sin. But now at the heavenly city we may join the "thousands upon thousands of angels in joyful assembly," the "church of the firstborn, whose names are written in heaven."[11] We have come to "God, the judge of all men," yet his holy glory does not judge us or terrify us, because we come also "to the spirits of righteous men made perfect" by the work of "Jesus the mediator of a new covenant," whose "sprinkled blood . . . speaks a better word than the blood of Abel."[12]

Although our citizenship is in heaven, we still walk on earth, and we still worship and serve a holy God. So the author draws upon the Sinai experience to warn God's church:

> See to it that you do not refuse him who speaks. If they did not escape when they refused him who warned them on earth, how much less will we, if we turn away from him who warns us from heaven? At that time his voice shook the earth, but now he has promised, "Once more I will shake not only the earth but also the heavens." The words "once more" indicate the removing of what can be shaken—that is, created things—so that what cannot be shaken may remain. (Heb 12:25–27).

The author uses a well-known *qal wahomer* argument: as we are heirs to a new and better covenant, so our obligation to obey God is more serious than that of Old Testament believers. If they did not escape when they refused God, how much less

---

[11] S. J. Kistemaker, *Hebrews* (Grand Rapids: Baker, 1984), notes, "Angels were commissioned to deliver the law at Mount Sinai (Acts 7:53; Gal. 3:19; cf. Deut. 33:2; Ps. 68:17); by contrast, they constitute a joyful assembly at Mount Zion, the heavenly Jerusalem (see Rev. 5:11–13). In heaven angels rejoice when they see that one sinner repents (Luke 15:10). They are sent out to serve all those who inherit salvation (Heb. 1:14)."

[12] Not inappropriately J. Calvin, *Hebrews and I and II Peter*, trans. Wm. B. Johnston (Grand Rapids: Eerdmans, 1963), 199, says, "Let us remember . . . that Gospel is here compared with Law, and secondly, that this comparison has two parts: the first that the glory of God shows itself more clearly in the Gospel than in the Law, and the second that the calling of God today is in friendship when previously it held nothing but sheer terror."

will we (cf. Heb 2:1–3)?[13] The author recalls that God "shook the earth" when he appeared at Mount Sinai, and he adds an eschatological prophecy of Haggai that "I will once more shake the heavens and the earth" (Hag 2:6; Heb 12:26). The "once more" is understood to mean, "Once more, as I did at Sinai." The interpretation is appropriate because, whereas the Sinai shaking accompanied the revelation of the Law, the eschatological shaking will come when God returns to judge all people according to that Law, most perfectly revealed in Jesus Christ (cf. Ro 2:12–16; 3:19). As he comes, he will remove all "created things" (i.e., the material heavens and earth) so that only "what cannot be shaken" (i.e., those spiritual things that are of God) will remain. Appropriately, the author concludes this eschatology with words born of the Sinai experience: "Therefore, since we are receiving a kingdom that cannot be shaken, let us be thankful, and so worship God acceptably with reverence and awe, for *our God is a consuming fire*" (Heb 12:28–29; cf. Dt 4:24). The consuming fire that terrified Israel at the foot of Mount Sinai will appear again when Jesus returns in his glory to judge humanity.

ALLUSIONS TO SINAI: REVELATION

The Throne

The judgment of humanity will take place before the throne of God. That throne was first implied in the account of the Mosaic elders' communion meal with God on Mount Sinai: "Moses and Aaron, Nadab and Abihu, and the seventy elders of Israel went up and saw the God of Israel. Under his feet was something like a pavement made of sapphire, clear as the sky itself" (Ex 24:9–10). The throne appears in Ezekiel, at

---

[13]Cf. R. Longenecker, *Biblical Exegesis in the Apostolic Period* (Grand Rapids: Eerdmans, 1975), 158–85, for a useful overall discussion of exegetical techniques and OT passages employed by the author of Hebrews.

SINAI THEOPHANY

the prophet's inaugural vision of God's chariot throne (Eze 1). Ezekiel's account is evocative of the Sinai event:

> Above the expanse over their heads was what looked like a throne of sapphire, and high above on the throne was a figure like that of a man. I saw that from what appeared to be his waist up he looked like glowing metal, as if full of fire, and that from there down he looked like fire; and brilliant light surrounded him. Like the appearance of a rainbow in the clouds on a rainy day, so was the radiance around him. (Eze 1:26–28)

God's appearance before the Mosaic elders revealed only his feet and a pavement of sapphire beneath. The fuller vision of Ezekiel shows, not only his feet, but the whole. The gemstone analogy is repeated, only this time it is applied to the throne.

Daniel's vision of God's seat also shows a chariot throne, and he emphasizes the fiery nature of the theophany:

> Thrones were set in place
>   and the Ancient of Days took his seat.
> His clothing was white as snow;
>   the hair of his head was white like wool.
> His throne was flaming with fire,
>   and its wheels were all ablaze.
> A river of fire was flowing,
>   coming out from before him.
> Thousands upon thousands attended him;
>   ten thousand times ten thousand stood before him.
> The court was seated,
>   and the books were opened. (Da 7:9–10)

Daniel's vision is another revelatory advance: God is portrayed on his throne in greater detail. Now he has clothing as white as snow and hair like wool. Not only is his chariot throne fiery—now a river of fire flows out from before it. The account recalls the theophanic judgment description of Psalm 97:2–3:

> Clouds and thick darkness surround him;
>   righteousness and justice are the foundation of his throne.
> Fire goes before him
>   and consumes his foes on every side.

The passages are related, because God is coming to judge the world in Daniel's vision; that is why "the court was seated, and the books were opened." The scene is the divine court—with "court" taken in both senses—as God is seated with his heavenly myriads to begin the judgment of humankind.

The latest development of this Sinaitic throne-vision motif in the Bible is John's vision of God's throne in Revelation 4. Here we find all of the elements of the earlier visions expanded and refined:

> At once I was in the Spirit, and there before me was a throne in heaven with someone sitting on it. And the one who sat there had the appearance of jasper and carnelian. A rainbow, resembling an emerald, encircled the throne. Surrounding the throne were twenty-four other thrones, and seated on them were twenty-four elders. They were dressed in white and had crowns of gold on their heads. From the throne came flashes of lightning, rumblings and peals of thunder. Before the throne, seven lamps were blazing. These are the seven spirits [sevenfold Spirit] of God. Also before the throne there was what looked like a sea of glass, clear as crystal. (Rev 4:2–6)

The passage goes on to portray the four living creatures who surround the throne and give glory to God—recalling the four living creatures in Ezekiel's vision. The echoes of the Old Testament throne theophanies are also clear. The Mosaic pavement beneath God's feet, described as an "expanse" by Ezekiel, is now a "sea of glass, clear as crystal" before the throne.[14] A gemstone analogy continues, so that as Moses compared the pavement to sapphire, and Ezekiel compared the throne to sapphire, John compares God to "jasper and carnelian." As Ezekiel saw a rainbow surrounding the throne, so John sees "a rainbow, resembling an emerald" encircling it.[15] The parallels may be illustrated as follows:

---

[14]Cf. Rev 15:2.

[15]Of the gemstones and the rainbow G. E. Ladd, *A Commentary on the Revelation of John* (Grand Rapids: Eerdmans, 1972), 73, rightly comments:

SINAI THEOPHANY

Descriptive element	Exodus	Ezekiel	Daniel	Revelation
Pavement/expanse	24:10	1:22–26		4:6
Gemstone analogy	24:10	1:26		4:3
Rainbow around throne		1:28		4:3
God-man on the throne	24:10	1:26–27	7:9	4:3
Fire of theophany		1:27	7:9–10	4:5
Divine court	[24:9.11]		7:9–10	4:4

In addition to the analogies already mentioned, two other features of these throne theophanies are highly significant. One is that God uniformly appears as a "man." In the Sinai event, Moses and the elders see his "feet." Ezekiel and Daniel both describe him as a man, and John's description assumes the same. The other point is that the divine or heavenly court, portrayed by Daniel and John, finds its counterpart and analogy in the Mosaic "court" on Mount Sinai. Moses and the elders of Israel sit before God and eat and drink. John sees the elders of

---

It is doubtful if any special symbolic meaning is intended by the choice of these three stones. They are sometimes associated together in classical literature. They were placed in different positions on the high priest's breastplate (Exod. 28:17ff.); they are third, sixth, and fourth in the twelve foundation stones of the Holy City (Rev. 21:19). Some take the crystal jasper to represent God's holiness, the fiery red carnelian to represent the consuming fire of his judgment, the emerald green to represent his mercy. While this may be a possible application, there is no hint that such ideas were in John's mind. Rather, we are reminded that different manifestations of light are often used in the Bible to represent the presence and the glory of God. Israel was led by a pillar of fire at night; the presence of God in the Holy of Holies was represented by the shekinah glory.... It is possible that the rainbow is meant as an allusion to the bow given to Noah as a promise of mercy that God would never again let his judgment fall upon the entire race. As such it may be taken as a sign of patience of the ruler of the world toward sinful men until the last judgment falls upon the whole world.

spiritual Israel sitting around God and worshiping.[16] The Sinai communion of God and the elders thus anticipates and foreshadows an eschatological fulfillment, when God and his elders—and his people—will commune in his glory.

A New Heaven and a New Earth

John portrays that consummation in terms that go back through Isaiah to Genesis 1:1: "Then I saw a new heaven and a new earth, for the first heaven and the first earth had passed away, and there was no longer any sea" (Rev 21:1). This remarkable verse says much about God's covenant faithfulness. It affirms that, surpassing any ancient Near Eastern emperor, he will not only restore what was damaged through the covenantal unfaithfulness of his vassal; he will remake it entirely, creating an altogether better state of affairs. Part of this new creation, oddly enough, is the lack of any sea. Umberto Cassuto has rightly connected this fact with the biblical background—which has Mesopotamian and Ugaritic analogies—of hostility between God and the powers of darkness and chaos, of which the sea is emblematic (e.g., Isa 27:1).[17] We may therefore take the statement of Revelation 21:1 about the sea as either sym-

---

[16]H. Gunkel, *Schöpfung und Chaos in Urzeit und Endzeit* (Göttingen: Vandenhoeck und Ruprecht, 1895). 302–8, suggested that the twenty-four Babylonian star gods were the original of the twenty-four elders, and that these gods were transformed by Judaism into angels. R. H. Charles, *The Revelation of St. John*, ICC (Edinburgh: T. & T. Clark, 1920), 1:131, notes: "The evidence of connection between the Babylonian conception and that which appears in our text is too slight to build upon. It seems to be, in fact, not more than a coincidence; for the points in common between the two can be explained within Judaism." He adds that "the most reasonable interpretation is that which identifies them with the angelic representatives of the twenty-four priestly orders."

[17]U. Cassuto, *Biblical and Oriental Studies* (Jerusalem: Magnes, 1975), 2:80–102 ("The Epic of the Revolt of the Sea; an Attempt to Reconstruct It"). One may disagree with Cassuto's attempt to "reconstruct" a hypothetical Hebrew epic along these mythopoeic lines, but his collocation of biblical and ancient Near Eastern data remains pioneering and valuable.

bolic or literal. Certainly the powers of chaos, symbolized by the sea, will be removed.[18] But the removal of the sea may be part of the new earth's formation in a manner analogous to its original form.

John sees the heavenly Jerusalem anticipated by Paul and the author of Hebrews descend from above. Now Isaiah's Sinaitic eschatological vision of Jerusalem (Isa 4:5-6) comes true. John also sees that the heavenly city "does not need the sun or the moon to shine on it, for the glory of God gives it light, and the Lamb is its lamp" (Rev 21:23). In this way the eschatological theophany of Isaiah is further realized: "The sun will no more be your light by day, nor will the brightness of the moon shine on you, for Yahweh will be your everlasting light, and your God will be your glory" (Isa 60:19). The apostle knows that "the kings of the earth will bring their splendor into it" (Rev 21:24), echoing Isaiah's promise that

> Yahweh rises upon you
> and his glory appears over you.
> Nations will come to your light,
> and kings to the brightness of your dawn.
>
> (Isa 60:2-3)

He understands that "the glory and honor of the nations will be brought into it" (Rev 21:26), echoing Haggai's prophecy that after God's Sinaitic "shaking" of the heavens and earth, "the desired of all nations will come, and I will fill this house with glory" (Hag 2:7).

Part of the glory of those days will be that God's servants—his people—"will see his face, and his name will be on their foreheads" (Rev 22:4). The face of God that gave a temporary radiance to Moses when he came down from Mount Sinai (Ex 34:29ff.) and that gradually transforms believers who look

---

[18] Cf. W. J. Harrington, *Revelation* (Collegeville: Liturgical Press, 1993), 207: "The sea is the primeval ocean, symbol of chaos; its disappearance is assurance of God's total victory."

upon it in Christ (2Co 3:18), will gaze directly on his people—as they gaze at God's face—and constantly supply them with eternal life. The "name" that God revealed to Moses on Mount Sinai will be on the foreheads of us all—that is, we will all bear the character of our God, being made like Him who became like us in order to save us. We will reflect his glory and be like the God-man on the throne, whose feet the Mosaic elders saw, but whom we shall see face to face.

Excursus: Tongues of Fire

Those who live in the already-not-yet of God's kingdom have, as the author of Hebrews says, tasted the "powers of the age to come" (Heb 6:5). That "taste" comes from the Holy Spirit in them who endows them with "authority to become children of God" (Jn 1:12). God's first historic endowment of that Spirit came at Pentecost, as Jesus had promised (Ac 1:8). At that time

> a sound like the blowing of a violent wind came from heaven and filled the whole house where they were sitting. They saw what seemed to be tongues of fire that separated and came to rest on each of them. All of them were filled with the Holy Spirit and began to speak in other tongues as the Spirit enabled them. (Ac 2:2–4)

Those followers of Jesus experienced a powerful and benign form of storm theophany.[19] God came in his glory to endow followers of Jesus with his fiery Spirit. The fiery aspect of that theophanic endowment takes the form of tongues because God was empowering his people to speak in the tongues of the multinational and multilingual crowd of Jews and Jewish converts who had come to celebrate Pentecost.

---

[19] S. J. Kistemaker, *Acts* (Grand Rapids: Baker, 1990), 66–67, fails to see the full storm-theophany implications of the event, but does usefully note that the term πνεῦμα, translated "wind," can mean either "wind" or "spirit/Spirit." Cf. Jn 3:8.

The donation of theophanic glory portrayed in Acts has an Old Testament and ancient Near Eastern background. Mesopotamian kings claimed to have a divine aura or *melammu* that endowed life, inspired awe, and cast all foes into utter confusion.

Like the Holy Spirit, the *melammu* could be endowed, and it could be taken away. The Enuma Elish, the Babylonian creation tablets dating from the early second millennium, include an example of its endowment. The sea dragon goddess Tiamat prepared terrible serpents/dragons to aid her in battle. Once she had created them, "she made them bear *an awesome radiance* [*melammu*], she made them [thus] like gods."[20]

The *melammu* could also be taken away, just as the Holy Spirit was taken away from king Saul (1Sa 16:14; cf. Ps 51:12[11]). One example comes from the law code of Hammurapi, king of Babylon (1792–1750 B.C.). At the end of the code Hammurapi invokes curses on any subsequent king who alters the law in any way. Among the curses we find this one: "May Anu [the sky god] take the *awesome radiance* [*melammu*] of kingship away from him."[21]

Another fact relevant to the endowment of the Spirit in Acts is that the *melammu* appeared about the head. The Enuma Elish makes this clear. When the god Marduk went forth to do battle with Tiamat, "the *awesome radiance* [*melammu*], overwhelming, [was] upon his head."[22]

Finally, the *melammu* was associated with life—both divine life and the gift of enhanced vitality to the mortal king who sought the god. This appears from a Babylonian inscription to the goddess Ishtar, which includes the prayer:

---

[20] Enuma Elish, II.24 (cf. III.28, 86).
[21] CH xlii.48. Cf. Oppenheim, *Ancient Mesopotamia*, 98: "This *melammu* terrifies and overwhelms the enemies of the king but is said to be taken away from him if he loses divine support."
[22] Enuma Elish, IV.58.

I have sought your brightness; may my face be bright.
I have turned to your dominion; may it be life and well-being for me.[23]

The Mesopotamian data show that a supernatural radiance associated with life was thought to be the possession of the gods. The same radiance could be associated with kings: it could be endowed by the gods or taken away by the gods.

This phenomenon has theological ramifications beyond the Mesopotamian milieu. A. Leo Oppenheim, in his book *Ancient Mesopotamia* has observed:

> The sanctity of the royal person is often, especially in Assyrian texts, said to be revealed by a supernatural and awe-inspiring radiance or aura which, according to the religious literature, is characteristic of deities and of all things divine. A number of terms refer to this phenomenon; among them the probably pre-Sumerian term *melammu*, something like "awe-inspiring luminosity," is most frequent, while other terms stress the *tremendum* inherent in this accepted phenomenon. The royal halo is also referred to in Middle Persian (Sassanian) texts as *xvarena*, in late classical as *aura,* and a corresponding nimbus is pictured about the living emperor as late as in early Christian representations.[24]

Perhaps the most striking pagan representation of the divine aura that can surround or rest upon the head of a king appears in Vergil's *Aeneid,* upon which the Roman poet was at work during the last ten years of his life (29–19 B.C.). In book 2 of Vergil's epic, Troy is being sacked by the Greeks. Aeneas is about to flee with his family when a divine luminosity rests upon the head of his little boy, Iulus. The passage reads as follows:

> ecce levis summo de vertice visus Iuli
> fundere lumen apex, tactuque innoxia mollis
> lambere flamma comas et circum tempora pasci.

---

[23]H. W. F. Saggs, *The Greatness That Was Babylon* (New York: Hawthorn, 1962), 328.
[24]Oppenheim, *Ancient Mesopotamia,* 98.

> Suddenly from above the head of Iulus
> a light tongue of flame seems to shed a gleam,
>   and harmless in its touch
> lick his soft locks and pasture round his temples.[25]

At this point Vergil adds a comic touch: Aeneas is afraid and pours water on his son's head to extinguish the tongue of supernatural flame that dances upon it. Iulus' grandfather Anchises, being older and wiser, recognizes a divine promise of kingship in what has happened and asks for a confirming omen, which he receives when a falling star crashes into a nearby forest.

The parallel with the Pentecost event is unmistakable, yet there are also differences. In the Acts account there came a sound from heaven like the rush of a mighty wind (2:2), and they were all filled with the Holy Spirit and began to speak in other tongues as the Spirit gave them utterance (2:3). But the differences should not obscure the central point of resemblance. A tongue of flame rested upon the head of Iulus as a divine promise of kingship because the future Roman Empire was to spring from him. Tongues of flame rested upon the assembled believers at Pentecost because they were God's royal priesthood from whom (as a secondary cause at least) the future *civitas dei* was to spring.

A background in pagan mythology—possibly reaching as far back as the Sumerians in the third millennium B.C.—lies behind the concept of a divine aura that can be imparted to human beings. Such endowment was restricted to kings in the pagan thought world. But it was extended to ordinary people—followers of Jesus—at Pentecost.

---

[25]Cf. H. R. Faircloth, *Virgil*, vol. 1 (London: Heinemann, 1925), 341.

FORM CRITICISM: THE GOSPELS

We turn now to the form criticism of theophanies in the New Testament: first the form criticism of gospel theophanies and then the form criticism of theophanies in the book of Revelation. It is useful to distinguish three theophanic categories in the Gospels: pre-resurrection theophanies, theophanies in eschatological discourse, and post-resurrection theophanies. As in the Old Testament, these involve angelic as well as divine appearances.

FORM CRITICISM: PRE-RESURRECTION THEOPHANIES

The pre-Resurrection theophanies include the angelic annunciations to Zechariah and Mary, Joseph's dreams, Jesus' baptism and walking on the water, and the Transfiguration.[26]

Gabriel and Zechariah: Luke 1:5-25

The apparition of the angel Gabriel to Zechariah follows the theophanic *Gattung* already established by numerous Old Testament examples:[27]

---

[26] Also some minor instances, dealt with below.

[27] Although not cognizant of the OT *Gattung* to which the pericope conforms, A. Plummer, *The Gospel According to St. Luke,* 5th ed., ICC (Edinburgh: T. & T. Clark, 1922), 7, remarks on the continuity of this birth announcement with Israel's past: "After more than three centuries of silence, Jehovah again speaks by prophecies and signs to Israel. But there is no violent rupture with the past in making this new departure. The announcement of the rise of a new Prophet is made in the temple at Jerusalem, to a priest of the old covenant, who is to be the Prophet's father." He then adds, "It is strong evidence of the historic truth of the narrative that no miracles are prophesied of the new Prophet, and that after his appearance his disciples attribute none to him."

Formal Element	Luke 1:5–25
1 Introductory description in the third person	1:5–11
2 Angel's utterance of name of (mortal) addressee	1:13a
3 Response of the addressee	1:18
4 Angel's self-asseveration	1:19
5 His quelling of human fear	1:13a
6 Assertion of his gracious presence	1:19
7 The *hieros logos* addressed to the particular situation	1:13b–17
8 Inquiry or protest by the addressee	1:18
9 Continuation of the *hieros logos* with perhaps some repetition of elements 4, 5, 6, 7, and/or 8	1:19–20
10 Concluding description in the third person	1:21–25

Zechariah's encounter with Gabriel contains all the elements of an Old Testament theophany. It also parallels in significant ways Gabriel's appearance to Mary, to which we now turn.

Gabriel and Mary: Luke 1:26–38

The apparition of the angel Gabriel to Mary also follows the Old Testament theophanic *Gattung* as the following analysis shows:

Formal Element	Luke 1:26–38
1 Introductory description in the third person	1:26–27
2 Angel's utterance of name of (mortal) addressee	1:30
3 Response of the addressee	1:34
5 Angel's quelling of human fear	1:30
6 Assertion of his gracious presence	1:28
7 The *hieros logos* addressed to the particular situation	1:31–33
8 Inquiry or protest by the addressee	1:34

9 Continuation of the *hieros logos* with
   perhaps some repetition of elements
   4, 5, 6, 7, and/or 8   1:35–38bα
10 Concluding description in the third person   1:38bβ

The encounters between Gabriel and Zechariah and Gabriel and Mary are parallel to the extent that they are complete exemplars of the Old Testament theophanic *Gattung*. But they are parallel in other ways that enable significant contrasts to emerge:

Formal Element	**Luke 1:5–25**	**1:26–38**
1 Appearance of angel	1:11	1:28
2 Fear	1:12	1:29–30
3 Divine birth announcement	1:13	1:31
4 Prophecy regarding the child	1:14–17	1:32–33
5 Reaction of Zechariah/Mary	1:18	1:34
6 Angelic reaffirmation of message	1:19–20	1:35–37
7 Angelic pronouncement of discipline	1:19	

Gabriel appears to announce the birth of a son in each case. Both births are supernatural in the sense that they are enabled by divine power. The birth of John the Baptist like that of Isaac will be to a woman far too old to have children in the normal course of nature. The birth of the Messiah will be to a virgin by the power of the Holy Spirit. As noted earlier, these annunciations parallel in form the annunciations to Sarah (Ge 18:10) and to the house of David (Isa 7:14).[28] As Sarah's reaction was skeptical, so is Zechariah's. God did not discipline Sarah for her doubt, but he does discipline Zechariah. Those who read the accounts can learn a lesson of faith from Zechariah's discipline. Zechariah, after all, posed what seems a reasonable question: "By what means can I be sure of this [Κατὰ τί γνώσομαι τοῦτο]? I am an old man and my wife is well along in years" (Lk

---

[28]See at chap. 7, 237–40.

1:18; cf. Ge 18:12). Mary poses a somewhat parallel question: "How will this be [Πῶς ἔσται τοῦτο] . . . since I am a virgin?" (Lk 1:34). Both questions follow the form: "How/by what means" plus a biological reason that appears to stand in the way of fulfillment. Yet, although the questions are parallel, the angelic responses are different. That is because Zechariah asks, in effect, for a sign: "By what means can I be sure of this?" Mary by contrast asks simply, "How will this come about?" That is why Gabriel disciplines Zechariah with muteness. His evaluation is that Zechariah, who asked for a sign, "did not believe my words, which will come true at their proper time" (1:20). Mary's question receives no such critique, and that implies an approval of her faith. She did not doubt God's ability to do this—but she wanted to know how it would come to pass.[29]

The Angels and the Shepherds: Luke 2:8–20

The angelic theophany to the shepherds—so often read at Christmastime—also follows the Old Testament theophanic *Gattung*:

Formal Element	Luke 2:8–20
1 Introductory description in the third person	2:8–10a
5 Angel's quelling of human fear	2:10b
6 Assertion of his gracious presence	2:10c
7 The *hieros logos* addressed to the particular situation	2:11–12

---

[29]Cf. Wm. Hendriksen, *The Gospel of Luke* (Grand Rapids: Baker, 1978), 88:

> It will be remembered that when Gabriel had told Zechariah that the latter's wife would have a son, the priest had answered, "How can I be sure of this?" His response amounted to "I can't believe it." Mary, on the other hand, is not guilty of lack of faith. She *believes*. . . . But she is befuddled, bewildered, mystified. She has correctly interpreted the angel's message to mean that without the assistance of a husband she is about to conceive a child. So far so good. But *how* was this possible?

| 9 | Continuation of the *hieros logos* with perhaps some repetition of elements 4, 5, 6, 7, and/or 8 | 2:13–14 |
| 10 | Concluding description in the third person | 2:15–20 |

The angel appears to shepherds with the good news of Messiah's birth. This is no accident. The shepherd was a royal type in the ancient Near East. Pharaonic iconography portrayed the king of Egypt with a shepherd's crook.[30] Mesopotamian royal ideology from ancient times propounded the idea that a king shepherded his people as a vice-regent of the gods. Hammurapi (1792–1750 B.C.) said that he was called to shepherd the people of Babylon by the gods Anu and Enlil,[31] and the phrase "the people of the god, Enlil," is attested from Sharkalisharri of Akkad (2212–2188 B.C.) to Ashurbanipal, who claimed, "I shepherded the people of the god, Enlil."[32] In Old Testament days God took David from "following the flock" to be ruler over Israel (2Sa 7:8). And David could also say, "Yahweh is my shepherd" (Ps 23:1). But now an angel announces to Judean shepherds the birth of that one who will say, "I am the good shepherd" (Jn 10:11). As God promised, he is the one "who will shepherd my people Israel" (Mic 5:2; Mt 2:6).

Joseph's Dreams:
Matthew 1:18–25; 2:13–15; and 2:19–21

Like his patriarchal namesake Joseph, the supposed father of Jesus (Lk 3:23) had revelatory dreams. These dreams, as recorded in Matthew's gospel, also partake of the theophanic *Gattung*. This is so because a divine or angelic appearance in a dream or vision—like an actual theophany—can be both revelatory and provocative of fear.

---

[30]Cf. Pritchard, *The Ancient Near East in Pictures,* 133 (fig. 379).
[31]CH I.1–25; cf. XXIV.R.10–15.
[32]Cf. Tallqvist, *Akkadische Götterepitheta,* 182–83.

Matthew 1:18–25

In this passage an angel appears to Joseph in a dream and reassures him that it is right to take Mary as his wife, because the child she carries is born of the Holy Spirit. It has the following form:

Formal Element	**Matthew 1:18–25**
1 Introductory description in the third person	1:18–20a
2 Angel's utterance of name of (mortal) addressee	1:20b
5 His quelling of human fear	1:20b
7 The *hieros logos* addressed to the particular situation	1:20c–21
10 Concluding description in the third person	1:22–25

Joseph's dream follows well the contours of the Old Testament theophanic *Gattung*. Revelatory dreams in the Old Testament could also entail a response (element 3) or protest or inquiry (element 8) by the addressee, as in the case of God's revelatory dream to Abimelech (Ge 20:3–8; cf. especially 20:4b–5). They might also include a continuation of the *hieros logos* (element 9), as at Genesis 20:6–7. But theophanies, whether in dream or otherwise, need not contain these optional discourse elements. Joseph's dream does contain a significant variation on the normal *Gattung:* the "fear" that the angel quells is not a fear of the angelic presence, but rather Joseph's fear of taking Mary as his wife.[33]

Matthew 2:13–15

In Joseph's second dream an angel appears and warns him to take both mother and child to Egypt for safety from Herod. It has the following form:

---

[33] By contrast, God speaks to Abimelech in a dream with a terrifying warning: if he does not return Sarah to Abraham, "you may be sure that you and all yours will die" (Ge 20:7).

Formal Element	Matthew 2:13-15
1 Introductory description in the third person	2:13a
7 The *hieros logos* addressed to the particular situation	2:13b
10 Concluding description in the third person	2:14-15

The account of Joseph's second dream is most economical: it introduces the dream (element 1), recounts the *hieros logos* (element 7), and concludes the account (element 10). This economy is warranted by the context, for the account of the dream simply functions to inform us of the divine guidance by which the child was protected.

Matthew 2:19-21

In Joseph's third dream an angel appears and tells him to take both mother and child from Egypt back to Israel. It has the following form:

Formal Element	Matthew 2:19-21
1 Introductory description in the third person	2:19
7 The *hieros logos* addressed to the particular situation	2:20
10 Concluding description in the third person	2:21

Matthew presents Joseph's third dream with the same economy he employed in the second. Here again the elegantly simple triad of introduction, *hieros logos,* and conclusion functions to carry the narrative forward and sustain the sense of divine protection and guidance for the messianic child. A fourth dream is also mentioned—namely, that Joseph was "warned in a dream" that Archelaus reigned in Judea in place of his father Herod (Mt 2:22). But it is reported in no greater detail.

"This Is My Son"—Theophany at Jesus' Baptism

The theophany that occurs at Jesus' baptism also follows the form of the Old Testament *Gattung* but again in a most economical way. A comparison of the synoptic passages displays the economy of form:[34]

Formal Element	Matthew	Mark	Luke
1 Introductory description, third person	3:13–17a	1:9–11a	3:21–22a
7 The *hieros logos*	3:17b	1:11b	3:22b

Important theophanic elements are the "voice" that speaks from "heaven" and the avian form of the Spirit, which recalls Genesis 1:2. I have already noted the importance of that form as an emblem of the Spirit's creative/recreative work.[35]

"Take Courage! It is I"–Jesus Walks on the Water

As the Spirit hovered over the waters at the Creation, the Son walks on the water–to the astonishment of his disciples. Only Matthew and Mark report this event. Their accounts are parallel although Matthew's is by far the most complete:

Formal Element	Matthew	Mark	John
1 Introductory description, third person	14:22–25	6:45–50a	6:16–20
4 Deity's self-asseveration	14:27a	6:50b	6:20a
5 His quelling of fear	14:27b	6:50b	6:20b
7 The *hieros logos*	14:29a		
8 Inquiry by addressee	14:28		
9 Continuation of *hieros logos* with perhaps repetition of elements 4, 5, 6, 7, and/or 8	14:29b–31		
10 Concluding description, third person	14:32–33	6:51–52	6:21

---

[34] John reports the baptism as a brief historical retrospective on the lips of John the Baptist (Jn 1:32–33).

[35] See above, chap. 5, 150–53.

Perhaps the most important aspect of Jesus' walk on the water is his supremacy over that element. Against the ancient Near Eastern and Old Testament background, it is clear that Jesus' walk demonstrates God's power over the forces of watery chaos like Moses' parting of the Reed Sea or Joshua's stopping of the Jordan. Moreover, Jesus walked on the water as "a strong wind was blowing and the waters grew rough" (Jn 6:18). He was supreme over those chaotic threats just as he was when he calmed the storm on the Sea of Galilee. Such a demonstration of power naturally evokes fear—even if it is the mistaken fear of thinking Jesus a ghost.

Luke's account also shows a human fear normal at theophanies: "In fear and amazement they asked one another, 'Who is this? He commands even the winds and the water, and they obey him'" (Lk 8:25b). The same awe appears at other demonstrations of the Spirit's power through Jesus: e.g., when he delivers the Gerasene demoniac (Lk 8:37) and when he heals a paralytic (Mt 9:8). Taken all together the theophanic fear reaction in these passages indicates a certain parallelism between the forces of watery chaos and the powers of darkness (sickness and demons)—for Jesus is supreme over them all, and that supremacy evokes fear on the part of mortals who see it displayed.

The Transfiguration

Analysis has shown how the Transfiguration account in Matthew 17 parallels the Sinaitic materials in Exodus, and how Jesus is compared to Moses and Elijah (who both experienced Sinai/Horeb theophanies) and is exalted above them by the comparison and by God's words in theophany. Now I will show the conformity of the synoptic Transfiguration accounts to the theophanic *Gattung* as it appears in both Testaments:

Formal Element	Matthew	Mark	Luke
1 Introductory description, third person	17:1–5a	9:2–7a	9:28–35a

5	God's quelling of fear	17:6–7		
7	The *hieros logos*	17:5b	9:7b	9:35b
10	Concluding description, third person	17:8–13	9:8–13	9:36

The account is virtually an Old Testament appearance of God's glory: he comes in cloud and is not seen but his voice is heard.[36] It parallels the way God appeared to Moses and Elijah. The cardinal difference is that God the Father now appears to God the Son incarnate. The work of the new covenant is under way. To quote Edersheim from another context:

> Even here also we mark the characteristic difference between the Old and the New Dispensations, to which St. Paul calls attention in another connection (2 Cor. iii. 13–18). For whereas, under the preparatory dispensation God dwelt in a "cloud" and in "thick darkness," we all now behold "the glory of God" in the Face of His Anointed.[37]

Or as another has said, "Nebula Deus se et representabat et velabat"[38]—but the glory of God now appears in the face of Christ.

Jesus' Death

The synoptic accounts of Jesus' death (Mt 27:45–56; Mk 15:33–41; Lk 23:44–49) contain elements that evoke Old Testa-

---

[36]The Father's approbation at the Transfiguration echoes that which occurred at Jesus' baptism, and it also resembles the brief account in Jn 12:28–33. There, when Jesus asked his Father to glorify his name, "A voice came from heaven, 'I have glorified it, and will glorify it again.' The crowd that was there and heard it said that it had thundered; others said an angel had spoken to him. Jesus said, 'This voice was for your benefit, not mine'" (Jn 12:28–30). The theophany is brief, but as in OT theophanies, the key element is the voice: God reveals himself not only gloriously but also propositionally.

[37]A. Edersheim, *History of Judah and Israel* (London: Religious Tract Society, 1880), 90.

[38]Ibid., 90, n. 3. I.e., "By cloud God both revealed and concealed himself."

ment theophanies and eschatological promise, and for that reason deserve form-critical discussion. The relevant elements are darkness and earthquake, which form a large part of the theophanic *Aufruhr der Natur* that one might expect in a theophany:

Formal Element	Matthew	Mark	Luke
1 Darkness	27:45	15:33	23:44–45
2 Earthquake	27:51		

Darkness and earthquake not only remind us of God's descent on Mount Sinai; they also elicit a human response that we have come to expect in any Sinaitic theophany: that of fear. When the centurion and others saw the earthquake and all that had happened, "they were terrified, and exclaimed, 'Surely he was the Son of God'" (Mt 27:54; cf. Mk 15:39; Lk 23:47). Their words resemble those of the widow of Zarephath when Elijah displayed God's power by raising her son from the dead: "Now I know that you are a man of God and that the word of Yahweh from your mouth is the truth" (1Ki 17:24). The purpose of any display of God's power is not simply to show force; it is to show God. So at Jesus' death God shows his approbation by a major demonstration of power: he darkens the sun and shakes the earth in accordance with an Old Testament promise soon to be quoted by Peter at Pentecost:

> I will show wonders in heaven above
>   and signs on the earth below . . .
> The sun will be turned to darkness
>   and the moon to blood
>   before the coming of the great and glorious day of the Lord.
> And everyone who calls
>   on the name of the Lord will be saved.
> (Ac 2:19–21 = Joel 2:30–32)

That death and the *Aufruhr der Natur* that mark its accomplishment and its approval are the necessary antecedents of the salvation promised by Joel and fulfilled by Jesus. That death goes before the gift of life–that natural upheaval goes before the final grand irruption of the eschaton.

FORM CRITICISM: THE ESCHATOLOGICAL DISCOURSES

This category includes what are commonly called the eschatological discourses of the synoptic gospels as well as Jesus' words to the Sanhedrin, which are also an eschatological allusion and even instruction to them.

Synoptic Eschatological Discourses

The accounts are parallel in the eschatological storm theophany phenomena they evoke:

Formal Element	Matthew	Mark	Luke
1 Son's advent like lightning	24:27		17:24
2 Sodom and Gomorrah simile			17:28–30
3 Isaiah 13:10; 34:4 citation	24:29	13:24–25	21:26b
4 Son of Man to come with clouds, power, and glory	24:30	13:26	21:27
5 Angels, trumpet call, elect, and four winds	24:31	13:27	

The central issue in these accounts is not form critical. It is rather God's advent in glory and power to save his elect. The accounts echo an ancient hope that Yahweh would descend in glory and rescue his chosen one from his foes. By God's Spirit that salvation could be—and was—portrayed as though it had already occurred:

> Out of the brightness of his presence clouds advanced,
>   with hailstones and bolts of lightning.
> Yahweh thundered from heaven,
>   the thunderous voice of the Most High resounded.
> He shot his arrows and scattered the enemies,
>   great bolts of lightning and scattered them.
> The valleys of the sea were exposed
>   and the foundations of the earth laid bare
> at your rebuke, Yahweh,
>   at the blast of breath from your nostrils.

> He reached down from on high and took hold of me;
>   he drew me out of deep waters.
> He rescued me from my powerful enemy,
>   from my foes, who were too strong for me.
>
> (Ps 18:13–18 [12–17])

Just as David anticipated Yahweh's intrusion to save, so Jesus says he will come one day in stormy glory to save. One theme of David's eschatological judgment intrusion scenario commands particular attention in light of the New Testament. Psalm 18 parallels the raging waters and the foes of the elect. The Lucan eschatological discourse perhaps echoes this ancient theme when Jesus says, "On the earth, nations will be in anguish and perplexity at the roaring and tossing of the sea" (Lk 21:25). And the parallel is made complete in Revelation, where John sees "the great prostitute, who sits on many waters" (17:1) and is told, "The waters you saw, where the prostitute sits, are peoples, multitudes, nations and languages" not submissive to God (17:15). Paul says the Lord will deal with these enemies when he returns:

> God is just. He will pay back trouble to those who trouble you and give relief to you who are troubled, and to us as well. This will happen when the Lord Jesus is revealed from heaven in blazing fire with his powerful angels. He will punish those who do not know God and do not obey the gospel of our Lord Jesus. They will be punished with everlasting destruction and shut out from the presence of the Lord and from the majesty of his power on the day he comes to be glorified in his holy people and to be marveled at among all those who have believed. (2Th 1:6–10)

To be "shut out from the presence of the Lord" means death as we have understood from the Old Testament and even from ancient Near Eastern parallels. That will be the fate of those who do not acknowledge God in Christ. And Jesus both warns and instructs a recalcitrant Sanhedrin along the same eschatological lines.

Jesus Before the Sanhedrin

Jesus' short testimony before the Sanhedrin contains three points or facts that they "will see." He is the Son of Man—a messianic title as we have noted. He will be seated at the right hand of the Mighty One. And he will come on the clouds of heaven (cf. Rev 1:7).

Formal Element	Matthew	Mark	Luke
1 Son of Man	26:64b	14:62b	22:69b
2 Session at God's right hand	26:64c	14:62c	22:69c
3 Advent on clouds of heaven	26:64d	14:62d	

Jesus' allusions to the "Son of Man" title (Ps 8:5[4]; 80:18[17]; cf. Eze 2:1 and passim) and to Psalm 110:1 (session at the right hand of God) and Daniel 7:13 (advent on the clouds of heaven) unite to claim for him the character of Messiah, king and priest (order of Melchizedek, cf. Ps 110:2.4), prophet (cf. Ezekiel), quintessential Israel, and indeed human being (cf. Pss 8:5[4]; 80:18[17]). The stumbling block for the Sanhedrin was Jesus' prophecy that they would see his eschatological return (Mt 26:64b; Mk 14:62b). Jesus portrayed that return as an Old Testament glory theophany of Yahweh—an application the Sanhedrin thought gave them ample warrant for crying, "Blasphemy!"

Messiah's eschatological return echoes the way God first came to Adam and Eve in the garden once they had sinned (Ge 3:8). Whenever God came in glory in the Old Testament, he came in that way: partly revealed in flashes of light and thunderous voice, partly concealed in dark cloud. Every such theophany was a judgment because the advent of light judges the darkness (cf. Jn 3:19–20). At the eschaton that judgment par excellence will take place of which all Old Testament glory theophanies—however powerful and glorious—are only a foreshadowing.

FORM CRITICISM: POST-RESURRECTION THEOPHANIES

In this category we include appearances of angels and Jesus after his resurrection but before his ascension. We have to deal in particular with those encounters that share theophanic characteristics already noted in the Old Testament *Gattung*. Our concern is not with synoptic issues (e.g., the notice of one angel in Matthew's and Mark's gospels, but two in Luke's and John's). Such issues appear also in ancient Near Eastern historical records and are usually matters of selective reportage (which occurs for a variety of reasons) rather than of inconsistency with regard to facts.

The Angels at the Tomb

The synoptics (Mt 28:1-8; Mk 16:1-8; Lk 24:1-12) and the gospel of John (Jn 20:10-18) report an appearance of angels at the tomb immediately after the resurrection of Christ. Examination of the synoptics and John in turn shows that angelic theophany has major characteristics of the theophanic *Gattung*:

	Formal Element	Matthew	Mark	Luke
1	Introductory description, third person	28:1-4	16:1-5a	24:1-5a
5	Angel quells human fear	28:5	16:6a	
7	The *hieros logos*	28:6-7	16:6b-7	24:5b-7
10	Concluding description, third person	28:8	16:8	24:8-12

As in other theophanies, the character of the messenger suffices to show his divine quality (cf. element 4), and the content of his message goes far to demonstrate the gracious presence of God (element 6).

John's gospel also contains an account of angels at the tomb, with the addition of an important discourse between Jesus and Mary of Magdala:

Formal Element	John
1 Introductory description, third person	20:10–12
2 Angels' address to mortal	20:13a
3 Response of the addressee	20:13b
2 Jesus' address to mortal	20:15a
3 Response of the addressee	20:15b
2 Jesus' address to mortal	20:16a
8 Inquiry or protest by the addressee	20:16b
7 The *hieros logos* addressed to the particular situation	20:17
10 Concluding description in the third person	20:18

The account begins with the angels' address to Mary but quickly shifts to her dialogue with Jesus. Her initial inability to recognize him (20:14) classes this part of the passage as theophanic because it demonstrates that post-Resurrection change in the quality of Jesus' appearance that elsewhere occasions fear (see below). His apparently obscure warning, "Do not hold on to me, for I have not yet returned to the Father" (20:17) may seem to add to this aspect of the narrative. Morris, however, interprets it–perhaps rightly–as follows: "The present imperative with a negative means 'Stop doing something' rather than 'Do not start something.' Here it will mean 'Stop clinging to me.'. . . . Evidently Mary in her joy at seeing the Lord laid hold on Him, possibly in the same way and for the same purpose as the ladies of whom Matthew writes."[39] Morris alludes to Matthew 28:9, where "Mary Magdalene and the other Mary" clasp Jesus' feet and worship him.[40] Such a conclusion cannot be proved but may be appropriate for the context.

---

[39] L. Morris, *The Gospel According to John* (Grand Rapids: Eerdmans, 1971), 840.
[40] Ibid., 840.

Despite Locked Doors

Although the disciples had locked every door for fear of the Jews, Jesus comes among his disciples. His coming frightens them as much as any theophany. Although Luke (24:36–49) and John (20:19–23) report it with a different selection of details, their accounts may with profit be examined together:

	Formal Element	Luke	John
1	Introductory description, third person	24:36a	20:19a
2	Deity's address to mortal	24:36b	20:19b
4	Deity's self-asseveration	24:39	20:21b
5	His quelling of human fear	24:37–43	20:20–21a
6	Assertion of his gracious presence		
7	The *hieros logos*	24:44–49	20:21b–23

The accounts are parallel in structure, but they vary in content.[41] Luke focuses on Jesus' physical demonstration of his bodily nature, even to the extent of eating fish in the disciples' presence. He adds Jesus' teaching on in the prophetic quality of the Scriptures that foretold him and the promise of the Spirit to empower them for kingdom life and work. John portrays Jesus' Spirit-breath upon them—apparently meant as a new version of

---

[41]Cf. John's account of Jesus' subsequent appearance for the benefit of Thomas:

	Formal Element	John
1	Introductory description in the third person	20:24–26a
2	Deity's address to mortal	20:26b
4	Deity's self-asseveration	20:27
3	Response of the addressee	20:28
5	His quelling of human fear	20:26b
7	The *hieros logos*	20:29
10	Concluding description in the third person	20:30–31

In this account, as in the earlier accounts of Luke and John, Jesus' demonstration of his bodily presence and his reassuring blessing of peace upon the disciples function virtually as element 6, "Assertion of his gracious presence." The "concluding description" in this case is actually a summary evaluation of Jesus' many miraculous signs and their import.

Genesis 2:7—and the reassurance, "If you forgive anyone his sins, they have been forgiven; if you do not forgive them, they have not been forgiven" (20:23). Morris again rightly observes:

> It should . . . be borne in mind that, according to the best text, the verbs "are forgiven" and "are retained" are in the perfect tense. The meaning of this is that the Spirit-filled church can pronounce with authority that the sins of such-and-such men have been forgiven or have been retained. If the church is really acting under the leadership of the Spirit it will be found that her pronouncements on this matter do but reveal what has already been determined in heaven.[42]

Morris' words verge on the homiletical and deserve emphasis. The church that lives by the Spirit should keep in step with the Spirit (Gal 5:25)—for that Spirit of Christ is our true life.

THEOPHANIES IN THE BOOK OF ACTS

The book of Acts contains three major theophanies of the Sinaitic type: the endowment of the Spirit at Pentecost; a lesser visitation of the Spirit in Acts 4, and the course-changing appearance of Jesus to Saul on the road to Damascus.[43]

Angels, Wind, and Tongues of Fire

Luke reports how Jesus "was taken up before their very eyes, and a cloud hid him from their sight" (Ac 1:9). Jesus' departure is evocative in a small way of the cloudy glory of his promised return (cf. Mt 26:64 and parallels). But a more immediate promise is that of the Spirit, as the angels who appear now remind Jesus' followers (Ac 1:10–11).

---

[42] Morris, *John*, 849.

[43] Visions in Acts such as those of Ananias (9:10–19a) and Peter (10:9–16) could also be included and should form part of a complete NT study. Even a cursory reading shows that they follow the pattern of the theophanic *Gattung*.

When the Spirit comes in power he does so as a wind (Ac 2:2; cf. Jn 3:8) and imparts himself as tongues of fire that separate and settle on different ones (2:3). The wind and fire are evocative of Old Testament storm theophanies—more or less explicitly from Genesis 3:8 onward. But there are now other and better meanings to be understood. The tongues are immediately symbolic of the Spirit-imparted human "tongues" that the disciples use to declare "the wonders of God" to the God-fearing Jews then visiting Jerusalem (vv. 4–12). That proclamation would lead to the salvation of many. But also, as noted above, the fiery Spirit-tongues that blossom upon their heads symbolize their royal election—just like the tongues of fire that pastured about the head of Iulus and the *melammu* that (supposedly) glorified Mesopotamian gods and royalty. Whether or not the followers of Jesus understood that at the time is unimportant to the symbolism, for in his providence God chose to adorn them with a symbol that spoke from the common grace of antiquity and can speak to us today.

The Spirit and Kingdom Warfare

The advent of the Spirit in Acts 4:31 has to do with kingdom warfare. The occasion of it is very like David's call for God's intervention (theophanically portrayed) in Psalm 18. David called for divine warfare against his foes. The followers of Jesus pray in a similar way after Peter and John return from their confrontation with the Sanhedrin (4:1–22). Their prayer combines God's attributes as Creator (v. 24) and Savior (vv. 29–30) much as do Psalms 77, 89, 135, and 136.[44] The logic is the same in all such cases: the God who created the world also and only has power to save his people and advance his kingdom.

God's kingdom advance is portrayed in Mosaic terms: "Stretch out your hand to heal and perform miraculous signs

---

[44]See discussion above, chap. 8, p. 286.

and wonders through the name of your holy servant Jesus" (Ac 4:30). In other words: may God act in a way evocative of the Exodus—may he "stretch out his hand" (= Ex 3:20; 7:5) to perform "signs and wonders" (= Ex 7:3) in his "name" (= Ex 3:15; 5:23; 9:16), which is now the name of Jesus. In Moses' day God's "signs and wonders" ravaged an earthly kingdom—Pharaoh's Egypt. But now God will stretch out his hand to heal (4:30). Every such act does, however, help to destroy a kingdom: it invades space formerly occupied by Satan (cf. Mt 12:22–29 and parallels). So it advances the kingdom of light against the kingdom of darkness. The Spirit comes again and shakes their place of assembly (4:31a). He comes to empower them for the miraculous works they seek. But since the advance of God's domain involves propositional revelation as well as miracles—"They were all filled with the Holy Spirit and spoke the word of God boldly" (4:31b). God would also choose another apostle to advance his kingdom by power and words. He would come to that man with words and in power.

Saul's Aborted Course

God showed unusual mercy, as well as sovereign choice, when Jesus appeared in glory above Saul on the road to Damascus. Paul later says, "Here is a trustworthy saying that deserves full acceptance: Christ Jesus came into the world to save sinners—of whom I am the worst" (1Ti 1:15). One can scarcely imagine a more dramatic and unasked for intrusion by God into a man's life. From a form-critical standpoint it conforms well to the ways that God appeared to Old Testament saints:

Formal Element	Acts 9:1–9
1 Introductory description in the third person	9:4a
2 Deity's utterance of name of (mortal) addressee	9:4b
3 Response of the addressee	9:5a
4 Deity's self-asseveration	9:5

7	The *hieros logos* addressed to the particular situation	9:6
10	Concluding description in the third person	9:7–9

Jesus comes in rebuke as well as commission. Perhaps for that reason he does not choose to quell Saul's fear (element 5) or "assert his gracious presence" (element 6). But his commission is a sign of favor, and Saul without inquiry or protest (element 8) does what he is told. Another response can hardly be imagined. As Amos said long before,

> The lion has roared;
>   who would not fear?[45]
> The Lord Yahweh has spoken—
>   who can but prophesy? (Am 3:8)

Once Jesus had appeared to Saul in glory, his life had to change forever. He let go the name of Israel's first king and took up a name that means "small"—as he must have felt before Israel's true King. "For I am the least of the apostles and do not even deserve to be called an apostle," he wrote, "because I persecuted the church of God. But by the grace of God I am what I am" (1Co 15:9–10a).[46]

---

[45]For the concept of Yahweh as a lion, cf. Niehaus, *Amos*, 1:381.

[46]Paul's own account of this encounter, as reported by Luke, follows essentially the same outline:

	Formal Element	Acts 22:2b–11
1	Introductory description in the third person	22:2b–7a
2	Deity's utterance of name of (mortal) addressee	22:7b
3	Response of the addressee	22:8a
4	Deity's self-asseveration	22:8b
8	Inquiry or protest by the addressee	22:10a
7	The *hieros logos* addressed to the particular situation	22:10b
10	Concluding description in the third person	22:11

Paul's account supplies the additional information that he asked: "What shall I do, Lord?" (22:10a = element 8). It may be that he mentions this to draw the listening crowd into the experience with him as he tells them about his God and theirs. For a comparision of the two passages cf. Kistemaker, *Acts*, 328–37.

THE REVELATION THEOPHANIES

The book of Revelation contains a number of theophanies that echo more or less directly the Old Testament theophanies we have examined. We have seen already how the throne appearance of God in Revelation 4:2-6 echoes his earlier appearances in Exodus, Ezekiel, and Daniel. We have seen how the appearance of a new heaven and new earth in Revelation 21 echoes the Old Testament promises, especially in Isaiah. It remains to examine form-critically the three major theophanies, which, in their own way, structure the book of Revelation: the appearance of the Lord to John (1:9-3:22), the throne appearance and its aftermath (4:1-9:21), and the appearance of the angel counselor and his instructions to John (10:1-22:17).[47]

---

[47]Other scholars have noted other aspects of structure without, however, understanding the role of the three theophanies as structural elements. R. H. Charles, *Revelation,* xxiii-xxviii, sees seven parts in strict chronological order: (1) 1:4-20, (2) 2-3, (3) 4-5, (4) 6-7:8. 8:1.3-5.2.6.13-19. 11:14-13. 15-20:8, (5) 21:9-22:2.14-15.17 20:4-10, (6) 20:11-15, and (7) 21:5a.4d.5b.1-4abc, 22:3-5. His approach is marred by the higher critical tendency to assign fragments of passages and verses to separate authors on the basis of the usual stylistic/vocabulary criteria (cf. xxix-xxxvii). Such assignments cut across form-critical unities in Revelation just as they do in OT books, a fact that constitutes one of many sane arguments against such methodology (cf. K. Baltzer, *Das Bundesformular* (Neukirchen: Neukirchener Verlag, 1960); Eng. version, *The Covenant Formulary,* trans. D. E. Green (Philadelphia: Fortress, 1971). R. H. Mounce, *The Book of Revelation* (Grand Rapids: Eerdmans, 1977), 31, comments:

> The unusually strong and early external evidence supporting apostolic authorship should cause us to hesitate before accepting a conclusion based on subjective appraisal of internal considerations. Since internal evidence is not entirely unfavorable to apostolic authorship and since external evidence is unanimous in its support, the wisest course of action is either to leave the question open or to accept in a tentative way that the Apocalypse was written by John the apostle, son of Zebedee and disciple of Jesus.

Mounce analyzes the structure in a fairly conventional way (47-49): I. Prologue (1:1-20), II. Letters to the Seven Churches (2:1-3:22), III. Adoration

GOD AT SINAI

The Appearance of the Lord to John (1:9–3:22)

The Lord appears to John in a way that echoes a number of Old Testament theophanies.

Descriptive Element	Revelation	Ezekiel	Daniel
"like a son of man"	1:13a	cf. 1:26b	7:13
robe reaching to his feet	1:13b		7:9b, 10:5[48]
golden sash	1:13b		10:5b
head/hair white like wool	1:14a		7:9b
head/hair white like snow	1:14b		7:9b
eyes like blazing fire	1:14c[49]	cf. 1:27	10:6b
feet like bronze glowing in a furnace	1:15a	cf. 1:27	10:6b
voice like the sound of rushing waters	1:15b	43:2b	cf. 10:6b
face shining brilliant like the sun	1:16b	cf. 1:27	cf. 10:6a

---

in the Court of Heaven (4:1–5:14), IV. The Seven Seals (6:1–8:1), Interlude: Visions of Security and Salvation (7:1–17), V. The Seven Trumpets (8:2–11:19), Interlude: Visions of the Prophetic Role (10:1–11:14), VI. Conflict Between the Church and the Powers of Evil (12:1–14:5), Interlude: Visions of Final Judgment (14:6–20), VII. The Seven Last Plagues (15:1–16:21), VIII. The Fall of Babylon (17:1–19:5), IX. The Final Victory (19:6–20:15), X. The New Heaven and the New Earth (21:1–22:5), XI. Epilogue (22:6–21). Other structural analyses include that of G. E. Ladd, *Revelation*, 15–17, who sees a six-part structure based on visions: I. Prologue (1:1–8), II. The First Vision (1:9–3:22), III. The Second Vision (4:1–16:21), IV. The Third Vision (17:1–21:8), V. The Fourth Vision (21:9–22:5), and VI. Epilogue (22:6–21). Such an analysis takes the visions well into account but fails to see some of them as contained within a larger framework of theophanic disclosure (e.g., 21:9–22:5 contained within 10:1–22:17[18–21], see below).

[48] Daniel does not mention the length of the robe; Scott, *Revelation*, 131, is probably right in comparing the full-length robe to the robe worn by a king or priest (cf. Ex 28:4.31 LXX).

[49] Cf. Rev 19:12.

As in the throne accounts, more detail is added now as the revelation of God's glory becomes more complete.[50]

Like the Old Testament accounts, the appearance of the risen Lord to John on Patmos follows the form of the theophanic *Gattung:*

Formal Element		**Revelation 1:9–3:22**
1	Introductory description, third person	1:9–10, 12–17a
7	The *hieros logos*	1:11
4	Deity's self-asseveration	1:17–18
5	His quelling of human fear	1:17b
9	Continuation of the *hieros logos*	1:19–3:22

In addition to its conformity to the Old Testament *Gattung,* the passage includes John's overall commission (1:19) and particular commissions to address by letter each of the seven churches (2:1, 8, 12, 18; 3:1, 7, 14; cf. 1:10b). Like some Old Testament theophanies, Jesus' revelation to John is essentially a prophetic commission (cf. Isa 6:1ff.). The Lord reveals himself most abruptly and does not utter the name of his prophet.[51] This may be in order to impress him more profoundly with the glory of Jesus, with whom John was on such personal terms during Jesus' Incarnation. Jesus now appears in that dread glory in which he will soon come to judge the quick and the dead. Yet his self-disclosure is gracious, and his very self-asseveration includes a promise of his second advent (1:17b–18), which John ought to find encouraging. The passage has no "concluding description" (element 10) but simply moves from the epistolary genre to the throne appearance of God.

---

[50] Cf. Charles, *Revelation,* lxviii-lxxxvi, for an excellent table of correlations between phrases in Revelation and counterparts in the OT, Pseudepigrapha, and NT.

[51] So there is no corresponding response (element 3). Likewise there is no protest or inquiry (element 8) by John.

The Throne Appearance and its Aftermath (4:1–9:21)

The throne appearance of God, already noted in comparison with its Old Testament counterparts, also introduces a long revelatory passage that conforms to the Old Testament *Gattung*:

	Formal Element	**Revelation 4:1–9:21**
1	Introductory description, third person	4:1a, 2–11
7	The *hieros logos*	4:1b
1	Further description in the third person	5:1–4
4	Deity's self-asseveration	4:8, 11[52]
9	Continuation of the *hieros logos*	5:5
1	Further description, third person	5:6–7:12
9	Continuation of the *hieros logos*	7:13
8	Inquiry or protest by the addressee	7:14a
9	Continuation of the *hieros logos*	7:14b–17
10	Concluding description in the third person	8:1–9:21

Again the Lord does not address John by name. He abruptly tells him to "come up here" for further revelation (4:1b). John then sees the Lord on his throne and is soon approached by an "elder" who speaks to him (5:5). Again it is an elder who speaks to John and identifies those who have come out of the Great Tribulation (7:14b–17). The passage therefore contains *hieroi logoi* from both the Lord and his elders. This is not unlike the experience of Ezekiel, who saw and talked with a "man" ("whose appearance was like bronze," 40:3; 47:6; et al.), but also was addressed by the Lord from his heavenly temple (accompanied by the "man," 43:6ff.). John's experience is more extensive (and perhaps more intense) and more complete because of what Christ has done as our forerunner (Heb 6:20). When John saw both the temple theophany and the elders in

---

[52]The "self-asseveration" is actually an affirmation of the Lord's nature and glory by the living creatures (4:8) and the elders (4:11). They function virtually as an asseveration of the Lord's being in the passage.

the context of eschatological judgment revelation, he experienced what the author of Hebrews affirmed: "You have come to God, the judge of all men, to the spirits of righteous men made perfect, to Jesus the mediator of a new covenant, and to the sprinkled blood that speaks a better word than the blood of Abel" (Heb 12:23-24).

The Angel Counselor and His Words to John (10:1-22:17)

John's encounter with an angel who plants one foot on the earth and one foot in the sea makes up half of the book of Revelation and also conforms to the Old Testament *Gattung:*

	Formal Element	**Revelation 10:1-22:17**
1	Introductory description, third person	10:1-4a
7	The *hieros logos* (the Lord)	10:4b
1	Further description, third person	10:5-8a
9	Continuation of the *hieros logos* (the Lord)	10:8b
1	Further description, third person	10:9a
9	Continuation of the *hieros logos* (the angel)	10:9b
1	Further description, third person	10:10
9	Continuation of the *hieros logos* (the angel)	10:11-11:3[53]
1	Further description, third person	11:4-14:12
9	Continuation of the *hieros logos* (the Lord)	14:13
1	Further description, third person	14:14-17:6
9	Continuation of the *hieros logos* (the angel)	17:7-18
1	Further description, third person	18:1-19:8
9	Continuation of the *hieros logos* (the angel)	19:9-10
1	Further description, third person	19:11-21:5a
9	Continuation of the *hieros logos* (the Lord)	21:5b-8
1	Further description, third person	21:9a
9	Continuation of the *hieros logos* (the angel)	21:9b

---

[53]Perhaps several angels address John at 10:11 (the verb is in the plural), whereas the angel of 10:9b addresses him at 11:1 (the singular participle), as Scott, *Revelation,* 216-17, has observed.

1	Further description, third person	21:10–22:5
9	Continuation of the *hieros logos* (the angel)	22:6–7
1	Further description, third person	22:8
9	Continuation of the *hieros logos* (the angel)	22:9–12
4	Deity's self-asseveration	22:13, 16
9	Continuation of the *hieros logos* (the angel?)	22:14–16a
10	Concluding description, third person	22:17(18–21)

The passage is significant as the execution of a further commission from the Lord. The commission involves first the eating of a scroll that is sweet in the mouth but bitter in the stomach (10:8–10; cf. Eze 2:8–3:3), then the command to prophesy accordingly "about many peoples, nations, languages and kings" (10:11). Form-critically a major feature of the passage is the alternation between third-person description (element 1) and *hieroi logoi* (element 9). The shift takes place ten times, and it is not always immediately clear who is speaking. In chapter 22 the words seem to pass from those of the angel (v. 6) to those of Christ (v. 7), but at this point the angel is probably only reporting the words of Christ.[54] It is more difficult to distinguish between angelic and divine utterance at 22:9–16a. Perhaps the discourse shifts abruptly from the angel (vv. 9–11) to the Lord (vv. 12–16a) as speaker. Probably it is better to take verses 12–16a as words of Christ reported by the angel, as at 22:7. Verse 16a especially ("I, Jesus, have sent my angel to give you this testimony for the churches") appears to point in this direction. Whatever the case, the divine self-asseveration (vv. 13, 16) is clear, as are the warnings (vv. 11–12, 15) and promises (vv. 12, 14) of the passage.

We have seen that there are three major theophanies, which, in their own way, structure the book of Revelation: the appearance of the Lord to John (1:9–3:22), the throne appearance and its aftermath (4:1–9:21), and the appearance of the angel counselor and his instructions to John (10:1–22:17). Rev-

---

[54]Cf. Scott, *Revelation*, 299.

elation is not the first biblical book to be structured largely by three long sections in which discourse plays a major role. Deuteronomy likewise consists of three major parts (the so-called Mosaic Discourses, Dt 1:6–4:43; 4:44–28:68; 29:1–30:20) that contribute to the book's structure in a way that complements the equally valid international treaty form of that book.[55] The comparison has a poetic aptness. For if Deuteronomy is the second and final major articulation of the Mosaic Law, Revelation shows the second advent of the one whose ministry fulfills that Law in every way.

SUMMARY

The role of Mount Sinai in the New Testament is both explicit and implicit. Explicit references to Sinai by Paul and the author of Hebrews focus on that mountain as the place where God gave the Law in terrible theophany. They place emphasis both on the dread quality of that event and on the legal consequences of it. The Law puts people under bondage because, although it shows God's goodly demands, it does not empower people to obey. When Jesus teaches on the Mount of the Beatitudes, he implies the same and demonstrates that the human case is even worse than the law indicates: he magisterially shows that God's demands are yet more far-reaching than a surface reading of the Law would suggest. That is why Christ must fulfill the Law for us—for only he is able.

Jesus' transfiguration on that second New Testament mount also echoes what happened on Sinai. It parallels the transfiguration of Moses and anticipates the transfiguration all Christians will know when they stand before the Lord in glory. On that day they will not need sun or moon for light, because

---

[55]Cf. J. A. Thompson, *Deuteronomy* (Leicester: Inter-Varsity Press, 1974), 14–15. Thompson's overall discussion of different aspects of the book's structure is worth reading (14–21).

Jesus himself will be their light. His luminous countenance will supply them eternally with glorious and abundant life in a way that exceeds the imaginings of ancient Near Eastern monarchs who claimed at best a shadow of such divine relationships for themselves.

Jesus' death on the cross was necessary to purchase that salvation for his people. On that third New Testament mount he paid the price for those who broke the Law. And there God answered with a theophanic darkening of the sun, clouds, and earthquake—echoing the Sinai theophany that gave the Law in the first place. He did so to fulfill his covenantal promise to Abram, made when he passed in theophanic glory between the cut up animals of the covenant ceremony almost two millennia before.

Those who live in the already-not-yet epoch of the human story can recall that glorious ministry of Christ. We look upon his theophanic transformation and anticipate our own with faith and great yearning. Although the terrors of God's final advent outstrip the awesomeness of his first judgment advent to Adam and Eve and far exceed anything he did against Pharaoh and the gods of Egypt, believers in Christ long for that coming. For when he comes again, we shall be like him. We shall then at last know as we are known.

Until that day we must wait patiently. And as we wait, we can also spend time in his presence. With unveiled faces we may reflect his glory and be transformed into his likeness with ever-increasing glory, which comes from the Lord, who is the Spirit.[56]

---

[56] For an excellent recent discussion of God's reflected glory and Moses' veil at 2Co 3, see S. J. Hafemann, "The Glory and Veil of Moses in 2 Cor 3:7–14: An Example of Paul's Contextual Exegesis of the OT–A Proposal," *Horizons in Biblical Theology* 14 (1992): 31–39. Hafemann not only does justice to the theology of Ex 32–34, but also clarifies the long misinterpreted καταργέω of 2Co 3:7, 13.

◆ Afterword ◆

A major hierarchy of ideas forms the background to God's glory theophanies in the Old and New Testaments. A parallel hierarchy applies in the ancient Near East—not because biblical thought is a derivative of that milieu, but because the Bible presents a universally true structure of ideas. That order of ideas is as follows: God as King, God's kingdom, God's covenant(s), and God's covenant administration. The order is both theological and logical.

God as King, and his kingdom. God is everywhere and always a Great King. So it makes sense both biblically and epistemologically to speak of God's kingdom. Consequently Jesus could proclaim the "Gospel of the Kingdom" (Mt 4:23). Theophany plays a signal role in that kingdom, if only because the location and the advance of God's kingdom are always a habitation for the Spirit of God. In New Testament terms, that glory Spirit who tabernacled among Israel now also tabernacles in Christians. He was dynamically active at the Creation and is dynamically active now when a person becomes a new creation through faith in Christ (or when God heals the sick, for example).

God's covenants. As a Great King, God chooses to live in a covenant relation with chosen creatures. He is their Suzerain, and they are his vassals. So it was with Adam and Eve in the Creation covenant. In fact, major Old Testament covenants—the Noahic, the Abrahamic, the Mosaic, and the Davidic—were all initiated by God to prepare the way for the new covenant of Jesus Christ, through whom the goals of the original Creation covenant are attained: a new heaven and a new earth, and a new humanity to be God's people. God's Spirit has also been at work in all of God's covenant initiations. He hovered over the face of the deep at the Creation; he was apparent in the symbolic rainbow of the Noahic (re-Creation) covenant; he was a theophanic fire as Abram's covenant was solemnized; he was a shekinah glory before Moses on Mount Sinai; and his glory invested the temple at its dedication to affirm the Davidic covenant. Finally, he hovered over Jesus in the form of a dove to affirm the onset of the Son's new covenant work, and he hovered above the faithful in tongues of fire as God anointed them to carry forward that kingdom work.

God's covenant administration. God's glory Spirit has led in the past and leads today those who choose to obey God's covenant (cf. Gal 5:25). Our glorious Lord has also appeared on days of covenantal judgment—an unhappy side of his covenant administration. So he came on the clouds to judge the world at the Flood, and so he will come again on theophanic clouds to judge the world by a cosmic conflagration.

God's theophanies form an essential part of his self-revelation in all of these biblical covenants. Moreover, our appreciation of the biblical theophanies has been enhanced by the ancient Near Eastern data. Further study may produce yet more instructive parallels from the ancient world. Study of this sort has another value: It can illustrate the truth that the whole earth has been—and is—"full of God's glory." In a day and a culture that glory in rebellion against all that is ancient and true—in a day when much biblical scholarship shows a profound disregard for the true implications of ancient (biblical and extrabiblical) data—such a study can bless those who undertake it. It can illuminate God's word (even out of the pagan past) for those who read it. Evangelical scholarship has done well to begin its journey along this road and will do well to continue. In this and other ways, may God, who said "Let there be light," continue to cause light to shine out of darkness.

◆ Bibliography ◆

Abba, R. "Name." Pp. 500–508 in G. A. Buttrick, ed., *The Interpreter's Dictionary of the Bible*. Vol. 3. New York: Abingdon, 1962.

Albright, W. F. *Archaeology and the Religion of Israel*. Baltimore: Johns Hopkins Press, 1942.

———. "The Babylonian Matter in the Predeuteronomic Primeval History (JE) in Gen 1–11." *JBL* 58, pt. 2 (June 1939): 91–103.

Allen, W. C. *Gospel According to St. Matthew*. ICC. Edinburgh: T. & T. Clark, 1912.

Allis, O. T. *The Five Books of Moses*. Nutley, N.J.: Presbyterian and Reformed, 1943.

———. *The Old Testament: Its Claims and Its Critics*. Grand Rapids: Baker, 1972.

Alt, A. *Die Landnahme der Israeliten in Palästina*. Leipzig: Reformationsprogramm der Universität Leipzig, 1925.

———. *Die Ursprünge des israelitischen Rechts*. Berichte über die Verhandlungen der Sächsischen Akademie der Wissenschaften zu Leipzig, Phil.-hist. Klasse, Bd. 86, H.1 (Leipzig, 1934).

Andersen, F. I. *The Sentence in Biblical Hebrew*. The Hague: Mouton, 1974.

Anderson, B. W. *Out of the Depths*. Philadelphia: Westminster, 1983.

Armerding, C. E. "Habakkuk." *Daniel–Minor Prophets*. EBC. Vol. 7. Grand Rapids: Zondervan, 1985.

Augustine. *The City of God*. Trans. M. Dodds. New York: Random House, 1950.

Bailey, L. "Horns of Moses." Crim, K., et al., eds., *The Interpreter's Dictionary of the Bible*, Supplementary Volume. Nashville: Abingdon, 1976. Pp. 419–20.

Baltzer, K. *Das Bundesformular*. Neukirchen: Neukirchener Verlag, 1960. English version, *The Covenant Formulary*. Trans. D. E. Green. Philadelphia: Fortress, 1971.

Barnes, Wm. E. *The First Book of the Kings*. Cambridge: Cambridge University Press, 1911.

Batto, B. F. *Slaying the Dragon*. Louisville: Westminster/John Knox Press, 1992.
Beyerlin, W. *Herkunft und Geschichte der ältesten Sinaitraditionen*. Tübingen: J. C. B. Mohr, 1961. English version, *Origins and History of the Oldest Sinaitic Traditions*. Trans. S. Rudman. Oxford: Basil Blackwell, 1965.
Binns, L. E. *The Book of Numbers*. London: Methuen, 1927.
Block, D. I. *The Gods of the Nations*. ETS Monograph Series 2. Jackson: Evangelical Theological Society, 1988.
Borger, R. *Die Inschriften Asarhaddons Königs von Assyrien*. Graz, 1956.
____. *Einleitung in die assyrischen Königsinschriften*, erster Theil. Leiden: Brill, 1961.
Breasted, J. H. *Development of Religion and Thought in Ancient Egypt*. Philadelphia: University of Pennsylvania Press, 1972.
Briggs, A. C., and E. G. Briggs, *The Book of Psalms*. ICC. Vol. 1. New York: Scribners, 1906.
Brownlee, Wm. H. *Ezekiel 1-19*. WBC 28. Waco: Word Books, 1986.
Bruce, F. F. *The Epistle to the Hebrews*. Grand Rapids: Eerdmans, 1964.
____. *Habakkuk*. In T. E. McComiskey, ed., *The Minor Prophets*. Vol. 2. Grand Rapids: Baker, 1993.
Budd, P. J. *Numbers*. WBC 5. Waco: Word, 1984.
Buis, P., and J. Leclercq. *Le Deutéronome*. Paris: Librarie Lecoffre, 1963.
Burrows, M. *An Outline of Biblical Theology*. Philadelphia: Westminster, 1946.
Calvin, J. *Commentaries on the First Book of Moses Called Genesis*. Vol. 1. Edinburgh: Calvin Translation Society, 1847.
____. *Commentaries on the Last Four Books of Moses*. Vol. 3. Trans. C. Wm. Bingham. Grand Rapids: Eerdmans, 1950.
____. *Commentaries on the Twelve Minor Prophets*. Vol. 4. Trans. J. Owen. Edinburgh: Calvin Translation Society, 1848.
____. *Hebrews and I and II Peter*. Trans. Wm. B. Johnston. Grand Rapids: Eerdmans, 1963.
Caquot, A., M. Sznycer, and A. Herdner. *Textes Ougaritiques*. Vol. 1. *Mythes et Legendes*. Paris: Editions du Cerf, 1974.
Carpenter, J. E., and G. Harford. *The Composition of the Hexateuch*. London: Longmans, Green & Co., 1902.

Cassuto, U. *A Commentary on the Book of Exodus.* Trans. I. Abrahams. Jerusalem: Magnes, 1967.
———. *A Commentary on the Book of Genesis.* Jerusalem: Magnes, 1961.
———. *Biblical and Oriental Studies.* Vol. 2. Jerusalem: Magnes, 1975.
———. *The Documentary Hypothesis.* Jerusalem: Magnes, 1961.
Charles, R. H. *The Revelation of St. John.* Vol. 1. ICC. Edinburgh: T. & T. Clark, 1920.
Clifford, R. J. *The Cosmic Mountain in Canaan and the Old Testament.* Cambridge: Harvard, 1972.
———. "The Tent of El and the Israelite Tent of Meeting." *CBQ* 33, no. 2 (April 1971): 221–29.
Cogan, M. *Imperialism and Religion: Assyria, Judah and Israel in the Eighth and Seventh Centuries B.C.E.* SBL Monograph Series 19. Missoula: Scholars Press, 1974.
Colenso, J. Wm. *The Pentateuch and Book of Joshua Critically Considered.* London: Longmans, Green, and Co., 1875.
Coogan, M. D. *Stories From Ancient Canaan.* Philadelphia: Westminster, 1978.
Cooper, J. S. *Sumerian and Akkadian Royal Inscriptions, I.* Presargonic Inscriptions. New Haven: The American Oriental Society, 1986.
Craigie, P. C. *The Book of Deuteronomy.* NICOT. Grand Rapids: Eerdmans, 1976.
———. *Ezekiel.* Philadelphia: Westminster, 1983.
———. *Psalms 1–50.* WBC. Waco: Word, 1983.
———. *Twelve Prophets.* Vol. 2. Philadelphia: Westminster, 1985.
Crim, K., et al., eds. *The Interpreter's Dictionary of the Bible,* Supplementary Volume. Nashville: Abingdon, 1976.
Cross, F. M. "Notes on a Canaanite Psalm in the Old Testament." *BASOR.* 117 (1950): 19–21.
———. *Canaanite Myth and Hebrew Epic.* Cambridge: Harvard University Press, 1973.
Cundall, A., and L. Morris. *Judges & Ruth.* London: Tyndale, 1968.
Dahood, M. "Hebrew-Ugaritic Lexicography I." *Biblica* 44 (1963): 289–303.
———. *Psalms I.* Anchor Bible. New York: Doubleday, 1966.
Davis, J. J. *Moses and the Gods of Egypt.* 2d ed. Grand Rapids: Baker, 1986.

Day, J. "Echoes of Baal's Seven Thunders and Lightnings in Psalm XXIX and Habakkuk III 9 and the Identity of the Seraphim in Isaiah VI." *VT* 29 (1979): 143–51.

Delitzsch, Franz. *Psalms, Commentary on the Old Testament.* Vol. 5. Grand Rapids: Eerdmans, 1976.

Delitzsch, Friedrich. *Babel and Bible.* New York: G. P. Putnam's Sons, 1903.

De Vries, S. J. "A Review of Recent Research in the Tradition History of the Pentateuch." *SBL* Abstracts and Seminar Papers 26 (1987). Pp. 459–502.

de Wette, W. M. L. *Dissertatio critica qua Deuteronomium a prioribus Pentateuchi libris diversum alius cuiusdam recentioris opus esse monstratur* (Jena, 1805).

_____. *Kritik der Israelitischen Geschichte, Erster Theil: Kritik der Mosäischen Geschichte.* Halle: Schimmelpfenning & Co., 1807.

_____, and E. Schrader. *Lehrbuch der historisch-kritischen Einleitung in die kanonischen und apokryphischen Bücher des Alten Testaments.* Berlin: Georg Reimer, 1869.

Dossin, G. "Les Archives Epistolaire du Palais de Mari." *Syria* (1938).

Douglas, J. D. ed. *The Illustrated Bible Dictionary.* Vol. 1. Leicester: Inter-Varsity Press, 1980.

Dozeman, T. B. *God on the Mountain.* SBL Monograph Series 37. Atlanta: Scholars Press, 1989.

Driver, S. R. *The Book of Daniel.* Cambridge: Cambridge University Press, 1922.

_____. *The Book of Exodus.* Cambridge: Cambridge University Press, 1911.

_____. *The Book of Genesis.* London: Methuen, 1904.

_____. *An Introduction to the Literature of the Old Testament.* 9th ed. Edinburgh: T. & T. Clark, 1913.

Dumbrell, W. I. *Covenant and Creation.* Nashville: Nelson, 1984.

Edersheim, A. *History of Judah and Israel.* London: Religious Tract Society, 1880.

Eichhorn, J. G. *Einleitung in das Alte Testament.* Göttingen: Karl Eduard Rosenbusch, 1823.

Eichrodt, W. *Ezekiel, A Commentary.* Trans. C. Quin. Philadelphia: Westminster, 1975.

_____. *Theology of the Old Testament.* Vol. 2. Trans. J. A. Baker. Philadelphia: Westminster, 1967.

Eissfeldt, O. *Einleitung in das Alte Testament.* Tübingen: J. C. B. Mohr, 1934. English translation by P. R. Ackroyd: O. Eissfeldt. *The Old Testament—An Introduction.* New York: Harper & Row, 1965.

Emerton, J. A. "Leviathan and *LTN:* The Vocalization of the Ugaritic Word for the Dragon." *VT* 32, fasc. 3 (1982): 327–31.

Frankfort, H. J. *Cylinder Seals.* London, 1939.

_____. *Kingship and the Gods: A Study of Ancient Near Eastern Religion as the Integration of Society and Nature.* Chicago: University of Chicago Press, 1948.

Gaballa, G. A. "Minor War Scenes of Ramesses II at Karnak." *JEA* 55 (1969).

Gaebelein, A. C. *The Prophet Daniel.* Grand Rapids: Kregel, 1955.

Garrett, D. *Rethinking Genesis.* Grand Rapids: Baker, 1991.

Gaster, T. H. "Psalm 29." *JQR* 37 (1946–47): 55–65.

Gibson, J. C. L. *Canaanite Myths and Legends.* Edinburgh: T. & T. Clark, 1978.

Ginsberg, H. L. "A Phoenician Hymn in the Psalter." *XIX Congresso Internazionale degli Orientalisti* (Rome, 1935): 472–76.

_____. "The Rebellion and Death of Ba^{c}lu." *Orientalia* 5 (1936).

Gispen, W. H. *Exodus.* Grand Rapids: Zondervan, 1982.

Gordon, C. "Higher Critics and Forbidden Fruit." *CT* 4 (1949): 3–6.

_____. *Ugaritic Textbook.* Rome: Pontificium Institutum Biblicum, 1965.

Götze, A. *Die Annalen des Muršiliš.* Darmstadt: Wissenschaftliche Buchgesellschaft, 1967.

Gray, J. *I & II Kings.* 2d ed. Philadelphia: Westminster, 1970.

_____, ed. *Joshua, Judges and Ruth.* Century Bible. London: Nelson, 1967.

Grayson, A. K. *Assyrian Royal Inscriptions.* Vol. 1. Wiesbaden: Harrassowitz, 1972.

_____. *Assyrian Royal Inscriptions.* Vol. 2. Wiesbaden: Harrassowitz, 1976.

_____. *Assyrian Rulers of the Third and Second Millennia B.C.* The Royal Inscriptions of Mesopotamia, Assyrian Periods. Vol. 1. Toronto: University of Toronto Press, 1987.

Greig, G., and K. Springer. *The Kingdom and the Power.* Ventura: Regal, 1993.
Gundry, R. H. *Matthew.* Grand Rapids: Eerdmans, 1982.
Gunkel, H. "Der Schreiberengel Nabu im Alten Testament und im Judentum." *Archiv fur Religionswissenschaft* 1 (1898).
_____. *Genesis.* 6th ed. Göttingen: Vandenhoeck & Ruprecht, 1964.
_____. *The Legends of Genesis.* New York: Schocken, 1964.
_____. *Schöpfung und Chaos in Urzeit und Endzeit.* Göttingen: Vandenhoeck & Ruprecht, 1895.
Gurney, O. R. *Some Aspects of Hittite Religion.* The Schweich Lectures 1976. Oxford: Oxford University Press, 1977.
Güterbock, H. G. "The Vocative in Hittite." *JAOS* 65 (1945): 248–57.
Hafemann, S. J. "The Glory and Veil of Moses in 2 Cor 3:7–14: An Example of Paul's Contextual Exegesis of the OT–A Proposal." *Horizons in Biblical Theology* 14 (1992): 31–39.
Hallo, Wm. W., and J. J. A. van Dijk. *The Exaltation of Inanna.* Yale Near Eastern Researches 3. New Haven: Yale University Press, 1968.
Harrington, W. J. *Revelation.* Collegeville: Liturgical Press, 1993.
Harrison, R. K. *Introduction to the Old Testament.* Grand Rapids, Eerdmans, 1969.
Hasel, G. "The Meaning of the Animal Rite in Gen. 15." *JSOT* 19 (1981): 61–78.
Heidel, A. *The Babylonian Genesis.* 2d ed. Chicago: University of Chicago Press, 1951.
Hendriksen, Wm. *The Gospel of Luke.* Grand Rapids: Baker, 1978.
Herdner, A. *Corpus des Tablettes en Cunéiformes Alphabétiques: découvertes à Ras Shamra-Ugarit de 1929 à 1939* (=Mission de Ras Shamra 10) Paris, 1963.
Hoffner, H. A., Jr. *Hittite Myths.* SBL Writings From the Ancient World 2. Atlanta: Scholars Press, 1990.
Holladay, Wm. *A Concise Hebrew and Aramaic Lexicon of the Old Testament.* Grand Rapids: Eerdmans: 1971.
Huffmon, H. B. "The Covenant Lawsuit in the Prophets." *JBL* 78 (1959): 285–95.
Isbell, C. D. *Corpus of the Aramaic Incantation Bowls.* Missoula: Scholars Press, 1975.

Jacobsen, T. *The Sumerian King List*. Chicago: University of Chicago Press, 1939.

Jeremias, J. *Theophanie: Die Geschichte einer alttestamentlichen Gattung, Wissenschaftliche Monographien zum Alten und Neuen Testament*. Neukirchen-Vluyn: Neukirchener Verlag, 1965.

Keil, C. F., and F. Delitzsch. *Commentary on the Old Testament in Ten Volumes*. Grand Rapids: Eerdmans, 1978.

Kidner, D. *Genesis*. London: Tyndale, 1967.

_____. *Psalms 1-72*. Leicester: Tyndale, 1973.

Kikawada I. M., and A. Quinn. *Before Abraham Was*. Nashville: Abingdon, 1985.

King, L. W. *Annals of the Kings of Assyria*. Vol. 1. Ed. E. A. W. Budge. London: Harrison and Sons, 1902.

Kirkpatrick, A. F. *The Psalms I-XLI*. Bk. 1. Cambridge: Cambridge University Press, 1891.

Kistemaker, S. J. *Acts*. Grand Rapids: Baker, 1990.

_____. *Hebrews*. Grand Rapids: Baker, 1984.

Kitchen, K. A. *Ancient Orient and Old Testament*. Chicago: InterVarsity Press, 1973.

_____. *The Bible in Its World*. Downers Grove: InterVarsity Press, 1978.

_____. "Egypt, Ugarit, Qatna and Covenant." *Ugarit-Forschungen*. Band 11. Neukirchen-Vluyn: Neukirchener Verlag, 1979. Pp. 453-64.

Kittel, G., and G. Friedrich. *Theologisches Handwörterbuch zum Neuen Testament*, Bd. IX. Stuttgart: W. Kohlhammer, 1973.

Kline, M. G. *Images of the Spirit*. Grand Rapids: Baker, 1980.

_____. *Kingdom Prologue*. South Hamilton: Gordon-Conwell Seminary, 1986.

_____. *Treaty of the Great King*. Grand Rapids: Eerdmans, 1963.

Knudtzon, J. A., ed. *Die El-Amarna Tafeln*. Leipzig: Otto Zeller, 1915.

Köhler, L. *Old Testament Theology*. Trans. A. S. Todd. Philadelphia: Westminster, 1957.

Kramer, S. F. "Kingship in Sumer and Akkad: The Ideal King." *RAI* 19, pp. 163-66.

Kuenen, A. *The Origin and Composition of the Hexateuch*. Trans. P. H. Wicksteed. London: Macmillan, 1886.

Kuntz, J. K. *The Self-Revelation of God*. Philadelphia: Westminster, 1967.

Kutscher, R. *Oh Angry Sea, The History of a Sumerian Congregational Lament.* New Haven: Yale University Press, 1975.
Ladd, G. E. *A Commentary on the Revelation of John.* Grand Rapids: Eerdmans, 1972.
Lambert, W. G. "Three Unpublished Fragments of the Tukulti-Ninurta Epic." *AfO* 18 (Graz: 1957–58): 38–51.
____, and A. R. Millard. *Atra-Ḫasis.* Oxford: Clarendon, 1969.
Langdon, S. *Die Neubabylonischen Königsinschriften.*VAB 4. Leipzig: J. C. Hinrichs, 1912.
Laughlin, J. C. H. "The 'Strange Fire' of Nadab and Abihu." *JBL* 95 (1976): 559–65.
Liddell, H. G., and R. Scott. *A Lexicon.* Oxford University Press: London, 1974.
Lindblom, J. "Theophanies in Holy Places in Hebrew Religion." *HUCA* 32 (1961): 91–106.
Lipinski, E. *La Royauté de Yahwé dans la poésie et le culte de l'ancien Israël.* Brussels: Paleis der Academiën, 1965.
Livingston, H. G. *The Pentateuch in Its Cultural Environment.* 2d ed. Grand Rapids: Baker, 1987.
Longenecker, R. *Biblical Exegesis in the Apostolic Period.* Grand Rapids: Eerdmans, 1975.
Longman, T. III. *Fictional Akkadian Autobiography.* Winona Lake: Eisenbrauns, 1991.
Luckenbill, D. D. *The Annals of Sennacherib.* Chicago: University of Chicago Press, 1924.
Lumby, J. R. *The First Book of the Kings.* Cambridge: Cambridge University Press, 1890.
Lust, J. "A Gentle Breeze or a Roaring Thunderous Sound?" *VT* 25 (1975): 110–15.
Machinist, P. "Literature as Politics: The Tukulti-Ninurta Epic and the Bible." *CBQ* 38 (1976): 455–82.
Maclaren, A. *The Psalms.* Vol. 1. London: Hodder & Stoughton, 1894.
Macmillan, K. D. "Some Cuneiform Tablets Bearing on the Religion of Babylonia and Assyria," in F. Delitzsch and P. Haupt, *Beiträge zur Assyriologie.* Leipzig: J. C. Hinrichs, 1906.
Mann, T. W. *Divine Presence and Guidance in Israelite Traditions.* Baltimore: Johns Hopkins University Press, 1977.

Matthews, I. G. *Ezekiel*. American Commentary on the Old Testament. Vol. 21. Chicago: American Baptist Publication Society, 1939.

May, H. G. "Some Cosmic Connotations of *Mayim Rabbim*, 'Many Waters,' " *JBL* 74 (1955): 9–21.

Mayes, A. D. H. *Israel in the Period of the Judges*. Studies in Biblical Theology, 2d ser., 59 Naperville: Alec R. Allenson, 1974.

McCarthy, D. J. "Three Covenants in Genesis." *CBQ* 26 (1964): 179–89.

———. *Treaty and Covenant*. Analecta Biblica 21A. Rome: Biblical Institute Press, 1978.

Mendenhall, G. E. "Covenant Forms in Israelite Tradition." *BA* 17 (1954): 49–76.

———. "The Hebrew Conquest of Palestine." *BA* 25, no. 3 (September 1962): 66–87; rpt. *The Biblical Archaeologist Reader* 3. New York: Anchor Books, 1970. Pp. 100–120.

———. *The Tenth Generation*. Baltimore: Johns Hopkins University Press, 1973.

Miller, P. D. *The Divine Warrior in Early Israel*. Harvard Semitic Monographs 5. Cambridge: Harvard University Press, 1973.

Moberly, R. W. L. *At the Mountain of God*. JSOT Supplement Series 22. Sheffield: JSOT Press, 1983.

Morgenstern, J. "Biblical Theophanies." ZA 25 (1911): 139–93; 28 (1913): 15–60.

Morris, L. *The Gospel According to John*. NICNT. Grand Rapids: Eerdmans, 1971.

Mounce, R. H. *The Book of Revelation*. Grand Rapids: Eerdmans, 1977.

Mowinckel, Sigmund. *He That Cometh*. Trans. G. W. Anderson. Nashville: Abingdon, 1954.

———. *Le Décalogue, Études d'Histoire et de Philosophie Religieuses*. Paris: F. Alcan 1927.

———. *The Psalms in Israel's Worship*. Vol. 1. Trans. D. R. Ap-Thomas. New York: Abingdon, 1962.

Nicholson, E. W. *Preaching to the Exiles*. Oxford: Basil Blackwell, 1970.

Niehaus, J. *Amos*. In T. E. McComiskey, ed., *The Minor Prophets: An Exegetical and Expository Commentary*. Vol. 1. Grand Rapids: Baker, 1992.

_____. "The Central Sanctuary: Where and When?" *TB* 43, no.1 (May 1992): 3–30.

_____. "In the Wind of the Storm: Another Look at Genesis iii 8." *VT* 44, no. 2 (April 1994): 263–67.

_____. "Joshua and Ancient Near Eastern Warfare." *JETS* 31, no. 1 (March 1988): 37–50.

_____. "Old Testament Foundations." Pp. 41–53 in G. Greig and K. Springer, eds, *The Kindgom and the Power*.Ventura: Regal, 1993.

_____. "*Pa'am 'ehat* and the Israelite Conquest." *VT* 30 (1980): 236–39.

_____. "RĀZ–PEŠAR, in Isaiah XXIV." *VT* 31, n. 3 (1981): 376–77.

Norden, E. *Agnostos Theos: Untersuchungen zur Formengeschichtliche religiöser Rede*. Leipzig/Berlin: B. G. Tuebner, 1913.

Noth, M. *Das Buch Josua*. Handbuch zum Alten Testament. Vol. 7. Tübingen: J. C. B. Mohr, 1953.

_____. *Exodus*. Philadelphia: Westminster, 1962.

_____. *The History of Israel*. 2d ed. New York: Harper & Row, 1960.

_____. *Leviticus*. Trans. J. E. Anderson. London: SCM Press, 1965.

_____. *Numbers*. Trans. J. D. Martin. Philadelphia: Westminster, 1968.

_____. *Das System der zwölf Stämme Israels, Beiträge zur Wissenschaft vom Alten und Neuen Testament*. Vol. 4.1. Stuttgart: W. Kohlhammer, 1930.

_____. *Überlieferungsgeschichte des Pentateuch*. Stuttgart, 1948. English translation by B. W. Anderson. *A History of Pentateuchal Traditions*. Englewood Cliffs: Prentice-Hall, 1972.

_____. *Überlieferungsgeschichtliche Studien*. 2d ed. Tübingen: Max Niemeyer, 1957. Pp. 1–110. Translated into English by J. Doull, J. Barton, et al. as *The Deuteronomistic History*. JSOT Supplement Series 15. Sheffield: JSOT Press, 1981.

Oppenheim, A. L. *Ancient Mesopotamia, Portrait of a Dead Civilization*. Chicago: University of Chicago Press, 1964.

Orr, J. *The Problem of the Old Testament*. New York: Scribners, 1907.

Piepkorn, A. C., *Historical Prism Inscriptions of Ashurbanipal*, I. Chicago: University of Chicago Press, 1933.

Plummer, A., *The Gospel According to St. Luke*. 5th ed. ICC. Edinburgh: T. & T. Clark, 1922.

Pritchard, J. B. *The Ancient Near East in Pictures*. Princeton: Princeton University Press, 1954.

_____. *Ancient Near Eastern Texts Relating to the Old Testament*. 3d ed. Princeton: Princton University Press, 1969.

Pythian-Adams, W. J. "The Volcanic Phenomena of the Exodus." *JPOS* 12 (1932): 86–103.

Rendtorff, R. *Das überlieferungsgeschichtliche Problem des Pentateuch*. Beihefte zur *ZAW* 147. Berlin: de Gruyter, 1977.

_____. "'Offenbarung' im Alten Testament." *Theologische Literaturzeitung*. Vol. 85 (1960), col. 833.

Ringren, H. *Israelite Religion*. Trans. D. E. Green. Philadelphia: Fortress, 1966.

_____. *Word and Wisdom*. Lund: Håkan Ohlssons Boktryckeri, 1947.

Robinson, H. W. *Inspiration and Revelation in the Old Testament*. Oxford: Clarendon, 1946.

Rost, P. *Die Keilschrifttexte Tiglat-Pilesers III*. Bd. 1. Leipzig: Verlag von Eduard Pfeiffer, 1893.

Rowley, H. H. *The Faith of Israel*. Philadelphia: Westminster, 1956.

Rudolph, W. *Micha–Nahum–Habakuk–Zephanja*. KAT 13.3. Gutersloh: Gerd Mohn, 1975.

Rushton, H. F. *Virgil*. Vol. 1. London: Heinemann, 1925.

Rylaarsdam, J. C. "Introduction and Exegesis to the Book of Exodus." *IB*. Vol. 1, pp. 833–1099.

Saggs, H. W. F. *The Greatness That Was Babylon*. New York: Hawthorn, 1962.

Sarna, N. F. *Exploring Exodus*. New York: Schocken, 1986.

Sayce, A. H. *Monument Facts and Higher Critical Fancies*. London: Religious Tract Society, 1904.

Schramm, W. F. "Die Annalen des Assyrischen Königs Tukulti-Ninurta II." *BO* 27, no. 3/4 (May–July): 1970, 147–60.

_____. *Einleitung in die assyrischen Königsinschriften*, zweiter Theil. Leiden: Brill, 1973.

Scott, C. A. *Revelation*. Edinburgh: T. C. & E. C. Jack, 1901.

Smith, G. A. *The Book of Isaiah*. Vol. 1. London: Hodder and Stoughton, 1897.

_____. *The Book of the Twelve Prophets*, Vol. II New York: A. C. Armstrong and Son, 1898.

Soden, W. F. von, *Akkadisches Handwörterbuch*, 3 Vols. Wiesbaden: Harrassowitz, 1965–68.

Sollberger, E. "Samsu-iluna's Bilingual Inscriptions C and D." *RA* LXIII, No. 1 1969, pp. 29–43.
Sperber, J. "Der Personenwechsel in der Bibel." *ZA* 21 1918/19, pp. 23–33.
Stek, J. H. "Elijah." *ISBE.* Vol 2. Grand Rapids: Eerdmans, 1982. Pp. 64–68.
Stuart, D. *Ezekiel*, The Communicator's Commentary 18 Dallas: Word, 1989.
____. *Hosea-Jonah.* WBC. Waco: Word, 1987.
Sturdy, J. *Numbers.* Cambridge: Cambridge University Press, 1972.
Tallqvist, K. *Akkadische Götterepitheta.* Helsinki: Druckerei-A.G. der finnischen Literaturgesellschaft, 1938.
Thompson, J. A. *Deuteronomy.* Leicester: Inter-Varsity Press, 1974.
Thompson, R. C., and R. W. Hutchinson. "The Excavations of the Temple of Nabu at Nineveh." *Archaeologia.* Vol. 79 (2d ser., vol. 29; 1929): 103–48.
Thompson, R. C., and M. E. L. Mallowen, "The British Museum Excavations at Nineveh, 1931–32." *University of Liverpool Annals of Archaeology and Anthropology.* Vol. 20 (1933): 71–127.
Thureau-Dangin, F. *Die Sumerischen und Akkadischen Königsinschriften.* Leipig: Hinrichs, 1907.
____. *Une Relation de la Huitième Campagne de Sargon.* Paris: Geuthner, Librarie Paul Geuthner, 1912.
Unger, M. F. *Introductory Guide to the Old Testament.* Grand Rapids: Zondervan, 1951.
von Rad, G. *Beiträge zur Wissenschaft vom Alten und Neuen Testament.* 4th ser. Vol. 26. Stuttgart, 1938.
____. *Old Testament Theology.* Vol. 1. Trans. D. M. G. Stalker. New York: Harper & Row, 1961.
____. *Old Testament Theology.* Vol. 2. Trans. D. M. G. Stalker. New York: Harper & Row, 1965.
____. *The Problem of the Hexateuch and Other Essays.* Edinburgh: Oliver & Boyd, 1966.
Vos, G. *Biblical Theology.* Grand Rapids: Eerdmans, 1948.
Vriezen, Th. C. *An Outline of Old Testament Theology.* Oxford: Basil Blackwell, 1958.
Wakeman, M. K. *God's Battle With the Monster.* Leiden: E. J. Brill, 1973.

Walvoord, J. F. *Daniel*. Chicago: Moody, 1971.
Weidner, E. F. *Die Inschriften Tukulti Ninurtas 1. und seiner Nachfolger*. Graz, 1959.
____. "Die Kämpfe Adadniraris I. gegen Ḫanigalbat." *AfO* 5 (Berlin, 1928–29): 89–100.
____. *Politische Dokumente aus Kleinasien, Die Staatsverträge in Akkadischer Sprache aus dem Archiv von Boghasköi*. Boghasköi Studien 8–9. Leipzig: J. C. Hinrichs, 1923.
Weinfeld, M. *Deuteronomy and the Deuteronomic School*. Oxford: Clarendon, 1972.
Weippert, M. *Die Landnahme der israelitischen Stämme in der neueren wissenschaftlichen Diskussion*. 1967.
Wellhausen, J. *Israelitische und Jüdische Geschichte*, zweite Ausgabe. Berlin: Georg Reimer, 1895.
____. *Prolegomena to the History of Ancient Israel*. Glocester: Peter Smith, 1973.
____. *Skizzen und Vorarbeiten*. Vol. 5. *Die kleinen Propheten übersetzt, mit Noten*. Berlin: Reimer, 1893.
Wenham, G. J. *The Book of Leviticus*, NICOT Grand Rapids: Eerdmans, 1979.
____. "Deuteronomy and the Central Sanctuary." *TB* 22 (1971): 103–18.
____. *Genesis 1–15*. Waco: Word, 1987.
____. "The Symbolism of the Animal Rite in Gen. 15: A Response to G. F. Hasel." *JSOT* 19 (1981): 61–78; 22 (1982): 134–37.
Whitehead, A. N. *Science and the Modern World*. New York: Free Press, 1967.
Whybray, R. N. *The Making of the Pentateuch*, JSOT Supplement Series 53. Sheffield: JSOT Press, 1987.
Winckler, H. *Die Gezetze Hammurabis*. Leipzig: J. C. Hinrichs, 1903.
Wiseman, D. J. "A New Stela of Aššur-naṣir-pal II." *Iraq* 14 (1952): 24–44.
Woudstra, M. H. *The Book of Joshua*. NICOT. Grand Rapids: Eerdmans, 1981.
Wright, G. E. "The Lawsuit of God: A Form-Critical Study of Deuteronomy 32." Pp. 26–46 in B. W. Anderson and W. Harrelson, eds., *Israel's Prophetic Heritage*. New York: Harper & Bros., 1962.

_____. "The Literary and Historical Problem of Joshua 10 and Judges 1." *JNES* 5 (April 1946): 105–14.

Yadin, Y. "Military and Archaeological Aspects of the Conquest of Canaan in the Book of Joshua." *'EL HA'AYIN* (Jerusalem, 1960): 1–13.

Young, E. J. *The Book of Isaiah*. Vol. 1. Grand Rapids: Eerdmans, 1965.

_____. *An Introduction to the Old Testament*. Grand Rapids: Eerdmans, 1949.

_____. *The Prophecy of Daniel*. Grand Rapids: Eerdmans, 1949.

Scripture Index

Genesis
1–11	46 n.13, 163 n.60
1	109, 145 n.12, 169, 174 n.91, 182, 287
1:1–2:3	84, 86, 91, 94, 143–47, 147 n.14, 152 n.29
1:1	145, 348
1:2	77, 142, 143, 146 n.13, 150–53, 153 n.34, 161 n.54, 171, 182, 205, 361
1:2–31	198
1:2–29	145
1:6	264
1:9–10	330
1:26	260
1:27–30	150, 154
1:27–28a	154
1:27	169, 203
1:28–30	23 n.50, 179
1:28b–30a	154
1:28	143, 145, 146, 170
1:29	170
1:30b	154
1:31	146
2:1	146
2:2	200
2:3	146
2:4a	143 n.5
2:7	371
2:15–17	150, 154–55
2:16–17a	145
2:16–17	23 n.50
2:16	146
2:17a	146
2:17b	146
2:21	172
3:8–24	33, 34
3:8–18	109
3:8–10	77
3:8	18, 23 n.19, 28, 33, 142, 143, 144, 150, 152, 155, 157 n.45, 158 nn.45–46, 158, 160 n.50, 161 n.52, 178, 255, 258, 314, 318, 367, 372
3:9	33
3:10	33, 159
3:11	33
3:12	33
3:13ab	33
3:14–19	33
3:14–15	33
3:15	179
3:16	33
3:17–19	33
3:20–24	33
3:22	179
3:24	258, 295
4:14	314
5:1	260
6–9	262 n.60
6:13–21	160
6:17	168 and n.78
7:1–4	160
7:6, 7, 11, 17	168 n.78
7:11	299, 320
7:16b	160 n.51
8:1	153–54 n.34, 161 n.54
8:1–2	153 n.34
8:15–17	160
9	261
9:1	169
9:1–17	94
9:2	169
9:3	169

9:6b	169
9:8–17	147 n.14
9:9	170
9:12ff.	146 n.13, 265
9:14	160
9:16	147 n.15
12:7	237 n.12
14	44 n.8
15	36 and n.56, 49, 77, 109, 142, 172, 174–77 and nn.99–100, 178 nn.102/104, 178
15:1	36, 172
15:1–6	36 n.57, 172 n.88
15:7–21	94
15:7–11	36 and n.57, 38, 172 n.88
15:7	36, 172, 174, 287
15:8	36
15:9	36
15:10–11	36
15:10	176
15:12–16	36 n.57, 172 and n.88
15:12–13a	172
15:13b–16	172
15:16	175
15:17–21	30, 172
15:17	173, 179, 318, 326, 331
15:17–18	36 n.57, 172 n.88, 173, 340
15:17–18a	173
15:18–21	175
15:18b–21	173
15:18a	173
15:18	173
16:7–14	19 n.8
17	49
18:1–2ff.	19 n.7
18:1ff.	233
18:10	238, 239, 356
18:11–14	239 n.18
18:11	239
18:12	357
18:25	25 n.28, 84
18:26	320
19:28	196
20:3–8	359
20:4b–5	359
20:6–7	359
20:7	359 n.33
26:23–25	32 n.49
26:24–25	237 n.12
26:26–31	197
26:30	198
31:11–13	19 n.9
31:40	236 n.11
31:44–54	197
32:24–30	19 n.7
32:31	221
35:7	237 n.12
49:24	185

Exodus

1–2	185
2:16	51
2:21–22	185
3–4, 19	109
3:1–4:17	186, 197
3:1–6, 9–14	53
3:1–4:7	185
3:1–4a	186
3:1	51, 54, 185
3:2–6	19 n.8
3:2–4a	54
3:2	187, 234 n.3, 307, 317, 331
3:4	187, 234 n.3
3:4b	54, 186
3:4c	186
3:5–6	186
3:5	24, 51, 54, 186, 188, 232, 236 n.8
3:6	27, 54, 186, 189, 227, 247
3:7–22	24
3:7–9a	54
3:7–8a	186
3:7–8	54, 186
3:7–8, 15–22	53
3:7	219
3:8b–10	186
3:8–4:17	188
3:9–15	54
3:9b–13	54
3:10ff.	30

SCRIPTURE INDEX

Reference	Page	Reference	Page
3:11	186	13–14	185
3:11, 13	188	13	135, 204
3:12	186, 235	13:5	287
3:13–14	241	13:19	219
3:13	186	13:21–22	179, 189, 195, 318
3:14–22	186	13:21	161 n.52, 179, 190, 201
3:14	24, 25 n.28, 54, 188	13:22	179, 190, 201
3:15	54, 373	14	135, 204
3:16–18	54	14:9	293
3:19–22	54	14:9, 23	293
3:19–21	54	14:13, 30–31	75
3:19	219	14:16ff.	293
3:20	373	14:19–24	19 n.9
4:1ff.	235	14:19	179, 189, 190, 266, 318
4:1, 10, 13	188, 235	14:20	179, 189, 218, 309
4:1	186	14:21	135
4:2ff.	236 n.9	14:22	296
4:2–9	186	14:24	179, 189, 204, 291, 318
4:8ff.	236 n.10	15	113, 135, 281, 301
4:10	186	15:1	215 n.46
4:11–12	186	15:1ff.	293
4:13	186	15:1, 21	293
4:14–17	186	15:2	293
4:18	186	15:2, 13	290, 299
4:21	231	15:3	297
5:16	308	15:4	293
5:23	373	15:5, 8	293, 299
6:2c–3	188 n.11	15:6–8	296
6:6	23 n.24, 308	15:6, 12	23 n.25
7:3	373	15:6	287, 305
7:3, 13, 14, 22	231	15:7	23 n.20, 319
7:5	373	15:8–10	114
7:8ff.	236 n.10	15:8	135, 303, 318
7:14–12:30	339 n.8	15:10	303, 307
9	196	15:11	240 n.22, 241 n.24, 242 and n.25, 285, 297, 305
9:8, 10	196	15:12	215 n.46
9:16	297, 373	15:13	299
9:27	319	15:14	291, 297
10:19	297	15:15–16	291
10:22	309	15:16–17	296
10:23	321	15:16	299, 300
12:7ff.	273	15:17	114, 284, 299
12:21–23	114	15:18	85
12:23	271	15:19	293
12:24	147		

16:5	84	19:20	224
16:32	215	19:20–25	53, 54
17:6	310	19:20–22	54
17:15	237 n.12	19:21b–22	196
18–21	197	19:22	209
19	52 n.35, 74	19:23	54, 196
19ff.	247	19:24	54, 196, 209
19–24	30, 62, 185	20	195
19:1–2a	54	20:1–31:18	197
19:1–2ab	53	20:1–17	63, 196
19:1–2	64	20:2	174
19:2b–8	63	20:3	140
19:2b–3a	54	20:13	336
19:2a	54	20:14	336
19:3c–19	54	20:18–21	63
19:3b–9	54	20:18–20	338
19:3b–6	54	20:18–19	295 n.24, 338
19:3a	54	20:18	158, 195, 326
19:4	153	20:19	236
19:6	197	20:20	237, 343, 338
19:6, 10, 14	26 n.30	20:21	195, 244, 309
19:7–11a	54	21:24	336
19:9a	63	23	195
19:9	74, 161 n.52, 179, 195, 303	23:17	331
19:9, 18	297	23:20–23	191
19:10–11a	54, 63	23:20–22	300
19:10–11	197	23:20	191
19:11b–13	54, 63	23:21	192, 194
19:11b	64 n.87	23:22	192
19:12–13	197	23:23	192
19:14–17	54	24	64, 197, 252, 258, 267
19:14–15	63	24:1–2, 9–11	63
19:16	23 n.19, 179, 195, 218, 248, 304, 307, 310, 326, 331, 340	24:3–8	63
		24:5	60
		24:5–8	99 n.80
19:16–21a	196	24:9–11	337
19:16–20:17	196	24:9–10	344
19:16–19	28, 248, 338	24:9	338
19:16–17, 19	63	24:9, 11	347
19:16, 18	318	24:10–11	323
19:16, 19	285	24:10	198, 252, 258, 290 n.11, 323
19:18	52 n.35, 54, 179, 195, 218, 248, 291, 297, 303, 305, 318, 340	24:11	198, 252
		24:11b	59
19:19	54, 74	24:15–18	198

24:15b–18a	64
24:15	338
24:16	251, 318, 337 n.5
24:17a	207 n.34
24:17	209, 218, 331
25:1–31:18	200
25:9	267 n.77
25:9, 40	117
25:18ff.	305
26:30	117
27:8	117
28:4, 31(LXX)	376 n.48
28:17ff.	347 n.15
28:33–34	117
29:42–43	25
30:9	208 n.37
30:27	307
31:3	117
32:19	245
33:7ff.	190, 191
33:7–11	185, 276
33:7	200
33:9ff.	243 n.26
33:9–11	201
33:9, 10	190, 268
33:10	265
33:11	121, 221, 310
33:12–23	212 n.42
33:14	191, 296
33:18–23	121 n.40, 185
33:18	245, 247
33:19–34:3	245
33:19	245, 246, 247
33:20	28, 221, 224
34	290 n.11
34:5–7	245, 246
34:6	247
34:8–9	245, 247
34:10–11	287
34:10	245, 247
34:11–26	246
34:11–14	245
34:11ff.	247
34:12	246
34:13	246
34:14	246
34:29ff.	338, 349
34:29–35	185, 188
34:29–32	226
34:29–30	121, 226
34:29–30, 34–35	311
34:29, 30, 35	290
34:34–35	121
34:34	227
40:2	185
40:34ff.	243 n.26
40:34–35	19 n.5, 185, 202, 251, 275, 279, 317
40:35	243
40:36–38	203

Leviticus

5:4	336
9:4	206
9:6	206
9:10a	207 n.34
9:13b	207 n.34
9:14b	207 n.34
9:17ab	207 n.34
9:20b	207 n.34
9:23–24	206
9:23	206, 207
9:24a	207 n.34
9:24	206, 207, 215, 236, 242, 262
10	208
10:1	208 n.37
10:2	207, 209, 215
10:6	209
14:2ff.	213 n.43
16:2	19 n.5
19:18	336
20:14	209
23:42–43	77
24:20	336

Numbers

5:2	213 n.43
6:22–27	311
6:24–26	121
6:25–26	227
6:25	287

6:27	122, 312	1:41, 42	105 n.103
7:89	206	2:12	104 n.103
9:15–23	204	2:21	105 n.103
10:2	210	3:22	105 n.103
10:11–13	204	3:28	105 n.103
10:33–34	204	4:1	147
11	208	4:1–40	217
11:1b–3	218	4:7	218
11:1–3	210	4:11–12	218
11:1	26 n.30, 210	4:11	244, 297, 303, 307, 309, 317, 331
11:1, 3	307		
11:3	210	4:12	218
12	208	4:15–20	218
12:2	211	4:15–16	260
12:3	211, 265	4:16–18	267 n.77
12:5	190, 204, 212	4:16–17	260 n.53
12:6–8	120, 212	4:24	209, 344
12:9–10	212	4:25	303, 307, 309, 331
12:11	213 n.43	4:26	146
12:14b	213 n.43	4:32–34	219, 220
14	208	4:33–35	22
14:9	213, 214	4:34	23 n.24, 219
14:10	213, 215	4:35	220
14:14	190, 201, 204, 213	4:44–28:68	21 n.15, 381
14:21	213	5:1–33	217, 221
14:22	213, 225	5:1–5	222
14:29–30	223	5:1–3	221, 222
14:31	223	5:4	221, 222
16	208	5:5	27, 221
16:3	214	5:6–27	222
16:13	215	5:6–21	222
16:14	215	5:6	174
16:19	215	5:15	23 n.24
16:32	215 n.46	5:22–27	222
16:35	215	5:22	222, 244, 309
20:1–13	298	5:23–27	222
20:24	296 n.25	5:23(20)	309, 331
27:14	296 n.25	5:26	224
27:20	290	5:28–31	223
30:2	336	5:28–29	222
		5:28b–29	224
Deuteronomy		6:20–24	57
1:6–4:43	21 n.15, 381	7:19	23 n.24
1:30	105 n.103	7:21	240 n.22, 242, 285, 305
1:31	185, 296	8:15b	298
1:38	105 n.103	8:19–20	274

SCRIPTURE INDEX

9:7–21	217	5:13–15	109, 231
10:17	240 n.22, 242, 285, 331	5:13	231, 232
10:21	287, 297	5:14	231, 232, 262
11:28	270	5:15a	232
12:5	297	5:15	25, 231
12:10	105 n.103	7:3	26 n.30
13:2ff.	236 n.10	7:15, 25	209
13:5	211, 254	7:24–26	215
13:17(16)	253	10:11	303, 308
17:7, 12	211	10:13	294
17:18(LXX)	336 n.4	10:42	214
18	223, 337	11:20	231
18:15–19	223	22:28	267 n.77
18:15	180 n.107, 194	24	57
19:3	105 n.103		
19:13, 19	211	**Judges**	
19:21	336	3:9, 15	237 n.13
21:21	211	5:2–31	281, 301
24:1	336	5:4–5	107, 281
24:20	233	5:4	28, 67, 284, 291, 310, 320
26:5ff.	57	5:5	68, 291
28:58	242, 285	6:11–18	233
29:1–30:20	21 n.15, 381	6:11–12a	234
31:17, 18	314	6:11–12	234
31:28	146	6:11	233
32:8	87 n.19	6:12b	234
32:15	289 n.9	6:12b, 14b, 18b	234
32:20	314	6:13	234, 235, 237
32:35	129	6:14a	234
32:41	326	6:14	234
33:2	68, 107, 289, 290 n.10, 343 n.11	6:15	234, 235
		6:16	234, 235
33:2–5	85	6:17–18a	234
33:17	227 n.67	6:17–18	235
33:26	285	6:19–24	234, 236
34	226	6:19–22a	236
34:7	226, 228, 311	6:19	236
34:10	121, 221, 228, 311	6:20	236 n.8
		6:21	236
Joshua		6:22	236, 237
1:2–9	39	6:22–23	242
1:5	232	6:22b	236
2:10	310	6:23	236, 237
3–5	75	6:24	236, 237
3:5	26 n.30	8:33	173
4:23	310	9:4	173

9:8	247 n.31	7:1–17	94
9:15	214 n.45	7:1–2	115
9:46	174	7:8	94, 358
13:3	237, 238	7:12–13	251
13:5	239 n.17	7:13	269
13:6	240	7:14	300
13:8	240	9:6–11	40
13:9	237	9:6abc	40
13:10	240	9:7ab	40
13:15	207	9:8	40
13:16	241	9:9–11a	40
13:17	241	9:11b	40
13:18	241	9:12–13	40
13:19–20	242	14:15	232
13:19	241	22:3	227 n.67
13:20b	262	22:13	260 n.54, 290
13:22	241, 242	22:15	326 n.66
13:23	242	24:16–17	271
15	239 n.17	24:18–25	271
16:20	214		
16:22–30	239 n.17	**1 Kings**	
		5:1(4:21)	176
Ruth		8:1–11	268
2:17	233	8:6–13	243
		8:6	244
1 Samuel		8:9	244
2:27	240 n.21	8:10–12	19
4:4	271	8:10–11	25, 275, 279
4:5–7	76	8:10	251
4:8–9	76 n.138	8:11	243, 251, 317
9:6, 7, 8, 10	240 n.21	8:12	244
10:6–7	277	8:13	244
10:9	277	8:15ff.	244
12:12	85	8:29	269
16:13	277	9:3	26
16:14	277, 351	12:22	240 n.21
17:9	111	13:1ff.	240 n.21
18:10–12	277	14:7–11	217 n.57
20:12–17	93	16:1–4, 11–13	217 n.57
26:12	172	16:29–33	246
28:15	214, 278	16:31	246 n.29
31:12	209	17:1	339 n.8
		17:24	364
2 Samuel		18:12	263
5:19–21	140	18:16ff.	109
6:2	271	18:16–29	20, 101
7	244		

18:19	246	18:33–35	102
18:38ff.	207	19:14ff.	271
18:39	242, 262	20:12	124
19:2	247		
19:9	249	**1 Chronicles**	
19:9b–18	109, 248	14:12	140
19:9b	248, 249	16:27	23 n.23, 317
19:10	248	21:16	242
19:11–13	27, 28, 306	21:26	236 n.10
19:11b–13a	249	28:11, 12, 18, 19	267 n.77
19:11b–13	245	28:18	256 n.46
19:11a	245		
19:11	247, 249	**2 Chronicles**	
19:11b	247, 310	3:1–2	271
19:11ff.	70	4:3	260 n.53
19:11b	247	5:13–14	279
19:11c	248	5:13b–6:1	243
19:12a	248	7:1–2	279
19:12b	248	7:11ff.	207
19:13	27, 247, 249, 338	16:14	209
19:13b	248, 249	34:5	253
19:14	245, 247, 249		
19:15–18	249	**Ezra**	
19:15–17	245, 246	6:11	217 n.57
19:15	246		
19:16	246	**Nehemiah**	
19:17	246	9:6ff.	57
19:18	245, 247		
20:28	240 n.21	**Esther**	
21:20–24	217 n.57	8:11	217 n.57
22:6	246	9:5–10	217 n.57
22:11	227 n.67		
22:19–23	227 n.67	**Job**	
		3:7	289 n.7
2 Kings		3:26	289 n.7
2:1, 11	310 n.51, 330, 331	4:13	173
2:1–11	23 n.18	7:19	315 n.54
2:11	256, 293, 339 n.8	9:13	182, 299
2:12	293	9:17	310
2:16	263	22:12	23 n.21
8:7–15	246 n.30	22:13ff.	23 n.21
9:3	246 n.30	33:15	173
15:5	84	36:29	318
16:10	267 n.77	37:2	289 n.7
17:36	23 n.24	37:4	131 n.68
18:19–25	42	37:22	290, 307
		38:1	23, 330
		39:20	290, 308

39:24	289 n.7	20:6	23 n.25, 207 n.35, 306 n.38
38:1	23 n.18	21:8	23 n.25, 306 n.38
40:6–14	14	22:25(24)	315
40:6	23 n.18, 330	22:29(28)	91
40:9	131 n.68	23:1	358
40:11–12	22	23:5(4)	236 n.9
		24:8–10	85

Psalms

1:4	157 n.44	27:5	318
2	317	27:10(9)	314
2:4	244, 252	29	142, 161, 163, 164 and n.66, 166, 167 n.75, 170, 171, 172, 178, 181, 294, 304 n.28, 307
2:7	300		
2:12	317		
4:7(6)	313, 321	29:1–9	165
5:2(3)	85	29:1–2	167
7:13–14(12–13)	305 n.33	29:1, 2, 3, 9	166
8:2, 10(1, 9)	305 n.35	29:1	170, 290
8:2(1)	290	29:3–9	167
8:5(4)	324, 367	29:3–5, 7–9	23 n.19
10:16	85	29:3–4, 7	167
11:3	23 n.23	29:3	23 n.19, 131 n.68, 168–70, 189, 259, 264 n.70, 303
11:4–7	317		
11:7(6)	313 n.53	29:4	317
13:2(1)	314	29:4, 11	286, 294
13:4(3)	313 n.53	29:5–6	167
17:7	23 n.25	29:5	307
17:8	214	29:6	1623
17:16(15)	313 n.53	29:7	166, 318
18	301, 305, 316, 366	29:8–9	167
18:5–20(4–19)	302	29:8	286, 294
18:5–15	302	29:9	168
18:5–6(4–5)	304	29:10–11	166
18:7ff.	28, 41	29:10	85, 252, 259
18:7–9	28	29:10b	168, 170
18:8(7)	303, 310, 320	29:11	170
18:9(8)	303	30:8(7)	315
18:10(9)	244, 283, 303	31:17(16)	313
18:11(10)	303	32:6	169
18:12	157 n.44, 318	33:1	207 n.35
18:12, 13(11, 12)	303	34:6(5)	313 n.53
18:13–18(12–17)	366	34:8(7)	305
18:13(12)	260 n.54, 303	35:5–6	305
18:14(13)	131 n.68, 304	35:27	207 n.35
18:15(14)	304, 326 n.66, 331	36:8(7)	214
18:16–20	303	36:10(9)	313 n.53
18:16(15)	303	37:7(6)	313 n.53

SCRIPTURE INDEX

38:3(2)	305 n.3	68:16(15)	283 n.3
39:14(13)	315 n.54	68:17–18(16–17)	283
43:3	313 n.53	68:17(16)	343 n.11
44:1–3	287	68:20–21(19–20)	285
44:3	287, 313 n.53	68:22–24(21–23)	285
44:4(3)	321	68:25–28(24–27)	283
44:25(24)	314	68:27(26)	285
45:5(4)	306	68:29, 31(28, 30)	285
45:7(6)	91	68:30(29)	285
46:7(6)	23 n.19, 305, 309	68:33–36(32–35)	284, 285
47:3(2)	240 n.22, 305 n.36	72	317
48:2	255	72:19	213, 305 n.37, 317
48:10	306 n.38	74:15	169 n.79, 310
50	284 n.4	75:2(1)	305 n.35
50:1–3ff.	305 n.34	75:5–6, 11(4–5, 10)	227 n.67
50:4	146	77	286, 287, 372
51:7	323	77:11(10)	306
51:11	277	77:12–15	286
51:12(11)	351	77:12, 15(11, 14)	241 n.24
56:14(13)	313 n.53	77:13–15	286
57:2(1)	214	77:14	287
57:6, 12(5, 11)	305n.37	77:15	287
59:17(16)	207 n.35	77:16–18	158
60:3(2)	305 n.37, 305	77:16–17	286, 287
60:6(5)	23 n.25	77:16b	287
63:3(2)	305 n.37	77:19(18)	23 n.19, 326 n.66
63:8(7)	214	77:20(19)	169
64:8(7)	305 n.33	78:12	241 n.24
66:2–5	305 n.37	78	285
66:3, 5	305 n.36	78:1–54	285
66:6	286, 292	78:14	286, 321
67:1–3	312	78:15	310
67	313	78:54	306
67:2(1)	313	78:70–71	94
67:7	312	79:5	305 n.34
68	283	79:9	305 nn.35, 37
68:2–3(1–2)	285	80:2(1)	271, 305
68:3(2)	283, 305 n.34	80:4, 7, 19(3, 6, 18)	313
68:5–7(4–6)	283, 285	80:15–16(14–15)	306
68:5(4)	283	81:1–7	285
68:8–9, 18–19(7–8, 17–18)	107	81:9(8)	285
68:8–9(7–8)	283	83:14–18	194
68:8–19(7–18)	285	83:16(15)	310, 330
68:9(8)	320	85:9	305 n.37
68:9, 18b	68	87:5(4)	183, 287 n.5

89	286, 287, 372
89:6(5)	241 n.24
89:9–12	286
89:9–10	286
89:9	287
89:10–12(9–11)	183
89:10	287, 299
89:11(10)	282, 287
89:11–12	286
89:14(13)	306 n.38
89:18(17)	227 n.67
89:47(46)	305 n.34, 315 n.54
90:8–9	315 n.54
91:1	214
93:1	23 n.22, 85
93:3	293 n.16
94:1	129 n.64
95:1	207 n.35
95:7b–11	287
96:6	317
96:10	85
97	135, 324
97:1–6	317
97:1–3	324
97:1	85
97:2–3	135, 345
97:2	244
97:4	326 n.66
97:11	313 n.53
99:1–3	317
99:1	85, 271, 305
99:3	305 nn.35–36
102:3(2)	315
103:6–7	287
103:19	91, 93 n.53
104:1	23 n.22
104:7	23 n.19
105	285
105:23–45	286
105:39	286
106:6, 47	286
106:7–33	286
106:7b–12, 22	286
106:9	396, 299, 300, 310
106:20	267 n.77
108:6(7)	23 n.25, 306 n.38
110	317
110:1	367
110:2, 4	317, 367
110:3	317
111:2–6	287
111:6	287
112:4	313 n.53
113:4	305 n.37
114	286, 294
114:3a, 5a	286, 294
114:3, 5	292
114:3b, 5b	286, 294
114:4, 6	286, 294
114:7	286, 294
114:8	286, 294
118:15–16	306 n.38
119:135	313
120:4	305 nn.33–34
121	220
135	23 n.22, 220, 286, 372
135:6–7	286
135:7	286
135:8–10	287
135:8–12	286
135:11–12	287
135:15–18	287
136	23 n.22, 220, 286, 372
136:5–9	220, 286
136:10–24	286
136:10–22	220
136:10–15	287
136:17–22	287
138:5	305 n.37
138:7	23 n.25, 306 n.38
139:6	241
139:7–10	21
140:11(10)	305 n.34
144	305
144:5–7	305
144:5	305
144:6	326 n.66
145:3–7	287
145:5	23 n.23
145:6	287
145:13	91

SCRIPTURE INDEX

Proverbs
3:21	236 n.11
4:21	236 n.11
19:15	172

Isaiah
1–39	308
1:2	146
1:18	323
2:9–22	23
2:10, 19, 21	23 n.20, 317
2:12, 13	252
2:19–21	308 n.45
2:19–20	308 n.44
4:2–6	318
4:2	318
4:4–6	308 n.44, 317, 318
4:4	318
4:5–6	331, 349
4:5	260 n.54, 290, 318
4:6	318
5:25	308 nn.44, 45
6	30, 109, 167 n.75
6:1–13	250
6:1–7	308 n.44
6:1–4	250
6:1	250 n.35, 252
6:3	213, 251, 253 n.39, 317
6:4	251
6:5	250, 253
6:6–7	250, 253
6:8a	250
6:8b	250
6:9–13	252
6:9–10	250
6:11b–13	250
6:11a	250
7:14	238, 356
9:6	241
10:15	236 n.9
10:16–17	308 n.46
10:16–17, 26	308 n.44
10:26	308
11:1	318
13:9–13	308 n.44, 317
13:10	321, 329
13:13	320
14:3	289 n.7
14:13	255
17:12–24	308
17:12–14	308 n.44
19:1–25	308 n.44, 317
24	329
24:1–13	319
24:5	147 n.15, 319
24:6–8	198
24:14–23	308 n.44, 317, 319
24:14	23 n.20, 319
24:15–18	198
24:16b–18a	319
24:16	319
24:16b	319 and n.57
24:16c	319
24:17–23	28
24:17	319
24:17b	319
24:18a	319
24:18b	319
24:18c	320
24:19	320
24:20	251, 320
24:21	29, 319, 320
24:22	319, 320
24:23	319, 320, 331
25:1	241 n.24
26:10–11	308 nn.44, 46
27:1	113, 169 n.79, 182, 184, 308 n.44, 308, 348
27:12	233
27:13	113
28:2	308 n.44, 309 n.47
28:6a	158 n.45
28:27	233
29:6	23 n.18, 308 nn.44–45, 309 n.47, 310 n.51
29:10	172
29:13	253
30:2–3	214 n.45
30:7	183, 299
30:23–26	307 n.41
30:27–33	307

30:27, 30, 31, 33	308 n.44	54:13	335
30:27	307, 308 and n.46	57:17	315
30:28	308 n.45	57:20	299 n.26
30:30	308, 309 n.47	58:8	308 n.44, 309 n.48
30:31	308	59:16	23 n.24
31:9	308 nn.44, 46, 331	59:19	308 n.44, 308 n.48
33:3	308 n.44, 309 n.47	60:1–20	317
34:8	129 n.64	60:1–3, 13, 19–20	308 n.44
35:2	308 n.44, 309 n.48	60:1, 2	309 n.48
37:16	320	60:2–3	349
38:7	236 n.10	60:19	21, 321, 349
39:1	124	61ff.	377
40–66	308	63:7–14	296, 297
40:5	308 n.44, 309 n.48, 317	63:9	191
40:24	23 n.18	63:10	296 n.25
41:16	23 n.18	63:15–19a	296
42:25	308 nn.44, 46	63:15–17	297
43:7	308 n.44, 309 n.48	63:18b–19	297
43:14	298	63:19b–64:11 (64:1–12)	296
43:15–17	199	63:19b	296, 297
43:16–17	298	64:1–12	297
43:19	298	64:1–3	308 nn.44–45
43:20	298	64:1, 2	297
44:13	267 n.77	64:1	297
44:27	299 n.26, 310	64:2	297
44:28	138	64:3	297
45:15–16	17 n.1	64:7	315, 316
45:18–19	17 n.1	65:1–7, 11–12	298
45:18	320	65:1–5	298
48:11	308 n.44, 309 n.48	65:6–7, 11–12	298
48:20	298	65:8–10, 13ff.	297
48:21	298	65:17	149, 320
49:2	214	65:20–25	149
49:13	207 n.35	66:15–16	308 n.44, 317
50:2	299 n.26	66:15	310
51:9–11	298	66:17–24	308 n.44, 317
51:9–10	183, 282	66:18–19	309 n.48
51:9	299	66:22	149, 320
51:10	299, 300	**Jeremiah**	
51:11	299	1:6	235
51:12–13b, 14, 16a, c	299	1:8, 17	263
51:13a, 15, 16b	299	1:18	263
51:15–16	299	4:13–16	132 n.78
51:15	299 n.26	7:8–15	269
53:5	23 n.24	7:9–15	26
54:9	299 n.26		

SCRIPTURE INDEX

7:11	269
11:16	259
17:18	308 n.43
23:19	23 n.18
25:30	329 and n.68
25:31	329
30:23–24	329
30:23	23 n.18, 330
31:7	207 n.35
31:32	185
31:35–36	147
32:17–23	300
33:20	147
33:25	147
34:18–20	177

Ezekiel

1	30, 109, 161, 261, 345
1:1–28	262
1:1–3:15	262
1:2	198, 265
1:3	265
1:4–28	19
1:4–21	274
1:4–21	274
1:4ff.	70
1:4	23 n.18, 255, 260, 303, 310 n.51, 318, 330, 331
1:4–21	274
1:5–14	256
1:5b–10	256
1:7	326
1:13	158, 258, 260, 326
1:15–21	256
1:16	326
1:18	275 n.90, 324
1:22–26	347
1:22, 23, 25, 26	258
1:22	264
1:24	259, 278, 326
1:25	259
1:26–28	345
1:26–27	323
1:26	258, 259, 274, 323, 347
1:26b	376
1:27–28	260
1:27	267, 347, 376
1:28	262, 265, 278, 279 347
2:1	262, 324, 367
2:2	262, 266
2:3–3:11	262
2:6	263
2:7	263
2:8–33	380
3:4	263
3:8–9	263
3:9	263
3:12–15	262, 267 n.78
3:12, 14	263
3:12	264, 267, 279
3:14, 22	266
3:15	264
3:22	265 n.73
3:23	262, 265, 279
3:24	266
7:20–22	269
7:21	276
7:22	269, 278
7:23–24	276
8–11	77
8:1	266
8:2	267, 327
8:3	267, 279
8:4	268
8:6	136, 268, 270
8:10	267 n.77
8:14	276 n.92
9:1–2	271
9:3–4	275
9:3ff.	276 n.92
9:3	271, 275, 303, 305
9:4	273
9:6	271, 273, 274
9:8	279 n.93
10	26
10:1ff.	256
10:2	274
10:3–4	275
10:4	260, 275, 290
10:5	259
10:6–7	254 n.44, 272 n.82, 274

10:6, 18	276	7:27	325
10:6	275	8:17	324
10:9–17	274	9:23	232
10:9	326	10:1–12:13	322, 325, 327
10:12	275	10:1–10	327
10:15, 20–22	274	10:4–6	326
10:15	303	10:5	376
10:18	275	10:5b	376
10:19	136, 236 n.11, 275	10:6a	376
11:1	267, 279	10:6	326 n.67
11:13	279 n.93	10:6b	376
11:21	270	10:7	295 n.24
11:22–23	136, 276	10:11	327
11:23	276	10:12b–14	327
16:1ff.	185	10:12a	327
20:16	270	10:12b	327
31:6	214 n.45	10:13, 20	87 n.19
34:12	244	10:15–16a	327
37:1	265 n.73, 267, 279 n.94	10:16b–17	327
40:1b–2	267, 279 n.94	10:18–19	327
40:3	267, 278, 326, 378	10:20–12:4	327
40:34–35	279	12:3	327
43:2–5	278	12:5–6a	327
43:2	278	12:6–7	272 n.82
43:2b	376	12:6b–7	327
43:3	262, 278	12:8	327
43:4	278	12:9–13	327
43:5	267, 279	12:13	328
43:6ff.	378		
44:4	262, 279	**Hosea**	
44:17–18	272 n.82	4:19	309
47:6	378	6:7	147
		8:14	309
Daniel		12:13	300
6:24	217 n.57	13:4–5	300
7:1–14	322		
7:8, 11, 24b–26	322	**Joel**	
7:9–14	91	2:1–11	109
7:9–10	256, 322, 345, 347	2:2	244, 309, 330
7:9	90, 323 and n.63, 347	2:10, 31(3:4)	321
7:9b	376	2:10	284
7:10a	324	2:11	23 n.19, 309
7:13	25 n.28, 324, 367, 376	2:28–32	328
7:14	325	2:28–29	329
7:15–27	322	2:30–32	328, 329, 364
7:16–17	322	2:31	328, 329

4:15(3:15)	329
4:16(3:16)	23 n.19, 284, 309. 320, 329 and n.68
4:21(3:21)	329

Amos

1:2	309
1:4ff.	309 n.49
1:5, 8	252 n.38
1:5	244
2:3	84
3:8	374
4:10	300
5:6	310
5:18–20	309
6:10	209 n.38
7:4	299
8:7	23 n.20
9:1	251
9:5	309

Obadiah

21	91

Jonah

1:3ff.	235

Micah

1:3–4	310
1:4	28
4:13–14	227 n.67
5:2	358
7:15	300

Nahum

1:3	310
1:4	310
1:5	284, 310
1:6	310

Habakkuk

1:4	290
1:13	326 n.66
2:3	291
3	288, 291 n.14
3:1	288 n.6
3:2a, 3–15	288
3:2	289 and n.7, 292 n.14, 295
3:2b	288
3:3–15	289 and n.8
3:3, 9, 13	288 n.6
3:3	289, 290
3:4	260 n.54, 290
3:4a	290 n.11
3:6	290, 297
3:7	291
3:8–11	292
3:8a	292
3:8	293
3:8b	292 n.14, 293
3:9	167 n.75
3:10	293, 294
3:11	331
3:13	292 n.15
3:15	295
3:16	288, 289
3:19	288
3:19b	288 n.6

Zephaniah

1:14	330
1:15	244, 330
1:18	330
2:2	330
2:2b–3	157 n.44
3:8	330

Haggai

2:6	330, 344
2:7	349

Zechariah

2:5	331
9:14	326 n.66, 331
10:10–11	300
12:8	300
12:9	300
13:9	331
14:3–4	331

Malachi

3:1	331
3:2	331
4:1(3:19)	331

Matthew

1:18–25	358, 359
1:18–20a	359
1:20c–21	359
1:20b	359
1:22–25	359
2:6	358
2:13–15	358, 359, 360
2:13a	360
2:13b	360
2:14–15	360
2:19–21	358, 360
2:19	360
2:20	360
2:21	360
2:22	360
3:13–17a	361
3:16–17	153
3:17	96
3:17b	361
4:23	383
5:1–2	334
5:17	335, 336
5:21–26	336
5:21–22	335
5:27–30	336
5:27, 31, 33, 38, 43	335
5:28, 32, 34, 39, 44	335
5:31–32	336
5:33–37	336
5:35	84, 251
5:38–42	336
5:43–48	336
6:33	91
7:28	335 n.2
9:8	362
12:22–29	373
12:43–45	272
13:43	189, 328
14:22–25	361
14:25–27	227
14:27a	361
14:27b	361
14:28	361
14:29a	361
14:29b–31	361
14:32–33	361
15:8a, 10b–11	253
17:1–8	336
17:1–5a	362
17:1	338
17:2	338
17:3	338
17:5	338
17:5b	363
17:6	337, 338
17:8–13	363
17:16–7	363
17:7	338
17:17	338
18:15–17	211
18:23–25	217 n.57
21:13	269
24:27	365
24:29	365
24:30	365
24:31	365
26:64	325, 371
26:64b	367
26:64c	367
26:64d	367
27:45–56	340, 363
27:45	340, 364
27:51	328, 340, 364
27:54	364
28:1–8	368
28:1–4	368
28:5	368
28:6–7	368
28:8	368
28:9	369
28:19–20	235

Mark

1:9–11a	361
1:11b	361
2:7	192
6:45–50a	361
6:50b	361
6:51–52	361
9:2–7a	362
9:7b	363

SCRIPTURE INDEX

9:8–13	363	2:15–20	358
13:24–25	365	3:21–22a	361
13:26	365	3:22b	361
13:27	365	3:23	358
14:62b	367	8:25b	362
14:62c	367	8:37	362
14:62d	367	9:28–35a	362
15:33–41	363	9:35b	363
15:33	364	9:36	363
15:39	364	12:48	274
16:1–5a	368	15:10	343 n.11
16:1–8	368	17:24	365
16:6a	368	17:28–30	365
16:6b–7	368	21:25	366
16:8	368	21:26b	365
		21:27	365
Luke		22:69b	367
1:5–25	239 n.19, 354, 355, 356	22:69c	367
1:5–11	355	23:44–49	363
1:11	356	23:44–45	328, 364
1:12	356	23:47	364
1:13	356	24:1–5a	368
1:13a	355	24:1–12	368
1:13b–17	355	24:5b–7	368
1:14–17	356	24:8–12	368
1:18	355, 356, 357	24:36–49	370
1:19–20	355, 356	24:36a	370
1:19	355, 356, 357	24:36b	370
1:21–25	355	24:37–43	370
1:26–38	239 n.19, 355, 356	24:39	370
1:26–27	355	24:44–49	370
1:28	355, 356		
1:29–30	356	**John**	
1:30	355	1:4	315
1:31	355, 356	1:9	315
1:32–33	356	1:12	300, 315, 350
1:34	355, 356, 357	1:14	319
1:35–38bα	356	1:21	180 n.107
1:35–37	356	1:32–33	361 n.34
1:38b	356	2:10	225
2:8–20	357	3:8	350 n.19, 372
2:8–10a	357	3:13	334
2:10b	357	3:16–21	24 n.26
2:10c	357	3:19–20	367
2:11–12	357	5:26	25 n.28
2:13–14	358	5:27	25 n.28

5:37	218	20:31	220
6:16–20	361	21:15, 16, 17	249 n.34
6:18	362	**Acts**	
6:21	361	1:8	350
7:40	180 n.107	1:9	339 n.8
10:10b	228	1:10–11	371
10:11	358	2:2–4	350
11:40	225	2:2	353, 372
12:28–33	363 n.36	2:3	353, 372
12:28–30	363 n.36	2:4–12	372
12:28–29	19 n.6	2:16–21	328
12:31	149	2:19–21	364
14:9	225	3:22–23	180 n.107, 194, 224
14:10	225	4	371
14:12	225	4:1–22	372
14:13	225	4:24	372
14:17	266	4:29–30	372
14:30	149	4:25–26	317
16:11	149	4:30	373
17:5	212	4:31	372
17:22–23a	225	4:31a	373
17:24	225	4:31b	373
20:10–20	369	5:1–11	210
20:10–18	368	7:53	343 n.11
20:13a	369	8:39	264
20:13b	369	9:1–9	373
20:14	369	9:4a	373
20:15a	369	9:4b	373
20:15b	369	9:5	373
20:16a	369	9:5a	373
20:16b	369	9:6	374
20:17	369	9:7–9	374
20:18	369	9:10–19a	371 n.43
20:19–23	370	10:9–16	371 n.43
20:19a	370	17:31	25 n.28
20:19b	370	22:2b–11	374 n.46
20:21b	370	22:2b–7a	374 n.46
20:20–21a	370	22:7b	374 n.46
20:21b–23	370	22:8a	374 n.46
20:23	371	22:8b	374 n.46
20:24–26a	370 n.41	22:10a	374 n.46
20:26b	370 n.41	22:10b	374 n.46
20:27	370 n.41	22:11	374 n.46
20:28	370 n.41		
20:29	370 n.41		
20:30–31	22 n.16, 370 n.41		

SCRIPTURE INDEX

Romans
1:21–23	82
2:12–16	344
3:19	344
3:20	341
7:7–25	341
8:31	214

1 Corinthians
3:12–18	227 n.67
5:1, 4	244
5:1–5	211
6:19	228, 244
15:9–10a	374

2 Corinthians
3	382 n.56
3:7–14	382 n.56
3:7, 11, 13	121
3:7, 13	382 n.56
3:13–18	363
3:16–18	229
3:18	350
4:4	149
4:6	315
5:1–4	276
5:1, 4	244

Galatians
3:2	341
3:5	341
3:19	343 n.11
3:29	178
4:24–26	341
5:25	205, 371, 384

Colossians
2:15	214

2 Thessalonians
1:6–10	366

1 Timothy
1:15	373

Hebrews
1:14	343 n.11
2:1–3	344
4:5–6	199
4:9–11	199
4:15	25 n.28
5:6	317
6:5	350
6:20	378
7:17, 21	317
8:5	117
10:39	222
12:18–24	342
12:18–21	330
12:22–24	330
12:23–24	379
12:25–27	343
12:26–27	330
12:26	344
12:27	251
12:28–29	344
12:28	331
12:29	331

1 Peter
4:17	274

2 Peter
1:13–14	244, 276

1 John
4:18	189

Revelation
1:1–20	375 n.47
1:1–8	376 n.47
1:7	367
1:4–20	375 n.47
1:9–10, 12–17a	377
1:9–3:22	375, 376 and n.47, 377, 380
1:10b	377
1:11	377
1:13a	376
1:13b	326, 376
1:14a	376
1:14b	376
1:14c	376
1:15a	376
1:15b	376

1:16b	376
1:14	323 and n.63, 326 n.67
1:15	326
1:16b	326
1:17–18	377
1:17	262, 295 n.24
1:17b–18	377
1:17b	377
1:19–3:22	377
1:19	377
2–3	375 n.47
2:1–3:22	375 n.47
2:1, 8, 12, 18	377
3:1, 7, 14	377
4–5	375 n.47
4	261, 346
4:1a, 2–11	378
4:1–16:21	376 n.47
4:1–9:21	375, 378, 380
4:1–5:14	376 n.47
4:1b	378
4:2–6	346, 375
4:3	261, 347
4:4	347
4:5	126 n.54, 347
4:6b–8	257
4:6	347
4:8, 11	378
4:8	378 n.52
4:11	378 n.52
5:1–4	378
5:5	378
5:6–7:12	378
5:11–13	343 n.11
6:1–8:1	376 n.47
6:1–7:8	375 n.47
7:1–17	376 n.47
7:2–3	273
7:13	378
7:14a	378
7:14b–17	378
8:1–9:21	378
8:1, 3–5, 2, 6, 13–19	375 n.47
8:2–11:19	376 n.47
10:1–22:17	375, 379, 380
10:1–11:14	376 n.47
10:1–4a	379
10:4b	379
10:5–8a	379
10:8–10	380
10:8b	379
10:9a	379
10:9b	379 and n.53
10:10	379
10:11–11:3	379
10:11	379 n.53, 380
11:1	379 n.53
11:3–13	339 n.8
11:4–14:12	379
11:6a	339 n.8
11:6b	339 n.8
11:9–11	339 n.8
11:12	339 n.8
11:14–13, 15–20:8	375 n.47
11:15	325
12:1–14:5	376 n.47
12:9	149, 299
13:16–17	273
13:16	273 n.86
14:1	273
14:6–20	376 n.47
14:13	379
14:14–17:6	379
15:1–16:21	376 n.47
15:2	346 n.14
17:1–21:8	376 n.47
17:1–19:5	376 n.47
17:1	366
17:7–18	379
17:15	366
18:1–19:8	379
18:8, 14	272 n.82
19:6–20:15	376 n.47
19:9–10	379
19:11–21:5a	379
19:12	376 n.49
19:16	89
20:4–10	375 n.47
20:11–15	375 n.47
21	375
21:1–22:5	376 n.47
21:1	149, 348

21:3	319
21:5a, 4d, 5b, 1–4abc, 22:3–5	375 n.47
21:5b–8	379
21:9a	379
21:9b	379
21:9–22:2, 14–15, 17	375 n.47
21:9–22:5	376 n.47
21:10–22:5	380
21:19	347 n.15
21:23	321, 349
21:25	349
21:26	349
22	380
22:4	349
22:5	325
22:6–21	376 n.47
22:6–7	380
22:6	380
22:7	380
22:8	380
22:9–16a	380
22:9–12	380
22:9–11	380
22:11–12, 15	380
22:12–16a	380
22:12, 14	380
22:13, 16	380
22:14–16a	380
22:16a	380
22:17(18–21)	380

♦ Author Index ♦

Abba, R., 192 (n.23)
Albright, W. F., 90, 91 n.45, 163 n.60
Allen, W. C., 335 n.2
Allis, O. T., 46 (n.17)
Alt, A., 57 n.48, 60 n.68, 69
Anderson, B. W., 282 n.1
Anderson, F. I., 188 n.11
Armerding, C. E., 290 n.10
Astruc, 48
Augustine, 81, 221 n.64, 291 n.14

Agustus, C. A., 168 n.78
Bailey, L., 227 n.67
Baltzer, K., 85 n.12, 375 n.47
Barnes, Wm. E., 246 nn.30–31, 249 (n.34)
Batto, B. F., 153–54 n.34, 182 (n.3), 183 n.4, 184 nn.5–6, 199 n.29, 227 n.67
Betz, O., 158 n.48
Beyerlin, W., 59–61 (nn.61–68, 75), 63 nn.85–86, 65, 66 n.96, 78
Binns, L. E., 214 n.44
Block, D. I., 89 n.38, 99 n.81
Borger, R., 79 n.145, 97 n.70, 101 n.86, 104 n.95, 118 n.33, 119 nn.34–35, 134 nn.83–85, 135 n.86, 136 n.87, 139 nn.97–98, 216 n.54
Breasted, J. H., 82 nn.4–5, 86 n.15, 87 n.18, 92 n.47, 95 n.61
Briggs, E. G., 168 n.78
Brownlee, Wm. H., 257 n.49, 267 n.78, 272 n.84, 273 n.87

Bruce, F. F., 118, 288 n.6, 290 n.11, 293 n.18, 342 n.10
Budd, P. J., 210 n.40
Buis, P., 221 n.64
Burrows, M., 29 n.35

Calvin, J., 157 n.45, 209, 210 n.39, 292 n.14, 295 (n.24), 343 n.12
Caquot, A., 169 n.79
Carpenter, J. E., 54 (n.39)
Cassuto, U., 24 (n.27), 47 (n.22), 157 n.45, 198 (nn.27–28), 348 (n.17)
Charles, R. H., 348 n.16, 375 n.47, 377 n.50
Clifford, R. J., 116 n.25, 117 (n.26), 118 (n.32)
Cogan, M., 104 (n.102), 107 n.109, 139, 140 n.100, 141 nn.100–101
Colenso, J. W., 50 n.29
Coogan, M. D., 106 n.107, 169 n.79
Cooper, J. S., 87 nn.20–22, 92 n.48, 96 nn.63/65, 97 nn.66–68, 71, 98 nn.74–75, 100 nn.83–84, 102 n.90, 103 nn.91–94, 115 n.23, 124 n.46
Craigie, P. C., 46 n.21, 163 (nn.67–68), 168 n.78, 168 (nn.80–81), 221 n.64, 256 n.46, 260, 261 n.55, 265 n.73, 273 n.88, 288 (n.6), 289 n.8
Cross, F. M., 43 (n.3), 71–72 (nn.120–26), 93 (n.60), 106 n.107, 163 (nn.63–64), 163 (n.66), 165 nn.69–71, 168 n.78
Cundall, A. E., 235 n.7

AUTHOR INDEX

Dahood, M., 163, 164 n.65, 165 nn.69/73, 170 n.73, 173 n.78
Davis, J. J., 114 n.19
Day, J., 167 n.75
Delitzsch, F., 46 (n, 14), 111 (n.7), , 166 n.74, 168 n.78, 169 n.80, 178 n.103, 208 n.37, 221 (n.64), 235 n.5, 239 n.17, 247 n.31, 254 n.44, 273 n.88, 209 nn.10–11, 291 nn.12–13, 292 n.15, 293(n.17)
de Vaux, R., 192 (n.19)
De Vries, S. J., 55 n.42
de Wette, W. M. L., 44, 48–50 (nn.25–28), 52 n.35, 53 (n.36), 54 nn.37–38
Dijk, J. J. A. van, 73 nn.128–129, 125 (n.51), 126 nn.52–53, 128 n.55, 139 n.99
Dossin, G., 270 n.80
Douglas, J. D., 294 n.19
Dozeman, T. B., 55 n.42
Driver, S. R., 52 n.35, 54 (n.40), 143 (n.1), 323 nn.60/62
Dumbrell, W. I., 143 (nn.4–5), 144 (n.6), 145 n.12, 171 (n.87), 177 (n.101)

Edersheim, A., 363 nn.37–38
Eichhorn, J. G., 48, 50 n.29
Eichrodt, W., 27 n.31, 257 (nn.47–48), 258 n.51, 264 nn.69/71, 277 n.71, 271 n.81, 273 n.85
Eissfeldt, O., 54, 55 n.41
Emerton, J. A., 112 n.13

Faircloth, H. R., 353 n.25
Frankfort, H., 96 n.64, 152 n.25
Freedman, D. N., 165 n.69

Gaballa, G. A., 219 nn.60–61
Gaebelein, A. C., 323 n.60
Garrett, D., 46 (n.12), 152 n.29, 188 n.11
Gaster, T. H., 163 (n.62)

Gibson, J. C. L., 14 n.6, 90 nn.39–44, 93 nn.53–55, 106 n.107, 112 (nn.11–12/14), 114 nn.17/20, 115 nn.21–22, 117 nn.27–29, 152 n.26, 167 n.76, 169 n.79, 194 (n.25), 238 n.14, 244 n.27, 283 n.2, 294 n.20, 304 nn.29, 30, 32
Ginsberg, H. L., 163 (n.61)
Gispen, W. H., 187 n.10
Gordon, C., 47 (n.23), 152 n.26, 190 n.17, 238 n.16, 244 n.27, 304 n.30
Götze, A., 88 n.28, 102 n.89, 128 nn.57–59, 129 nn.60–63/65
Gray, J., 232 n.1, 234 n.4, 235 n.6, 243 n.26, 246 n.31
Grayson, A. K., 78 n.143, 97 nn.69–70, 104 n.95, 105 nn.104–6, 107 n.110, 118 n.33, 119 n.36, 131 n.71, 132 nn.74/79–80, 134 n.82, 153 n.31, 175 n.97, 215 n.47, 216 nn.48/50, 217 n.56
Gundry, R. H., 335 n.1, 336 n.3, 337 n.5, 339 n.7
Gunkel, H., 31 (n.41), 44 (n.8), 52 n.35, 53, 110 n.3, 272 nn.83–84, 348 n.16
Gurney, O. R., 82 n.1, 88 nn.25–27, 29, 92 n.50, 93 n.51, 99 n.80, 113 n.16
Güterbock, H. G., 99 n.79

Hafemann, S. J., 382 n.56
Hallo, Wm. W., 73–74 (nn.128–29), 125 (n.51), 126 nn.52–53, 128 n.55, 139 n.99, 140
Harrington, W. J., 349 n.18
Harrison, R. K., 46 (n.19), 50 n.29
Harford, G., 54 (n.39)
Hasel, G., 177 (nn.99–100)
Heidel, A., 110 n.4, 111 (n.6)
Heimpel, W., 13 nn.1–2
Hendricksen, Wm., 357 n.29

Herdner, A., 158 n.48, 165 n.70, 168–69 n.79
Hoffner, H. A. Jr., 88 n.27
Homer, 14 n.4
Huffmon, H. B., 30 n.39
Hutchinson, R. W., 100 n.82

Isbell, Ch. D., 82 n.3

Jacobsen, T., 87 n.23
Jeremias, J., 27 n.33, 31 (n.44), 43 (n.1), 55, 65–72 (nn.95/97–105, 108–18), 80 n.147, 158 n.48, 291

Keats, John, 17
Keil, C. F., 46 (n.14), 85 n.11, 178 n.103, 208 n.37, 221 (nn.64–65), 235 n.5, 239 n.17, 247 n.31, 254 n.44, 273 n.88, 290 nn.10–11, 291 nn.12–13, 292 n.15, 293 (n.17), 323 (n.61), 324 (n.64)
Kidner, D., 143 (n.2), 168 n.78
Kikawada, I. M., 46 n.13, 143 (n.3)
King, L. W., 79 n.144, 97 nn.69–70, 118 n.33, 119 nn.34–35, 131 n.73, 132 nn.74–75
Kirkpatrick, A. F., 169 n.80
Kistemaker, S. J., 343 n.11, 350 n.19, 375 n.46
Kitchen, K. A., 30 n.38, 61 n.77, 94 n.58, 174 (nn.89/93), 174 n.93
Kline, M., 30 n.38, 43 (nn.5–6), 44, 61 n.77, 84 n.9, 94 nn.56/58, 143, 146 n.13, 150 (nn.21–22), 157 n.45, 158 n.46, 160 nn.50–51, 160 (nn.53–54), 174 (n.92), 177 (nn.102/104), 178 (n.105), 204 n.33, 261 n.56
Knudtzon, J. A., 130 n.67, 171 n.86, 192 n.21, 220 (n.62)
Köhler, L., 20 n.11, 156
Kramer, S. N., 95 n.62
Kuenen, A., 50 n.29

Kuntz, J. K., 20 (nn.10–13), 31 (n.45), 32 (nn.47–49), 39 (n.61), 43 (n.2), 55, 62–64 (nn.80–92), 65 nn.93–94, 187 n.7, 284 n.4
Kutscher, R., 193 n.24

Ladd, G. E., 346 n.15, 376 n.47
Lambert, W. G., 96 n.62, 131 nn.68/72, 138 n.89
Langdon, S., 124 n.47
Laughlin, J. C. H., 208 n.37
Leclercq, J., 221 n.64
Lewis, C. S., 333, 334
Lindblom, J., 19 n.10
Lipinski, E., 56 n.44
Livingston, G. H., 46 (n.20)
Longenecker, R., 343 n.13
Longman, T. III, 99 n.81
Luckenbill, 119 nn.34–35, 132 n.77, 138 n.94, 139 n.95, 216 n.53
Lumby, J. R., 246 n.31
Lust, J., 27 n.34, 248 (nn.32–33)

Machinist, P., 138 n.90
Maclaren, A., 168 n.78, 169 n.80, 171 n.85
Macmillan, K. D., 156 n.42
Mallowen, M. E. L., 100 n.82, 138 n.93
Mann, T. W., 43 (n.4), 70 n.118, 71 n.119, 73 (nn.130–37), 77 n.140, 92 n.49, 95 n.62, 106 n.107, 128 n.56, 133 n.81, 135 n.86, 162 n.59
Masefield, John, 280
Matthews, I. G., 257 (n.49), 258, 262 n.61, 266 n.75
May, H. G., 169 (nn.82–83)
Mayes, A. D. H., 239 n.17
McCarthy, D. J., 95 (n.59), 101 (n.88), 102 (n.89), 197 n.26
Mendenhall, G. E., 60 (n.70), 61 n.76, 151 (nn.23–24), 152 (nn.25/27–28), 153 nn.30/33, 160, 161

AUTHOR INDEX

n.52, 178, 187 (n.9), 190 n.16, 191, 261 (nn.57–59), 262 n.60
Millard, A. R., 131 n.68
Miller, P. D., 106 n.107
Milton, John, 142, 181
Moberly, R. W. L., 62 n.78
Morgenstern, J., 31 (n.42)
Morris, L., 235 n.7, 263 n.62, 369 (nn.39–40), 371 (n.42)
Mounce, R. H., 375 n.47
Mowinckel, S., 34 n.53, 39, 55–57 (nn.44–45), 65, 77, 78, 324 n.65

Neihaus, J., 23 n.20, 26 n.29, 30 n.40, 60 n.74, 84 n.10, 104 nn.97–101, 157 n.45, 209 n.38, 244 n.28, 251 n.36, 309 n.49, 319 n.57, 329 n.68, 339 n.8, 374 n.45
Nicholson, E. W., 30 n.39
Norden, E., 31 (n.43)
Noth, M., 52 n.34, 55, 57–58 (nn.52–60), 60 (n.69), 62, 70, 77 (n.141), 78 n.142, 79, 80 (n.147), 109 (n.2), 110 n.3, 207 n.34, 208 n.37, 211 n.41, 214 n.44, 217 (n.58), 233 n.2

Oppenheim, A. L., 82 n.5, 83 n.6, 88 (n.24), 91 n.46, 131 (n.70), 351 nn.21–22, 352 (n.24)
Orr, J., 46 (n.16)

Piepkorn, A. C., 34 n.54, 38 n.59, 68 n.107, 97 n.70, 118 n.33, 176 n.98, 216 n.55
Plummer, A., 354 n.27
Pritchard, J. B., 85 n.14, 86 nn.15–16, 87 n.23, 88 n.27, 89 n.37, 92 n.50, 99 n.77, 144 nn.7–9, 145 nn.10–11, 148 nn.16/18, 169 n.79, 227 n.67, 294 n.19
Pythian-Adams, W. J., 52 n.35

Quinn, A., 46 n.13, 143 (n.3)

Rad, G. von, 26 n.30, 29 (n.36), 55–58 (nn.43/46–51), 60, 61, 62, 77, 78
Reiner, E., 82 n.2, 254 n.41
Rendtorff, R., 18 n.3, 55 n.42
Ringren, H., 63 n.85, 254 n.43
Robinson, H. W., 20, 21 n.14
Rost, P., 134 n.82, 216 n.51
Rowley, H. H., 20 n.11
Rudolph, W., 157 n.44
Rylaarsdam, J. C., 52 n.35

Saggs, H. W. F., 352 n.23
Sarna, N. M., 52 n.35
Sayce, A. H., 46 (n.15)
Schrader, E., 53 (n.36), 54 nn.37–38
Schramm, W., 79 n.145, 216 n.50
Scott, C. A., 319 n.56, 376 n.48, 379 n.53, 380 n.54
Shelley, Percy Bysshe, 43
Smith, G. A., 250 n.35, 253 (nn.39–40), 289 n.7, 292 n.14
Sollberger, E., 123 n.43, 311 n.52
Sperber, J., 85 n.13, 216 n.50
Stevens, Wallace, 81, 230
Streck, M., 227 n.67
Stuart, D., 8, 257 n.49, 258 n.50, 266 n.74, 272 n.82, 273 n.89, 309 n.50
Sturdy, J., 214 n.44
Sznycer, M., 169 n.79

Tallqvist, K., 89 nn.30–36, 98 n.73, 113 n.16, 156 nn.40–41
Thompson, J. A., 381 n.55
Thompson, R. C., 100 n.82, 138 n.93
Thureau-Dangin, F., 98 n.74, 113 n.16, 119 n.37, 120 nn.38–39, 132 n.76, 216 n.52

Unger, M. F., 52 n.33

Vergil, 138 n.91, 303 n.27, 352, 353 (n.25)

Volz, P., 56 n.44
Vos, G., 44 (n.7), 94 n.56
Vriezen, Th. C., 27 n.32

Wakeman, M. K., 112 nn.9–10, 113 n.15, 114 n.18, 168 n.78, 169 n.80, 182 n.2
Walvoord, J. F., 323 n.60
Weidner, E. F., 97 n.70, 100 n.85, 148 n.19, 175 n.97, 216 n.49
Weinfeld, M., 98 n.76, 174 n.90, 174 (nn.94–95), 176, 192 (n.22), 219 (n.63)
Weippert, M., 60 n.71
Wellhausen, J., 50–51 (nn.30–32), 52 n.35, 58, 227 n.67, 244 n.26
Wenham, G. J., 26 n.29, 46 n.21, 175–77 (nn.96/100), 192 (n.20), 207 (n.34), 208 nn.36–37
Whitehead, A. N., 45 (nn.9–10)
Whybray, R. N., 47 n.24
Wilson, J. A., 86 nn.15–16, 87 n.17
Winckler, H., 98 n.72, 99 n.78, 358 n.31
Wiseman, D. J., 100 n.82
Woudstra, M. H., 47 n.21, 232 n.1
Wright, G. E., 30 n.39, 60 (n.72)

Yadin, Y., 60 (n.73)
Yeats, William Butler, 108
Young, E. J., 46 (n.18), 239, 240 n.20, 242 n.25, 249 n.35, 252 n.38, 254 n.43, 323 n.60